P9-CMF-475

THE
STONES OF VENICE.

VOLUME THE SECOND.
The Sea-Stories.

BY JOHN RUSKIN.

AUTHOR OF "THE SEVEN LAMPS OF ARCHITECTURE," "MODERN PAINTERS," ETC., ETC.

WITH ILLUSTRATIONS ON WOOD.

NEW YORK:

JOHN WILEY & SON, PUBLISHERS,

15 ASTOR PLACE.

1873.

NA1121
.V4 R7
1873
vol. 2

Phi.
173.724
Mar. 2/75

ADVERTISEMENT.

It was originally intended that this Work should consist of two volumes only; the subject has extended to three. The second volume, however, will conclude the account of the ancient architecture of Venice. The third will embrace the Early, the Roman, and the Grotesque Renaissance; and an Index, which, as it gives, in alphabetical order, a brief account of all the buildings in Venice, or references to the places where they are mentioned in the text, will be found a convenient guide for the traveller. In order to make it more serviceable, I have introduced some notices of the pictures which I think most interesting in the various churches, and in the Scuola di San Rocco.

The third, and last, volume is already in the press.

CONTENTS.

(library stamp)

THE

STONES OF VENICE.

FIRST, OR BYZANTINE, PERIOD.

CHAPTER I.

THE THRONE.

§ I. In the olden days of travelling, now to return no more, in which distance could not be vanquished without toil, but in which that toil was rewarded, partly by the power of deliberate survey of the countries through which the journey lay, and partly by the happiness of the evening hours, when, from the top of the last hill he had surmounted, the traveller beheld the quiet village where he was to rest, scattered among the meadows beside its valley stream; or, from the long hoped for turn in the dusty perspective of the causeway, saw, for the first time, the towers of some famed city, faint in the rays of sunset—hours of peaceful and thoughtful pleasure, for which the rush of the arrival in the railway station is perhaps not always, or to all men, an equivalent,—in those days, I say, when there was something more to be anticipated and remembered in the first aspect of each successive halting-place, than a new arrangement of glass roofing and iron girder, there were few moments of which the recollection was more fondly che-

1

rished by the traveller than that which, as I endeavored to describe in the close of the last chapter, brought him within sight of Venice, as his gondola shot into the open lagoon from the canal of Mestre.   Not but that the aspect of the city itself was generally the source of some slight disappointment, for, seen in this direction, its buildings are far less characteristic than those of the other great towns of Italy; but this inferiority was partly disguised by distance, and more than atoned for by the strange rising of its walls and towers out of the midst, as it seemed, of the deep sea, for it was impossible that the mind or the eye could at once comprehend the shallowness of the vast sheet of water which stretched away in leagues of rippling lustre to the north and south, or trace the narrow line of islets bounding it to the east.   The salt breeze, the white moaning sea-birds, the masses of black weed separating and disappearing gradually, in knots of heaving shoal, under the advance of the steady tide, all proclaimed it to be indeed the ocean on whose bosom the great city rested so calmly; not such blue, sfot, lake-like ocean as bathes the Neapolitan promontories, or sleeps beneath the marble rocks of Genoa, but a sea with the bleak power of our own northern waves, yet subdued into a strange spacious rest, and changed from its angry pallor into a field of burnished gold, as the sun declined behind the belfry tower of the lonely island church, fitly named "St. George of the Seaweed."   As the boat drew nearer to the city, the coast which the traveller had just left sank behind him into one long, low, sad-colored line, tufted irregularly with brushwood and willows: but, at what seemed its northern extremity, the hills of Arqua rose in a dark cluster of purple pyramids, balanced on the bright mirage of the lagoon; two or three smooth surges of inferior hill extended themselves about their roots, and beyond these, beginning with the craggy peaks above Vicenza, the chain of the Alps girded the whole horizon to the north—a wall of jagged blue, here and

there showing through its clefts a wilderness of misty pre
cipices, fading far back into the recesses of Cadore, and itself
rising and breaking away eastward, where the sun struck
opposite upon its snow, into mighty fragments of peaked light
standing up behind the barred clouds of evening, one after
another, countless, the crown of the Adrian Sea, until the eye
turned back from pursuing them, to rest upon the nearer
burning of the campaniles of Murano, and on the great city,
where it magnified itself along the waves, as the quick silent
pacing of the gondola drew nearer and nearer. And at last,
when its walls were reached, and the outmost of its untrodden
streets was entered, not through towered gate or guarded
rampart, but as a deep inlet between two rocks of coral in the
Indian sea; when first upon the traveller's sight opened the
long ranges of columned palaces,—each with its black boat
moored at the portal,—each with its image cast down, beneath
its feet, upon that green pavement which every breeze broke
into new fantasies of rich tessellation; when first, at the extremity of the bright vista, the shadowy Rialto threw its colossal
curve slowly forth from behind the palace of the Camerlenghi;
that strange curve, so delicate, so adamantine, strong as a
mountain cavern, graceful as a bow just bent; when first,
before its moonlike circumference was all risen, the gondolier's
cry, "Ah! Stalì,"* struck sharp upon the ear, and the prow
turned aside under the mighty cornices that half met over the
narrow canal, where the plash of the water followed close and
loud, ringing along the marble by the boat's side; and when
at last that boat darted forth upon the breadth of silver sea,
across which the front of the Ducal palace, flushed with its
sanguine veins, looks to the snowy dome of Our Lady of Salvation,† it was no marvel that the mind should be so deeply

---

* Appendix 1.: "The Gondolier's Cry."
† Appendix 2.: "Our Lady of Salvation."

entranced by the visionary charm of a scene so beautiful and so strange, as to forget the darker truths of its history and its being. Well might it seem that such a city had owed her existence rather to the rod of the enchanter, than the fear of the fugitive; that the waters which encircled her had been chosen for the mirror of her state, rather than the shelter of her nakedness; and that all which in nature was wild or merciless,—Time and Decay, as well as the waves and tempests,—had been won to adorn her instead of to destroy, and might still spare, for ages to come, that beauty which seemed to have fixed for its throne the sands of the hour-glass as well as of the sea.

§ II. And although the last few eventful years, fraught with change to the face of the whole earth, have been more fatal in their influence on Venice than the five hundred that preceded them; though the noble landscape of approach to her can now be seen no more, or seen only by a glance, as the engine slackens its rushing on the iron line; and though many of her palaces are for ever defaced, and many in desecrated ruins, there is still so much of magic in her aspect, that the hurried traveller, who must leave her before the wonder of that first aspect has been worn away, may still be led to forget the humility of her origin, and to shut his eyes to the depth of her desolation. They, at least, are little to be envied, in whose hearts the great charities of the imagination lie dead, and for whom the fancy has no power to repress the importunity of painful impressions, or to raise what is ignoble, and disguise what is discordant, in a scene so rich in its remembrances, so surpassing in its beauty. But for this work of the imagination there must be no permission during the task which is before us. The impotent feelings of romance, so singularly characteristic of this century, may indeed gild, but never save the remains of those mightier ages to which they are attached like climbing flowers; and they must be torn away from the magnificent fragments, if we would see them as they stood in their own strength. Those feelings, always as fruitless as they are fond, are in Venice not only incapable of protecting, but even of discerning, the objects to which they ought to have been attached. The Venice of modern fiction and drama is a thing of yesterday, a mere efflorescence of decay, a stage dream which the first ray of daylight must dissipate into dust. No prisoner, whose name is worth remembering, or whose sorrow deserved sympathy, ever crossed that "Bridge of Sighs," which is the centre of the Byronic ideal of Venice; no great merchant of Venice ever saw that Rialto under which the traveller now passes with breathless interest: the statue which Byron makes Faliero address as of one of his great ancestors was erected to a soldier of fortune a hundred and fifty years after Faliero's death; and the most conspicuous parts of the city have been so entirely altered in the course of the last three centuries, that if Henry Dandolo or Francis Foscari could be summoned from their tombs, and stood each on the deck of his galley at the entrance of the Grand Canal, that renowned entrance, the painter's favorite subject, the novelist's favorite scene, where the water first narrows by the steps of the Church of La Salute,—the mighty Doges would not know in what spot of the world they stood, would literally not recognize one stone of the great city, for whose sake, and by whose ingratitude, their grey hairs had been brought down with bitterness to the grave. The remains of *their* Venice lie hidden behind the cumbrous masses which were the delight of the nation in its dotage; hidden in many a grass-grown court, and silent pathway, and lightless canal, where the slow waves have sapped their foundations for five hundred years, and must soon prevail over them for ever. It must be our task to glean and gather them forth, and restore out of them some faint image of the lost city, more gorgeous a thousand-fold than that which now exists, yet not created in the day-

dream of the prince, nor by the ostentation of the noble, but
built by iron hands and patient hearts, contending against
the adversity of nature and the fury of man, so that its won
derfulness cannot be grasped by the indolence of imagination,
but only after frank inquiry into the true nature of that wild
and solitary scene, whose restless tides and trembling sands
did indeed shelter the birth of the city, but long denied her
dominion.

§ III. When the eye falls casually on a map of Europe, there
is no feature by which it is more likely to be arrested than the
strange sweeping loop formed by the junction of the Alps and
Apennines, and enclosing the great basin of Lombardy. This
return of the mountain chain upon itself causes a vast difference in the character of the distribution of its debris on its
opposite sides. The rock fragments and sediment which the
torrents on the north side of the Alps bear into the plains are
distributed over a vast extent of country, and, though here
and there lodged in beds of enormous thickness, soon permit the firm substrata to appear from underneath them; but
all the torrents which descend from the southern side of the
High Alps, and from the northern slope of the Apennines,
meet concentrically in the recess or mountain bay which the
two ridges enclose; every fragment which thunder breaks out
of their battlements, and every grain of dust which the summer rain washes from their pastures, is at last laid at rest in
the blue sweep of the Lombardic plain; and that plain must
have risen within its rocky barriers as a cup fills with
wine, but for two contrary influences which continually
depress, or disperse from its surface, the accumulation of the
ruins of ages.

§ IV. I will not tax the reader's faith in modern science by
insisting on the singular depression of the surface of Lombardy,
which appears for many centuries to have taken place steadily
and continually; the main fact with which we have to do is

the gradual transport, by the Po and its great collateral rivers, of vast masses of the finer sediment to the sea. The character of the Lombardic plains is most strikingly expressed by the ancient walls of its cities, composed for the most part of large rounded Alpine pebbles alternating with narrow courses of brick; and was curiously illustrated in 1848, by the ramparts of these same pebbles thrown up four or five feet high round every field, to check the Austrian cavalry in the battle under the walls of Verona. The finer dust among which these pebbles are dispersed is taken up by the rivers, fed into continual strength by the Alpine snow, so that, however pure their waters may be when they issue from the lakes at the foot of the great chain, they become of the color and opacity of clay before they reach the Adriatic; the sediment which they bear is at once thrown down as they enter the sea, forming a vast belt of low land along the eastern coast of Italy. The powerful stream of the Po of course builds forward the fastest; on each side of it, north and south, there is a tract of marsh, fed by more feeble streams, and less liable to rapid change than the delta of the central river. In one of these tracts is built RAVENNA, and in the other VENICE.

§ v. What circumstances directed the peculiar arrangement of this great belt of sediment in the earliest times, it is not here the place to inquire. It is enough for us to know that from the mouths of the Adige to those of the Piave there stretches, at a variable distance of from three to five miles from the actual shore, a bank of sand, divided into long islands by narrow channels of sea. The space between this bank and the true shore consists of the sedimentary deposits from these and other rivers, a great plain of calcareous mud, covered, in the neighborhood of Venice, by the sea at high water, to the depth in most places of a foot or a foot and a half, and nearly everywhere exposed at low tide, but divided by an intricate network of narrow and winding channels, from which the sea never retires. In some places, according to the run of the currents, the land has risen into marshy islets, consolidated, some by art, and some by time, into ground firm enough to be built upon, or fruitful enough to be cultivated : in others, on the contrary, it has not reached the sea level; so that, at the average low water, shallow lakelets glitter among its irregularly exposed fields of seaweed. In the midst of the largest of these, increased in importance by the confluence of several large river channels towards one of the openings in the sea bank, the city of Venice itself is built, on a crowded cluster of islands; the various plots of higher ground which appear to the north and south of this central cluster, have at different periods been also thickly inhabited, and now bear, according to their size, the remains of cities, villages, or isolated convents and churches, scattered among spaces of open ground, partly waste and encumbered by ruins, partly under cultivation for the supply of the metropolis.

§ VI. The average rise and fall of the tide is about three feet (varying considerably with the seasons *) ; but this fall, on so flat a shore, is enough to cause continual movement in the waters, and in the main canals to produce a reflux which frequently runs like a mill stream. At high water no land is visible for many miles to the north or south of Venice, except in the form of small islands crowned with towers or gleaming with villages : there is a channel, some three miles wide, between the city and the mainland, and some mile and a half wide between it and the sandy breakwater called the Lido, which divides the lagoon from the Adriatic, but which is so ow as hardly to disturb the impression of the city's having neen built in the midst of the ocean, although the secret of its true position is partly, yet not painfully, betrayed by the clusters of piles set to mark the deep-water channels, which

---

* Appendix 3. : "Tides of Venice."

undulate far away in spotty chains like the studded backs of huge sea-snakes, and by the quick glittering of the crisped and crowded waves that flicker and dance before the strong winds upon the unlifted level of the shallow sea. But the scene is widely different at low tide. A fall of eighteen or twenty inches is enough to show ground over the greater part of the lagoon; and at the complete ebb the city is seen standing in the midst of a dark plain of sea-weed, of gloomy green, except only where the larger branches of the Brenta and its associated streams converge towards the port of the Lido. Through this salt and sombre plain the gondola and the fishing-boat advance by tortuous channels, seldom more than four or five feet deep, and often so choked with slime that the heavier keels furrow the bottom till their crossing tracks are seen through the clear sea water like the ruts upon a wintry road, and the oar leaves blue gashes upon the ground at every stroke, or is entangled among the thick weed that fringes the banks with the weight of its sullen waves, leaning to and fro upon the uncertain sway of the exhausted tide. The scene is often profoundly oppressive, even at this day, when every plot of higher ground bears some fragment of fair building: but, in order to know what it was once, let the traveller follow in his boat at evening the windings of some unfrequented channel far into the midst of the melancholy plain; let him remove, in his imagination, the brightness of the great city that still extends itself in the distance, and the walls and towers from the islands that are near; and so wait, until the bright investiture and sweet warmth of the sunset are withdrawn from the waters, and the black desert of their shore lies in its nakedness beneath the night, pathless, comfortless, infirm, lost in dark languor and fearful silence, except where the salt runlets plash into the tideless pools, or the sea-birds flit from their margins with a questioning cry; and he will be enabled to enter in some sort into the horror of heart with

1*

which this solitude was anciently chosen by man for his habitation. They little thought, who first drove the stakes into the sand, and strewed the ocean reeds for their rest, that their children were to be the princes of that ocean, and their palaces its pride; and yet, in the great natural laws that rule that sorrowful wilderness, let it be remembered what strange preparation had been made for the things which no human imagination could have foretold, and how the whole existence and fortune of the Venetian nation were anticipated or compelled, by the setting of those bars and doors to the rivers and the sea. Had deeper currents divided their islands, hostile navies would again and again have reduced the rising city into servitude; had stronger surges beaten their shores, all the richness and refinement of the Venetian architecture must have been exchanged for the walls and bulwarks of an ordinary sea-port. Had there been no tide, as in other parts of the Mediterranean, the narrow canals of the city would have become noisome, and the marsh in which it was built pestiferous. Had the tide been only a foot or eighteen inches higher in its rise, the water-access to the doors of the palaces would have been impossible : even as it is, there is sometimes a little difficulty, at the ebb, in landing without setting foot upon the lower and slippery steps : and the highest tides sometimes enter the courtyards, and overflow the entrance halls. Eighteen inches more of difference between the level of the flood and ebb would have rendered the doorsteps of every palace, at low water, a treacherous mass of weeds and limpets, and the entire system of water-carriage for the higher classes, in their easy and daily intercourse, must have been done away with. The streets of the city would have been widened, its network of canals filled up, and all the peculiar character of the place and the people destroyed.

§ VII. The reader may perhaps have felt some pain in the contrast between this faithful view of the site of the Venetian

Throne, and the romantic conception of it which we ordinarily form ; but this pain, if he have felt it, ought to be more than counterbalanced by the value of the instance thus afforded to us at once of the inscrutableness and the wisdom of the ways of God. If, two thousand years ago, we had been permitted to watch the slow settling of the slime of those turbid rivers into the polluted sea, and the gaining upon its deep and fresh waters of the lifeless, impassable, unvoyageable plain, how little could we have understood the purpose with which those islands were shaped out of the void, and the torpid waters enclosed with their desolate walls of sand ! How little could we have known, any more than of what now seems to us most distressful, dark, and objectless, the glorious aim which was then in the mind of Him in whose hand are all the corners of the earth ! how little imagined that in the laws which were stretching forth the gloomy margins of those fruitless banks, and feeding the bitter grass among their shallows, there was indeed a preparation, and *the only preparation possible*, for the founding of a city which was to be set like a golden clasp on the girdle of the earth, to write her history on the white scrolls of the sea-surges, and to word it in their thunder, and to gather and give forth, in world-wide pulsation, the glory of the West and of the East, from the burning heart of her Fortitude and Splendor.

CHAPTER II.

TORCELLO.

§ I. SEVEN miles to the north of Venice, the banks of sand,
which near the city rise little above low-water mark, attain by
degrees a higher level, and knit themselves at last into fields
of salt morass, raised here and there into shapeless mounds,
and intercepted by narrow creeks of sea. One of the feeblest
of these inlets, after winding for some time among buried
fragments of masonry, and knots of sunburnt weeds whitened
with webs of fucus, stays itself in an utterly stagnant pool
beside a plot of greener grass covered with ground ivy and
violets. On this mound is built a rude brick campanile, of
the commonest Lombardic type, which if we ascend towards
evening (and there are none to hinder us, the door of its
ruinous staircase swinging idly on its hinges), we may command from it one of the most notable scenes in this wide
world of ours. Far as the eye can reach, a waste of wild sea
moor, of a lurid ashen grey; not like our northern moors
with their jet-black pools and purple heath, but lifeless, the
color of sackcloth, with the corrupted sea-water soaking
through the roots of its acrid weeds, and gleaming hither
and thither through its snaky channels. No gathering of
fantastic mists, nor coursing of clouds across it; but melancholy clearness of space in the warm sunset, oppressive,
reaching to the horizon of its level gloom. To the very
horizon, on the north-east; but, to the north and west, there

is a blue line of higher land along the border of it, and above this, but farther back, a misty band of mountains, touched with snow. To the east, the paleness and roar of the Adriatic, louder at momentary intervals as the surf breaks on the bars of sand ; to the south, the widening branches of the calm lagoon, alternately purple and pale green, as they reflect the evening clouds or twilight sky ; and almost beneath our feet, on the same field which sustains the tower we gaze from, a group of four buildings, two of them little larger than cottages (though built of stone, and one adorned by a quaint belfry), the third an octagonal chapel, of which we can see but little more than the flat red roof with its rayed tiling, the fourth, a considerable church with nave and aisles, but of which, in like manner, we can see little but the long central ridge and lateral slopes of roof, which the sunlight separates in one glowing mass from the green field beneath and grey moor beyond. There are no living creatures near the buildings, nor any vestige of village or city round about them. They lie like a little company of ships becalmed on a far-away sea.

§ II. Then look farther to the south. Beyond the widening branches of the lagoon, and rising out of the bright lake into which they gather, there are a multitude of towers, dark, and scattered among square-set shapes of clustered palaces, a long and irregular line fretting the southern sky.

Mother and daughter, you behold them both in their widowhood,—TORCELLO, and VENICE.

Thirteen hundred years ago, the grey moorland looked as it does this day, and the purple mountains stood as radiantly in the deep distances of evening; but on the line of the horizon, there were strange fires mixed with the light of sunset, and the lament of many human voices mixed with the fretting of the waves on their ridges of sand. The flames rose from the ruins of Altinum ; the lament from the multitude of its people, seeking, like Israel of old, a refuge from the sword in the paths of the sea.

The cattle are feeding and resting upon the site of the city that they left; the mower's scythe swept this day at dawn over the chief street of the city that they built, and the swathes of soft grass are now sending up their scent into the night air, the only incense that fills the temple of their ancient worship. Let us go down into that little space of meadow land.

§ III. The inlet which runs nearest to the base of the campanile is not that by which Torcello is commonly approached. Another, somewhat broader, and overhung by alder copse, winds out of the main channel of the lagoon up to the very edge of the little meadow which was once the Piazza of the city, and there, stayed by a few grey stones which present some semblance of a quay, forms its boundary at one extremity. Hardly larger than an ordinary English farmyard, and roughly enclosed on each side by broken palings and hedges of honeysuckle and briar, the narrow field retires from the water's edge, traversed by a scarcely traceable footpath, for some forty or fifty paces, and then expanding into the form of a small square, with buildings on three sides of it, the fourth being that which opens to the water. Two of these, that on our left and that in front of us as we approach from the canal, are so small that they might well be taken for the out-houses of the farm, though the first is a conventual building, and the other aspires to the title of the " Palazzo publico," both dating as far back as the beginning of the fourteenth century; the third, the octagonal church of Santa Fosca, is far more ancient than either, yet hardly on a larger scale. Though the pillars of the portico which surrounds it are of pure Greek marble, and their capitals are enriched with delicate sculpture, they, and the arches they sustain, together only raise the roof to the height of a cattle-shed; and the first strong impression which the spectator receives from the whole scene is, that whatever sin it may have been which has on this spot been visited with so utter a desolation, it could not at least have been ambition. Nor will this impression be diminished as we approach, or enter, the larger church to which the whole group of building is subordinate. It has evidently been built by men in flight and distress*, who sought in the hurried erection of their island church such a shelter for their earnest and sorrowful worship as, on the one hand, could not attract the eyes of their enemies by its splendor, and yet, on the other, might not awaken too bitter feelings by its contrast with the churches which they had seen destroyed. There is visible everywhere a simple and tender effort to recover some of the form of the temples which they had loved, and to do honor to God by that which they were erecting, while distress and humiliation prevented the desire, and prudence precluded the admission, either of luxury of ornament or magnificence of plan. The exterior is absolutely devoid of decoration, with the exception only of the western entrance and the lateral door, of which the former has carved sideposts and architrave, and the latter, crosses of rich sculpture; while the massy stone shutters of the windows, turning on huge rings of stone, which answer the double purpose of stanchions and brackets, cause the whole building rather to resemble a refuge from Alpine storm than the cathedral of a populous city; and, internally, the two solemn mosaics of the eastern and western extremities,—one representing the Last Judgment, the other the Madonna, her tears falling as her hands are raised to bless,—and the noble range of pillars which enclose the space between, terminated by the high throne for the pastor and the semicircular raised seats for the superior clergy, are expressive at once of the deep sorrow and the sacred courage of men who had no home

* Appendix 4.: "Date of the Duomo of Torcello."

left them upon earth, but who looked for one to come, of men "persecuted but not forsaken, cast down but not destroyed."

§ IV. I am not aware of any other early church in Italy which has this peculiar expression in so marked a degree; and it is so consistent with all that Christian architecture ought to express in every age (for the actual condition of the exiles who built the cathedral of Torcello is exactly typical of the spiritual condition which every Christian ought to recognize in himself, a state of homelessness on earth, except so far as he can make the Most High his habitation), that I would rather fix the mind of the reader on this general character than on the separate details, however interesting, of the architecture itself. I shall therefore examine these only so far as is necessary to give a clear idea of the means by which the peculiar expression of the building is attained.

§ V. On the opposite page, the uppermost figure, 1., is a rude plan of the church. I do not answer for the thickness and external disposition of the walls, which are not to our present purpose, and which I have not carefully examined; but the interior arrangement is given with sufficient accuracy. The church is built on the usual plan of the Basilica,* that is to say, its body divided into a nave and aisles by two rows of massive shafts, the roof of the nave being raised high above the aisles by walls sustained on two ranks of pillars, and pierced with small arched windows. At Torcello the aisles are also lighted in the same manner, and the nave is nearly twice their breadth.†

The capitals of all the great shafts are of white marble, and are among the best I have ever seen, as examples of perfectly calculated effect from every touch of the chisel. Mr. Hope

---

* For a full account of the form and symbolical meaning of the Basilica, see Lord Lindsay's "Christian Art," vol. i. p. 12. It is much to be regretted that the Chevalier Bunsen's work on the Basilicas of Rome is not translated into English.

† The measures are given in Appendix 3.

calls them " indifferently imitated from the Corinthian :"* but the expression is as inaccurate as it is unjust; every one of them is different in design, and their variations are as graceful as they are fanciful. I could not, except by an elaborate drawing, give any idea of the sharp, dark, deep penetrations of the chisel into their snowy marble, but a single example is given in the opposite Plate, fig. 1., of the nature of the changes effected in them from the Corinthian type. In this capital, although a kind of acanthus (only with rounded lobes) is indeed used for the upper range of leaves, the lower range is not acanthus at all, but a kind of vine, or at least that species of plant which stands for vine in all early Lombardic and Byzantine work (vide Vol. I. Appendix 8.); the leaves are trefoiled, and the stalks cut clear so that they might be grasped with the hand, and cast sharp dark shadows, perpetually changing, across the bell of the capital behind them. I have drawn one of these vine plants larger in fig. 2., that the reader may see how little imitation of the Corinthian there is in them, and how boldly the stems of the leaves are detached from the ground. But there is another circumstance in this ornament still more noticeable. The band which encircles the shaft beneath the spring of the leaves is copied from the common

Fig. 1.

classical wreathed or braided fillet, of which the reader may see examples on almost every building of any pretensions in modern London. But the mediæval builders could not be content with the dead and meaningless scroll: the Gothic energy and love of life, mingled with the early Christian religious symbolism, were struggling daily into more vigorous expression, and they turned the wreathed band into a serpent of three times the length necessary to undulate

* Hope's "Historical Essay on Architecture," (third edition, 1840) chap. ix. p. 95. In other respects Mr. Hope has done justice to this building, and to the style of the early Christian churches in general.

round the shaft, which, knotting itself into a triple chain, shows at one side of the shaft its tail and head, as if perpetually gliding round it beneath the stalks of the vines. The vine, as is well known, was one of the early symbols of Christ, and the serpent is here typical either of the eternity of his dominion, or of the Satanic power subdued.

§ VI. Nor even when the builder confines himself to the acanthus leaf (or to that representation of it, hereafter to be more particularly examined, constant in Romanesque work) can his imagination allow him to rest content with its accustomed position. In a common Corinthian capital the leaves nod forward only, thrown out on every side from the bell which they surround: but at the base of one of the capitals on the opposite side of the nave from this of the vines,* two leaves are introduced set with their sides outwards, forming spirals by curling back, half-closed, in the position shown in fig. 4. in Plate II., there represented as in a real acanthus leaf; for it will assist our future inquiries into the ornamentation of capitals that the reader should be acquainted with the form of the acanthus leaf itself. I have drawn it, therefore, in the two positions, figs. 3. and 4. in Plate II.; while fig. 5. is the translation of the latter form into marble by the sculptor of Torcello. It is not very like the acanthus, but much liker than any Greek work; though still entirely conventional in its cinquefoiled lobes. But these are disposed with the most graceful freedom of line, separated at the roots by deep drill holes, which tell upon the eye far away like beads of jet; and changed, before they become too crowded to be effective, into a vigorous and simple zigzagged edge, which saves the designer some embarrassment in the perspective of the terminating spiral. But his feeling of nature was greater than his knowledge of perspective; and it is delightful to see how he has rooted the whole leaf in the strong rounded under-stem,

* A sketch has been given of this capital in my folio work.

the indication of its closing with its face inwards, and has thus given organization and elasticity to the lovely group of spiral lines; a group of which, even in the lifeless sea-shell, we are never weary, but which becomes yet more delightful when the ideas of elasticity and growth are joined to the sweet succession of its involution.

§ VII. It is not, however, to be expected that either the mute language of early Christianity (however important a part of the expression of the building at the time of its erection), or the delicate fancies of the Gothic leafage springing into new life, should be read, or perceived, by the passing traveller who has never been taught to expect any thing in architecture except five orders: yet he can hardly fail to be struck by the simplicity and dignity of the great shafts themselves; by the frank diffusion of light, which prevents their severity from becoming oppressive; by the delicate forms and lovely carving of the pulpit and chancel screen; and, above all, by the peculiar aspect of the eastern extremity of the church, which, instead of being withdrawn, as in later cathedrals, into a chapel dedicated to the Virgin, or contributing by the brilliancy of its windows to the splendor of the altar, and theatrical effect of the ceremonies performed there, is a simple and stern semicircular recess, filled beneath by three ranks of seats, raised one above the other, for the bishop and presbyters, that they might watch as well as guide the devotions of the people, and discharge literally in the daily service the functions of bishops or *overseers* of the flock of God.

§ VIII. Let us consider a little each of these characters in succession; and first (for of the shafts enough has been said already), what is very peculiar to this church, its luminousness. This perhaps strikes the traveller more from its contrast with the excessive gloom of the Church of St. Mark's; but it is remarkable when we compare the Cathedral of Torcello with any of the contemporary basilicas in South Italy or Lombardic churches in the North. St. Ambrogio at Milan, St. Michele at Pavia, St. Zeno at Verona, St. Frediano at Lucca, St. Miniato at Florence, are all like sepulchral caverns compared with Torcello, where the slightest details of the sculptures and mosaics are visible, even when twilight is deepening. And there is something especially touching in our finding the sunshine thus freely admitted into a church built by men in sorrow. They did not need the darkness; they could not perhaps bear it. There was fear and depression upon them enough, without a material gloom. They sought for comfort in their religion, for tangible hopes and promises, not for threatenings or mysteries; and though the subjects chosen for the mosaics on the walls are of the most solemn character, there are no artificial shadows cast upon them, nor dark colors used in them : all is fair and bright, and intended evidently to be regarded in hopefulness, and not with terror.

§ IX. For observe this choice of subjects. It is indeed possible that the walls of the nave and aisles, which are now whitewashed, may have been covered with fresco or mosaic, and thus have supplied a series of subjects, on the choice of which we cannot speculate. I do not, however, find record of the destruction of any such works ; and I am rather inclined to believe that at any rate the central division of the building was originally decorated, as it is now, simply by mosaics representing Christ, the Virgin, and the apostles, at one extremity, and Christ coming to judgment at the other. And if so, I repeat, observe the significance of this choice. Most other early churches are covered with imagery sufficiently suggestive of the vivid interest of the builders in the history and occupations of the world. Symbols or representations of political events, portraits of living persons, and sculptures of satirical, grotesque, or trivial subjects are of constant occurrence, mingled with the more strictly appointed representations of scriptural or ecclesiastical history ; but at Torcello even these

usual, and one should have thought almost necessary, successions of Bible events do not appear. The mind of the worshipper was fixed entirely upon two great facts, to him the
most precious of all facts,—the present mercy of Christ to His
Church, and His future coming to judge the world. That
Christ's mercy was, at this period, supposed chiefly to be
attainable through the pleading of the Virgin, and that therefore beneath the figure of the Redeemer is seen that of the
weeping Madonna in the act of intercession, may indeed be
matter of sorrow to the Protestant beholder, but ought not
to blind him to the earnestness and singleness of the faith with
which these men sought their sea-solitudes; not in hope of
founding new dynasties, or entering upon new epochs of prosperity, but only to humble themselves before God, and to pray
that in His infinite mercy He would hasten the time when the
sea should give up the dead which were in it, and Death and
Hell give up the dead which were in them, and when they
might enter into the better kingdom, " where the wicked cease
from troubling and the weary are at rest."

§ x. Nor were the strength and elasticity of their minds,
even in the least matters, diminished by thus looking forward
to the close of all things. On the contrary, nothing is more
remarkable than the finish and beauty of all the portions of the
building, which seem to have been actually executed for the
place they occupy in the present structure. The rudest are
those which they brought with them from the mainland; the
best and most beautiful, those which appear to have been
carved for their island church: of these, the new capitals
already noticed, and the exquisite panel ornaments of the
chancel screen, are the most conspicuous; the latter form a
low wall across the church between the six small shafts whose
places are seen in the plan, and serve to enclose a space raised
two steps above the level of the nave, destined for the singers,
and indicated also in the plan by an open line $a\ b\ c\ d$. The

bas-reliefs on this low screen are groups of peacocks and lions two face to face on each panel, rich and fantastic beyond description, though not expressive of very accurate knowledge either of leonine or pavonine forms. And it is not until we pass to the back of the stair of the pulpit, which is connected with the northern extremity of this screen, that we find evidence of the haste with which the church was constructed.

§ XI. The pulpit, however, is not among the least noticeable of its features. It is sustained on the four small detached shafts marked at p in the plan, between the two pillars at the north side of the screen; both pillars and pulpit studiously plain, while the staircase which ascends to it is a compact mass of masonry (shaded in the plan), faced by carved slabs of marble; the parapet of the staircase being also formed of solid blocks like paving-stones, lightened by rich, but not deep, exterior carving. Now these blocks, or at least those which adorn the staircase towards the aisle, have been brought from the main land; and, being of size and shape not easily to be adjusted to the proportions of the stair, the architect has cut out of them pieces of the size he needed, utterly regardless of the subject or symmetry of the original design. The pulpit is not the only place where this rough procedure has been permitted: at the lateral door of the church are two crosses, cut out of slabs of marble, formerly covered with rich sculpture over their whole surfaces, of which portions are left on the surface of the crosses; the lines of the original design being, of course, just as arbitrarily cut by the incisions between the arms, as the patterns upon a piece of silk which has been shaped anew. The fact is, that in all early Romanesque work, large surfaces are covered with sculpture for the sake of enrichment only; sculpture which indeed had always meaning, because it was easier for the sculptor to work with some chain of thought to guide his chisel, than without any; but it was not always intended, or at least not always hoped, that this chain of thought might be traced by the spectator. All that was proposed appears to have been the enrichment of surface, so as to make it delightful to the eye; and this being once understood, a decorated piece of marble became to the architect just what a piece of lace or embroidery is to a dressmaker, who takes of it such portions as she may require, with little regard to the places where the patterns are divided. And though it may appear, at first sight, that the procedure is indicative of bluntness and rudeness of feeling, we may perceive, upon reflection, that it may also indicate the redundance of power which sets little price upon its own exertion. When a barbarous nation builds its fortress-walls out of fragments of the refined architecture it has overthrown, we can read nothing but its savageness in the vestiges of art which may thus chance to have been preserved; but when the new work is equal, if not superior, in execution, to the pieces of the older art which are associated with it, we may justly conclude that the rough treatment to which the latter have been subjected is rather a sign of the hope of doing better things, than of want of feeling for those already accomplished. And, in general, this careless fitting of ornament is, in very truth, an evidence of life in the school of builders, and of their making a due distinction between work which is to be used for architectural effect, and work which is to possess an abstract perfection; and it commonly shows also that the exertion of design is so easy to them, and their fertility so inexhaustible, that they feel no remorse in using somewhat injuriously what they can replace with so slight an effort.

§ XII. It appears however questionable in the present instance, whether, if the marbles had not been carved to his hand, the architect would have taken the trouble to enrich them. For the execution of the rest of the pulpit is studiously simple, and it is in this respect that its design possesses, it seems to me, an interest to the religious spectator greater

than he will take in any other portion of the building. It is
supported, as I said, on a group of four slender shafts; itself
of a slightly oval form, extending nearly from one pillar of the
nave to the next, so as to give the preacher free room for the
action of the entire person, which always gives an unaffected
impressiveness to the eloquence of the southern nations. In
the centre of its curved front, a small bracket and detached
shaft sustain the projection of a narrow marble desk (occupying the place of a cushion in a modern pulpit), which is hollowed out into a shallow curve on the upper surface, leaving a
ledge at the bottom of the slab, so that a book laid upon it, or
rather into it, settles itself there, opening as if by instinct, but
without the least chance of slipping to the side, or in any way
moving beneath the preacher's hands.* Six balls, or rather
almonds, of purple marble veined with white are set round
the edge of the pulpit, and form its only decoration. Perfectly
graceful, but severe and almost cold in its simplicity, built for
permanence and service, so that no single member, no stone
of it, could be spared, and yet all are firm and uninjured as
when they were first set together, it stands in venerable contrast both with the fantastic pulpits of mediæval cathedrals
and with the rich furniture of those of our modern churches.
It is worth while pausing for a moment to consider how far
the manner of decorating a pulpit may have influence on the
efficiency of its service, and whether our modern treatment
of this, to us all-important, feature of a church be the best
possible.

§ XIII. When the sermon is good we need not much concern
ourselves about the form of the pulpit. But sermons cannot
always be good; and I believe that the temper in which the
congregation set themselves to listen may be in some degree
modified by their perception of fitness or unfitness, impressiveness or vulgarity, in the disposition of the place appointed for

* Appendix 5 : "Modern Pulpits."

the speaker,—not to the same degree, but somewhat in the same way, that they may be influenced by his own gestures or expression, irrespective of the sense of what he says. I believe, therefore, in the first place, that pulpits ought never to be highly decorated; the speaker is apt to look mean or diminutive if the pulpit is either on a very large scale or covered with splendid ornament, and if the interest of the sermon should flag the mind is instantly tempted to wander. I have observed that in almost all cathedrals, when the pulpits are peculiarly magnificent, sermons are not often preached from them; but rather, and especially if for any important purpose, from some temporary erection in other parts of the building: and though this may often be done because the architect has consulted the effect upon the eye more than the convenience of the ear in the placing of his larger pulpit, I think it also proceeds in some measure from a natural dislike in the preacher to match himself with the magnificence of the rostrum, lest the sermon should not be thought worthy of the place. Yet this will rather hold of the colossal sculptures, and pyramids of fantastic tracery which encumber the pulpits of Flemish and German churches, than of the delicate mosaics and ivory-like carving of the Romanesque basilicas, for when the form is kept simple, much loveliness of color and costliness of work may be introduced, and yet the speaker not be thrown into the shade by them.

§ XIV. But, in the second place, whatever ornaments we admit ought clearly to be of a chaste, grave, and noble kind; and what furniture we employ, evidently more for the honoring of God's word than for the ease of the preacher. For there are two ways of regarding a sermon, either as a human composition, or a Divine message. If we look upon it entirely as the first, and require our clergymen to finish it with their utmost care and learning, for our better delight whether of ear or intellect, we shall necessarily be led to expect much formality and stateliness in its delivery, and to think that all is not well if the pulpit have not a golden fringe round it, and a goodly cushion in front of it, and if the sermon be not fairly written in a black book, to be smoothed upon the cushion in a majestic manner before beginning; all this we shall duly come to expect: but we shall at the same time consider the treatise thus prepared as something to which it is our duty to listen without restlessness for half an hour or three quarters, but which, when that duty has been decorously performed, we may dismiss from our minds in happy confidence of being provided with another when next it shall be necessary. But if once we begin to regard the preacher, whatever his faults, as a man sent with a message to us, which it is a matter of life or death whether we hear or refuse; if we look upon him as set in charge over many spirits in danger of ruin, and having allowed to him but an hour or two in the seven days to speak to them; if we make some endeavor to conceive how precious these hours ought to be to him, a small vantage on the side of God after his flock have been exposed for six days together to the full weight of the world's temptation, and he has been forced to watch the thorn and the thistle springing in their hearts, and to see what wheat had been scattered there snatched from the way-side by this wild bird and the other, and at last, when breathless and weary with the week's labor they give him this interval of imperfect and languid hearing, he has but thirty minutes to get at the separate hearts of a thousand men, to convince them of all their weaknesses, to shame them for all their sins, to warn them of all their dangers, to try by this way and that to stir the hard fastenings of those doors where the Master himself has stood and knocked yet none opened, and to call at the openings of those dark streets where Wisdom herself hath stretched forth her hands and no man regarded,—thirty minutes to aise the dead in,—let us but once understand and feel this, and we shall look with changed eyes upon that frippery of gay furniture about the place from which the message of judgment must be delivered, which either breathes upon the dry bones that they may live, or, if ineffectual, remains recorded in condemnation, perhaps against the utterer and listener alike, but assuredly against one of them. We shall not so easily bear with the silk and gold upon the seat of judgment, nor with ornament of oratory in the mouth of the messenger: we shall wish that his words may be simple, even when they are sweetest, and the place from which he speaks like a marble rock in the desert, about which the people have gathered in their thirst.

§ xv. But the severity which is so marked in the pulpit at Torcello is still more striking in the raised seats and episcopal throne which occupy the curve of the apse. The arrangement at first somewhat recalls to the mind that of the Roman amphitheatres; the flight of steps which lead up to the central throne divides the curve of the continuous steps or seats (it appears in the first three ranges questionable which were intended, for they seem too high for the one, and too low and close for the other), exactly as in an amphitheatre the stairs for access intersect the sweeping ranges of seats. But in the very rudeness of this arrangement, and especially in the want of all appliances of comfort (for the whole is of marble, and the arms of the central throne are not for convenience, but for distinction, and to separate it more conspicuously from the undivided seats), there is a dignity which no furniture of stalls nor carving of canopies ever could attain, and well worth the contemplation of the Protestant, both as sternly significative of an episcopal authority which in the early days of the Church was never disputed, and as dependent for all its impressiveness on the utter absence of any expression either of pride or self-indulgence.

§ xvi. But there is one more circumstance which we ought

to remember as giving peculiar significance to the position which the episcopal throne occupies in this island church, namely, that in the minds of all early Christians the Church itself was most frequently symbolized under the image of a ship, of which the bishop was the pilot. Consider the force which this symbol would assume in the imaginations of men to whom the spiritual Church had become an ark of refuge in the midst of a destruction hardly less terrible than that from which the eight souls were saved of old, a destruction in which the wrath of man had become as broad as the earth and as merciless as the sea, and who saw the actual and literal edifice of the Church raised up, itself like an ark in the midst of the waters. No marvel if with the surf of the Adriatic rolling between them and the shores of their birth, from which they were separated for ever, they should have looked upon each other as the disciples did when the storm came down on the Tiberias Lake, and have yielded ready and loving obedience to those who ruled them in His name, who had there rebuked the winds and commanded stillness to the sea. And if the stranger would yet learn in what spirit it was that the dominion of Venice was begun, and in what strength she went forth conquering and to conquer, let him not seek to estimate the wealth of her arsenals or number of her armies, nor look upon the pageantry of her palaces, nor enter into the secrets of her councils; but let him ascend the highest tier of the stern ledges that sweep round the altar of Torcello, and then, looking as the pilot did of old along the marble ribs of the goodly temple-ship, let him repeople its veined deck with the shadows of its dead mariners, and strive to feel in himself the strength of heart that was kindled within them, when first, after the pillars of it had settled in the sand, and the roof of it had been closed against the angry sky that was still reddened by the fires of their homesteads,—first, within the shelter of its knitted walls, amidst the murmur of the waste of waves and

the beating of the wings of the sea-birds round the rock that
was strange to them,—rose that ancient hymn, in the power
of their gathered voices:

THE SEA IS HIS, AND HE MADE IT:

AND HIS HANDS PREPARED THE DRY LAND.

CHAPTER III.

MURANO.

§ I. THE decay of the city of Venice is, in many respects, like that of an outwearied and aged human frame; the cause of its decrepitude is indeed at the heart, but the outward appearances of it are first at the extremities. In the centre of the city there are still places where some evidence of vitality remains, and where, with kind closing of the eyes to signs, too manifest even there, of distress and declining fortune, the stranger may succeed in imagining, for a little while, what must have been the aspect of Venice in her prime. But this lingering pulsation has not force enough any more to penetrate into the suburbs and outskirts of the city; the frost of death has there seized upon it irrevocably, and the grasp of mortal disease is marked daily by the increasing breadth of its belt of ruin. Nowhere is this seen more grievously than along the great north-eastern boundary, once occupied by the smaller palaces of the Venetians, built for pleasure or repose; the nobler piles along the grand canal being reserved for the pomp and business of daily life. To such smaller palaces some garden ground was commonly attached, opening to the water-side; and, in front of these villas and gardens, the lagoon was wont to be covered in the evening by gondolas: the space of it between this part of the city and the island group of Murano being to Venice, in her time of power, what its parks are to London; only gondolas were used instead of carriages, and the crowd of the population did not come out till towards sunset, and prolonged their pleasures far into the night, company answering to company with alternate singing.

§ II. If, knowing this custom of the Venetians, and with a vision in his mind of summer palaces lining the shore, and myrtle gardens sloping to the sea, the traveller now seeks thi suburb of Venice, he will be strangely and sadly surprised to find a new but perfectly desolate quay, about a mile in length, extending from the arsenal to the Sacca della Misericordia, in front of a line of miserable houses built in the course of the last sixty or eighty years, yet already tottering to their ruin ; and not less to find that the principal object in the view which these houses (built partly in front and partly on the ruins of the ancient palaces) now command is a dead brick wall, about a quarter of a mile across the water, interrupted only by a kind of white lodge, the cheerfulness of which prospect is not enhanced by his finding that this wall encloses the principal public cemetery of Venice. He may, perhaps, marvel for a few moments at the singular taste of the old Venetians in taking their pleasure under a churchyard wall : but, on further inquiry, he will find that the building on the island, like those on the shore, is recent, that it stands on the ruins of the Church of St. Cristoforo della Pace ; and that with a singular, because unintended, moral, the modern Venetians have replaced the Peace of the Christ-bearer by the Peace of Death, and where they once went, as the sun set daily, to their pleasure, now go, as the sun sets to each of them for ever, to their graves.

§ III. Yet the power of Nature cannot be shortened by the folly, nor her beauty altogether saddened by the misery, of man. The broad tides still ebb and flow brightly about the island of the dead, and the linked conclave of the Alps know no decline from their old preeminence, nor stoop from their golden thrones in the circle of the horizon. So lovely is the scene still, in spite of all its injuries, that we shall find ourselves drawn there again and again at evening out of the narrow canals and streets of the city, to watch the wreaths of the sea-mists weaving themselves like mourning veils around the mountains far away, and listen to the green waves as they fret and sigh along the cemetery shore.

§ IV. But it is morning now: we have a hard day's work to do at Murano, and our boat shoots swiftly from beneath the last bridge of Venice, and brings us out into the open sea and sky.

The pure cumuli of cloud lie crowded and leaning against one another, rank beyond rank, far over the shining water, each cut away at its foundation by a level line, trenchant and clear, till they sink to the horizon like a flight of marble steps, except where the mountains meet them, and are lost in them, barred across by the grey terraces of those cloud foundations, and reduced into one crestless bank of blue, spotted here and there with strange flakes of wan, aerial, greenish light, strewed upon them like snow. And underneath is the long dark line of the mainland, fringed with low trees; and then the wide-waving surface of the burnished lagoon trembling slowly, and shaking out into forked bands of lengthening light the images of the towers of cloud above. To the north, there is first the great cemetery wall, then the long stray buildings of Murano, and the island villages beyond, glittering in intense crystalline vermilion, like so much jewellery scattered on a mirror, their towers poised apparently in the air a little above the horizon, and their reflections, as sharp and vivid and substantial as themselves, thrown on the vacancy between them and the sea. And thus the villages seem standing on the air; and, to the east, there is a cluster of ships that seem sailing on the land; for the sandy line of the Lido stretches itself between us and them, and we can see the tall white sails moving beyond it, but not the sea, only there is a sense of the

great sea being indeed there, and a solemn strength of gleam
ing light in sky above.

§ v. The most discordant feature in the whole scene is the
cloud which hovers above the glass furnaces of Murano; but
this we may not regret, as it is one of the last signs left of
human exertion among the ruinous villages which surround us.
The silent gliding of the gondola brings it nearer to us every
moment; we pass the cemetery, and a deep sea-channel which
separates it from Murano, and finally enter a narrow water-
street, with a paved footpath on each side, raised three or
four feet above the canal, and forming a kind of quay between
the water and the doors of the houses. These latter are, for
the most part, low, but built with massy doors and windows
of marble or Istrian stone, square set, and barred with iron;
buildings evidently once of no mean order, though now inhabited only by the poor. Here and there an ogee window of
the fourteenth century, or a doorway deeply enriched with
cable mouldings, shows itself in the midst of more ordinary
features; and several houses, consisting of one story only
carried on square pillars, forming a short arcade along the
quay, have windows sustained on shafts of red Verona marble,
of singular grace and delicacy. All now in vain: little care
is there for their delicacy or grace among the rough fishermen
sauntering on the quay with their jackets hanging loose from
their shoulders, jacket and cap and hair all of the same dark-
greenish sea-grey. But there is some life in the scene, more
than is usual in Venice: the women are sitting at their doors
nitting busily, and various workmen of the glass-houses sift-
ing glass dust upon the pavement, and strange cries coming
from one side of the canal to the other, and ringing far along
the crowded water, from venders of figs and grapes, and
gourds and shell-fish; cries partly descriptive of the eatables
in question, but interspersed with others of a character unintelligible in proportion to their violence, and fortunately so if

2*

we may judge by a sentence which is stencilled in black, within a garland, on the whitewashed walls of nearly every other house in the street, but which, how often soever written, no one seems to regard: "Bestemme non più. Lodate Gesù."

§ VI. We push our way on between large barges laden with fresh water from Fusina, in round white tubs seven feet across, and complicated boats full of all manner of nets that look as if they could never be disentang'ed, hanging from their masts and over their sides; and presently pass under a bridge with the lion of St. Mark on its archivolt, and another on a pillar at the end of the parapet, a small red lion with much of the puppy in his face, looking vacantly up into the air (in passing we may note that, instead of feathers, his wings are covered with hair, and in several other points the manner of his sculpture is not uninteresting). Presently the canal turns a little to the left, and thereupon becomes more quiet, the main bustle of the water-street being usually confined to the first straight reach of it, some quarter of a mile long, the Cheapside of Murano. We pass a considerable church on the left, St. Pietro, and a little square opposite to it with a few acacia trees, and then find our boat suddenly seized by a strong green eddy, and whirled into the tide-way of one of the main channels of the lagoon, which divides the town of Murano into two parts by a deep stream some fifty yards over, crossed only by one wooden bridge. We let ourselves drift some way down the current, looking at the low line of cottages on the other side of it, hardly knowing if there be more cheerfulness or melancholy in the way the sunshine glows on their ruinous but white-washed walls, and sparkles on the rushing of the green water by the grass-grown quay. It needs a strong stroke of the oar to bring us into the mouth of another quiet canal on the farther side of the tide-way, and we are still somewhat giddy when we run the head of the gondola into the sand on the left-hand side of this more sluggish stream, and land under the east end of the Church of San Donato, the "Matrice" or "Mother" Church of Murano.

§ VII. It stands, it and the heavy campanile detached from it a few yards, in a small triangular field of somewhat fresher grass than is usual near Venice, traversed by a paved walk with green mosaic of short grass between the rude squares of its stones, bounded on one side by ruinous garden walls, on another by a line of low cottages, on the third, the base of the triangle, by the shallow canal from which we have just landed. Near the point of the triangular space is a simple well, bearing date 1502 ; in its widest part, between the canal and campanile, is a four-square hollow pillar, each side formed by a separate slab of stone, to which the iron hasps are still attached that once secured the Venetian standard.

The cathedral itself occupies the northern angle of the field, encumbered with modern buildings, small outhouse-like chapels, and wastes of white wall with blank square windows, and itself utterly defaced in the whole body of it, nothing but the apse having been spared ; the original plan is only discoverable by careful examination, and even then but partially. The whole impression and effect of the building are irretrievably lost, but the fragments of it are still most precious.

We must first briefly state what is known of its history.

§ VIII. The legends of the Romish Church, though generally more insipid and less varied than those of Paganism, deserve audience from us on this ground, if on no other, that they have once been sincerely believed by good men, and have had no ineffective agency in the foundation of the existent European mind. The reader must not therefore accuse me of trifling, when I record for him the first piece of information I have been able to collect respecting the cathedral of Murano : namely, that the emperor Otho the Great, being

overtaken by a storm on the Adriatic, vowed, if he were preserved, to build and dedicate a church to the Virgin, in whatever place might be most pleasing to her; that the storm
thereupon abated; and the Virgin appearing to Otho in a
dream showed him, covered with red lilies, that very triangular field on which we were but now standing, amidst the
ragged weeds and shattered pavement. The emperor obeyed
the vision; and the church was consecrated on the 15th of
August, 957.

§ IX. Whatever degree of credence we may feel disposed
to attach to this piece of history, there is no question that a
church was built on this spot before the close of the tenth
century: since in the year 999 we find the incumbent of the
Basilica (note this word, it is of some importance) di Santa
Maria Plebania di Murano taking an oath of obedience to the
Bishop of the Altinat church, and engaging at the same time
to give the said bishop his dinner on the Domenica in Albis,
when the prelate held a confirmation in the mother church, as
it was then commonly called, of Murano. From this period,
for more than a century, I can find no records of any alterations made in the fabric of the church, but there exist very
full details of the quarrels which arose between its incumbents
and those of San Stefano, San Cipriano, San Salvatore, and
the other churches of Murano, touching the due obedience
which their less numerous or less ancient brotherhoods owed
to St. Mary's.

These differences seem to have been renewed at the election
of every new abbot by each of the fraternities, and must have
been growing serious when the patriarch of Grado, Henry
Dandolo, interfered in 1102, and, in order to seal a peace
between the two principal opponents, ordered that the abbot
of St. Stephen's should be present at the service in St. Mary's
on the night of the Epiphany, and that the abbot of St. Mary's
should visit him of St. Stephen's on St. Stephen's day; and

that then the two abbots " should eat apples and drink good wine together, in peace and charity."*

§ x. But even this kindly effort seems to have been without result: the irritated pride of the antagonists remained unsoothed by the love-feast of St. Stephen's day; and the breach continued to widen until the abbot of St. Mary's obtained a timely accession to his authority in the year 1125. The Doge Domenico Michele, having in the second crusade secured such substantial advantages for the Venetians as might well counterbalance the loss of part of their trade with the East, crowned his successes by obtaining possession in Cephalonia of the body of St. Donato, bishop of Eurœa; which treasure he having presented on his return to the Murano basilica, that church was thenceforward called the church of Sts. Mary and Donato. Nor was the body of the saint its only acquisition: St. Donato's principal achievement had been the destruction of a terrible dragon in Epirus; Michele brought home the bones of the dragon as well as of the saint; the latter were put in a marble sarcophagus, and the former hung up over the high altar.

§ xi. But the clergy of St. Stefano were indomitable. At the very moment when their adversaries had received this formidable accession of strength, they had the audacity " ad onta de' replicati giuramenti, e dell' inveterata consuetudine,"† to refuse to continue in the obedience which they had vowed to their mother church. The matter was tried in a provincial council; the votaries of St. Stephen were condemned, and remained quiet for about twenty years, in wholesome dread

* " Mela, e buon vino, con pace e carità." Memorie Storiche de' Veneti Primi e Secondi, di Jacopo Filiasi, (Padua, 1811) tom. iii. cap. 23. Perhaps, in the choice of the abbot's cheer, there was some occult reference to the verse of Solomon's Song: "Stay me with flagons, comfort me with apples."

† Notizie Storiche delle Chiese di Venezia, illustrate da Flaminio Corner, (Padua, 1758) p. 615.

of the authority conferred on the abbot of St. Donato, by the Pope's legate, to suspend any of the clergy of the island from their office if they refused submission.   In 1172, however, they appealed to Pope Alexander III., and were condemned again: and we find the struggle renewed at every promising opportunity, during the course of the 12th and 13th centuries; until at last, finding St. Donato and the dragon together too strong for him, the abbot of St. Stefano " discovered" in his church the bodies of two hundred martyrs at once!—a discovery, it is to be remembered, in some sort equivalent in those days to that of California in ours. The inscription, however, on the façade of the church, recorded it with quiet dignity :—" MCCCLXXIV. a dì XIV. di Aprile. Furono trovati nella presente chiesa del protomartire San Stefano, duecento e più corpi de' Santi Martiri, dal Ven. Prete Matteo Fradello, piovano della chiesa."* Corner, who gives this inscription, which no longer exists, goes on to explain with infinite gravity, that the bodies in question, " being of infantile form and stature, are reported by tradition to have belonged to those fortunate innocents who suffered martyrdom under King Herod ; but that when, or by whom, the church was enriched with so vast a treasure, is not manifested by any document."†

§ XII. The issue of the struggle is not to our present purpose. We have already arrived at the fourteenth century without finding record of any effort made by the clergy of St. Mary's to maintain their influence by restoring or beautifying their basilica; which is the only point at present of importance to us. That great alterations were made in it at the time of the acquisition of the body of St. Donato is however highly probable, the mosaic pavement of the interior, which bears its

---

* "On the 14th day of April, 1374, there were found, in this church of the first martyr St. Stefano, two hundred and more bodies of holy martyrs, by the venerable priest, Matthew Fradello, incumbent of the church."

† Notizie Storiche, p. 620.

date inscribed, 1140, being probably the last of the additions.
I believe that no part of the ancient church can be shown to
be of more recent date than this; and I shall not occupy the
reader's time by any inquiry respecting the epochs or authors
of the destructive modern restorations; the wreck of the old
fabric, breaking out beneath them here and there, is generally
distinguishable from them at a glance; and it is enough for
the reader to know that none of these truly ancient fragments
can be assigned to a more recent date than 1140, and that
some of them may with probability be looked upon as remains
of the shell of the first church, erected in the course of the
latter half of the tenth century. We shall perhaps obtain
some further reason for this belief as we examine these
remains themselves.

§ XIII. Of the body of the church, unhappily, they are few
and obscure; but the general form and extent of the building, as shown in the plan, Plate I. fig. 2., are determined,
first, by the breadth of the uninjured east end D E; secondly,
by some remains of the original brickwork of the clerestory,
and in all probability of the side walls also, though these have
been refaced; and finally by the series of nave shafts, which
are still perfect. The doors A and B may or may not be in
their original positions; there must of course have been
always, as now, a principal entrance at the west end. The
ground plan is composed, like that of Torcello, of nave and
aisles only, but the clerestory has transepts extending as far
as the outer wall of the aisles. The semicircular apse, thrown
out in the centre of the east end, is now the chief feature of
interest in the church, though the nave shafts and the eastern
extremities of the aisles, outside, are also portions of the
original building; the latter having been modernized in the
interior, it cannot now be ascertained whether, as is probable,
the aisles had once round ends as well as the choir. The
spaces F G form small chapels, of which G has a straight ter-

minal wall behind its altar, and F a curved one, marked by the dotted line; the partitions which divide these chapels from the presbytery are also indicated by dotted lines, being modern work.

§ XIV. The plan is drawn carefully to scale, but the relation in which its proportions are disposed can hardly be appreciated by the eye. The width of the nave from shaft to opposite shaft is 32 feet 8 inches; of the aisles, from the shaft to the wall, 16 feet 2 inches, or allowing 2 inches for the thickness of the modern wainscot, 16 feet 4 inches, half the breadth of the nave exactly. The intervals between the shafts are exactly one fourth of the width of the nave, or 8 feet 2 inches, and the distance between the great piers which form the pseudo-transept is 24 feet 6 inches, exactly three times the interval of the shafts. So the four distances are accurately in arithmetical proportion; i. e.

	Ft.	In.
Interval of shafts	8	2
Width of aisle	16	4
Width of transept	24	6
Width of nave	32	8

The shafts average 5 feet 4 inches in circumference, as near the base as they can be got at, being covered with wood; and the broadest sides of the main piers are 4 feet 7 inches wide, their narrowest sides 3 feet 6 inches. The distance $a\ c$ from the outmost angle of these piers to the beginning of the curve of the apse is 25 feet, and from that point the apse is nearly semicircular, but it is so encumbered with renaissance fittings that its form cannot be ascertained with perfect accuracy. It is roofed by a concha, or semi-dome; and the external arrangement of its walls provides for the security of this dome by what is, in fact, a system of buttresses as effective and definite as that of any of the northern churches, although the buttresses are obtained entirely by adaptations of the Roman shaft and arch, the lower story being formed by a thick mass of wall lightened by ordinary semicircular round-headed niches, like those used so extensively afterwards in renaissance architecture, each niche flanked by a pair of shafts standing clear of the wall, and bearing deeply moulded arches thrown over the niche. The wall with its pillars thus forms a series of massy buttresses (as seen in the ground plan), on the top of which is an open gallery, backed by a thinner wall, and roofed by arches whose shafts are set above the pairs of shafts below. On the heads of these arches rests the roof. We have, therefore, externally a heptagonal apse, chiefly of rough and common brick, only with marble shafts and a few marble ornaments; but for that very reason all the more interesting, because it shows us what may be done, and what was done, with materials such as are now at our own command; and because in its proportions, and in the use of the few ornaments it possesses, it displays a delicacy of feeling rendered doubly notable by the roughness of the work in which laws so subtle are observed, and with which so thoughtful ornamentation is associated.

§ xv. First, for its proportions: I shall have occasion in Chapter V. to dwell at some length on the peculiar subtlety of the early Venetian perception for ratios of magnitude; the relations of the sides of this heptagonal apse supply one of the first and most curious instances of it. The proportions above given of the nave and aisles might have been dictated by a mere love of mathematical precision; but those of the apse could only have resulted from a true love of harmony.

In fig. 6. Plate I. the plan of this part of the church is given on a large scale, showing that its seven external sides are arranged on a line less than a semicircle, so that if the figure were completed, it would have sixteen sides; and it will be observed also, that the seven sides are arranged in four mag-

nitudes, the widest being the central one. The brickwork is
so much worn away, that the measures of the arches are not
easily ascertainable, but those of the plinth on which they
stand, which is nearly uninjured, may be obtained accurately.
This plinth is indicated by the open line in the ground plan,
and its sides measure respectively :

		Ft.	In.
1st. *a b* in plan	. . . .	6	7
2nd. *b c*	. . . .	7	7
3rd. *c d*	. . . .	7	5
4th. *d e* (central)	. . .	7	10
5th. *e f*	. . . .	7	5
6th. *f g*	. . . .	7	8
7th. *g h*	. . . .	6	10

§ XVI. Now observe what subtle feeling is indicated by this
delicacy of proportion. How fine must the perceptions of
grace have been in those builders who could not be content
without *some* change between the second and third, the fifth
and sixth terms of proportion, such as should oppose the general direction of its cadence, and yet *were* content with a diminution of two inches on a breadth of seven feet and a half!
For I do not suppose that the reader will think the curious
lessening of the third and fifth arch a matter of accident, and
even if he did so, I shall be able to prove to him hereafter that
it was not, but that the early builders were always desirous
of obtaining some alternate proportion of this kind. The relations of the numbers are not easily comprehended in the form
of feet and inches, but if we reduce the first four of them into
inches, and then subtract some constant number, suppose 75,
from them all, the remainders 4, 16, 14, 19, will exhibit the
ratio of proportion in a clearer, though exaggerated form.

§ XVII. The pairs of circular spots at *b, c, d,* &c., on the
ground plan fig. 6. represent the bearing shafts, which are all
of solid marble as well as their capitals. Their measures and

various other particulars respecting them are given in Appendix 6. "Apse of Murano;" here I only wish the reader to note the coloring of their capitals. Those of the two single shafts in the angles (*a*, *h*) are both of deep purple marble; the two next pairs, *b* and *g*, are of white marble; the pairs *c* and *f* are of purple, and *d* and *e* are of white: thus alternating with each other on each side; two white meeting in the centre. Now observe, *the purple capitals are all left plain ; the white are all sculptured.* For the old builders knew that by carving the purple capitals they would have injured them in two ways : first, they would have mixed a certain quantity of grey shadow with the surface hue, and so adulterated the purity of the color; secondly, they would have drawn away the thoughts from the color, and prevented the mind from fixing upon it or enjoying it, by the degree of attention which the sculpture would have required. So they left their purple capitals full broad masses of color; and sculptured the white ones, which would otherwise have been devoid of interest.

§ xviii. But the feature which is most to be noted in this apse is a band of ornament, which runs round it like a silver girdle, composed of sharp wedges of marble, preciously inlaid, and set like jewels into the brickwork ; above it there is another band of triangular recesses in the bricks, of nearly similar shape, and it seems equally strange that all the marbles should have fallen from it, or that it should have been originally destitute of them. The reader may choose his hypothesis; but there is quite enough left to interest us in the lower band, which is fortunately left in its original state, as is sufficiently proved by the curious niceties in the arrangement of its colors, which are assuredly to be attributed to the care of the first builder. A word or two, in the first place, respecting the means of color at his disposal.

§ xix. I stated that the building was, for the most part, composed of yellow brick. This yellow is very nearly pure, much more positive and somewhat darker than that of our English light brick, and the material of the brick is very good and hard, looking, in places, almost vitrified, and so compact as to resemble stone. Together with this brick occurs another of a deep full red, and more porous substance, which is used for decoration chiefly, while all the parts requiring strength are composed of the yellow brick. Both these materials are *cast into any shape and size* the builder required, either into curved pieces for the arches, or flat tiles for filling the triangles ; and, what is still more curious, the thickness of the yellow bricks used for the walls varies considerably, from two inches to four ; and their length also, some of the larger pieces used in important positions being a foot and a half long.

With these two kinds of brick, the builder employed five or six kinds of marble : pure white, and white veined with purple ; a brecciated marble of white and black ; a brecciated marble of white and deep green ; another, deep red, or nearly of the color of Egyptian porphyry ; and a grey and black marble, in fine layers.

§ xx. The method of employing these materials will be understood at once by a reference to the opposite plate (Plate III.), which represents two portions of the lower band. I could not succeed in expressing the variation and chequering of color in marble, by real tints in the print ; and have been content, therefore, to give them in line engraving. The different triangles are, altogether, of ten kinds :

a. Pure white marble with sculptured surface (as the third and fifth in the upper series of Plate III.).

b. Cast triangle of red brick with a sculptured round-headed piece of white marble inlaid (as the first and seventh of the upper series, Plate III.).

c. A plain triangle of greenish black marble, now perhaps considerably paler in color than when first employed (as the second and sixth of the upper series of Plate III.).

d. Cast red brick triangle, with a diamond inlaid of the above-mentioned black marble (as the fourth in the upper series of Plate III.).

e. Cast white brick, with an inlaid round-headed piece of marble, variegated with black and yellow, or white and violet (not seen in the plate).

f. Occurs only once, a green-veined marble, forming the upper part of the triangle, with a white piece below.

g. Occurs only once. A brecciated marble of intense black and pure white, the centre of the lower range in Plate III.

h. Sculptured white marble with a triangle of veined purple marble inserted (as the first, third, fifth, and seventh of the lower range in Plate III.).

i. Yellow or white marble veined with purple (as the second and sixth of the lower range in Plate III.).

k. Pure purple marble, not seen in this plate.

§ XXI. The band, then, composed of these triangles, set close to each other in varied but not irregular relations, is thrown, like a necklace of precious stones, round the apse and along the ends of the aisles; each side of the apse taking, of course, as many triangles as its width permits. If the reader will look back to the measures of the sides of the apse, given before, p. 42., he will see that the first and seventh of the series, being much narrower than the rest, cannot take so many triangles in their band. Accordingly, they have only six each, while the other five sides have seven. Of these groups of seven triangles each, that used for the third and fifth sides of the apse is the uppermost in Plate III.; and that used for the centre of the apse, and of the whole series, is the lowermost in the same plate; *the piece of black and white marble being used to emphasize the centre of the chain*, exactly as a painter would use a dark touch for a similar purpose.

§ XXII. And now, with a little trouble, we can set before the reader, at a glance, the arrangement of the groups along the entire extremity of the church.

There are thirteen recesses, indicative of thirteen arches, seen in the ground plan, fig. 2. Plate I. Of these, the second and twelfth arches rise higher than the rest; so high as to break the decorated band; and the groups of triangles we have to enumerate are, therefore, only eleven in number; one above each of the eleven low arches. And of these eleven, the first and second, tenth and eleventh, are at the ends of the aisles; while the third to the ninth, inclusive, go round the apse. Thus, in the following table, the numerals indicate the place of each entire group (counting from the south to the north side of the church, or from left to right), and the letters indicate the species of triangle of which it is composed, as described in the list given above.

<pre>
                        6. h. i. h. g. h. i. h.
          5. b. c. a. d. a. c. b.   7. b. c. a. d. a. c. b.
       4. b. a. b. c. a. e. a.   8. a. e. a. c. b. a. b.
       3. b. a. b. e. b. a.   9. a. b. e. b. a. b.
2. a. b. c.   10. a. b. c. b.
1. a. b. c. b. a.   11. b. a. c. a. f. a. a.
</pre>

The central group is put first, that it may be seen how the series on the two sides of the apse answer each other. It was a very curious freak to insert the triangle e, in the outermost place *but one* of both the fourth and eighth sides of the apse, and in the outermost *but two* in the third and ninth; in neither case having any balance to it in its own group, and the real balance being only effected on the other side of the apse, which it is impossible that any one should see at the same time. This is one of the curious pieces of system which so often occur in mediæval work, of which the key is now lost. The groups at the ends of the transepts correspond neither in number nor arrangement; we shall presently see why, but must first examine more closely the treatment of the triangles themselves, and the nature of the floral sculpture employed upon them.

§ XXIII. As the scale of Plate III. is necessarily small, I have given three of the sculptured triangles on a larger scale in Plate IV. opposite. Fig. 3. is one of the four in the lower series of Plate IV., and figs. 4. and 5. from another group. The forms of the trefoils are here seen more clearly; they, and all the other portions of the design, are thrown out in low and flat relief, the intermediate spaces being cut out to the depth of about a quarter of an inch. I believe these vacant spaces were originally filled with a black composition, which is used in similar sculptures at St. Mark's, and of which I found some remains in an archivolt moulding here, though not in the triangles. The surface of the whole would then be perfectly smooth, and the ornamental form relieved by a ground of dark grey; but, even though this ground is lost, the simplicity of the method insures the visibility of all its parts at the necessary distance (17 or 18 feet), and the quaint trefoils have a crispness and freshness of effect which I found it almost impossible to render in a drawing. Nor let us fail to note in passing how strangely delightful to the human mind the trefoil always is. We have it here repeated five or six hundred times in the space of a few yards, and yet are never weary of it. In fact, there are two mystical feelings at the root of our enjoyment of this decoration: the one is the love of trinity in unity, the other that of the sense of fulness with order; of every place being instantly filled, and yet filled with propriety and ease; the leaves do not push each other, nor put themselves out of their own way, and yet whenever there is a vacant space, a leaf is always ready to step in and occupy it.

§ XXIV. I said the trefoil was five or six hundred times repeated. It is so, but observe, it is hardly ever twice of the same size; and this law is studiously and resolutely observed

In the carvings *a* and *b* of the upper series, Plate III., the diminution of the leaves might indeed seem merely representative of the growth of the plant. But look at the lower: the triangles of inlaid purple marble are made much more nearly equilateral than those of white marble, into whose centres they are set, so that the leaves may continually diminish in size as the ornament descends at the sides. The reader may perhaps doubt the accuracy of the drawing on the smaller scale, but in that given larger, fig. 3. Plate IV., the angles are all measured, and the *purposeful* variation of width in the border therefore admits of no dispute.* Remember how absolutely this principle is that of nature; the same leaf continually repeated, but never twice of the same size. Look at the clover under your feet, and then you will see what this Murano builder meant, and that he was not altogether a barbarian.

§ xxv. Another point I wish the reader to observe is, the importance attached to *color* in the mind of the designer. Note especially—for it is of the highest importance to see how the great principles of art are carried out through the whole building—that, as only the white capitals are sculptured below, only the white triangles are sculptured above. No colored triangle is touched with sculpture; note also, that in the two principal groups of the apse, given in Plate III., the centre of the group is color, not sculpture, and the eye is evidently intended to be drawn as much to the chequers of the stone, as to the intricacies of the chiselling. It will be noticed also how much more precious the lower series, which is central in the apse, is rendered, than the one above it in the plate, which flanks it : there is no brick in the lower one, and three kinds of variegated marble are used in it, whereas

---

* The intention is farther confirmed by the singular variation in the breadth of the small fillet which encompasses the inner marble. It is much narrower at the bottom than at the sides, so as to recover the original breadth in the lower border.

the upper is composed of brick, with black and white marble only; and lastly—for this is especially delightful—see how the workman made his chiselling finer where it was to go with the variegated marbles, and used a bolder pattern with the coarser brick and dark stone. The subtlety and perfection of artistical feeling in all this are so redundant, that in the building itself the eye can rest upon this colored chain with the same kind of delight that it has in a piece of the embroidery of Paul Veronese.

§ XXVI. Such being the construction of the lower band, that of the upper is remarkable only for the curious change in its proportions. The two are sepa-

Fig. II.

rated, as seen in the little woodcut here at the side, by a string-course composed of two layers of red bricks, of which the uppermost projects as a cornice, and is sustained by an intermediate course of irregular brackets, obtained by setting the thick yellow bricks edgeways, in the manner common to this day. But the wall above is carried up perpendicularly from this projection, so that the whole upper band is advanced to the thickness of a brick over the lower one. The result of this is, of course, that each side of the apse is four or five inches broader above than below; so that the same number of triangles which filled a whole side of the lower band, leave an inch or two blank at each angle in the upper. This would have looked awkward, if there had been the least appearance of its being an accidental error; so that, in order to draw the eye to it, and show that it is done on purpose, the upper triangles are made about two inches higher than the lower ones, so as to be much more acute in proportion and effect, and actually to look considerably narrower, though of the same width at the base. By this means they are made lighter in effect, and subordinated to the richly decorated series of the lower band, and the two courses, instead of repeating, unite with each other, and become a harmonious whole.

In order, however, to make still more sure that this difference in the height of the triangles should not escape the eye, another course of plain bricks is added above their points, increasing the width of the band by another two inches. There are five courses of bricks in the lower band, and it measures 1 ft. 6 in. in height: there are seven courses in the upper (of which six fall between the triangles), and it measures 1 ft. 10 in. in height, except at the extremity of the northern aisle, where for some mysterious reason the intermediate cornice is sloped upwards so as to reduce the upper triangles to the same height as those below. And here, finally, observe how determined the builder was that the one series should not be a mere imitation of the other; he could not now make them acute by additional height—so he here, and here only, *narrowed their bases*, and we have seven of them above, to six below.

§ XXVII. We come now to the most interesting portion of the whole east end, the archivolt at the end of the northern aisle.

It was above stated, that the band of triangles was broken by two higher arches at the ends of the aisles. That, however, on the northern side of the apse does not entirely interrupt, but lifts it, and thus forms a beautiful and curious archivolt, drawn opposite, in Plate V. The upper band of triangles cannot rise together with the lower, as it would otherwise break the cornice prepared to receive the second story; and the curious zigzag with which its triangles die away against the sides of the arch, exactly as waves break upon the sand, is one of the most curious features in the structure.

It will be also seen that there is a new feature in the treatment of the band itself when it turns the arch. Instead of leaving the bricks projecting between the sculptured or colored stones, reversed triangles of marble are used, inlaid to an equal depth with the others in the brickwork, but projecting beyond them so as to produce a sharp dark line of zigzag at their junctions. Three of these supplementary stones have unhappily fallen out, so that it is now impossible to determine the full harmony of color in which they were originally arranged. The central one, corresponding to the keystone in a common arch, is, however, most fortunately left, with two lateral ones on the right hand, and one on the left.

§ XXVIII. The keystone, if it may be so called, is of white marble, the lateral voussoirs of purple; and these are the only colored stones in the whole building which are sculptured; but they are sculptured in a way which more satisfactorily proves that the principle above stated was understood by the builders, than if they had been left blank. The object, observe, was to make the archivolt as rich as possible; eight of the white sculptured marbles were used upon it in juxtaposition. Had the purple marbles been left altogether plain, they would have been out of harmony with the elaboration of the rest. It became necessary to touch them with sculpture as a mere sign of carefulness and finish, but at the same time destroying their colored surface as little as possible. *The ornament is merely outlined upon them with a fine incision,* as if it had been etched out on their surface preparatory to being carved. In two of them it is composed merely of three concentric lines, parallel with the sides of the triangle; in the third, it is a wreath of beautiful design, which I have drawn of larger size in fig. 2. Plate V., that the reader may see how completely the surface is left undestroyed by the delicate incisions of the chisel, and may compare the method of working with that employed on the white stones, two of which are given in that plate, figs. 4. and 5. The keystone, of which we have not yet spoken, is the only white stone worked with the light incision; its design not being capable of the kind of workmanship given to the floral ornaments, and requiring either to be carved in complete relief, or left as we see it. It is given at fig. 1. of Plate IV. The sun and moon on each side of the cross are, as we shall see in the fifth Chapter, constantly employed on the keystones of Byzantine arches.

§ XXIX. We must not pass without notice the grey and green pieces of marble inserted at the flanks of the arch. For, observe, there was a difficulty in getting the forms of the triangle into anything like reconciliation at this point, and a mediæval artist always delights in a difficulty: instead of concealing it, he boasts of it; and just as we saw above that he directed the eye to the difficulty of filling the expanded sides of the upper band by elongating his triangles, so here, having to put in a piece of stone of awkward shape, he makes that very stone the most conspicuous in the whole arch, on both sides, by using in one case a dark, cold grey; in the other a vigorous green, opposed to the warm red and purple and white of the stones above and beside it. The green and white piece on the right is of a marble, as far as I know, exceedingly rare. I at first thought the white fragments were inlaid, so sharply are they defined upon their ground. They are indeed inlaid, but I believe it is by nature; and that the stone is a calcareous breccia of great mineralogical inte- rest. The white spots are of singular value in giving piquancy to the whole range of more delicate transitional hues above. The effect of the whole is, however, generally injured by the loss of the three large triangles above. I have no doubt they were purple, like those which remain, and that the whole arch was thus one zone of white, relieved on a purple ground, encircled by the scarlet cornices of brick, and the whole chord of color contrasted by the two precious fragments of grey and green at either side.

§ xxx. The two pieces of carved stone inserted at each side of the arch, as seen at the bottom of Plate V., are of different workmanship from the rest; they do not match each other, and form part of the evidence which proves that portions of the church had been brought from the mainland. One bears an inscription, which, as its antiquity is confirmed by the shapelessness of its letters, I was much gratified by not being able to read; but M. Lazari, the intelligent author of the latest and best Venetian guide, with better skill, has given as much of it as remains, thus:

T SCEMARIEDIGENETRICISETBEATIESTEFANIMART
IRIEGOINDIGNVSETPECCATVRDOMENICVST

I have printed the letters as they are placed in the inscription, in order that the reader may form some idea of the difficulty of reading such legends when the letters, thus thrown into one heap, are themselves of strange forms, and half worn away; any gaps which at all occur between them, coming in the wrong places. There is no doubt, however, as to the reading of this fragment:—"T . . . Sancte Marie Domini Genetricis et beati Estefani martiri ego indignus et peccator Domenicus T." On these two initial and final Ts, expanding one into Templum, the other into Torcellanus, M. Lazari founds an ingenious conjecture that the inscription records the elevation of the church under a certain bishop Dominic of Torcello (named in the Altinat Chronicle), who flourished in the middle of the ninth century. If this were so, as the inscription occurs broken off on a fragment inserted scornfully in the present edifice, this edifice must be of the twelfth century, worked with fragments taken from the ruins of that built in the ninth. The two Ts are, however, hardly a foundation large enough to build the church upon, a hundred years before the date assigned to it both by history and tradition (see above, § VIII.) : and the reader has yet to be made aware of the principal fact bearing on the question.

§ XXXI. Above the first story of the apse runs, as he knows already, a gallery under open arches, protected by a light balustrade. This balustrade is worked on the *outside* with mouldings, of which I shall only say at present that they are of exactly the same school as the greater part of the work of the existing church. But the great horizontal pieces of stone which form the top of this balustrade are fragments of an older building turned inside out. They are covered with sculptures on the back, only to be seen by mounting into the gallery. They have once had an arcade of low wide arches traced on their surface, the spandrils filled with leafage, and archivolts enriched with studded chainwork and with crosses in their centres. These pieces have been used as waste marble by the architect of the existing apse. The small arches of the present balustrade are cut mercilessly through the old work, and the profile of the balustrade is cut out of what was once the back of the stone ; only some respect is shown for the crosses in the old design, the blocks are cut so that these shall be not only left uninjured, but come in the centre of the balustrades.

§ XXXII. Now let the reader observe carefully that this balustrade of Murano is a fence of other things than the low gallery round the deserted apse. It is a barrier between two great schools of early architecture. On one side it was cut by Romanesque workmen of the early Christian ages, and furnishes us with a distinct type of a kind of ornament which, as we meet with other examples of it, we shall be able to describe in generic terms, and to throw back behind this balustrade, out of our way. The *front* of the balustrade presents us with a totally different condition of design, less rich, more graceful,

and here shown in its simplest possible form. From the outside of this bar of marble we shall commence our progress in
the study of existing Venetian architecture. The only question is, do we begin from the tenth or from the twelfth century?

§ XXXIII. I was in great hopes once of being able to determine this positively; but the alterations in all the early buildings of Venice are so numerous, and the foreign fragments
introduced so innumerable, that I was obliged to leave the
question doubtful. But one circumstance must be noted, bearing upon it closely.

Fig. III.

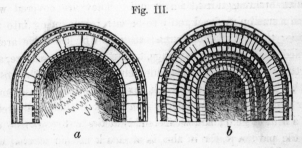

a   b

In the woodcut above, Fig. III., *b* is an archivolt of Murano,
a one of St. Mark's; the latter acknowledged by all historians
and all investigators to be of the twelfth century.

All the twelfth century archivolts in Venice, without exception, are on the model of *a*, differing only in their decorations
and sculpture. There is not one which resembles that of
Murano.

But the deep mouldings of Murano are almost exactly similar to those of St. Michele of Pavia, and other Lombard
churches built, some as early as the seventh, others in the
eighth, ninth, and tenth centuries.

On this ground it seems to me probable that the existing
apse of Murano is part of the original earliest church, and that
the inscribed fragments used in it have been brought from the

main land. The balustrade, however, may still be later than the rest; it will be examined, hereafter, more carefully.*

I have not space to give any farther account of the exterior of the building, though one half of what is remarkable in it remains untold. We must now see what is left of interest within the walls.

§ XXXIV. All hope is taken away by our first glance; for it falls on a range of shafts whose bases are concealed by wooden panelling, and which sustain arches decorated in the most approved style of Renaissance upholstery, with stucco roses in squares under the soffits, and egg and arrow mouldings on the architraves, gilded, on a ground of spotty black and green, with a small pink-faced and black-eyed cherub on every key-stone; the rest of the church being for the most part concealed either by dirty hangings, or dirtier whitewash, or dim pictures on warped and wasting canvass; all vulgar, vain, and foul. Yet let us not turn back, for in the shadow of the apse our more careful glance shows us a Greek Madonna, pictured on a field of gold; and we feel giddy at the first step we make on the pavement, for it, also, is of Greek mosaic waved like the sea, and dyed like a dove's neck.

§ XXXV. Nor are the original features of the rest of the edifice altogether indecipherable; the entire series of shafts marked in the ground plan on each side of the nave, from the western entrance to the apse, are nearly uninjured; and I believe the stilted arches they sustain are those of the original fabric, though the masonry is covered by the Renaissance stucco mouldings. Their capitals, for a wonder, are left bare, and appear to have sustained no farther injury than has resulted from the insertion of a large brass chandelier into each of their abaci, each chandelier carrying a sublime wax candle two 'nches thick, fastened with wire to the wall above. The due arrangement of these appendages, previous to festa days, can

* Its elevation is given to scale in fig. 4. Plate XIII. below.

only be effected from a ladder set against the angle of the abacus; and ten minutes before I wrote this sentence, I had the privilege of watching the candlelighter at his work, knocking his ladder about the heads of the capitals as if they had given him personal offence. He at last succeeded in breaking away one of the lamps altogether, with a bit of the marble of the abacus; the whole falling in ruin to the pavement, and causing much consultation and clamor among a tribe of beggars who were assisting the sacristan with their wisdom respecting the festal arrangements.

§ xxxvi. It is fortunate that the capitals themselves, being somewhat rudely cut, can bear this kind of treatment better than most of those in Venice. They are all founded on the Corinthian type, but the leaves are in every one different: those of the easternmost capital of the southern range are the best, and very beautiful, but presenting no feature of much interest, their workmanship being inferior to most of the imitations of Corinthian common at the period; much more to the rich fantasies which we have seen at Torcello. The apse itself, to-day (12th September, 1851), is not to be described; for just in front of it, behind the altar, is a magnificent curtain of new red velvet with a gilt edge and two golden tassels, held up in a dainty manner by two angels in the upholsterer's service; and above all, for concentration of effect, a star or sun, some five feet broad, the spikes of which conceal the whole of the figure of the Madonna except the head and hands.

§ xxxvii. The pavement is however still left open, and it is of infinite interest, although grievously distorted and defaced. For whenever a new chapel has been built, or a new altar erected, the pavement has been broken up and readjusted so as to surround the newly inserted steps or stones with some appearance of symmetry; portions of it either covered or carried away, others mercilessly shattered or replaced by

3*

modern imitations, and those of very different periods, with pieces of the old floor left here and there in the midst of them, and worked round so as to deceive the eye into acceptance of the whole as ancient. The portion, however, which occupies the western extremity of the nave, and the parts immediately adjoining it in the aisles, are, I believe, in their original positions, and very little injured: they are composed chiefly of groups of peacocks, lions, stags, and griffins,—two of each in a group, drinking out of the same vase, or shaking claws together,—enclosed by interlacing bands, and alternating with chequer or star patterns, and here and there an attempt at representation of architecture, all worked in marble mosaic. The floors of Torcello and of St. Mark's are executed in the same manner; but what remains at Murano is finer than either, in the extraordinary play of color obtained by the use of variegated marbles. At St. Mark's the patterns are more intricate, and the pieces far more skilfully set together; but each piece is there commonly of one color: at Murano every fragment is itself variegated, and all are arranged with a skill and feeling not to be taught, and to be observed with deep reverence, for that pavement is not dateless, like the rest of the church; it bears its date on one of its central circles, 1140, and is, in my mind, one of the most precious monuments in Italy, showing thus early, and in those rude chequers which the bared knee of the Murano fisher wears in its daily bending, the beginning of that mighty spirit of Venetian color, which was to be consummated in Titian.

§ XXXVIII. But we must quit the church for the present, for its garnishings are completed; the candles are all upright in their sockets, and the curtains drawn into festoons, and a pasteboard crescent, gay with artificial flowers, has been attached to the capital of every pillar, in order, together with the gilt angels, to make the place look as much like Paradise as possible. If we return to-morrow, we shall find it filled with woful groups of aged men and women, wasted and fever-struck, fixed in paralytic supplication, half-kneeling, half-couched upon the pavement; bowed down, partly in feeble-ness, partly in a fearful devotion, with their grey clothes cast far over their faces, ghastly and settled into a gloomy animal misery, all but the glittering eyes and muttering lips.

Fit inhabitants, these, for what was once the Garden of Venice, " a terrestrial paradise,—a place of nymphs and demigods!" *

§ XXXIX. We return, yet once again, on the following day. Worshippers and objects of worship, the sickly crowd and gilded angels, all are gone ; and there, far in the apse, is seen the sad Madonna standing in her folded robe, lifting her hands in vanity of blessing. There is little else to draw away our thoughts from the solitary image. An old wooden tablet, carved into a rude effigy of San Donato, which occupies the central niche in the lower part of the tribune, has an interest of its own, but is unconnected with the history of the older church. The faded frescoes of saints, which cover the upper tier of the wall of the apse, are also of comparatively recent date, much more the piece of Renaissance workmanship, shaft and entablature, above the altar, which has been thrust into the midst of all, and has cut away part of the feet of the Madonna. Nothing remains of the original structure but the semidome itself, the cornice whence it springs, which is the same as that used on the exterior of the church, and the border and face-arch which surround it. The ground of the dome is of gold, unbroken except by the upright Madonna, and usual inscription, $\widehat{MR}$ ΘV. The figure wears a robe of blue, deeply fringed with gold, which seems to be gathered on the head and thrown back on the shoulders, crossing the

* "Luogo de' ninfe e de' semidei."—*M. Andrea Calmo*, quoted by Muti-nelli, Annali Urbani di Venezia (Venice, 1841), p. 362.

breast, and falling in many folds to the ground. The under robe, shown beneath it where it opens at the breast, is of the same color; the whole, except the deep gold fringe, being simply the dress of the women of the time. "Le donne, anco elle del 1100, vestivano *di turchino con manti in spalla*, che le coprivano dinanzi e di dietro." [*]

Round the dome there is a colored mosaic border; and on the edge of its arch, legible by the whole congregation, this inscription:

"QUOS EVA CONTRIVIT, PIA VIRGO MARIA REDEMIT;
HANC CUNCTI LAUDENT, QUI CRISTI MUNERE GAUDENT." [†]

The whole edifice is, therefore, simply a temple to the Virgin: to her is ascribed the fact of Redemption, and to her its praise.

§ XL. "And is this," it will be asked of me, "the time, is this the worship, to which you would have us look back with reverence and regret?" Inasmuch as redemption is ascribed to the Virgin, No. Inasmuch as redemption is a thing desired, believed, rejoiced in, Yes,—and Yes a thousand times. As far as the Virgin is worshipped in place of God, No; but as far as there is the evidence of worship itself, and of the sense of a Divine presence, Yes. For there is a wider division of men than that into Christian and Pagan: before we ask what a man worships, we have to ask whether he worships at all. Observe Christ's own words on this head:

[*] "The women, even as far back as 1100, wore dresses of blue, with mantles on the shoulder, which clothed them before and behind."—*Sansovino.*

It would be difficult to imagine a dress more modest and beautiful. See Appendix 7.

[†] "Whom Eve destroyed, the pious Virgin Mary redeemed; All praise her, who rejoice in the Grace of Christ."

Vide Appendix 8.

"God is a spirit; and they that worship Him must worship Him in spirit, *and* in truth." The worshipping in spirit comes first, and it does not necessarily imply the worshipping in truth. Therefore, there is first the broad division of men into Spirit worshippers and Flesh worshippers; and then, of the Spirit worshippers, the farther division into Christian and Pagan,—worshippers in Falsehood or in Truth. I therefore, for the moment, omit all inquiry how far the Mariolatry of the early church did indeed eclipse Christ, or what measure of deeper reverence for the Son of God was still felt through all the grosser forms of Madonna worship. Let that worship be taken at its worst; let the goddess of this dome of Murano be looked upon as just in the same sense an idol as the Athene of the Acropolis, or the Syrian Queen of Heaven; and then, on this darkest assumption, balance well the difference between those who worship and those who worship not; —that difference which there is in the sight of God, in all ages, between the calculating, smiling, self-sustained, self-governed man, and the believing, weeping, wondering, struggling, Heaven-governed man;—between the men who say in their hearts "there is no God," and those who acknowledge a God at every step, "if haply they might feel after Him and find Him." For that is indeed the difference which we shall find, in the end, between the builders of this day and the builders on that sand island long ago. They *did* honor something out of themselves; they did believe in spiritual presence judging, animating, redeeming them; they built to its honor and for its habitation; and were content to pass away in nameless multitudes, so only that the labor of their hands might fix in the sea-wilderness a throne for their guardian angel. In this was their strength, and there was indeed a Spirit walking with them on the waters, though they could not discern the form thereof, though the Master's voice came not to them, "It is I." What their error cost

them, we shall see hereafter ; for it remained when the
majesty and the sincerity of their worship had departed, and
remains to this day.   Mariolatry is no special characteristic
of the twelfth century; on the outside of that very tribune
of San Donato, in its central recess, is an image of the Virgin
which receives the reverence once paid to the blue vision
upon the inner dome.   With rouged cheeks and painted
brows, the frightful doll stands in wretchedness of rags,
blackened with the smoke of the votive lamps at its feet ;
and if we would know what has been lost or gained by Italy
in the six hundred years that have worn the marbles of
Murano, let us consider how far the priests who set up this
to worship, the populace who have this to adore, may be
nobler than the men who conceived that lonely figure standing on the golden field, or than those to whom it seemed to
receive their prayer at evening, far away, where they only
saw the blue clouds rising out of the burning sea.

CHAPTER IV.

ST. MARK'S.

assoc. of Paul

§ I. "AND so Barnabas took Mark, and sailed unto Cyprus."
If as the shores of Asia lessened upon his sight, the spirit of
prophecy had entered into the heart of the weak disciple who
had turned back when his hand was on the plough, and
who had been judged, by the chiefest of Christ's captains,
unworthy thenceforward to go forth with him to the work,*
how wonderful would he have thought it, that by the lion
symbol in future ages he was to be represented among men!
how woful, that the war-cry of his name should so often re-
animate the rage of the soldier, on those very plains where he
himself had failed in the courage of the Christian, and so
often dye with fruitless blood that very Cypriot Sea, over
whose waves, in repentance and shame, he was following the
Son of Consolation!

§ II. That the Venetians possessed themselves of his body
in the ninth century, there appears no sufficient reason to
doubt, nor that it was principally in consequence of their
having done so, that they chose him for their patron saint.
There exists, however, a tradition that before he went into
Egypt he had founded the Church at Aquileia, and was thus,
in some sort, the first bishop of the Venetian isles and people.
I believe that this tradition stands on nearly as good grounds

* Acts, xiii. 13. ; xv. 38, 39.

as that of St. Peter having been the first bishop of Rome ;[*] but, as usual, it is enriched by various later additions and embellishments, much resembling the stories told respecting the church of Murano. Thus we find it recorded by the Santo Padre who compiled the " Vite de' Santi spettanti alle Chiese di Venezia,"[†] that " St. Mark having seen the people of Aquileia well grounded in religion, and being called to Rome by St. Peter, before setting off took with him the holy bishop Hermagoras, and went in a small boat to the marshes of Venice. There were at that period some houses built upon a certain high bank called Rialto, and the boat being driven by the wind was anchored in a marshy place, when St. Mark, snatched into ecstasy, heard the voice of an angel saying to him : 'Peace be to thee, Mark ; here shall thy body rest.' " The angel goes on to foretell the building of " una stupenda, ne più veduta Città ; " but the fable is hardly ingenious enough to deserve farther relation.

§ III. But whether St. Mark was first bishop of Aquileia or not, St. Theodore was the first patron of the city ; nor can he yet be considered as having entirely abdicated his early right, as his statue, standing on a crocodile, still companions the winged lion on the opposing pillar of the piazzetta. A church erected to this Saint is said to have occupied, before the ninth century, the site of St. Mark's ; and the traveller, dazzled by the brilliancy of the great square, ought not to leave it without endeavoring to imagine its aspect in that early time, when it was a green field, cloister-like and quiet,[‡]

* The reader who desires to investigate it may consult Galliciolli, "Delle Memorie Venete," (Venice, 1795) tom. ii. p. 332., and the authorities quoted by him.

† Venice, 1761, tom. i. p. 126.

‡ St. Mark's Place, " partly covered by turf, and planted with a few trees; and on account of its pleasant aspect called Brollo or Broglio, that is to say, Garden." The canal passed through it, over which is built the bridge of the Malpassi. Galliciolli, lib. I. cap. viii.

divided by a small canal, with a line of trees on each side; and extending between the two churches of St. Theodore and St. Geminian, as the little piazza of Torcello lies between its "palazzo" and cathedral.

§ IV. But in the year 813, when the seat of government was finally removed to the Rialto, a Ducal Palace, built on the spot where the present one stands, with a Ducal Chapel beside it,* gave a very different character to the Square of St. Mark; and fifteen years later, the acquisition of the body of the Saint, and its deposition in the Ducal Chapel, perhaps not yet completed, occasioned the investiture of that chapel with all possible splendor. St. Theodore was deposed from his patronship, and his church destroyed, to make room for the aggrandizement of the one attached to the Ducal Palace, and thenceforward known as "St. Mark's."†

§ V. This first church was however destroyed by fire, when the Ducal Palace was burned in the revolt against Candiano, in 976. It was partly rebuilt by his successor, Pietro Orseolo, on a larger scale; and, with the assistance of Byzantine architects, the fabric was carried on under successive Doges for nearly a hundred years; the main building being completed in 1071, but its incrustation with marble not till considerably later. It was consecrated on the 8th of October, 1085,‡ according to Sansovino and the author of the "Chiesa

* My authorities for this statement are given below, in the chapter on the Ducal Palace.

† In the Chronicles, "Sancti Marci Ducalis Cappella."

‡ "To God the Lord, the glorious Virgin Annunciate, and the Protector St. Mark."—*Corner*, p. 14. It is needless to trouble the reader with the various authorities for the above statements: I have consulted the best. The previous inscription once existing on the church itself:

> "Anno milleno transacto bisque trigeno
> Desuper undecimo fuit facta primo,"

is no longer to be seen, and is conjectured by Corner, with much probability to have perished "in qualche ristauro."

Ducale di S. Marco," in 1094 according to Lazari, but certainly between 1084 and 1096, those years being the limits of the reign of Vital Falier; I incline to the supposition that it was soon after his accession to the throne in 1085, though Sansovino writes, by mistake, Ordelafo instead of Vital Falier. But, at all events, before the close of the eleventh century the great consecration of the church took place. It was again injured by fire in 1106, but repaired; and from that time to the fall of Venice there was probably no Doge who did not in some slight degree embellish or alter the fabric, so that few parts of it can be pronounced boldly to be of any given date. Two periods of interference are, however, notable above the rest: the first, that in which the Gothic school had superseded the Byzantine towards the close of the fourteenth century, when the pinnacles, upper archivolts, and window traceries were added to the exterior, and the great screen, with various chapels and tabernacle-work, to the interior; the second, when the Renaissance school superseded the Gothic, and the pupils of Titian and Tintoret substituted, over one half of the church, their own compositions for the Greek mosaics with which it was originally decorated;* happily, though with no good will, having left enough to enable us to imagine and lament what they destroyed. Of this irreparable loss we shall have more to say hereafter; meantime, I wish only to fix in the reader's mind the succession of periods of alteration as firmly and simply as possible.

§ VI. We have seen that the main body of the church may be broadly stated to be of the eleventh century, the Gothic additions of the fourteenth, and the restored mosaics of the seventeenth. There is no difficulty in distinguishing at a glance the Gothic portions from the Byzantine; but there is considerable difficulty in ascertaining how long, during the

---

* Signed Bartolomeus Bozza, 1634, 1647, 1656, &c.

course of the twelfth and thirteenth centuries, additions were
made to the Byzantine church, which cannot be easily distinguished from the work of the eleventh century, being pur-
posely executed in the same manner. Two of the most important pieces of evidence on this point are, a mosaic in the south
transept, and another over the northern door of the façade;
the first representing the interior, the second the exterior, of
the ancient church.

§ VII. It has just been stated that the existing building was
consecrated by the Doge Vital Falier. A peculiar solemnity
was given to that act of consecration, in the minds of the Venetian people, by what appears to have been one of the best
arranged and most successful impostures ever attempted by
the clergy of the Romish church. The body of St. Mark had,
without doubt, perished in the conflagration of 976; but the
revenues of the church depended too much upon the devotion
excited by these relics to permit the confession of their loss.
The following is the account given by Corner, and believed to
this day by the Venetians, of the pretended miracle by which
it was concealed.

"After the repairs undertaken by the Doge Orseolo, the
place in which the body of the holy Evangelist rested had
been altogether forgotten; so that the Doge Vital Falier was
entirely ignorant of the place of the venerable deposit. This
was no light affliction, not only to the pious Doge, but to all
the citizens and people; so that at last, moved by confidence
in the Divine mercy, they determined to implore, with prayer
and fasting, the manifestation of so great a treasure, which
did not now depend upon any human effort. A general fast
being therefore proclaimed, and a solemn procession appointed
for the 25th day of June, while the people assembled in the
church interceded with God in fervent prayers for the desired
boon, they beheld, with as much amazement as joy, a slight
shaking in the marbles of a pillar (near the place where the

altar of the Cross is now), which, presently falling to the earth, exposed to the view of the rejoicing people the chest of bronze in which the body of the Evangelist was laid."

§ VIII. Of the main facts of this tale there is no doubt. They were embellished afterwards, as usual, by many fanciful traditions; as, for instance, that, when the sarcophagus was discovered, St. Mark extended his hand out of it, with a gold ring on one of the fingers, which he permitted a noble of the Dolfin family to remove; and a quaint and delightful story was further invented of this ring, which I shall not repeat here, as it is now as well known as any tale of the Arabian Nights. But the fast and the discovery of the coffin, by whatever means effected, are facts; and they are recorded in one of the best-preserved mosaics of the north transept, executed very certainly not long after the event had taken place, closely resembling in its treatment that of the Bayeux tapestry, and showing, in a conventional manner, the interior of the church, as it then was, filled by the people, first in prayer, then in thanksgiving, the pillar standing open before them, and the Doge in the midst of them, distinguished by his crimson bonnet embroidered with gold, but more unmistakably by the inscription "Dux" over his head, as uniformly is the case in the Bayeux tapestry, and most other pictorial works of the period. The church is, of course, rudely represented, and the two upper stories of it reduced to a small scale in order to form a background to the figures; one of those bold pieces of picture history which we, in our pride of perspective and a thousand things besides, never dare attempt. We should have put in a column or two, of the real or perspective size, and subdued it into a vague background: the old workman crushed the church together that he might get it all in, up to the cupolas; and has, therefore, left us some useful notes of its ancient form, though any one who is familiar with the method of drawing employed at the period will not push the evidence too far. The two pulpits are there, however, as they are at this day, and the fringe of mosaic flowerwork which then encompassed the whole church, but which modern restorers have destroyed, all but one frag ment still left in the south aisle. There is no attempt to represent the other mosaics on the roof, the scale being too small to admit of their being represented with any success; but some at least of those mosaics had been executed at that period, and their absence in the representation of the entire church is especially to be observed, in order to show that we must not trust to any negative evidence in such works. M. Lazari has rashly concluded that the central archivolt of St. Mark's *must* be posterior to the year 1205, because it does not appear in the representation of the exterior of the church over the northern door;* but he justly observes that this mosaic (which is the other piece of evidence we possess respect- ing the ancient form of the building) cannot itself be earlier than 1205, since it represents the bronze horses which were brought from Constantinople in that year. And this one fact renders it very difficult to speak with confidence respecting the date of any part of the exterior of St. Mark's; for we have above seen that it was consecrated in the eleventh cen- tury, and yet here is one of its most important exterior deco- rations assuredly retouched, if not entirely added, in the thir- teenth, although its style would have led us to suppose it had been an original part of the fabric. However, for all our pur- poses, it will be enough for the reader to remember that the earliest parts of the building belong to the eleventh, twelfth, and first part of the thirteenth century; the Gothic portions to the fourteenth; some of the altars and embellishments to the fifteenth and sixteenth; and the modern portion of the mosaics to the seventeenth.

§ IX. This, however, I only wish him to recollect in order

* Guida di Venezia, p. 6.

that I may speak generally of the Byzantine architecture of St. Mark's, without leading him to suppose the whole church to have been built and decorated by Greek artists. Its later portions, with the single exception of the seventeenth century mosaics, have been so dexterously accommodated to the original fabric that the general effect is still that of a Byzantine building; and I shall not, except when it is absolutely necessary, direct attention to the discordant points, or weary the reader with anatomical criticism. Whatever in St. Mark's arrests the eye, or affects the feelings, is either Byzantine, or has been modified by Byzantine influence; and our inquiry into its architectural merits need not therefore be disturbed by the anxieties of antiquarianism, or arrested by the obscurities of chronology.

§ x. And now I wish that the reader, before I bring him into St. Mark's Place, would imagine himself for a little time in a quiet English cathedral town, and walk with me to the west front of its cathedral. Let us go together up the more retired street, at the end of which we can see the pinnacles of one of the towers, and then through the low grey gateway, with its battlemented top and small latticed window in the centre, into the inner private-looking road or close, where nothing goes in but the carts of the tradesmen who supply the bishop and the chapter, and where there are little shaven grass-plots, fenced in by neat rails, before old-fashioned groups of somewhat diminutive and excessively trim houses, with little oriel and bay windows jutting out here and there, and deep wooden cornices and eaves painted cream color and white, and small porches to their doors in the shape of cockle-shells, or little, crooked, thick, indescribable wooden gables warped a little on one side; and so forward till we come to larger houses, also old-fashioned, but of red brick, and with gardens behind them, and fruit walls, which show here and there, among the nectarines, the vestiges of an old cloister arch or shaft, and looking in front on the cathedral square itself, laid out in rigid divisions of smooth grass and gravel walk, yet not uncheerful, especially on the sunny side where the canons' children are walking with their nurserymaids. And so, taking care not to tread on the grass, we will go along the straight walk to the west front, and there stand for a time, looking up at its deep-pointed porches and the dark places between their pillars where there were statues once, and where the fragments, here and there, of a stately figure are still left, which has in it the likeness of a king, perhaps indeed a king on earth, perhaps a saintly king long ago in heaven; and so higher and higher up to the great mouldering wall of rugged sculpture and confused arcades, shattered, and grey, and grisly with heads of dragons and mocking fiends, worn by the rain and swirling winds into yet unseemlier shape, and colored on their stony scales by the deep russet-orange lichen, melancholy gold; and so, higher still, to the bleak towers, so far above that the eye loses itself among the bosses of their traceries, though they are rude and strong, and only sees like a drift of eddying black points, now closing, now scattering, and now settling suddenly into invisible places among the bosses and flowers, the crowd of restless birds that fill the whole square with that strange clangor of theirs, so harsh and yet so soothing, like the cries of birds on a solitary coast between the cliffs and sea.

§ XI. Think for a little while of that scene, and the meaning of all its small formalisms, mixed with its serene sublimity. Estimate its secluded, continuous, drowsy felicities, and its evidence of the sense and steady performance of such kind of duties as can be regulated by the cathedral clock; and weigh the influence of those dark towers on all who have passed through the lonely square at their feet for centuries, and on all who have seen them rising far away over the wooded plain, or catching on their square masses the last rays of the sunset,

when the city at their feet was indicated only by the mist at
the bend of the river. And then let us quickly recollect that
we are in Venice, and land at the extremity of the Calle Lunga
San Moisè, which may be considered as there answering to
the secluded street that led us to our English cathedral
gateway.

§ XII. We find ourselves in a paved alley, some seven feet
wide where it is widest, full of people, and resonant with cries
of itinerant salesmen,—a shriek in their beginning, and dying
away into a kind of brazen ringing, all the worse for its con-
finement between the high houses of the passage along which
we have to make our way. Over-head an inextricable confusion of rugged shutters, and iron balconies and chimney flues
pushed out on brackets to save room, and arched windows
with projecting sills of Istrian stone, and gleams of green
leaves here and there where a fig-tree branch escapes over a
lower wall from some inner cortile, leading the eye up to the
narrow stream of blue sky high over all. On each side, a row
of shops, as densely set as may be, occupying, in fact, intervals between the square stone shafts, about eight feet high,
which carry the first floors: intervals of which one is narrow
and serves as a door; the other is, in the more respectable
shops, wainscotted to the height of the counter and glazed
above, but in those of the poorer tradesmen left open to the
ground, and the wares laid on benches and tables in the open
air, the light in all cases entering at the front only, and fading
away in a few feet from the threshold into a gloom which the
eye from without cannot penetrate, but which is generally
broken by a ray or two from a feeble lamp at the back of the
shop, suspended before a print of the Virgin. The less pious
shopkeeper sometimes leaves his lamp unlighted, and is contented with a penny print; the more religious one has his
print colored and set in a little shrine with a gilded or figured
fringe, with perhaps a faded flower or two on each side, and

his lamp burning brilliantly. Here at the fruiterer's, where the dark-green water-melons are heaped upon the counter like cannon balls, the Madonna has a tabernacle of fresh laurel leaves; but the pewterer next door has let his lamp out, and there is nothing to be seen in his shop but the dull gleam of the studded patterns on the copper pans, hanging from his roof in the darkness. Next comes a "Vendita Frittole e Liquori," where the Virgin, enthroned in a very humble manner beside a tallow candle on a back shelf, presides over certain ambrosial morsels of a nature too ambiguous to be defined or enumerated. But a few steps farther on, at the regular wine-shop of the calle, where we are offered "Vino Nostrani a Soldi 28·32," the Madonna is in great glory, enthroned above ten or a dozen large red casks of three-year-old vintage, and flanked by goodly ranks of bottles of Maraschino, and two crimson lamps; and for the evening, when the gondoliers will come to drink out, under her auspices, the money they have gained during the day, she will have a whole chandelier.

§ XIII. A yard or two farther, we pass the hostelry of the Black Eagle, and, glancing as we pass through the square door of marble, deeply moulded, in the outer wall, we see the shadows of its pergola of vines resting on an ancient well, with a pointed shield carved on its side; and so presently emerge on the bridge and Campo San Moisè, whence to the entrance into St. Mark's Place, called the Bocca di Piazza (mouth of the square), the Venetian character is nearly destroyed, first by the frightful façade of San Moisè, which we will pause at another time to examine, and then by the modernizing of the shops as they near the piazza, and the mingling with the lower Venetian populace of lounging groups of English and Austrians. We will push fast through them into the shadow of the pillars at the end of the "Bocca di Piazza," and then we forget them all; for between those

4

pillars there opens a great light, and, in the midst of it, as we advance slowly, the vast tower of St. Mark seems to lift itself visibly forth from the level field of chequered stones; and, on each side, the countless arches prolong themselves into ranged symmetry, as if the rugged and irregular houses that pressed together above us in the dark alley had been struck back into sudden obedience and lovely order, and all their rude casements and broken walls had been transformed into arches charged with goodly sculpture, and fluted shafts of delicate stone.

§ XIV. And well may they fall back, for beyond those troops of ordered arches there rises a vision out of the earth, and all the great square seems to have opened from it in a kind of awe, that we may see it far away;—a multitude of pillars and white domes, clustered into a long low pyramid of colored light; a treasure-heap, it seems, partly of gold, and partly of opal and mother-of-pearl, hollowed beneath into five great vaulted porches, ceiled with fair mosaic, and beset with sculpture of alabaster, clear as amber and delicate as ivory,—sculpture fantastic and involved, of palm leaves and lilies, and grapes and pomegranates, and birds clinging and fluttering among the branches, all twined together into an endless network of buds and plumes; and, in the midst of it, the solemn forms of angels, sceptred, and robed to the feet, and leaning to each other across the gates, their figures indistinct among the gleaming of the golden ground through the leaves beside them, interrupted and dim, like the morning light as it faded back among the branches of Eden, when first its gates were angel-guarded long ago. And round the walls of the porches there are set pillars of variegated stones, jasper and porphyry, and deep-green serpentine spotted with flakes of snow, and marbles, that half refuse and half yield to the sunshine, Cleopatra-like, "their bluest veins to kiss"—the shadow, as it steals back from them, revealing line after line of azure undalation, as a receding tide leaves the waved sand; their capitals rich with interwoven tracery, rooted knots of herbage, and drifting leaves of acanthus and vine, and mystical signs, all beginning and ending in the Cross; and above them, in the broad archivolts, a continuous chain of language and of life—angels, and the signs of heaven, and the labors of men, each in its appointed season upon the earth; and above these, another range of glittering pinnacles, mixed with white arches edged with scarlet flowers,—a confusion of delight, amidst which the breasts of the Greek horses are seen blazing in their breadth of golden strength, and the St. Mark's Lion, lifted on a blue field covered with stars, until at last, as if in ecstacy, the crests of the arches break into a marble foam, and toss themselves far into the blue sky in flashes and wreaths of sculptured spray, as if the breakers on the Lido shore had been frost-bound before they fell, and the sea-nymphs had inlaid them with coral and amethyst.

Between that grim cathedral of England and this, what an interval! There is a type of it in the very birds that haunt them; for, instead of the restless crowd, hoarse-voiced and sable-winged, drifting on the bleak upper air, the St. Mark's porches are full of doves, that nestle among the marble foliage, and mingle the soft iridescence of their living plumes, changing at every motion, with the tints, hardly less lovely, that have stood unchanged for seven hundred years.

§ xv. And what effect has this splendor on those who pass beneath it? You may walk from sunrise to sunset, to and fro, before the gateway of St. Mark's, and you will not see an eye lifted to it, nor a countenance brightened by it. Priest and layman, soldier and civilian, rich and poor, pass by it alike regardlessly. Up to the very recesses of the porches, the meanest tradesmen of the city push their counters; nay, the foundations of its pillars are themselves the seats—not " of them that sell doves " for sacrifice, but of the vendors of toys and caricatures. Round the whole square in front of the church there is almost a continuous line of cafés, where the idle Venetians of the middle classes lounge, and read empty journals; in its centre the Austrian bands play during the time of vespers, their martial music jarring with the organ notes,—the march drowning the miserere, and the sullen crowd thickening round them,—a crowd, which, if it had its will, would stiletto every soldier that pipes to it. And in the recesses of the porches, all day long, knots of men of the lowest classes, unemployed and listless, lie basking in the sun like lizards; and unregarded children,—every heavy glance of their young eyes full of desperation and stony depravity, and their throats hoarse with cursing,—gamble, and fight, and snarl, and sleep, hour after hour, clashing their bruised centesimi upon the marble ledges of the church porch. And the images of Christ and His angels look down upon it continually.

That we may not enter the church out of the midst of the horror of this, let us turn aside under the portico which looks towards the sea, and passing round within the two massive pillars brought from St. Jean d'Acre, we shall find the gate of the Baptistery; let us enter there. The heavy door closes behind us instantly, and the light, and the turbulence of the Piazzetta, are together shut out by it.

§ XVI. We are in a low vaulted room; vaulted, not with arches, but with small cupolas starred with gold, and chequered with gloomy figures: in the centre is a bronze font charged with rich bas-reliefs, a small figure of the Baptist standing above it in a single ray of light that glances across the narrow room, dying as it falls from a window high in the wall, and the first thing that it strikes, and the only thing that it strikes brightly, is a tomb. We hardly know if it be a tomb indeed; for it is like a narrow couch set beside the window, low-roofed and curtained, so that it might seem, but that it has some height above the pavement, to have been drawn towards the window, that the sleeper might be wakened early;—Only there are two angels who have drawn the curtain back, and are looking down upon him. Let us look also, and thank that gentle light that rests upon his forehead for ever, and dies away upon his breast.

The face is of a man in middle life, but there are two deep furrows right across the forehead, dividing it like the foundations of a tower: the height of it above is bound by the fillet of the ducal cap. The rest of the features are singularly small and delicate, the lips sharp, perhaps the sharpness of death being added to that of the natural lines; but there is a sweet smile upon them, and a deep serenity upon the whole countenance. The roof of the canopy above has been blue, filled with stars; beneath, in the centre of the tomb on which the figure rests, is a seated figure of the Virgin, and the border of it all around, is of flowers and soft leaves, growing rich and deep, as if in a field in summer.

It is the Doge Andrea Dandolo, a man early great among the great of Venice; and early lost. She chose him for her king in his 36th year; he died ten years later, leaving behind him that history to which we owe half of what we know of her former fortunes.

§ XVII. Look round at the room in which he lies. The floor of it is of rich mosaic, encompassed by a low seat of red marble, and its walls are of alabaster, but worn and shattered, and darkly stained with age, almost a ruin,—in places the slabs of marble have fallen away altogether, and the rugged brickwork is seen through the rents, but all beautiful; the ravaging fissures fretting their way among the islands and channelled zones of the alabaster, and the time-stains on its translucent masses darkened into fields of rich golden brown, like the color of seaweed when the sun strikes on it through deep sea. The light fades away into the recess of the chamber towards the altar, and the eye can hardly trace the lines of the bas-relief behind it of the baptism of Christ: but on the vaulting of the roof the figures are distinct, and there are seen upon it two great circles, one surrounded by the "Principalities and powers in heavenly places," of which Milton has expressed the ancient division in the single massy line,

"Thrones, Dominations, Princedoms, Virtues, Powers,"

and around the other, the Apostles; Christ the centre of both; and upon the walls, again and again repeated, the gaunt figure of the Baptist, in every circumstance of his life and death; and the streams of the Jordan running down between their cloven rocks; the axe laid to the root of a fruitless tree that springs upon their shore. "Every tree that bringeth not forth good fruit shall be hewn down, and cast into the fire." Yes, verily: to be baptized with fire, or to be cast therein; it is the choice set before all men. The march-notes still murmur through the grated window, and mingle with the sounding in our ears of the sentence of judgment, which the old Greek has written on that Baptistery wall. Venice has made her choice.

§ XVIII. He who lies under that stony canopy would have taught her another choice, in his day, if she would have listened to him; but he and his counsels have long been forgotten by her, and the dust lies upon his lips.

Through the heavy door whose bronze network closes the place of his rest, let us enter the church itself. It is lost in still deeper twilight, to which the eye must be accustomed for some moments before the form of the building can be traced; and then there opens before us a vast cave, hewn out into the form of a Cross, and divided into shadowy aisles by many pillars. Round the domes of its roof the light enters only through narrow apertures like large stars; and here and there a ray or two from some far away casement wanders into the darkness, and casts a narrow phosphoric stream upon the waves of marble that heave and fall in a thousand colors along the floor. What else there is of light is from torches, or silver lamps, burning ceaselessly in the recesses of the chapels; the roof sheeted with gold, and the polished walls covered with alabaster, give back at every curve and angle some feeble gleaming to the flames; and the glories round the heads of the sculptured saints flash out upon us as we pass them, and sink again into the gloom. Under foot and over head, a continual succession of crowded imagery, one picture passing into another, as in a dream; forms beautiful and terrible mixed together; dragons and serpents, and ravening beasts of prey, and graceful birds that in the midst of them drink from running fountains and feed from vases of crystal; the passions and the pleasures of human life symbolized together, and the mystery of its redemption; for the mazes of interwoven lines and changeful pictures lead always at last to the Cross, lifted and carved in every place and upon every stone; sometimes with the serpent of eternity wrapt round it, sometimes with doves beneath its arms, and sweet herbage growing forth from its feet; but conspicuous most of all on the great rood that crosses the church before the altar, raised in bright blazonry against the shadow of the apse. And although in the recesses of the aisles and chapels, when the mist of the incense hangs heavily, we may see continually a figure traced in faint lines upon their marble, a woman standing with her eyes raised to heaven, and the inscription above her, " Mother of God," she is not here the presiding deity. It is the Cross that is first seen, and always, burning in the centre of the temple; and every dome and hollow of its roof has the figure of Christ in the utmost height of it, raised in power, or returning in judgment.

§ XIX. Nor is this interior without effect on the minds of the people. At every hour of the day there are groups collected before the various shrines, and solitary worshippers

scattered through the darker places of the church, evidently
in prayer both deep and reverent, and, for the most part,
profoundly sorrowful. The devotees at the greater number
of the renowned shrines of Romanism may be seen mur-
muring their appointed prayers with wandering eyes and
unengaged gestures; but the step of the stranger does not
disturb those who kneel on the pavement of St. Mark's; and
hardly a moment passes, from early morning to sunset, in
which we may not see some half-veiled figure enter beneath
the Arabian porch, cast itself into long abasement on the
floor of the temple, and then rising slowly with more confirmed step, and with a passionate kiss and clasp of the arms
given to the feet of the crucifix, by which the lamps burn
always in the northern aisle, leave the church, as if comforted.

§ xx. But we must not hastily conclude from this that the
nobler characters of the building have at present any influence
in fostering a devotional spirit. There is distress enough in
Venice to bring many to their knees, without excitement
from external imagery; and whatever there may be in the
temper of the worship offered in St. Mark's more than can
be accounted for by reference to the unhappy circumstances
of the city, is assuredly not owing either to the beauty of its
architecture or to the impressiveness of the Scripture histories
embodied in its mosaics. That it has a peculiar effect, however slight, on the popular mind, may perhaps be safely conjectured from the number of worshippers which it attracts,
while the churches of St. Paul and the Frari, larger in size
and more central in position, are left comparatively empty.*
But this effect is altogether to be ascribed to its richer assem-
blage of those sources of influence which address themselves

* The mere warmth of St. Mark's in winter, which is much greater than
that of the other two churches above named, must, however, be taken into
consideration, as one of the most efficient causes of its being then more
frequented.

to the commonest instincts of the human mind, and which, in all ages and countries, have been more or less employed in the support of superstition. Darkness and mystery; confused recesses of building; artificial light employed in small quantity, but maintained with a constancy which seems to give it a kind of sacredness; preciousness of material easily comprehended by the vulgar eye; close air loaded with a sweet and peculiar odor associated only with religious services, solemn music, and tangible idols or images having popular legends attached to them,—these, the stage properties of superstition, which have been from the beginning of the world, and must be to the end of it, employed by all nations, whether openly savage or nominally civilized, to produce a false awe in minds incapable of apprehending the true nature of the Deity, are assembled in St. Mark's to a degree, as far as I know, unexampled in any other European church. The arts of the Magus and the Brahmin are exhausted in the animation of a paralyzed Christianity; and the popular sentiment which these arts excite is to be regarded by us with no more respect than we should have considered ourselves justified in rendering to the devotion of the worshippers at Eleusis, Ellora, or Edfou.*

§ XXI. Indeed, these inferior means of exciting religious emotion were employed in the ancient Church as they are at this day, but not employed alone. Torchlight there was, as there is now; but the torchlight illumined Scripture histories

* I said above that the larger number of the devotees entered by the "Arabian" porch; the porch, that is to say, on the north side of the church, remarkable for its rich Arabian archivolt, and through which access is gained immediately to the northern transept. The reason is, that in that transept is the chapel of the Madonna, which has a greater attraction for the Venetians than all the rest of the church besides. The old builders kept their images of the Virgin subordinate to those of Christ; but modern Romanism has retrograded from theirs, and the most glittering portions of the whole church are the two recesses behind this lateral altar, covered with silver hearts dedicated to the Virgin.

on the walls, which every eye traced and every heart com
prehended, but which, during my whole residence in Venice,
I never saw one Venetian regard for an instant. I never
heard from any one the most languid expression of interest
in any feature of the church, or perceived the slightest evidence of their understanding the meaning of its architecture;
and while, therefore, the English cathedral, though no longer
dedicated to the kind of services for which it was intended
by its builders, and much at variance in many of its characters with the temper of the people by whom it is now
surrounded, retains yet so much of its religious influence that
no prominent feature of its architecture can be said to exist
altogether in vain, we have in St. Mark's a building apparently still employed in the ceremonies for which it was
designed, and yet of which the impressive attributes have
altogether ceased to be comprehended by its votaries. The
beauty which it possesses is unfelt, the language it uses is forgotten; and in the midst of the city to whose service it has
so long been consecrated, and still filled by crowds of the
descendants of those to whom it owes its magnificence, it
stands, in reality, more desolate than the ruins through which
the sheep-walk passes unbroken in our English valleys; and
the writing on its marble walls is less regarded and less
powerful for the teaching of men, than the letters which the
shepherd follows with his finger, where the moss is lightest
on the tombs in the desecrated cloister.

§ XXII. It must therefore be altogether without reference to
its present usefulness, that we pursue our inquiry into the
merits and meaning of the architecture of this marvellous
building; and it can only be after we have terminated that
inquiry, conducting it carefully on abstract grounds, that
we can pronounce with any certainty how far the present
neglect of St. Mark's is significative of the decline of the
Venetian character, or how far this church is to be con-

sidered as the relic of a barbarous age, incapable of attracting the admiration, or influencing the feelings of a civilized community.

The inquiry before us is twofold. Throughout the first volume, I carefully kept the study of *expression* distinct from that of abstract architectural perfection; telling the reader that in every building we should afterwards examine, he would have first to form a judgment of its construction and decorative merit, considering it merely as a work of art; and then to examine farther, in what degree it fulfilled its expressional purposes. Accordingly, we have first to judge of St. Mark's merely as a piece of architecture, not as a church; secondly, to estimate its fitness for its special duty as a place of worship, and the relation in which it stands, as such, to those northern cathedrals that still retain so much of the power over the human heart, which the Byzantine domes appear to have lost for ever.

§ XXIII. In the two succeeding sections of this work, devoted respectively to the examination of the Gothic and Renaissance buildings in Venice, I have endeavored to analyze, and state, as briefly as possible, the true nature of each school,—first in Spirit, then in Form. I wished to have given a similar analysis, in this section, of the nature of Byzantine architecture; but could not make my statements general, because I have never seen this kind of building on its native soil. Nevertheless, in the following sketch of the principles exemplified in St. Mark's, I believe that most of the leading features and motives of the style will be found clearly enough distinguished to enable the reader to judge of it with tolerable fairness, as compared with the better known systems of European architecture in the middle ages.

§ XXIV. Now the first broad characteristic of the building, and the root nearly of every other important peculiarity in it, is its confessed *incrustation*. It is the purest example in Italy of the great school of architecture in which the ruling principle is the incrustation of brick with more precious materials; and it is necessary before we proceed to criticise any one of its arrangements, that the reader should carefully consider the principles which are likely to have influenced, or might legitimately influence, the architects of such a school, as distinguished from those whose designs are to be executed in massive materials.

It is true, that among different nations, and at different times, we may find examples of every sort and degree of incrustation, from the mere setting of the larger and more compact stones by preference at the outside of the wall, to the miserable construction of that modern brick cornice, with its coating of cement, which, but the other day, in London, killed its unhappy workmen in its fall.* But just as it is perfectly possible to have a clear idea of the opposing characteristics of two different species of plants or animals, though between the two there are varieties which it is difficult to assign either to the one or the other, so the reader may fix decisively in his mind the legitimate characteristics of the incrusted and the massive styles, though between the two there are varieties which confessedly unite the attributes of both. For instance, in many Roman remains, built of blocks of tufa and incrusted with marble, we have a style, which, though truly solid, possesses some of the attributes of incrustation; and in the Cathedral of Florence, built of brick and coated with marble, the marble facing is so firmly and exquisitely set, that the building, though in reality incrusted, assumes the attributes of solidity. But these intermediate examples need not in the least confuse our generally distinct ideas of the two families of buildings: the one in which the substance is alike throughout, and the forms and conditions of the ornament assume or prove that it is so, as in the best

* Vide "Builder," for October, 1851.

Greek buildings, and for the most part in our early Norman
and Gothic; and the other, in which the substance is of two
kinds, one internal, the other external, and the system of
decoration is founded on this duplicity, as pre-eminently in
St. Mark's.

§ xxv. I have used the word duplicity in no depreciatory
sense. In chapter ii. of the "Seven Lamps," § 18., I especially guarded this incrusted school from the imputation of
insincerity, and I must do so now at greater length. It
appears insincere at first to a Northern builder, because,
accustomed to build with solid blocks of freestone, he is in
the habit of supposing the external superficies of a piece of
masonry to be some criterion of its thickness. But, as soon
as he gets acquainted with the incrusted style, he will find
that the Southern builders had no intention to deceive him.
He will see that every slab of facial marble is fastened to the
next by a confessed *rivet*, and that the joints of the armor
are so visibly and openly accommodated to the contours of
the substance within, that he has no more right to complain
of treachery than a savage would have, who, for the first
time in his life seeing a man in armor, had supposed him to
be made of solid steel. Acquaint him with the customs of
chivalry, and with the uses of the coat of mail, and he ceases
to accuse of dishonesty either the panoply or the knight.

These laws and customs of the St. Mark's architectural
chivalry it must be our business to develope.

§ xxvi. First, consider the natural circumstances which
give rise to such a style. Suppose a nation of builders,
placed far from any quarries of available stone, and having
precarious access to the mainland where they exist; compelled therefore either to build entirely with brick, or to
import whatever stone they use from great distances, in ships
of small tonnage, and for the most part dependent for speed
on the oar rather than the sail. The labor and cost of car-

riage are just as great, whether they import common or precious stone, and therefore the natural tendency would always be to make each shipload as valuable as possible. But in proportion to the preciousness of the stone, is the limitation of its possible supply; limitation not determined merely by cost, but by the physical conditions of the material, for of many marbles, pieces above a certain size are not to be had for money. There would also be a tendency in such circumstances to import as much stone as possible ready sculptured, in order to save weight; and therefore, if the traffic of their merchants led them to places where there were ruins of ancient edifices, to ship the available fragments of them home. Out of this supply of marble, partly composed of pieces of so precious a quality that only a few tons of them could be on any terms obtained, and partly of shafts, capitals, and other portions of foreign buildings, the island architect has to fashion, as best he may, the anatomy of his edifice. It is at his choice either to lodge his few blocks of precious marble here and there among his masses of brick, and to cut out of the sculptured fragments such new forms as may be necessary for the observance of fixed proportions in the new building; or else to cut the colored stones into thin pieces, of extent sufficient to face the whole surface of the walls, and to adopt a method of construction irregular enough to admit the insertion of fragmentary sculptures; rather with a view of displaying their intrinsic beauty, than of setting them to any regular service in the support of the building.

An architect who cared only to display his own skill, and had no respect for the works of others, would assuredly have chosen the former alternative, and would have sawn the old marbles into fragments in order to prevent all interference with his own designs. But an architect who cared for the preservation of noble work, whether his own or others', and more regarded the beauty of his building than his own fame, would have done what those old builders of St. Mark's did for us, and saved every relic with which he was entrusted.

§ XXVII. But these were not the only motives which influenced the Venetians in the adoption of their method of architecture. It might, under all the circumstances above stated, have been a question with other builders, whether to import one shipload of costly jaspers, or twenty of chalk flints; and whether to build a small church faced with porphyry and paved with agate, or to raise a vast cathedral in freestone. But with the Venetians it could not be a question for an instant; they were exiles from ancient and beautiful cities, and had been accustomed to build with their ruins, not less in affection than in admiration: they had thus not only grown familiar with the practice of inserting older fragments in modern buildings, but they owed to that practice a great part of the splendor of their city, and whatever charm of association might aid its change from a Refuge into a Home. The practice which began in the affections of a fugitive nation, was prolonged in the pride of a conquering one; and beside the memorials of departed happiness, were elevated the trophies of returning victory. The ship of war brought home more marble in triumph than the merchant vessel in speculation; and the front of St. Mark's became rather a shrine at which to dedicate the splendor of miscellaneous spoil, than the organized expression of any fixed architectural law, or religious emotion.

§ XXVIII. Thus far, however, the justification of the style of this church depends on circumstances peculiar to the time of its erection, and to the spot where it arose. The merit of its method, considered in the abstract, rests on far broader grounds.

In the fifth chapter of the "Seven Lamps," § 14. the reader will find the opinion of a modern architect of some reputation, Mr. Wood, that the chief thing remarkable in this church "is its extreme ugliness;" and he will find this opi-

nion associated with another, namely, that the works of the
Caracci are far preferable to those of the Venetian painters.
This second statement of feeling reveals to us one of the prin
cipal causes of the first; namely, that Mr. Wood had not
any perception of color, or delight in it. / The perception
of color is a gift just as definitely granted to one person,
and denied to another, as an ear for music; and the very
first requisite for true judgment of St. Mark's, is the perfection of that color-faculty which few people ever set themselves seriously to find out whether they possess or not.
For it is on its value as a piece of perfect and unchangeable
coloring, that the claims of this edifice to our respect are
finally rested; and a deaf man might as well pretend to pronounce judgment on the merits of a full orchestra, as an architect trained in the composition of form only, to discern the
beauty of St. Mark's.   It possesses the charm of color in common with the greater part of the architecture, as well as of the
manufactures, of the East; but the Venetians deserve especial
note as the only European people who appear to have sympathized to the full with the great instinct of the Eastern races.
They indeed were compelled to bring artists from Constantinople to design the mosaics of the vaults of St. Mark's, and
to group the colors of its porches; but they rapidly took up
and developed, under more masculine conditions, the system of
which the Greeks had shown them the example: while the
burghers and barons of the North were building their dark
streets and grisly castles of oak and sandstone, the merchants
of Venice were covering their palaces with porphyry and
gold; and at last, when her mighty painters had created for
her a color more priceless than gold or porphyry, even this,
the richest of her treasures, she lavished upon walls whose
foundations were beaten by the sea; and the strong tide, as
it runs beneath the Rialto, is reddened to this day by the
reflection of the frescoes of Giorgione.

§ XXIX. If, therefore, the reader does not care for color, I must protest against his endeavor to form any judgment whatever of this church of St. Mark's. But, if he both cares for and loves it, let him remember that the school of incrusted architecture is *the only one in which perfect and permanent chromatic decoration is possible;* and let him look upon every piece of jasper and alabaster given to the architect as a cake of very hard color, of which a certain portion is to be ground down or cut off, to paint the walls with. Once understand this thoroughly, and accept the condition that the body and availing strength of the edifice are to be in brick, and that this under muscular power of brickwork is to be clothed with the defence and the brightness of the marble, as the body of an animal is protected and adorned by its scales or its skin, and all the consequent fitnesses and laws of the structure will be easily discernible: These I shall state in their natural order.

§ XXX. LAW I. / *That the plinths and cornices used for binding the armor are to be light and delicate.* A certain thickness, at least two or three inches, must be required in the covering pieces (even when composed of the strongest stone, and set on the least exposed parts), in order to prevent the chance of fracture, and to allow for the wear of time. And the weight of this armor must not be trusted to cement; the pieces must not be merely glued to the rough brick surface, but connected with the mass which they protect by binding cornices and string courses; and with each other, so as to secure mutual support, aided by the rivetings, but by no means dependent upon them. And, for the full honesty and straightforwardness of the work, it is necessary that these string courses and binding plinths should not be of such proportions as would fit them for taking any important part in the hard work of the inner structure, or render them liable to be mistaken for the great cornices and plinths already explained as essential parts of the best solid building. They must be delicate, slight, and visibly incapable of severer work than that assigned to them.

§ XXXI. LAW II. *Science of inner structure is to be abandoned.* As the body of the structure is confessedly of inferior, and comparatively incoherent materials, it would be absurd to attempt in it any expression of the higher refinements of construction. It will be enough that by its mass we are assured of its sufficiency and strength; and there is the less reason for endeavoring to diminish the extent of its surface by delicacy of adjustment, because on the breadth of that surface we are to depend for the better display of the color, which is to be the chief source of our pleasure in the building. The main body of the work, therefore, will be composed of solid walls and massive piers; and whatever expression of finer structural science we may require, will be thrown either into subordinate portions of it, or entirely directed to the support of the external mail, where in arches or vaults it might otherwise appear dangerously independent of the material within.

§ XXXII. LAW III. *All shafts are to be solid.* Wherever, by the smallness of the parts, we may be driven to abandon the incrusted structure at all, it must be abandoned altogether. The eye must never be left in the least doubt as to what is solid and what is coated. Whatever appears *probably* solid, must be *assuredly* so, and therefore it becomes an inviolable law that no shaft shall ever be incrusted. Not only does the whole virtue of a shaft depend on its consolidation, but the labor of cutting and adjusting an incrusted coat to it would be greater than the saving of material is worth. Therefore the shaft, of whatever size, is always to be solid; and because the incrusted character of the rest of the building renders it more difficult for the shafts to clear themselves from suspicion, they must not, in this incrusted style, be in any place jointed. No shaft must ever be used but of one block; and this the more, because the permission given to the builder to have his walls and piers as ponderous as he likes, renders it quite unnecessary for him to use shafts of any fixed size. In our Norman and Gothic, where definite support is required at a definite point, it becomes lawful to build up a tower of small stones in the shape of a shaft. But the Byzantine is allowed to have as much support as he wants from the walls in every direction, and he has no right to ask for further license in the structure of his shafts. Let him, by generosity in the substance of his pillars, repay us for the permission we have given him to be superficial in his walls. The builder in the chalk valleys of France and England may be blameless in kneading his clumsy pier out of broken flint and calcined lime; but the Venetian, who has access to the riches of Asia and the quarries of Egypt, must frame at least his shafts out of flawless stone.

§ xxxiii. And this for another reason yet. Although, as we have said, it is impossible to cover the walls of a large building with color, except on the condition of dividing the stone into plates, there is always a certain appearance of meanness and niggardliness in the procedure. It is necessary that the builder should justify himself from this suspicion; and prove that it is not in mere economy or poverty, but in the real impossibility of doing otherwise, that he has sheeted his walls so thinly with the precious film. Now the shaft is exactly the portion of the edifice in which it is fittest to recover his honor in this respect. For if blocks of jasper or porphyry be inserted in the walls, the spectator cannot tell their thickness, and cannot judge of the costliness of the sacrifice. But the shaft he can measure with his eye in an instant, and estimate the quantity of treasure both in the mass of its existing substance, and in that which has been hewn away to bring it into its perfect and symmetrical form. And thus the shafts of all buildings of this kind are justly regarded as an expres sion of their wealth, and a form of treasure, just as much as the jewels or gold in the sacred vessels; they are, in fact, nothing else than large jewels,* the block of precious serpentine or jasper being valued according to its size and brilliancy of color, like a large emerald or ruby; only the bulk required to bestow value on the one is to be measured in feet and tons, and on the other in lines and carats. The shafts must therefore be, without exception, of one block in all buildings of this kind; for the attempt in any place to incrust or joint them would be a deception like that of introducing a false stone among jewellery (for a number of joints of any precious stone are of course not equal in value to a single piece of equal weight), and would put an end at once to the spectator's confidence in the expression of wealth in any portion of the structure, or of the spirit of sacrifice in those who raised it.

§ XXXIV. LAW IV. *The shafts may sometimes be independent of the construction.* Exactly in proportion to the importance which the shaft assumes as a large jewel, is the diminution of its importance as a sustaining member; for the delight which we receive in its abstract bulk, and beauty of color, is altogether independent of any perception of its adaptation to mechanical necessities. Like other beautiful things in this world, its end is to *be* beautiful; and, in proportion to its beauty, it receives permission to be otherwise useless. We do not blame emeralds and rubies because we cannot make them into heads of hammers. Nay, so far from our admiration of the jewel shaft being dependent on its doing work for us, it is very possible that a chief part of its precious-

---

* "Quivi presso si vedi una colonna di tanta bellezza e finezza che e riputato *piutosto gioia che pietra.*"—*Sansovino,* of the verd-antique pillar in San Jacomo dell' Orio. A remarkable piece of natural history and moral philosophy, connected with this subject, will be found in the second chapter of our third volume, quoted from the work of a Florentine architect of the fifteenth century.

ness may consist in a delicacy, fragility, and tenderness of material, which must render it utterly unfit for hard work; and therefore that we shall admire it the more, because we perceive that if we were to put much weight upon it, it would be crushed. But, at all events, it is very clear that the primal object in the placing of such shafts must be the display of their beauty to the best advantage, and that therefore all imbedding of them in walls, or crowding of them into groups, in any position in which either their real size or any portion of their surface would be concealed, is either inadmissible altogether, or objectionable in proportion to their value; that no symmetrical or scientific arrangements of pillars are therefore ever to be expected in buildings of this kind, and that all such are even to be looked upon as positive errors and misapplications of materials: but that, on the contrary, we must be constantly prepared to see, and to see with admiration, shafts of great size and importance set in places where their real service is little more than nominal, and where the chief end of their existence is to catch the sunshine upon their polished sides, and lead the eye into delighted wandering among the mazes of their azure veins.

§ XXXV. LAW V. *The shafts may be of variable size.* Since the value of each shaft depends upon its bulk, and diminishes with the diminution of its mass, in a greater ratio than the size itself diminishes, as in the case of all other jewellery, it is evident that we must not in general expect perfect symmetry and equality among the series of shafts, any more than definiteness of application; but that, on the contrary, an accurately observed symmetry ought to give us a kind of pain, as proving that considerable and useless loss has been sustained by some of the shafts, in being cut down to match with the rest. It is true that symmetry is generally sought for in works of smaller jewellery; but, even there, not a perfect symmetry, and obtained under circumstances quite different from those which affect the placing of shafts in architecture. First: the symmetry is usually imperfect. The stones that seem to match each other in a ring or necklace, appear to do so only because they are so small that their differences are not easily measured by the eye; but there is almost always such difference between them as would be strikingly apparent if it existed in the same proportion between two shafts nine or ten feet in height. Secondly: the quantity of stones which pass through a jeweller's hands, and the facility of exchange of such small objects, enable the tradesman to select any number of stones of approximate size; a selection, however, often requiring so much time, that perfect symmetry in a group of very fine stones adds enormously to their value. But the architect has neither the time nor the facilities of exchange. He cannot lay aside one column in a corner of his church till, in the course of traffic, he obtain another that will match it; he has not hundreds of shafts fastened up in bundles, out of which he can match sizes at his ease; he cannot send to a brother-tradesman and exchange the useless stones for available ones, to the convenience of both. His blocks of stone, or his ready hewn shafts, have been brought to him in limited number, from immense distances; no others are to be had; and for those which he does not bring into use, there is no demand elsewhere. His only means of obtaining symmetry will therefore be, in cutting down the finer masses to equality with the inferior ones; and this we ought not to desire him often to do. And therefore, while sometimes in a Baldacchino, or an important chapel or shrine, this costly symmetry may be necessary, and admirable · in proportion to its probable cost, in the general fabric we must expect to see shafts introduced of size and proportion continually varying, and such symmetry as may be obtained among them never altogether perfect, and dependent for its charm frequently on strange complexities and unexpected rising and falling of weight and accent in its marble syllables;

bearing the same relation to a rigidly chiselled and proportioned architecture that the wild lyric rhythm of Æschylus or Pindar bears to the finished measures of Pope.

§ XXXVI. The application of the principles of jewellery to the smaller as well as the larger blocks, will suggest to us another reason for the method of incrustation adopted in the walls. It often happens that the beauty of the veining in some varieties of alabaster is so great, that it becomes desirable to exhibit it by dividing the stone, not merely to economise its substance, but to display the changes in the disposition of its fantastic lines. By reversing one of two thin plates successively taken from the stone, and placing their corresponding edges in contact, a perfectly symmetrical figure may be obtained, which will enable the eye to comprehend more thoroughly the position of the veins. And this is actually the method in which, for the most part, the alabasters of St. Mark are employed; thus accomplishing a double good,—directing the spectator, in the first place, to close observation of the nature of the stone employed, and in the second, giving him a farther proof of the honesty of intention in the builder: for wherever similar veining is discovered in two pieces, the fact is declared that they have been cut from the same stone. It would have been easy to disguise the similarity by using them in different parts of the building; but on the contrary they are set edge to edge, so that the whole system of the architecture may be discovered at a glance by any one acquainted with the nature of the stones employed. Nay, but, it is perhaps answered me, not by an ordinary observer; a person ignorant of the nature of alabaster might perhaps fancy all these symmetrical patterns to have been found in the stone itself, and thus be doubly deceived, supposing blocks to be solid and symmetrical which were in reality subdivided and irregular. I grant it; but be it remembered, that in all things, ignorance is liable to be deceived, and has no right to accuse anything but itself as the source of the deception. The style and the words are dishonest, not which are liable to be misunderstood if subjected to no inquiry, but which are deliberately calculated to lead inquiry astray. There are perhaps no great or noble truths, from those of religion downwards, which present no mistakeable aspect to casual or ignorant contemplation. Both the truth and the lie agree in hiding themselves at first, but the lie continues to hide itself with effort, as we approach to examine it; and leads us, if undiscovered, into deeper lies; the truth reveals itself in proportion to our patience and knowledge, discovers itself kindly to our pleading, and leads us, as it is discovered, into deeper truths.

§ XXXVII. LAW VI. *The decoration must be shallow in cutting.* The method of construction being thus systematized, it is evident that a certain style of decoration must arise out of it, based on the primal condition that over the greater part of the edifice there can be *no deep cutting*. The thin sheets of covering stones do not admit of it; we must not cut them through to the bricks; and whatever ornaments we engrave upon them cannot, therefore, be more than an inch deep at the utmost. Consider for an instant the enormous differences which this single condition compels between the sculptural decoration of the incrusted style, and that of the solid stones of the North, which may be hacked and hewn into whatever cavernous hollows and black recesses we choose; struck into grim darknesses and grotesque projections, and rugged ploughings up of sinuous furrows, in which any form or thought may be wrought out on any scale,—mighty statues with robes of rock and crowned foreheads burning in the sun, or venomous goblins and stealthy dragons shrunk into lurking-places of untraceable shade: think of this, and of the play and freedom given to the sculptor's hand and temper, to smite out and in, hither and thither, as he will; and then consider what must be the different spirit of the design which is to be wrought on the smooth surface of a film of marble, where every line and shadow must be drawn with the most tender pencilling and cautious reserve of resource,—where even the chisel must not strike hard, lest it break through the delicate stone, nor the mind be permitted in any impetuosity of conception inconsistent with the fine discipline of the hand. Consider that whatever animal or human form is to be suggested, must be projected on a flat surface; that all the features of the countenance, the folds of the drapery, the involutions of the limbs, must be so reduced and subdued that the whole work becomes rather a piece of fine drawing than of sculpture; and then follow out, until you begin to perceive their endlessness, the resulting differences of character which will be necessitated in every part of the ornamental designs of these incrusted churches, as compared with that of the Northern schools. I shall endeavor to trace a few of them only.

§ xxxviii. The first would of course be a diminution of the builder's dependence upon human form as a source of ornament: since exactly in proportion to the dignity of the form itself is the loss which it must sustain in being reduced to a shallow and linear bas-relief, as well as the difficulty of expressing it at all under such conditions. Wherever sculpture can be solid, the nobler characters of the human form at once lead the artist to aim at its representation, rather than at that of inferior organisms; but when all is to be reduced to outline, the forms of flowers and lower animals are always more intelligible, and are felt to approach much more to a satisfactory rendering of the objects intended, than the outlines of the human body. This inducement to seek for resources of ornament in the lower fields of creation was powerless in the minds of the great Pagan nations, Ninevite, Greek, or Egyptian: first, because their thoughts were so concentrated on their own capacities and fates, that they preferred the rudest suggestion of human form to the best of an inferior organism;

secondly, because their constant practice in solid sculpture, often colossal. enabled them to bring a vast amount of science into the treatment of the lines, whether of the low relief, the monochrome vase, or shallow hieroglyphic.

§ xxxix. But when various ideas adverse to the representation of animal, and especially of human, form, originating with the Arabs and iconoclast Greeks, had begun at any rate to direct the builders' minds to seek for decorative materials in inferior types, and when diminished practice in solid sculpture had rendered it more difficult to find artists capable of satisfactorily reducing the high organisms to their elementary outlines, the choice of subject for surface sculpture would be more and more uninterruptedly directed to floral organisms, and human and animal form would become diminished in size, frequency, and general importance. So that, while in the Northern solid architecture we constantly find the effect of its noblest features dependent on ranges of statues, often colossal, and full of abstract interest, independent of their architectural service, in the Southern incrusted style we must expect to find the human form for the most part subordinate and diminutive, and involved among designs of foliage and flowers, in the manner of which endless examples had been furnished by the fantastic ornamentation of the Romans, from which the incrusted style had been directly derived.

§ xl. Farther. In proportion to the degree in which his subject must be reduced to abstract outline will be the tendency in the sculptor to abandon naturalism of representation, and subordinate every form to architectural service. Where the flower or animal can be hewn into bold relief, there will always be a temptation to render the representation of it more complete than is necessary, or even to introduce details and intricacies inconsistent with simplicity of distant effect. Very often a worse fault than this is committed; and in the endeavor to give vitality to the stone, the original ornamental purpose of the design is sacrificed or forgotten. But when nothing of this kind can be attempted, and a slight outline is all that the sculptor can command, we may anticipate that this outline will be composed with exquisite grace; and that the richness of its ornamental arrangement will atone for the feebleness of its power of portraiture. On the porch of a Northern cathedral we may seek for the images of the flowers that grow in the neighboring fields, and as we watch with wonder the grey stones that fret themselves into thorns, and soften into blossoms, we may care little that these knots of ornament, as we retire from them to contemplate the whole building, appear unconsidered or confused. On the incrusted building we must expect no such deception of the eye or thoughts. It may sometimes be difficult to determine, from the involutions of its linear sculpture, what were the natural forms which originally suggested them : but we may confidently expect that the grace of their arrangement will always be complete ; that there will not be a line in them which could be taken away without injury, nor one wanting which could be added with advantage.

§ XLI. Farther. While the sculptures of the incrusted school will thus be generally distinguished by care and purity rather than force, and will be, for the most part, utterly wanting in depth of shadow, there will be one means of obtaining darkness peculiarly simple and obvious, and often in the sculptor's power. Wherever he can, without danger, leave a hollow behind his covering slabs, or use them, like glass, to fill an aperture in the wall, ne can, by piercing them with holes, obtain points or spaces of intense blackness to contrast with the light tracing of the rest of his design. And we may expect to find this artifice used the more extensively, because, while it will be an effective means of ornamentation on the exterior of the build ing, it will be also the safest way of admitting light to the interior, still totally excluding both rain and wind. And it will naturally follow that the architect, thus familiarized with the effect of black and sudden points of shadow, will often seek to carry the same principle into other portions of his ornamentation, and by deep drill-holes, or perhaps inlaid portions of black color, to refresh the eye where it may be wearied by the lightness of the general handling.

§ XLII. Farther. Exactly in proportion to the degree in which the force of sculpture is subdued, will be the importance attached to color as a means of effect or constituent of beauty. I have above stated that the incrusted style was the only one in which perfect or permanent color decoration was *possible*. It is also the only one in which a true system of color decoration was ever likely to be invented. In order to understand this, the reader must permit me to review with some care the nature of the principles of coloring adopted by the Northern and Southern nations.

§ XLIII. I believe that from the beginning of the world there has never been a true or fine school of art in which color was despised. It has often been imperfectly attained and injudiciously applied, but I believe it to be one of the essential signs of life in a school of art, that it loves color ; and I know it to be one of the first signs of death in the Renaissance schools, that they despised color.

Observe, it is not now the question whether our Northern cathedrals are better with color or without. Perhaps the great monotone grey of Nature and of Time is a better color than any that the human hand can give; but that is nothing to our present business. The simple fact is, that the builders of those cathedrals laid upon them the brightest colors they could obtain, and that there is not, as far as I am aware, in Europe, any monument of a truly noble school which has not been either painted all over, or vigorously touched with paint, mosaic, and gilding in its prominent parts. Thus far Egyptians, Greeks, Goths, Arabs, and mediæval Christians all agree: none of them, when in their right senses, ever think of doing without paint; and, therefore, when I said above that the Venetians were the only people who had thoroughly sympathized with the Arabs in this respect, I referred, first, to their intense love of color, which led them to lavish the most expensive decorations on ordinary dwelling-houses; and, secondly, to that perfection of the color-instinct in them, which enabled them to render whatever they did, in this kind, as just in principle as it was gorgeous in appliance. It is this principle of theirs, as distinguished from that of the Northern builders, which we have finally to examine.

§ XLIV. In the second chapter of the first volume, it was noticed that the architect of Bourges Cathedral liked hawthorn, and that the porch of his cathedral was therefore decorated with a rich wreath of it; but another of the predilections of that architect was there unnoticed, namely, that he did not at all like *grey* hawthorn, but preferred it green, and he painted it green accordingly, as bright as he could. The color is still left in every sheltered interstice of the foliage. He had, in fact, hardly the choice of any other color; he might have gilded the thorns, by way of allegorizing human life, but if they were to be painted at all, they could hardly be painted anything but green, and green all over. People would have been apt to object to any pursuit of abstract harmonies of color, which might have induced him to paint his hawthorn blue.

§ XLV. In the same way, whenever the subject of the sculpture was definite, its color was of necessity definite also ; and, in the hands of the Northern builders, it often became, in consequence, rather the means of explaining and animating the stories of their stone-work, than a matter of abstract decorative science. Flowers were painted red, trees green, and faces flesh-color ; the result of the whole being often far more entertaining than beautiful. And also, though in the lines of the mouldings and the decorations of shafts or vaults, a richer and more abstract method of coloring was adopted (aided by the rapid development of the best principles of color in early glass-painting), the vigorous depths of shadow in the Northern sculpture confused the architect's eye, compelling him to use violent colors in the recesses, if these were to be seen as color at all, and thus injured his perception of more delicate color harmonies; so that in innumerable instances it becomes very disputable whether monuments even of the best times were improved by the color bestowed upon them, or the contrary. But, in the South, the flatness and comparatively vague forms of the sculpture, while they appeared to call for color in order to enhance their interest, presented exactly the conditions which would set it off to the greatest advantage ; breadth of surface displaying even the most delicate tints in the lights, and faintness of shadow joining with the most delicate and pearly greys of color harmony ; while the subject of the design being in nearly all cases reduced to mere intricacy of ornamental line, might be colored in any way the architect chose without any loss of rationality. Where oak-leaves and roses were carved into fresh relief and perfect bloom, it was necessary to paint the one green and the other red ; but in portions of ornamentation where there was nothing which could be definitely construed into either an oak-leaf or a rose, but a mere labyrinth of beautiful lines, becoming here something like a leaf, and there something like a flower, the whole tracery of the sculpture might be left white, and grounded with gold or blue, or treated in any other manner best harmonizing with the colors around it. And as the necessarily feeble character of the sculpture called for and was ready to display the best arrangements of color, so the precious marbles in the architect's hands give him at once the best examples and the best means of color. The best examples, for the tints of all natural stones are as exquisite in quality as endless in change; and the best means, for they are all permanent.

§ XLVI. Every motive thus concurred in urging him to the study of chromatic decoration, and every advantage was given him in the pursuit of it; and this at the very moment when, as presently to be noticed, the *naïveté* of barbaric Christianity could only be forcibly appealed to by the help of colored pictures: so that, both externally and internally, the architectural construction became partly merged in pictorial effect; and the whole edifice is to be regarded less as a temple wherein to pray, than as itself a Book of Common Prayer, a vast illuminated missal, bound with alabaster instead of parchment, studded with porphyry pillars instead of jewels, and written within and without in letters of enamel and gold.

§ XLVII. LAW VII. *That the impression of the architecture is not to be dependent on size.* And now there is but one final consequence to be deduced. The reader understands, I trust, by this time, that the claims of these several parts of the building upon his attention will depend upon their delicacy of design, their perfection of color, their preciousness of material, and their legendary interest. All these qualities are independent of size, and partly even inconsistent with it. Neither delicacy of surface sculpture, nor subtle gradations of color, can be appreciated by the eye at a distance; and since we have seen that our sculpture is generally to be only an inch or two in depth, and that our coloring is in great part to be produced with the soft tints and veins of natural stones, it will follow necessarily that none of the parts of the building can be removed far from the eye, and therefore that the whole mass of it cannot be large. It is not even desirable that it should be so; for the temper in which the mind addresses itself to contemplate minute and beautiful details is altogether different from that in which it submits itself to vague impressions of space and size. And therefore we must not be disappointed, but grateful, when we find all the best work of the building concentrated within a space comparatively small; and that, for the great cliff-like buttresses and mighty piers of the North, shooting up into indiscernible height, we have here low walls spread before us like the pages of a book, and shafts whose capitals we may touch with our hand.

§ XLVIII. The due consideration of the principles above stated will enable the traveller to judge with more candor and justice of the architecture of St. Mark's than usually it would have been possible for him to do while under the influence of the prejudices necessitated by familiarity with the very different schools of Northern art. I wish it were in my power to lay also before the general reader some exemplification of the manner in which these strange principles are developed in the lovely building. But exactly in proportion to the nobility of any work, is the difficulty of conveying a just impression of it; and wherever I have occasion to bestow high praise, there it is exactly most dangerous for me to endeavor to illustrate my meaning, except by reference to the work itself. And, in fact, the principal reason why architectural criticism is at this day so far behind all other, is the impossibility of illustrating the best architecture faithfully. Of the various schools of painting, examples are accessible to every one, and reference to the works themselves is found sufficient for all purposes of criticism; but there is nothing like St. Mark's or the Ducal Palace to be referred to in the National Gallery, and no faithful illustration of them is possible on the scale of such a volume as this. And it is exceedingly difficult on any scale. Nothing is so rare in art, as far as my own experience goes, as a fair illustration of architecture; *perfect* illustration of it does not exist. For all good architecture depends upon the adaptation of its chiselling

to the effect at a certain distance from the eye; and to render
the peculiar confusion in the midst of order, and uncertainty
in the midst of decision, and mystery in the midst of trenchant
lines, which are the result of distance, together with perfect
expression of the peculiarities of the design, requires the skill
of the most admirable artist, devoted to the work with the
most severe conscientiousness, neither the skill nor the determination having as yet been given to the subject. And in
the illustration of details, every building of any pretensions
to high architectural rank would require a volume of plates,
and those finished with extraordinary care. With respect to
the two buildings which are the principal subjects of the
present volume, St. Mark's and the Ducal Palace, I have
found it quite impossible to do them the slightest justice by
any kind of portraiture; and I abandoned the endeavor in
the case of the latter with less regret, because in the new
Crystal Palace (as the poetical public insist upon calling it,
though it is neither a palace, nor of crystal) there will be
placed, I believe, a noble cast of one of its angles. As for
St. Mark's, the effort was hopeless from the beginning. For
its effect depends not only upon the most delicate sculpture
in every part, but, as we have just stated, eminently on its
color also, and that the most subtle, variable, inexpressible
color in the world,—the color of glass, of transparent alabaster, of polished marble, and lustrous gold. It would be
easier to illustrate a crest of Scottish mountain, with its purple
heather and pale harebells at their fullest and fairest, or a
glade of Jura forest, with its floor of anemone and moss,
than a single portico of St. Mark's. The fragment of one of
its archivolts, given at the bottom of the opposite Plate, is
not to illustrate the thing itself, but to illustrate the impossibility of illustration.

§ XLIX. It is left a fragment, in order to get it on a larger
scale ; and yet even on this scale it is too small to show the

5*

sharp folds and points of the marble vine-leaves with sufficient
clearness. The ground of it is gold, the sculpture in the spandrils is not more than an inch and a half deep, rarely so much.
It is in fact nothing more than an exquisite sketching of outlines in marble, to about the same depth as in the Elgin frieze;
the draperies, however, being filled with close folds, in the
manner of the Byzantine pictures, folds especially necessary
here, as large masses could not be expressed in the shallow
sculpture without becoming insipid; but the disposition of
these folds is always most beautiful, and often opposed by
broad and simple spaces, like that obtained by the scroll in
the hand of the prophet, seen in the Plate.

The balls in the archivolt project considerably, and the
interstices between their interwoven bands of marble are
filled with colors like the illuminations of a manuscript;
violet, crimson, blue, gold, and green, alternately: but no
green is ever used without an intermixture of blue pieces in
the mosaic, nor any blue without a little centre of pale green;
sometimes only a single piece of glass a quarter of an inch
square, so subtle was the feeling for color which was thus to
be satisfied.* The intermediate circles have golden stars set
on an azure ground, varied in the same manner; and the
small crosses seen in the intervals are alternately blue and
subdued scarlet, with two small circles of white set in the
golden ground above and beneath them, each only about half
an inch across (this work, remember, being on the outside of
the building, and twenty feet above the eye), while the blue
crosses have each a pale green centre. Of all this exquisitely
mingled hue, no plate, however large or expensive, could give
any adequate conception; but, if the reader will supply in

* The fact is, that no two tesseræ of the glass are exactly of the same tint,
the greens being all varied with blues, the blues of different depths, the reds
of different clearness, so that the effect of each mass of color is full of variety,
like the stippled color of a fruit piece.

imagination to the engraving what he supplies to a common woodcut of a group of flowers, the decision of the respective merits of modern and of Byzantine architecture may be allowed to rest on this fragment of St. Mark's alone.

From the vine-leaves of that archivolt, though there is no direct imitation of nature in them, but on the contrary a studious subjection to architectural purpose more particularly to be noticed hereafter, we may yet receive the same kind of pleasure which we have in seeing true vine-leaves and wreathed branches traced upon golden light; its stars upon their azure ground ought to make us remember, as its builder remembered, the stars that ascend and fall in the great arch of the sky: and I believe that stars, and boughs, and leaves, and bright colors are everlastingly lovely, and to be by all men beloved; and, moreover, that church walls grimly seared with squared lines, are not better nor nobler things than these. I believe the man who designed and the men who delighted in that archivolt to have been wise, happy, and holy. Let the reader look back to the archivolt I have already given out of the streets of London (Plate XIII. Vol. I.), and see what there is in it to make us any of the three. Let him remember that the men who design such work as that call St. Mark's a barbaric monstrosity, and let him judge between us.

§ L. Some farther details of the St. Mark's architecture, and especially a general account of Byzantine capitals, and of the principal ones at the angles of the church, will be found in the following chapter.* Here I must pass on to the second part of our immediate subject, namely, the inquiry now far the exquisite and varied ornament of St. Mark's fits it, as a Temple, for its sacred purpose, and would be applicable in the churches of modern times. We have here evidently two

* Some illustration, also, of what was said in § XXXIII. above, respecting the value of the shafts of St. Mark's as large jewels, will be found in Appendix 9. "Shafts of St. Mark's."

questions: the first, that wide and continually agitated one, whether richness of ornament be right in churches at all; the second, whether the ornament of St. Mark's be of a truly ecclesiastical and Christian character.

§ LI. In the first chapter of the "Seven Lamps of Architecture" I endeavored to lay before the reader some reasons why churches ought to be richly adorned, as being the only places in which the desire of offering a portion of all precious things to God could be legitimately expressed. But I left wholly untouched the question: whether the church, as such, stood in need of adornment, or would be better fitted for its purposes by possessing it. This question I would now ask the reader to deal with briefly and candidly.

The chief difficulty in deciding it has arisen from its being always presented to us in an unfair form. It is asked of us, or we ask of ourselves, whether the sensation which we now feel in passing from our own modern dwelling-house, through a newly built street, into a cathedral of the thirteenth century, be safe or desirable as a preparation for public worship. But we never ask whether that sensation was at all calculated upon by the builders of the cathedral.

§ LII. Now I do not say that the contrast of the ancient with the modern building, and the strangeness with which the earlier architectural forms fall upon the eye, are at this day disadvantageous. But I do say, that their effect, whatever it may be, was entirely uncalculated upon by the old builder. He endeavored to make his work beautiful, but never expected it to be strange. And we incapacitate ourselves altogether from fair judgment of its intention, if we forget that, when it was built, it rose in the midst of other work fanciful and beautiful as itself; that every dwelling-house in the middle ages was rich with the same ornaments and quaint with the same grotesques which fretted the porches or animated the gargoyles of the cathedral; that what we now regard with doubt and wonder, as well as with delight, was then the natural continuation, into the principal edifice of the city, of a style which was familiar to every eye throughout all its lanes and streets; and that the architect had often no more idea of producing a peculiarly devotional impression by the richest color and the most elaborate carving, than the builder of a modern meeting-house has by his white-washed walls and square-cut casements.*

§ LIII. Let the reader fix this great fact well in his mind, and then follow out its important corollaries. We attach, in modern days, a kind of sacredness to the pointed arch and the groined roof, because, while we look habitually out of square windows and live under flat ceilings, we meet with the more beautiful forms in the ruins of our abbeys. But when those abbeys were built, the pointed arch was used for every shop door, as well as for that of the cloister, and the feudal baron and freebooter feasted, as the monk sang, under vaulted roofs; not because the vaulting was thought especially appropriate to either the revel or psalm, but because it was then the form in which a strong roof was easiest built. We have destroyed the goodly architecture of our cities; we have substituted one wholly devoid of beauty or meaning; and then we reason respecting the strange effect upon our minds of the fragments which, fortunately, we have left in our churches, as if those churches had always been designed to stand out in strong relief from all the buildings around them, and Gothic architecture had always been, what it is now, a religious language, like Monkish Latin. Most readers know, if they would arouse their knowledge, that this was not so; but they take no pains to reason the matter out: they abandon themselves drowsily to the impression that Gothic is a peculiarly ecclesiastical style; and sometimes, even, that richness in church ornament is a condition or furtherance of the Romish religion

* See the farther notice of this subject in Vol. III. Chap. IV.

Undoubtedly it has become so in modern times : for there being no beauty in our recent architecture, and much in the remains of the past, and these remains being almost exclusively ecclesiastical, the High Church and Romanist parties have not been slow in availing themselves of the natural instincts which were deprived of all food except from this source ; and have willingly promulgated the theory, that because all the good architecture that is now left is expressive of High Church or Romanist doctrines, all good architecture ever has been and must be so,—a piece of absurdity from which, though here and there a country clergyman may innocently believe it, I hope the common sense of the nation will soon manfully quit itself. It needs but little inquiry into the spirit of the past, to ascertain what, once for all, I would desire here clearly and forcibly to assert, that wherever Christian church architecture has been good and lovely, it has been merely the perfect development of the common dwelling-house architecture of the period; that when the pointed arch was used in the street, it was used in the church; when the round arch was used in the street, it was used in the church ; when the pinnacle was set over the garret window, it was set over the belfry tower ; when the flat roof was used for the drawing-room, it was used for the nave. There is no sacredness in round arches, nor in pointed ; none in pinnacles, nor in buttresses; none in pillars, nor in traceries. Churches were larger than most other buildings, because they had to hold more people ; they were more adorned than most other buildings, because they were safer from violence, and were the fitting subjects of devotional offering : but they were never built in any separate, mystical, and religious style ; they were built in the manner that was common and familiar to everybody at the time. The flamboyant traceries that adorn the façade of Rouen Cathedral had once their fellows in every window of every house in the market-place ; the sculptures that adorn the porches of St. Mark's had once their match on the walls of every palace on the Grand Canal; and the only difference between the church and the dwelling-house was, that there existed a symbolical meaning in the distribution of the parts of all buildings meant for worship, and that the painting or sculpture was, in the one case, less frequently of profane subject than in the other. A more severe distinction cannot be drawn: for secular history was constantly introduced into church architecture; and sacred history or allusion generally formed at least one half of the ornament of the dwelling-house.

§ LIV. This fact is so important, and so little considered, that I must be pardoned for dwelling upon it at some length, and accurately marking the limits of the assertion I have made. I do not mean that every dwelling-house of mediæval cities was as richly adorned and as exquisite in composition as the fronts of their cathedrals, but that they presented features of the same kind, often in parts quite as beautiful; and that the churches were not separated by any change of style from the buildings round them, as they are now, but were merely more finished and full examples of a universal style, rising out of the confused streets of the city as an oak tree does out of an oak copse, not differing in leafage, but in size and symmetry. Of course the quainter and smaller forms of turret and window necessary for domestic service, the inferior materials, often wood instead of stone, and the fancy of the inhabitants, which had free play in the design, introduced oddnesses, vulgarities, and variations into house architecture, which were prevented by the traditions, the wealth, and the skill of the monks and freemasons; while, on the other hand, conditions of vaulting, buttressing, and arch and tower building, were necessitated by the mere size of the cathedral, of which it would be difficult to find examples elsewhere. But there was nothing more in these features than the adaptation of mechanical skill to vaster requirements; there was nothing intended to be, or felt to be, especially ecclesiastical in any of the forms so developed; and the inhabitants of every village and city, when they furnished funds for the decoration of their church, desired merely to adorn the house of God as they adorned their own, only a little more richly, and with a somewhat graver temper in the subjects of the carving. Even this last difference is not always clearly discernible : all manner of ribaldry occurs in the details of the ecclesiastical buildings of the North, and at the time when the best of them were built, every man's house was a kind of temple ; a figure of the Madonna, or of Christ, almost always occupied a niche over the principal door, and the Old Testament histories were curiously interpolated amidst the grotesques of the brackets and the gables.

§ LV. And the reader will now perceive that the question respecting fitness of church decoration rests in reality on totally different grounds from those commonly made foundations of argument. So long as our streets are walled with barren brick, and our eyes rest continually, in our daily life, on objects utterly ugly, or of inconsistent and meaningless design, it may be a doubtful question whether the faculties of eye and mind which are capable of perceiving beauty, having been left without food during the whole of our active life, should be suddenly feasted upon entering a place of worship; and color, and music, and sculpture should delight the senses, and stir the curiosity of men unaccustomed to such appeal, at the moment when they are required to compose themselves for acts of devotion ;—this, I say, may be a doubtful question: but it cannot be a question at all, that if once familiarized with beautiful form and color, and accustomed to see in whatever human hands have executed for us, even for the lowest services, evidence of noble thought and admirable skill, we shall desire to see this evidence also in whatever is built or labored for the house of prayer; that the absence of the accustomed loveliness would disturb instead of assisting devotion; and that we should feel it as vain to ask whether, with our own house full of goodly craftsmanship, we should worship God in a house destitute of it, as to ask whether a pilgrim whose day's journey had led him through fair woods and by sweet waters, must at evening turn aside into some barren place to pray.

§ LVI. Then the second question submitted to us, whether the ornament of St. Mark's be truly ecclesiastical and Christian, is evidently determined together with the first; for, if not only the permission of ornament at all, but the beautiful execution of it, be dependent on our being familiar with it in daily life, it will follow that no style of noble architecture *can* be exclusively ecclesiastical. It must be practised in the dwelling before it be perfected in the church, and it is the test of a noble style that it shall be applicable to both; for if essentially false and ignoble, it may be made to fit the dwelling-house, but never can be made to fit the church: and just as there are many principles which will bear the light of the world's opinion, yet will not bear the light of God's word, while all principles which will bear the test of Scripture will also bear that of practice, so in architecture there are many forms which expediency and convenience may apparently justify, or at least render endurable, in daily use, which will yet be found offensive the moment they are used for church service; but there are none good for church service, which cannot bear daily use. Thus the Renaissance manner of building is a convenient style for dwelling-houses, but the natural sense of all religious men causes them to turn from it with pain when it has been used in churches; and this has given rise to the popular idea that the Roman style is good for houses and the Gothic for churches. This is not so; the Roman style is essentially base, and we can bear with it only so long as it gives us convenient windows and spacious rooms; the moment the question of convenience is set aside, and the expression or beauty of the style is tried by its being used in a church, we find it fail. But because the Gothic and Byzantine styles are fit for churches they are not therefore less fit for dwellings. They are in the highest sense fit and good for both, nor were they ever brought to perfection except where they were used for both.

§ LVII. But there is one character of Byzantine work which, according to the time at which it was employed, may be considered as either fitting or unfitting it for distinctly ecclesiastical purposes; I mean the essentially pictorial character of its decoration. We have already seen what large surfaces it leaves void of bold architectural features, to be rendered interesting merely by surface ornament or sculpture. In this respect Byzantine work differs essentially from pure Gothic styles, which are capable of filling every vacant space by features purely architectural, and may be rendered, if we please, altogether independent of pictorial aid. A Gothic church may be rendered impressive by mere successions of arches, accumulations of niches, and entanglements of tracery. But a Byzantine church requires expression and interesting decoration over vast plane surfaces,—decoration which becomes noble only by becoming pictorial; that is to say, by representing natural objects,—men, animals, or flowers. And, therefore, the question whether the Byzantine style be fit for church service in modern days, becomes involved in the inquiry, what effect upon religion has been or may yet be produced by pictorial art, and especially by the art of the mosaicist?

§ LVIII. The more I have examined the subject the more dangerous I have found it to dogmatize respecting the character of the art which is likely, at a given period, to be most useful to the cause of religion. One great fact first meets me. I cannot answer for the experience of others, but I never yet met with a Christian whose heart was thoroughly set upon the world to come, and, so far as human judgment could pronounce, perfect and right before God, who cared about art at all. I have known several very noble Christian men who loved it intensely, but in them there was always traceable some entanglement of the thoughts with the matters of this world, causing them to fall into strange distresses and doubts, and often leading them into what they themselves would confess to be errors in understanding, or even failures in duty. I do not say that these men may not, many of them, be in very deed nobler than those whose conduct is more consistent; they may be more tender in the tone of all their feelings, and farther-sighted in soul, and for that very reason exposed to greater trials and fears, than those whose hardier frame and naturally narrower vision enable them with less effort to give their hands to God and walk with Him. But still, the general fact is indeed so, that I have never known a man who seemed altogether right and calm in faith, who seriously cared about art; and when casually moved by it, it is quite impossible to say beforehand by what class of art this impression will on such men be made. Very often it is by a theatrical commonplace, more frequently still by false sentiment. I believe that the four painters who have had, and still have, the most influence, such as it is, on the ordinary Protestant Christian mind, are Carlo Dolci, Guercino, Benjamin West, and John Martin. Raphael, much as he is talked about, is, I believe in very fact, rarely looked at by religious people; much less his master, or any of the truly great religious men of old. But a smooth Magdalen of Carlo Dolci with a tear on each cheek, or a Guercino Christ or St. John, or a Scripture illustration of West's, or a black cloud with a flash of lightning in it of Martin's, rarely fails of being verily, often deeply, felt for the time.

§ LIX. There are indeed many very evident reasons for this; the chief one being that, as all truly great religious painters

have been hearty Romanists, there are none of their works
which do not embody, in some portions of them, definitely
Romanist doctrines. The Protestant mind is instantly struck
by these, and offended by them, so as to be incapable of entering, or at least rendered indisposed to enter, farther into the
heart of the work, or to the discovering those deeper characters of it, which are not Romanist, but Christian, in the everlasting sense and power of Christianity. Thus most Protestants, entering for the first time a Paradise of Angelico, would
be irrevocably offended by finding that the first person the
painter wished them to speak to was St. Dominic; and would
retire from such a heaven as speedily as possible,—not giving
themselves time to discover, that whether dressed in black,
or white, or grey, and by whatever name in the calendar they
might be called, the figures that filled that Angelico heaven
were indeed more saintly, and pure, and full of love in every
feature, than any that the human hand ever traced before or
since. And thus Protestantism, having foolishly sought for
the little help it requires at the hand of painting from the
men who embodied no Catholic doctrine, has been reduced
to receive it from those who believed neither Catholicism
nor Protestantism, but who read the Bible in search of the
picturesque. We thus refuse to regard the painters who
passed their lives in prayer, but are perfectly ready to be
taught by those who spent them in debauchery. There is
perhaps no more popular Protestant picture than Salvator's
" Witch of Endor," of which the subject was chosen by the
painter simply because, under the names of Saul and the
Sorceress, he could paint a captain of banditti, and a Neapolitan hag.

§ LX. The fact seems to be that strength of religious feeling
is capable of supplying for itself whatever is wanting in the
rudest suggestions of art, and will either, on the one hand,
purify what is coarse into inoffensiveness, or, on the other,

raise what is feeble into impressiveness. Probably all art, as such, is unsatisfactory to it; and the effort which it makes to supply the void will be induced rather by association and accident than by the real merit of the work submitted to it. The likeness to a beloved friend, the correspondence with a habitual conception, the freedom from any strange or offensive particularity, and, above all, an interesting choice of incident, will win admiration for a picture when the noblest efforts of religious imagination would otherwise fail of power. How much more, when to the quick capacity of emotion is joined a childish trust that the picture does indeed represent a fact! It matters little whether the fact be well or ill told; the moment we believe the picture to be true, we complain little of its being ill-painted. Let it be considered for a moment, whether the child, with its colored print, inquiring eagerly and gravely which is Joseph, and which is Benjamin, is not more capable of receiving a strong, even a sublime, impression from the rude symbol which it invests with reality by its own effort, than the connoisseur who admires the grouping of the three figures in Raphael's "Telling of the Dreams;" and whether also, when the human mind is in right religious tone, it has not always this childish power—I speak advisedly, this power—a noble one, and possessed more in youth than at any period of after life, but always, I think, restored in a measure by religion—of raising into sublimity and reality the rudest symbol which is given to it of accredited truth.

§ LXI. Ever since the period of the Renaissance, however, the truth has not been accredited; the painter of religious subject is no longer regarded as the narrator of a fact, but as the inventor of an idea.* We do not severely criticise the

* I do not mean that modern Christians believe less in the *facts* than ancient Christians, but they do not believe in the representation of the facts as true. We look upon the picture as this or that painter's conception; the elder Christians looked upon it as this or that painter's description of what

manner in which a true history is told, but we become harsh
investigators of the faults of an invention; so that in the
modern religious mind, the capacity of emotion, which renders
judgment uncertain, is joined with an incredulity which
renders it severe; and this ignorant emotion, joined with
ignorant observance of faults, is the worst possible temper in
which any art can be regarded, but more especially sacred
art. For as religious faith renders emotion facile, so also it
generally renders expression simple; that is to say a truly
religious painter will very often be ruder, quainter, simpler,
and more faulty in his manner of working, than a great
irreligious one. And it was in this artless utterance, and
simple acceptance, on the part of both the workman and the
beholder, that all noble schools of art have been cradled; it
is in them that they *must* be cradled to the end of time. It
is impossible to calculate the enormous loss of power in
modern days, owing to the imperative requirement that art
shall be methodical and learned: for as long as the constitution of this world remains unaltered, there will be more
intellect in it than there can be education; there will be
many men capable of just sensation and vivid invention, who
never will have time to cultivate or polish their natural
powers. And all unpolished power is in the present state of
society lost; in other things as well as in the arts, but in the
arts especially: nay, in nine cases out of ten, people mistake
the polish for the power. Until a man has passed through a

had actually taken place. And in the Greek Church all painting is, to this
day, strictly a branch of tradition. See M. Dideron's admirably written
introduction to his Iconographie Chrétienne, p. 7.:—"Un de mes compagnons
s'étonnait de retrouver à la Panagia de St. Luc, le saint Jean Chrysostome
qu'il avait dessiné dans le baptistère de St. Marc. à Venise. Le costume des
personnages est partout et en tout temps le même, non-seulement pour la
forme, mais pour la couleur, mais pour le dessin, mais jusque pour le nombre
et l'épaisseur des plis."

course of academy studentship, and can draw in an approved manner with French chalk, and knows foreshortening, and perspective, and something of anatomy, we do not think he can possibly be an artist; what is worse, we are very apt to think that we can *make* him an artist by teaching him anatomy, and how to draw with French chalk; whereas the real gift in him is utterly independent of all such accomplishments: and I believe there are many peasants on every estate, and laborers in every town, of Europe, who have imaginative powers of a high order, which nevertheless cannot be used for our good, because we do not choose to look at anything but what is expressed in a legal and scientific way. I believe there is many a village mason who, set to carve a series of Scripture or any other histories, would find many a strange and noble fancy in his head, and set it down, roughly enough indeed, but in a way well worth our having. But we are too grand to let him do this, or to set up his clumsy work when it is done; and accordingly the poor stone-mason is kept hewing stones smooth at the corners, and we build our church of the smooth square stones, and consider ourselves wise.

§ LXII. I shall pursue this subject farther in another place; but I allude to it here in order to meet the objections of those persons who suppose the mosaics of St. Mark's, and others of the period, to be utterly barbarous as representations of religious history. Let it be granted that they are so; we are not for that reason to suppose they were ineffective in religious teaching. I have above spoken of the whole church as a great Book of Common Prayer; the mosaics were its illuminations, and the common people of the time were taught their Scripture history by means of them, more impressively perhaps, though far less fully, than ours are now by Scripture reading. They had no other Bible, and—Protestants do not often enough consider this—*could* have no other. We find it somewhat difficult to furnish our poor with printed Bibles;

consider what the difficulty must have been when they could be given only in manuscript. The walls of the church necessarily became the poor man's Bible, and a picture was more easily read upon the walls than a chapter. Under this view, and considering them merely as the Bible pictures of a great nation in its youth, I shall finally invite the reader to examine the connexion and subjects of these mosaics; but in the mean time I have to deprecate the idea of their execution being in any sense barbarous. I have conceded too much to modern prejudice, in permitting them to be rated as mere childish efforts at colored portraiture: they have characters in them of a very noble kind; nor are they by any means devoid of the remains of the science of the later Roman empire. The character of the features is almost always fine, the expression stern and quiet, and very solemn, the attitudes and draperies always majestic in the single figures, and in those of the groups which are not in violent action;* while the bright coloring and disregard of chiaroscuro cannot be regarded as imperfections, since they are the only means by which the figures could be rendered clearly intelligible in the distance and darkness of the vaulting. So far am I from considering them barbarous, that I believe of all works of religious art whatsoever, these, and such as these, have been the most effective. They stand exactly midway between the debased manufacture of wooden and waxen images which is the support of Romanist idolatry all over the world, and the great art which

---

* All the effects of Byzantine art to represent violent action are inadequate, most of them ludicrously so, even when the sculptural art is in other respects far advanced. The early Gothic sculptors, on the other hand, fail in all points of refinement, but hardly ever in expression of action. This distinction is of course one of the necessary consequences of the difference in all respects between the repose of the Eastern, and activity of the Western, mind, which we shall have to trace out completely in the inquiry into the nature of Gothic.

leads the mind away from the religious subject to the art itself. Respecting neither of these branches of human skill is there, nor can there be, any question. The manufacture of puppets, however influential on the Romanist mind of Europe, is certainly not deserving of consideration as one of the fine arts. It matters literally nothing to a Romanist what the image he worships is like. Take the vilest doll that is screwed together in a cheap toy-shop, trust it to the keeping of a large family of children, let it be beaten about the house by them till it is reduced to a shapeless block, then dress it in a satin frock and declare it to have fallen from heaven, and it will satisfactorily answer all Romanist purposes. Idolatry,* it cannot be too often repeated, is no encourager of the fine arts. But, on the other hand, the highest branches of the fine arts are no encouragers either of idolatry or of religion. No picture of Leonardo's or Raphael's, no statue of Michael Angelo's, has ever been worshipped, except by accident. Carelessly regarded, and by ignorant persons, there is less to attract in them than in commoner works. Carefully regarded, and by intelligent persons, they instantly divert the mind from their subject to their art, so that admiration takes the place of devotion. I do not say that the Madonna di S. Sisto, the Madonna del Cardellino, and such others, have not had considerable religious influence on certain minds, but I say that on the mass of the people of Europe they have had none whatever; while by far the greater number of the most celebrated statues and pictures are never regarded with any other feelings than those of admiration of human beauty, or reverence for human skill. Effective religious art, therefore, has always lain, and I believe must always lie, between the two extremes—of barbarous idol-fashioning on one side, and magnificent craftsmanship on the other. It consists partly in missal-painting, and such book-illustrations as, since the inven-

* Appendix 10.: "Proper Sense of the word Idolatry."

tion of printing, have taken its place; partly in glass-painting, partly in rude sculpture on the outsides of buildings; partly in mosaics; and partly in the frescoes and tempera pictures which, in the fourteenth century, formed the link between this powerful, because imperfect, religious art, and the impotent perfection which succeeded it.

§ LXIII. But of all these branches the most important are the inlaying and mosaic of the twelfth and thirteenth centuries, represented in a central manner by these mosaics of St. Mark's. Missal-painting could not, from its minuteness, produce the same sublime impressions, and frequently merged itself in mere ornamentation of the page. Modern book-illustration has been so little skilful as hardly to be worth naming. Sculpture, though in some positions it becomes of great importance, has always a tendency to lose itself in architectural effect; and was probably seldom deciphered, in all its parts, by the common people, still less the traditions annealed in the purple burning of the painted window. Finally, tempera pictures and frescoes were often of limited size or of feeble color. But the great mosaics of the twelfth and thirteenth centuries covered the walls and roofs of the churches with inevitable lustre; they could not be ignored or escaped from; their size rendered them majestic, their distance mysterious, their color attractive. They did not pass into confused or inferior decorations; neither were they adorned with any evidences of skill or science, such as might withdraw the attention from their subjects. They were before the eyes of the devotee at every interval of his worship; vast shadowings forth of scenes to whose realization he looked forward, or of spirits whose presence he invoked. And the man must be little capable of receiving a religious impression of any kind, who, to this day, does not acknowledge some feeling of awe, as he looks up at the pale countenances and ghastly forms which haunt the dark roofs of the Baptisteries of Parma and

Florence, or remains altogether untouched by the majesty of the colossal images of apostles, and of Him who sent apostles, that look down from the darkening gold of the domes of Venice and Pisa.

§ LXIV. I shall, in a future portion of this work, endeavor to discover what probabilities there are of our being able to use this kind of art in modern churches; but at present it remains for us to follow out the connexion of the subjects represented in St. Mark's so as to fulfil our immediate object, and form an adequate conception of the feelings of its builders, and of its uses to those for whom it was built.

Now there is one circumstance to which I must, in the outset, direct the reader's special attention, as forming a notable distinction between ancient and modern days. Our eyes are now familiar and wearied with writing; and if an inscription is put upon a building, unless it be large and clear, it is ten to one whether we ever trouble ourselves to decipher it. But the old architect was sure of readers. He knew that every one would be glad to decipher all that he wrote; that they would rejoice in possessing the vaulted leaves of his stone manuscript; and that the more he gave them, the more grateful would the people be. We must take some pains, therefore, when we enter St. Mark's, to read all that is inscribed, or we shall not penetrate into the feeling either of the builder or of his times.

§ LXV. A large atrium or portico is attached to two sides of the church, a space which was especially reserved for unbaptized persons and new converts. It was thought right that, before their baptism, these persons should be led to contemplate the great facts of the Old Testament history; the history of the Fall of Man, and of the lives of Patriarchs up to the period of the Covenant by Moses: the order of the subjects in this series being very nearly the same as in many Northern churches, but significantly closing with the Fall of the Manna, in order to mark to the catechumen the insufficiency of the Mosaic covenant for salvation,—"Our fathers did eat manna in the wilderness, and are dead,"—and to turn his thoughts to the true Bread of which that manna was the type.

§ LXVI. Then, when after his baptism he was permitted to enter the church, over its main entrance he saw, on looking back, a mosaic of Christ enthroned, with the Virgin on one side and St. Mark on the other, in attitudes of adoration. Christ is represented as holding a book open upon his knee, on which is written: "I AM THE DOOR; BY ME IF ANY MAN ENTER IN, HE SHALL BE SAVED." On the red marble moulding which surrounds the mosaic is written: "I AM THE GATE OF LIFE; LET THOSE WHO ARE MINE ENTER BY ME." Above, on the red marble fillet which forms the cornice of the west end of the church, is written, with reference to the figure of Christ below: "WHO HE WAS, AND FROM WHOM HE CAME, AND AT WHAT PRICE HE REDEEMED THEE, AND WHY HE MADE THEE, AND GAVE THEE ALL THINGS, DO THOU CONSIDER."

Now observe, this was not to be seen and read only by the catechumen when he first entered the church; every one who at any time entered, was supposed to look back and to read this writing; their daily entrance into the church was thus made a daily memorial of their first entrance into the spiritual Church; and we shall find that the rest of the book which was opened for them upon its walls continually led them in the same manner to regard the visible temple as in every part a type of the invisible Church of God.

§ LXVII. Therefore the mosaic of the first dome, which is over the head of the spectator as soon as he has entered by the great door (that door being the type of baptism), represents the effusion of the Holy Spirit, as the first consequence and seal of the entrance into the Church of God. In the centre of the cupola is the Dove, enthroned in the Greek manner, as the Lamb is enthroned, when the Divinity of the Second and

Third Persons is to be insisted upon together with their peculiar offices. From the central symbol of the Holy Spirit twelve streams of fire descend upon the heads of the twelve apostles, who are represented standing around the dome; and below them, between the windows which are pierced in its walls, are represented, by groups of two figures for each separate people, the various nations who heard the apostles speak, at Pentecost, every man in his own tongue. Finally, on the vaults, at the four angles which support the cupola, are pictured four angels, each bearing a tablet upon the end of a rod in his hand: on each of the tablets of the three first angels is inscribed the word "Holy;" on that of the fourth is written "Lord;" and the beginning of the hymn being thus put into the mouths of the four angels, the words of it are continued around the border of the dome, uniting praise to God for the gift of the Spirit, with welcome to the redeemed soul received into His Church:

"HOLY, HOLY, HOLY, LORD GOD OF SABAOTH:
HEAVEN AND EARTH ARE FULL OF THY GLORY.
HOSANNA IN THE HIGHEST:
BLESSED IS HE THAT COMETH IN THE NAME OF THE LORD."

And observe in this writing that the convert is required to regard the outpouring of the Holy Spirit especially as a work of *sanctification*. It is the *holiness* of God manifested in the giving of His Spirit to sanctify those who had become His children, which the four angels celebrate in their ceaseless praise; and it is on account of this holiness that the heaven and earth are said to be full of His glory.

§ LXVIII. After thus hearing praise rendered to God by the angels for the salvation of the newly-entered soul, it was thought fittest that the worshipper should be led to contemplate, in the most comprehensive forms possible, the past evidence and the future hopes of Christianity, as summed up in three facts without assurance of which all faith is vain; namely that Christ died, that He rose again, and that He ascended into heaven, there to prepare a place for His elect. On the vault between the first and second cupolas are represented the crucifixion and resurrection of Christ, with the usual series of intermediate scenes,—the treason of Judas, the judgment of Pilate, the crowning with thorns, the descent into Hades, the visit of the women to the Sepulchre, and the apparition to Mary Magdalene. The second cupola itself, which is the central and principal one of the church, is entirely occupied by the subject of the Ascension. At the highest point of it Christ is represented as rising into the blue heaven, borne up by four angels, and throned upon a rainbow, the type of reconciliation. Beneath him, the twelve apostles are seen upon the Mount of Olives, with the Madonna, and, in the midst of them, the two men in white apparel who appeared at the moment of the Ascension, above whom, as uttered by them, are inscribed the words, " Ye men of Galilee, why stand ye gazing up into heaven ? This Christ, the Son of God, as He is taken from you, shall so come, the arbiter of the earth, trusted to do judgment and justice."

§ LXIX. Beneath the circle of the apostles, between the windows of the cupola, are represented the Christian virtues, as sequent upon the crucifixion of the flesh, and the spiritual ascension together with Christ. Beneath them, on the vaults which support the angles of the cupola, are placed the four Evangelists, because on their evidence our assurance of the fact of the ascension rests; and, finally, beneath their feet, as symbols of the sweetness and fulness of the Gospel which they declared, are represented the four rivers of Paradise, Pison, Gihon, Tigris, and Euphrates.

§ LXX. The third cupola, that over the altar, represents the witness of the Old Testament to Christ; showing him enthroned in its centre, and surrounded by the patriarchs and prophets. But this dome was little seen by the people;* their contemplation was intended to be chiefly drawn to that of the centre of the church, and thus the mind of the worship-per was at once fixed on the main groundwork and hope of Christianity,—"Christ is risen," and "Christ shall come." If he had time to explore the minor lateral chapels and cupolas, he could find in them the whole series of New Testament history, the events of the Life of Christ, and the Apostolic miracles in their order, and finally the scenery of the Book of Revelation ;† but if he only entered, as often the common people do to this hour, snatching a few moments before begin-ning the labor of the day to offer up an ejaculatory prayer, and advanced but from the main entrance as far as the altar screen, all the splendor of the glittering nave and variegated dome, if they smote upon his heart, as they might often, in strange contrast with his reed cabin among the shallows of the lagoon, smote upon it only that they might proclaim the two great messages—"Christ is risen," and "Christ shall come." Daily, as the white cupolas rose like wreaths of sea-foam in the dawn, while the shadowy campanile and frowning palace were still withdrawn into the night, they rose with the Easter Voice of Triumph,—"Christ is risen ;" and daily, as they looked down upon the tumult of the people, deepening and eddying in the wide square that opened from their feet to the sea, they uttered above them the sentence of warning,—"Christ shall come."

§ LXXI. And this thought may surely dispose the reader to look with some change of temper upon the gorgeous building and wild blazonry of that shrine of St. Mark's. He now per-

* It is also of inferior workmanship, and perhaps later than the rest   Vide Lord Lindsay, vol. i. p. 124. note.

† The old mosaics from the Revelation have perished, and have been replaced by miserable work of the seventeenth century.

ceives that it was in the hearts of the old Venetian people far more than a place of worship. It was at once a type of the Redeemed Church of God, and a scroll for the written word of God. It was to be to them, both an image of the Bride, all glorious within, her clothing of wrought gold; and the actual Table of the Law and the Testimony, written within and without. And whether honored as the Church or as the Bible, was it not fitting that neither the gold nor the crystal should be spared in the adornment of it; that, as the symbol of the Bride, the building of the wall thereof should be of jasper,* and the foundations of it garnished with all manner of precious stones; and that, as the channel of the World, that triumphant utterance of the Psalmist should be true of it, —" I have rejoiced in the way of thy testimonies, as much as in all riches?" And shall we not look with changed temper down the long perspective of St. Mark's Place towards the sevenfold gates and glowing domes of its temple, when we know with what solemn purpose the shafts of it were lifted above the pavement of the populous square? Men met there from all countries of the earth, for traffic or for pleasure; but, above the crowd swaying for ever to and fro in the restlessness of avarice or thirst of delight, was seen perpetually the glory of the temple, attesting to them, whether they would hear or whether they would forbear, that there was one treasure which the merchantmen might buy without a price, and one delight better than all others, in the word and the statues of God. Not in the wantonness of wealth, not in vain ministry to the desire of the eyes or the pride of life, were those marbles hewn into transparent strength, and those arches arrayed in the colors of the iris. There is a message written in the dyes of them, that once was written in blood; and a sound in the echoes of their vaults, that one day shall fill the vault of heaven,—" He shall return, to do judgment

* Rev. xxi. 18.

and justice." The strength of Venice was given her, so long
as she remembered this: her destruction found her when she
had forgotten this; and it found her irrevocably, because she
forgot it without excuse. Never had city a more glorious
Bible. Among the nations of the North, a rude and shadowy
sculpture filled their temples with confused and hardly legible
imagery; but, for her, the skill and the treasures of the East
had gilded every letter, and illumined every page, till the
Book-Temple shone from afar off like the star of the Magi.
In other cities, the meetings of the people were often in places
withdrawn from religious association, subject to violence and
to change; and on the grass of the dangerous rampart, and
in the dust of the troubled street, there were deeds done and
counsels taken, which, if we cannot justify, we may sometimes
forgive. But the sins of Venice, whether in her palace or in
her piazza, were done with the Bible at her right hand. The
walls on which its testimony was written were separated but
by a few inches of marble from those which guarded the
secrets of her councils, or confined the victims of her policy.
And when in her last hours she threw off all shame and all
restraint, and the great square of the city became filled with
the madness of the whole earth, be it remembered how much
her sin was greater, because it was done in the face of the
House of God, burning with the letters of His Law. Mounte-
bank and masquer laughed their laugh, and went their way;
and a silence has followed them, not unforetold; for amidst
them all, through century after century of gathering vanity
and festering guilt, that white dome of St. Mark's had uttered
in the dead ear of Venice, "Know thou, that for all these
things God will bring thee into judgment."

CHAPTER V.

BYZANTINE PALACES.

§ I. THE account of the architecture of St. Mark's given in the previous chapter has, I trust, acquainted the reader sufficiently with the spirit of the Byzantine style: but he has probably, as yet, no clear idea of its generic forms. Nor would it be safe to define these after an examination of St. Mark's alone, built as it was upon various models, and at various periods. But if we pass through the city, looking for buildings which resemble St. Mark's—first, in the most important feature of incrustation; secondly, in the character of the mouldings,—we shall find a considerable number, not indeed very attractive in their first address to the eye, but agreeing perfectly, both with each other, and with the earliest portions of St. Mark's, in every important detail; and to be regarded, therefore, with profound interest, as indeed the remains of an ancient city of Venice, altogether different in aspect from that which now exists. From these remains we may with safety deduce general conclusions touching the forms of Byzantine architecture, as practised in Eastern Italy, during the eleventh, twelfth, and thirteenth centuries.

§ II. They agree in another respect, as well as in style. All are either ruins, or fragments disguised by restoration. Not one of them is uninjured or unaltered; and the impossibility of finding so much as an angle or a single story in perfect condition is a proof, hardly less convincing than the method of their architecture, that they were indeed raised during the earliest phases of the Venetian power. The mere fragments, dispersed in narrow streets, and recognizable by a single capital, or the segment of an arch, I shall not enumerate: but, of important remains, there are six in the immediate neighborhood of the Rialto, one in the Rio di Ca' Foscari, and one conspicuously placed opposite the great Renaissance Palace known as the Vendramin Calerghi, one of the few palaces still inhabited* and well maintained; and noticeable, moreover, as having a garden beside it, rich with evergreens, and decorated by gilded railings and white statues that cast long streams of snowy reflection down into the deep water. The vista of canal beyond is terminated by the Church of St. Geremia, another but less attractive work of the Renaissance; a mass of barren brickwork, with a dull leaden dome above, like those of our National Gallery. So that the spectator has the richest and meanest of the late architecture of Venice before him at once: the richest, let him observe, a piece of private luxury; the poorest, that which was given to God. Then, looking to the left, he will see the fragment of the work of earlier ages, testifying against both, not less by its utter desolation than by the nobleness of the traces that are still left of it.

§ III. It is a ghastly ruin; whatever is venerable or sad in its wreck being disguised by attempts to put it to present uses of the basest kind. It has been composed of arcades borne by marble shafts, and walls of brick faced with marble: but the covering stones have been torn away from it like the shroud from a corpse; and its walls, rent into a thousand chasms, are filled and refilled with fresh brickwork, and the seams and hollows are choked with clay and whitewash, oozing and trickling over the marble,—itself blanched into dusty decay by the frosts of centuries. Soft grass and wandering

* In the year 1851, by the Duchesse de Berri.

leafage have rooted themselves in the rents, but they are not
suffered to grow in their own wild and gentle way, for the
place is in a sort inhabited; rotten partitions are nailed across
its corridors, and miserable rooms contrived in its western
wing; and here and there the weeds are indolently torn
down, leaving their haggard fibres to struggle again into
unwholesome growth when the spring next stirs them: and
thus, in contest between death and life, the unsightly heap is
festering to its fall.

Of its history little is recorded, and that little futile. That
it once belonged to the dukes of Ferrara, and was bought
from them in the sixteenth century, to be made a general recep-
tacle for the goods of the Turkish merchants, whence it is now
generally known as the Fondaco, or Fontico, de' Turchi, are
facts just as important to the antiquary, as that, in the year
1852, the municipality of Venice allowed its lower story to be
used for a "deposito di Tabacchi." Neither of this, nor of
any other remains of the period, can we know anything but
what their own stones will tell us.

§ IV. The reader will find in Appendix 11., written chiefly
for the traveller's benefit, an account of the situation and present state of the other seven Byzantine palaces. Here I shall
only give a general account of the most interesting points in
their architecture.

They all agree in being round-arched and incrusted with
marble, but there are only six in which the original disposition
of the parts is anywise traceable; namely, those distinguished
in the Appendix as the Fondaco de' Turchi, Casa Loredan,
Caso Farsetti, Rio-Foscari House, Terraced House, and Madonnetta House*: and these six agree farther in having continuous arcades along their entire fronts from one angle to the

---

* Of the Braided House and Casa Businello, described in the Appendix,
only the great central arcades remain.

other, and in having their arcades divided, in each case, into a centre and wings; both by greater size in the midmost arches, and by the alternation of shafts in the centre, with pilasters, or with small shafts, at the flanks.

§ v. So far as their structure can be traced, they agree also in having tall and few arches in their lower stories, and shorter and more numerous arches above : but it happens most unfortunately that in the only two cases in which the second stories are left the ground floors are modernized, and in the others where the sea stories are left the second stories are modernized; so that we never have more than two tiers of the Byzantine arches, one above the other. These, however, are quite enough to show the first main point on which I wish to insist, namely, the subtlety of the feeling for proportion in the Greek architects; and I hope that even the general reader will not allow himself to be frightened by the look of a few measurements, for, if he will only take the little pains necessary to compare them, he will, I am almost certain, find the result not devoid of interest.

§ vi. I had intended originally to give elevations of all these palaces; but have not had time to prepare plates requiring so much labor and care. I must, therefore, explain the position of their parts in the simplest way in my power.

The Fondaco de' Turchi has sixteen arches in its sea story, and twenty-six above them in its first story, the whole based on a magnificent foundation, built of blocks of red marble, some of them seven feet long by a foot and a half thick, and raised to a height of about five feet above high-water mark. At this level, the elevation of one half of the building, from its flank to the central pillars of its arcades, is rudely given in Fig. IV., in the next page. It is only drawn to show the arrangement of the parts, as the sculptures which are indicated by the circles and upright oblongs between the arches are too delicate to be shown in a sketch three times the size of this. The building once was crowned with an Arabian parapet; but it was taken down some years since, and I am aware of no authentic representation of its details. The greater part of the sculptures between the arches, indicated in the woodcut only by blank circles, have also fallen, or been removed, but enough remain on the two flanks to justify the representation given in the diagram of their original arrangement.

Fig. IV.

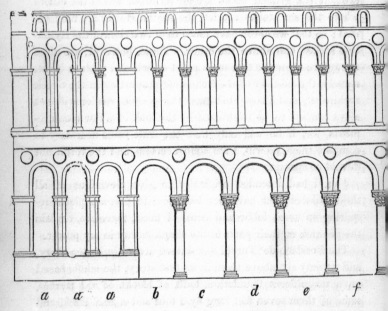

And now observe the dimensions. The small arches of the wings in the ground story, *a, a, a,* measure, in breadth, from

			Ft.	In.
shaft to shaft	.	.	4	5
interval *b*	.	.	7	6½
interval *c*	.	.	7	11
intervals *d, e, f,* &c.	.	.	8	1

The difference between the width of the arches b and c is necessitated by the small recess of the cornice on the left hand as compared with that of the great capitals; but this sudden difference of half a foot between the two extreme arches of the centre offended the builder's eye, so he diminished the next one, *unnecessarily*, two inches, and thus obtained the gradual cadence to the flanks, from eight feet down to four and a half, in a series of continually increasing steps. Of course the effect cannot be shown in the diagram, as the first difference is less than the thickness of its lines. In the upper story the capitals are all nearly of the same height, and there was no occasion for the difference between the extreme arches. Its twenty-six arches are placed, four small ones above each lateral three of the lower arcade, and eighteen larger above the central ten; thus throwing the shafts into all manner of relative positions, and completely confusing the eye in any effort to count them : but there is an exquisite symmetry running through their apparent confusion; for it will be seen that the four arches in each flank are arranged in two groups, of which one has a large single shaft in the centre, and the other a pilaster and two small shafts. The way in which the large shaft is used as an echo of those in the central arcade, dovetailing them, as it were, into the system of the pilasters,—just as a great painter, passing from one tone of color to another, repeats, over a small space, that which he has left,—is highly characteristic of the Byzantine care in composition. There are other evidences of it in the arrangement of the capitals, which will be noticed below in the seventh chapter. The lateral arches of this upper arcade measure 3 ft. 2 in. across, and the central 3 ft. 11 in., so that the arches in the building are altogether of six magnitudes.

§ VII. Next let us take the Casa Loredan. The mode of arrangement of its pillars is precisely like that of the Fondaco

de' Turchi, so that I shall merely indicate them by vertical
lines in order to be able to letter the intervals. It has five
arches in the centre of the lower story, and two in each
of its wings.

				Ft.	In.
The midmost interval, *a*, of the central five, is				6	1
The two on each side, *b, b*	.	.	.	5	2
The two extremes, *c, c* .	.	.	.	4	9
Inner arches of the wings, *d, d* .	.	.	.	4	4
Outer arches of the wings, *e, e* .	.	.	.	4	6

The gradation of these dimensions is visible at a glance;
the boldest step being here taken nearest the centre, while in
the Fondaco it is farthest from the centre. The first loss here
is of eleven inches, the second of five, the third of five, and
then there is a most subtle increase of two inches in the
extreme arches, as if to contradict the principle of diminution,
and stop the falling away of the building by firm resistance at
its flanks.

I could not get the measures of the upper story accurately,
the palace having been closed all the time I was in Venice;
but it has seven central arches above the five below, and
three at the flanks above the two below, the groups being
separated by double shafts.

§ VIII. Again, in the Casa Farsetti, the lower story has a
centre of five arches, and wings of two. Referring, therefore, to the last figure, which will answer for this palace also,
the measures of the intervals are :

				Ft.	In.
a	.	.	.	8	0
b	.	.	.	5	10
c	.	.	.	5	4
d and *e*	.	.	.	5	3

It is, however, possible that the interval *c* and the wing arches may have been intended to be similar; for one of the wing arches measures 5ft. 4 in. We have thus a simpler proportion than any we have hitherto met with; only two losses taking place, the first of 2 ft. 2 in., the second of 6 inches.

The upper story has a central group of seven arches, whose widths are 4 ft. 1 in.

	Ft.	In.
The next arch on each side .	3	5
The three arches of each wing .	3	6

Here again we have a most curious instance of the subtlety of eye which was not satisfied without a third dimension, but *could* be satisfied with a difference of an inch on three feet and a half.

§ IX In the Terraced House, the ground floor is modernized, but the first story is composed of a centre of five arches, with wings of two, measuring as follows:

	Ft.	In.
Three midmost arches of the central group .	4	0
Outermost arch of the central group .	4	6
Innermost arch of the wing .	4	10
Outermost arch of the wing* .	5	0

Here the greatest step is towards the centre; but the increase, which is unusual, is towards the outside, the gain being successively six, four, and two inches.

* Only one wing of the first story is left. See Appendix 11.

I could not obtain the measures of the second story, in which only the central group is left; but the two outermost arches are visibly larger than the others, thus beginning a correspondent proportion to the one below, of which the lateral quantities have been destroyed by restorations.

§ x. Finally, in the Rio-Foscari House, the central arch is the principal feature, and the four lateral ones form one magnificent wing; the dimensions being from the centre to the side:

				Ft.	In.
Central arch	.	.	.	9	9
Second „	.	.	.	3	8
Third „	.	.	.	3	10
Fourth „	.	.	.	3	10
Fifth „	.	.	.	3	8

The difference of two inches on nearly three feet in the two midmost arches being all that was necessary to satisfy the builder's eye.

§ xi. I need not point out to the reader that these singular and minute harmonies of proportion indicate, beyond all dispute, not only that the buildings in which they are found are of one school, but (so far as these subtle coincidences of measurement can still be traced in them) in their original form. No modern builder has any idea of connecting his arches in this manner, and restorations in Venice are carried on with too violent hands to admit of the supposition that such refinements would be even noticed in the progress of demolition, much less imitated in heedless reproduction. And as if to direct our attention especially to this character, as indicative of Byzantine workmanship, the most interesting example of all will be found in the arches of the front of St. Mark's itself, whose proportions I have not noticed before, in order that they might here be compared with those of the contemporary palaces.

§ XII. The doors actually employed for entrance in the western façade are as usual five, arranged as at *a* in the annexed woodcut, fig. V.; but the Byzantine builder could

Fig. V.

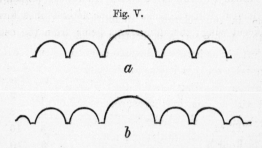

not be satisfied with so simple a group, and he introduced, therefore, two minor arches at the extremities, as at *b*, by adding two small porticos which are of *no use whatever* except to consummate the proportions of the façade, and themselves to exhibit the most exquisite proportions in arrangements of shaft and archivolt with which I am acquainted in the entire range of European architecture.

Into these minor particulars I cannot here enter; but observe the dimensions of the range of arches in the façade, as thus completed by the flanking porticos:

		Ft.	In.
The space of its central archivolt is	. .	31	8
,, the two on each side, about*	. .	19	8
,, the two succeeding, about	. .	20	4
,, small arches at flanks, about	. .	6	0

* I am obliged to give these measures approximately, because, this front having been studied by the builder with unusual care, not one of its measures is the same as another; and the symmetries between the correspondent arches are obtained by changes in the depth of their mouldings and varia

I need not make any comment upon the subtle difference of
eight inches on twenty feet between the second and third
dimensions. If the reader will be at the pains to compare
the whole evidence now laid before him, with that deduced
above from the apse of Murano, he cannot but confess that it
amounts to an irrefragable proof of an intense perception of
harmony in the relation of quantities, on the part of the
Byzantine architects; a perception which we have at present
lost so utterly as hardly to be able even to conceive it. And
let it not be said, as it was of the late discoveries of subtle
curvature in the Parthenon,* that what is not to be demon-
strated without laborious measurement, cannot have influence
on the beauty of the design. The eye is continually influenced by what it cannot detect; nay, it is not going too far to
say, that it is most influenced by what it detects least. Let
the painter define, if he can, the variations of lines on which
depend the changes of expression in the human countenance.
The greater he is, the more he will feel their subtlety, and
the intense difficulty of perceiving all their relations, or
answering for the consequences of a variation of a hair's

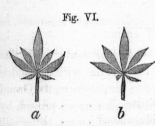

Fig. VI.

a   *b*

breadth in a single curve. Indeed, there is nothing truly
noble either in color or in form,
but its power depends on circumstances infinitely too intricate to be explained, and almost
too subtle to be traced. And
as for these Byzantine buildings,
we only do not feel them because we do not *watch* them;

tions in their heights, far too complicated for me to enter into here; so that
of the two arches stated as 19 ft. 8 in. in span, one is in reality 19 ft. 6½ in.
the other 19 ft. 10 in., and of the two stated as 20 ft. 4 in., one is 20 ft. and
the other 20 ft. 8 in.

* By Mr. Penrose.

otherwise we should as much enjoy the variety of proportion in their arches, as we do at present that of the natural architecture of flowers and leaves. Any of us can feel in an instant the grace of the leaf group, b, in the annexed figure; and yet that grace is simply owing to its being proportioned like the façade of St. Mark's; each leaflet answering to an arch,—the smallest at the root, to those of the porticos. I have tried to give the proportion quite accurately in b; but as the difference between the second and third leaflets is hardly discernible on so small a scale, it is somewhat exaggerated in a.* Nature is often far more subtle in her proportions. In looking at some of the nobler species of lilies, full in the front of the flower, we may fancy for a moment that they form a symmetrical six-petaled star; but on examining them more closely, we shall find that they are thrown into a group of three magnitudes by the expansion of two of the inner petals above the stamens to a breadth greater than any of the four others; while the third inner petal, on which the stamens rest, contracts itself into the narrowest of the six, and the

Fig. VII.

three under petals remain of one intermediate magnitude, as seen in the annexed figure.

§ XIII. I must not, however, weary the reader with this subject, which has always been a favorite one with me, and is apt to lead too far; we will return to the palaces on the Grand Canal. Admitting, then, that their fragments are proved, by the minute correspondences of their arrangement, to be still in their original positions, they indicate to us a form, whether of palace or dwelling-house, in which there were, universally, central galleries, or loggias, opening into apartments on each

---

* I am sometimes obliged, unfortunately, to read my woodcuts backwards, owing to my having forgotten to reverse them on the wood.

wing, the amount of light admitted being immense; and the general proportions of the building, slender, light, and graceful in the utmost degree, it being in fact little more than an aggregate of shafts and arches. Of the interior disposition of these palaces there is in no instance the slightest trace left, nor am I well enough acquainted with the existing architecture of the East to risk any conjecture on this subject. I pursue the statement of the facts which still are ascertainable respecting their external forms.

§ XIV. In every one of the buildings above mentioned, except the Rio-Foscari House (which has only one great entrance between its wings), the central arcades are sustained, at least in one story, and generally in both, on bold detached cylindrical shafts, with rich capitals, while the arches of the wings are carried on smaller shafts assisted by portions of wall, which become pilasters of greater or less width.

And now I must remind the reader of what was pointed out above (Vol. I. Chap. XXVII. §§ III. XXXV. XL.), that there are two great orders of capitals in the world; that one of these is convex in its contour, the other concave; and that richness of ornament, with all freedom of fancy, is for the most part found in the one, and severity of ornament, with stern discipline of the fancy, in the other.

Of these two families of capitals, both occur in the Byzantine period, but the concave group is the longest-lived, and extends itself into the Gothic times. In the account which I gave of them in the first volume, they were illustrated by giving two portions of a simple curve, that of a salvia leaf. We must now investigate their characters more in detail; and these may be best generally represented by considering both families as formed upon the types of flowers,—the one upon that of the water-lily, the other upon that of the convolvulus. There was no intention in the Byzantine architects to imitate either one or the other of these flowers; but, as I have already

so often repeated, all beautiful works of art must either inten-
tionally imitate or accidentally resemble natural forms; and
the direct comparison with the natural forms which these
capitals most resemble, is the likeliest mode of fixing their
distinctions in the reader's mind.

The one then, the convex family, is modelled according to
the commonest shapes of that great group of flowers which
form rounded cups, like that of the water-lily, the leaves
springing horizontally from the stalk, and closing together
upwards. The rose is of this family, but her cup is filled with
the luxuriance of her leaves; the crocus, campanula, ranuncu-
lus, anemone, and almost all the loveliest children of the field,
are formed upon the same type.

The other family resembles the convolvulus, trumpet-
flower, and such others, in which the lower part of the bell is
slender, and the lip curves outwards at the top. There are
fewer flowers constructed on this than on the convex model ;
but in the organization of trees and of clusters of herbage it is
seen continually. Of course, both of these conditions are
modified, when applied to capitals, by the enormously greater
thickness of the stalk or shaft, but in other respects the paral-
lelism is close and accurate ; and the reader had better at
once fix the flower outlines in his mind,* and remember them
as representing the only two orders of capitals that the world
has ever seen, or can see.

§ xv. The examples of the concave family in the Byzantine
times are found principally either in large capitals founded on
the Greek Corinthian, used chiefly for the nave pillars of
churches, or in the small lateral shafts of the palaces. It
appears somewhat singular that the pure Corinthian form
should have been reserved almost exclusively for nave pillars,
as at Torcello, Murano, and St. Mark's; it occurs, indeed,
together with almost every other form, on the exterior of St.

* Vide Plate X. figs. 1. and 4.

Mark's also, but never so definitely as in the nave and transept shafts. Of the conditions assumed by it at Torcello enough has been said; and one of the most delicate of the varieties occurring in St. Mark's is given in Plate VIII., fig. 15., remarkable for the cutting of the sharp thistle-like leaves into open relief, so that the light sometimes shines through them from behind, and for the beautiful curling of the extremities of the leaves outwards, joining each other at the top, as in an undivided flower.

§ XVI. The other characteristic examples of the concave groups in the Byzantine times are as simple as those resulting from the Corinthian are rich. They occur on the *small* shafts at the flanks of the Fondaco de' Turchi, the Casa Farsetti, Casa Loredan, Terraced House, and upper story of the Madonnetta House, in forms so exactly similar that the two figures 1. and 2. in Plate VIII. may sufficiently represent them all. They consist merely of portions cut out of the plinths or stringcourses which run along all the faces of these palaces, by four truncations in the form of arrowy leaves (fig. 1., Fondaco de' Turchi), and the whole rounded a little at the bottom so as to fit the shaft. When they occur between two arches they assume the form of the group fig. 2. (Terraced House). fig. 3. is from the central arches of the Casa Farsetti, and is only given because either it is a later restoration or a form absolutely unique in the Byzantine period.

§ XVII. The concave group, however, was not naturally pleasing to the Byzantine mind. Its own favorite capital was of the bold convex or cushion shape, so conspicuous in all the buildings of the period that I have devoted Plate VII., opposite, entirely to its illustration. The form in which it is first used is practically obtained from a square block laid on the head of the shaft (fig. 1. Plate VII.), by first cutting off the lower corners, as in fig. 2., and then rounding the edges, as in fig. 3.; this gives us the bell stone: on this is laid a simple abacus, as seen in fig. 4., which is the actual form used in the upper arcade of Murano, and the framework of the capital is complete. Fig. 5. shows the general manner and effect of its decoration on the same scale; the other figures, 6. and 7. both from the apse of Murano, 8. from the Terraced House, and 9. from the Baptistery of St. Mark's, show the method of chisel ling the surfaces in capitals of average richness, such as occur everywhere, for there is no limit to the fantasy and beauty of the more elaborate examples.

§ XVIII. In consequence of the peculiar affection entertained for these massy forms by the Byzantines, they were apt, when they used any condition of capital founded on the Corinthian, to modify the concave profile by making it bulge out at the bottom. Fig. 1. *a*, Plate X., is the profile of a capital of the pure concave family ; and observe, it needs a fillet or cord round the neck of the capital to show where it separates from the shaft. Fig. 4. *a*, on the other hand, is the profile of the pure convex group, which not only needs no such projecting fillet, but would be encumbered by it ; while fig. 2. *a* is the profile of one of the Byzantine capitals (Fondaco de' Turchi, lower arcade) founded on Corinthian, of which the main sweep is concave, but which bends below into the convex bell-shape, where it joins the shaft. And, lastly, fig. 3. *a* is the profile of the nave shafts of St. Mark's, where, though very delicately granted, the concession to the Byzantine temper is twofold ; first at the spring of the curve from the base, and secondly at the top, where it again becomes convex, though the expression of the Corinthian bell is still given to it by the bold concave leaves.

§ XIX. These, then, being the general modifications of Byzantine profiles, I have thrown together in Plate VIII., opposite, some of the most characteristic examples of the decoration of the concave and transitional types ; their localities are given in the note below*, and the following are the principal points to be observed respecting them.

The purest concave forms, 1. and 2., were never decorated in the earliest times, except sometimes by an incision or rib down the centre of their truncations on the angles.

Figures 4. 5. 6. and 7. show some of the modes of application of a peculiarly broad-lobed acanthus leaf, very characteristic of native Venetian work; 4. and 5. are from the same building, two out of a group of four, and show the boldness of the variety admitted in the management even of the capitals most closely derived from the Corinthian. I never saw one of these Venetian capitals in all respects like another. The trefoils into which the leaves fall at the extremities are, however, for the most part similar, though variously disposed, and generally niche themselves one under the other, as very characteristically in fig. 7. The form 8. occurs in St. Mark's only, and there very frequently: 9. at Venice occurs, I think, in St. Mark's only; but it is a favorite early Lombardic form. 10. 11. and 12. are all highly characteristic. 10. occurs with more fantastic interweaving upon its sides in the upper stories of St. Mark's; 11. is derived, in the Casa Loredan, from the great lily capitals of St. Mark's, of which more presently. 13. and 15. are peculiar to St. Mark's. 14. is a lovely condition, occurring both there and in the Fondaco de' Turchi.

The modes in which the separate portions of the leaves are executed in these and other Byzantine capitals, will be noticed

---

* 1. Fondaco de' Turchi, lateral pillars.   8. St. Mark's.
  2. Terraced House, lateral pillars.   9. St. Mark's.
  3. Casa Farsetti, central pillars,   10. Braided House, upper arcade.
     upper arcade.   11. Casa Loredan, upper arcade.
  4. Casa Loredan, lower arcade.   12. St. Mark's.
  5. Casa Loredan, lower arcade.   13. St. Mark's.
  6. Fondaco de' Turchi, upper arcade.   14. Fondaco de' Turchi, upper arcade.
  7. Casa Loredan, upper arcade.   15. St. Mark's.

more at length hereafter. Here I only wish the reader to observe two things, both with respect to these and the capitals of the convex family on the former Plate: first the Life, secondly, the Breadth, of these capitals, as compared with Greek forms.

§ XX. I say, first, the Life. Not only is every one of these capitals differently fancied, but there are many of them which *have no two sides alike.* Fig. 5., for instance, varies on every side in the arrangement of the pendent leaf in its centre; fig. 6. has a different plant on each of its four upper angles. The birds are each cut with a different play of plumage in figs. 9. and 12., and the vine-leaves are every one varied in their position in fig. 13. But this is not all. The differences in the character of ornamentation between them and the Greek capitals, all show a greater love of nature; the leaves are, every one of them, more founded on realities, sketched, however rudely, more directly from the truth; and are continually treated in a manner which shows the mind of the workman to have been among the living herbage, not among Greek precedents. The hard outlines in which, for the sake of perfect intelligibility, I have left this Plate, have deprived the examples of the vitality of their light and shade; but the reader can nevertheless observe the *ideas* of life occurring perpetually: at the top of fig. 4., for instance, the small leaves turned sideways; in fig. 5., the formal volutes of the old Corinthian transformed into a branching tendril; in fig. 6., the bunch of grapes thrown carelessly in at the right-hand corner, in defiance of all symmetry; in fig. 7., the volutes knitted into wreaths of ivy; in fig. 14., the leaves, drifted, as it were, by a whirlwind round the capital by which they rise; while figs. 13. and 15. are as completely living leaves as any of the Gothic time. These designs may or may not be graceful; what grace or beauty they have is not to be rendered in mere outline,—but they are indisputably more *natural* than any Greek ones, and therefore healthier, and tending to greatness.

§ XXI. In the second place, note in all these examples, the excessive breadth of the masses, however afterwards they may be filled with detail. Whether we examine the contour of the simpler convex bells, or those of the leaves which bend outwards from the richer and more Corinthian types, we find they are all outlined by grand and simple curves, and that the whole of their minute fretwork and thistle-work is cast into a gigantic mould which subdues all their multitudinous points and foldings to its own inevitable dominion. And the fact is, that in the sweeping lines and broad surfaces of these Byzantine sculptures we obtain, so far as I know, for the first time in the history of art, the germ of that unity of perfect ease in every separate part, with perfect subjection to an enclosing form or directing impulse, which was brought to its most intense expression in the compositions of the two men in whom the art of Italy consummated itself and expired— Tintoret and Michael Angelo.

I would not attach too much importance to the mere habit of working on the rounded surface of the stone, which is often as much the result of haste or rudeness as of the desire for breadth, though the result obtained is not the less beautiful. But in the capital from the Fondaco de' Turchi, fig. 6., it will be seen that while the sculptor had taken the utmost care to make his leaves free, graceful, and sharp in effect, he was dissatisfied with their separation, and could not rest until he had enclosed them with an unbroken line, like that of a pointed arch; and the same thing is done in many different ways in other capitals of the same building, and in many of St. Mark's: but one such instance would have been enough to prove, if the loveliness of the profiles themselves did not do so, that the sculptor understood and loved the laws of generalization; and that the feeling which bound his prickly leaves, as they waved or drifted round the ridges of his capital, into those broad masses of unbroken flow, was indeed one with that which made Michael Angelo encompass the principal figure in his Creation of Adam with the broad curve of its cloudy drapery. It may seem strange to assert any connexion between so great a conception and these rudely hewn fragments of ruined marble; but all the highest principles of art are as universal as they are majestic, and there is nothing too small to receive their influence. They rule at once the waves of the mountain outline, and the sinuosities of the minutest lichen that stains its shattered stones.

§ XXII. We have not yet spoken of the three braided and chequered capitals, numbered 10. 11. and 12. They are representations of a group, with which many most interesting associations are connected. It was noticed in the last chapter, that the method of covering the exterior of buildings with thin pieces of marble was likely to lead to a system of lighting the interior by minute perforation. In order to obtain both light and air, without admitting any unbroken body of sunshine, in warm countries, it became a constant habit of the Arabian architects to pierce minute and starlike openings in slabs of stone; and to employ the stones so pierced where the Gothic architects employ traceries. Internally, the form of stars assumed by the light as it entered* was, in itself, an exquisite decoration; but, externally, it was felt necessary to add some slight ornament upon the surface of the perforated stone; and it was soon found that, as the small perforations had a tendency to look scattered and spotty, the most effective treatment of the intermediate surfaces would be one which bound them together, and gave unity and repose to the pierced and disturbed stone : universally, therefore, those intermediate spaces were carved into the semblance of interwoven fillets, which alternately sank beneath and rose above each other as they

* Compare "Seven Lamps," chap. ii. § 22.

met. This system of braided or woven ornament was not con fined to the Arabs; it is universally pleasing to the instinct of mankind. I believe that nearly all early ornamentation is full of it,—more especially, perhaps, Scandinavian and Anglo-Saxon; and illuminated manuscripts depend upon it for their loveliest effects of intricate color, up to the close of the thirteenth century. There are several very interesting metaphysical reasons for this strange and unfailing delight, felt in a thing so simple. It is not often that any idea of utility has power to enhance the true impressions of beauty; but it is possible that the enormous importance of the art of weaving to mankind may give some interest, if not actual attractiveness, to any type or image of the invention to which we owe, at once, our comfort and our pride. But the more pro found reason lies in the innate love of mystery and unity; in the joy that the human mind has in contemplating any kind of maze or entanglement, so long as it can discern, through its confusion, any guiding clue or connecting plan: a pleasure increased and solemnized by some dim feeling of the setting forth, by such symbols, of the intricacy, and alternate rise and fall, subjection and supremacy, of human fortune; the

"Weave the warp, and weave the woof,"

of Fate and Time.

§ XXIII. But be this as it may, the fact is that we are never tired of contemplating this woven involution; and that, in some degree, the sublime pleasure which we have in watching the branches of trees, the intertwining of the grass, and the tracery of the higher clouds, is owing to it, not less than that which we receive from the fine meshes of the robe, the braiding of the hair, and the various glittering of the linked net or wreathed chain. Byzantine ornamentation, like that of almost all nations in a state of progress, is full of this kind of work: but it occurs most conspicuously, though most simply, in the minute traceries which surround their most solid capitals; sometimes merely in a reticulated veil, as in the tenth figure in the Plate, sometimes resembling a basket, on the edges of which are perched birds and other animals. The diamonded ornament in the eleventh figure is substituted for it in the Casa Loredan, and marks a somewhat later time and a tendency to the ordinary Gothic chequer; but the capitals which show it most definitely are those already so often spoken of as the lily capitals of St. Mark's, of which the northern one is carefully drawn in Plate IX.

§ XXIV. These capitals, called barbarous by our architects, are without exception the most subtle pieces of composition in broad contour which I have ever met with in architecture. Their profile is given in the opposite Plate X. fig. 3. *b;* the inner line in the figure being that of the stone behind the lily, the outer that of the external network, taken through the side of the capital; while fig. 3. *c* is the outer profile at its angle; and the reader will easily understand that the passing of the one of these lines into the other is productive of the most exquisite and wonderful series of curvatures possible within such compass, no two views of the capital giving the same contour. Upon these profoundly studied outlines, as remarkable for their grace and complexity as the general mass of the capital is for solid strength and proportion to its necessary service, the braided work is wrought with more than usual care; perhaps, as suggested by the Marchese Selvatico, with some idea of imitating those "nets of chequerwork and wreaths of chainwork" on the chapiters of Solomon's temple, which are, I suppose, the first instances on record of an ornamentation of this kind thus applied. The braided work encloses on each of the four sides of the capital a flower whose form, derived from that of the lily, though as usual modified, in every instance of its occurrence, in some minor particulars, is generally seen as represented in fig. 11. of Plate

VIII. It is never without the two square or oblong objects at the extremity of the tendrils issuing from its root, set like vessels to catch the dew from the points of its leaves; but I do not understand their meaning. The abacus of the capital has already been given at *a* Plate XVI. Vol. I.; but no amount of illustrations or eulogium would be enough to make the reader understand the perfect beauty of the thing itself, as the sun steals from interstice to interstice of its marble veil, and touches with the white lustre of its rays at midday the pointed leaves of its thirsty lilies.

In all the capitals hitherto spoken of, the form of the head of the bell has been square, and its varieties of outline have been obtained in the transition from the square of the abacus to the circular outline of the shafts. A far more complex series of forms results from the division of the bell by recesses into separate lobes or leaves, like those of a rose or tulip, which are each in their turn covered with flowerwork or hollowed into reticulation. The example (fig. 10. Plate VII.) from St. Mark's will give some idea of the simplest of these conditions: perhaps the most exquisite in Venice, on the whole, is the central capital of the upper arcade of the Fondaco de' Turchi.

Such are the principal generic conditions of the Byzantine capital; but the reader must always remember that the examples given are single instances, and those not the most beautiful but the most intelligible, chosen out of thousands: the designs of the capitals of St. Mark's alone would form a volume.

§ xxv. Of the archivolts which these capitals generally sustain, details are given in the Appendix and in the notice of Venetian doors in Chapter VII. In the private palaces, the ranges of archivolt are for the most part very simple, with dentilled mouldings; and all the ornamental effect is entrusted to pieces of sculpture set in the wall above or between the arches, in the manner shown in Plate XV. below, Chapter VII. These pieces of sculpture are either crosses, upright oblongs, or circles: of all the three forms an example is given in Plate XI. opposite. The cross was apparently an invariable ornament, placed either in the centre of the archivolt of the doorway, or in the centre of the first story above the windows; on each side of it the circular and oblong ornaments were used in various alternation. In too many instances the wall marbles have been torn away from the earliest Byzantine palaces, so that the crosses are left on their archivolts only. The best examples of the cross set above the windows are found in houses of the transitional period: one in the Campo Stᵃ M. Formosa; another, in which a cross is placed between every window, is still well preserved in the Campo Stᵃ Maria Mater Domini; another, on the Grand Canal, in the parish of the Apostoli, has two crosses, one on each side of the first story, and a bas-relief of Christ enthroned in the centre; and finally, that from which the larger cross in the Plate was taken in the house once belonging to Marco Polo, at San Giovanni Grisostomo.

§ XXVI. This cross, though graceful and rich, and given because it happens to be one of the best preserved, is uncharacteristic in one respect; for, instead of the central rose at the meeting of the arms, we usually find a hand raised in the attitude of blessing, between the sun and moon, as in the two smaller crosses seen in the Plate. In nearly all representations of the Crucifixion, over the whole of Europe, at the period in question, the sun and the moon are introduced, one on each side of the cross,—the sun generally, in paintings, as a red star; but I do not think with any purpose of indicating the darkness at the time of the agony; especially because, had this been the intention, the moon ought not to have been visible, since it could not have been in the heavens during the day at the time of passover. I believe rather that the two luminaries are set there in

7*

order to express the entire dependence of the heavens and the earth upon the work of the Redemption: and this view is confirmed by our frequently finding the sun and moon set in the same manner beside the figure of Christ, as in the centre of the great archivolt of St. Mark's, or beside the hand signifying benediction, without any cross, in some other early archivolts ;* while, again, not unfrequently they are absent from the symbol of the cross itself, and its saving power over the whole of creation is indicated only by fresh leaves spring-ing from its foot, or doves feeding beside it ; and so also, in illuminated Bibles, we find the series of pictures representing the Creation terminate in the Crucifixion, as the work by which all the families of created beings subsist, no less than that in sympathy with which " the whole creation groaneth and travaileth in pain together until now."

§ XXVII. This habit of placing the symbol of the Christian faith in the centres of their palaces was, as I above said, universal in early Venice; it does not cease till about the middle of the fourteenth century. The other sculptures, which were set above or between the arches, consist almost invariably of groups of birds or beasts; either standing opposite to each other with a small pillar or spray of leafage between them, or else tearing and devouring each other. The multitude of these sculptures, especially of the small ones enclosed in circles, as figs. 5. and 6. Plate XI., which are now scattered through the city of Venice, is enormous, but they are seldom to be seen in their original positions. When the Byzantine palaces were destroyed, these fragments were generally preserved, and inserted again in the walls of the new buildings, with more or less attempt at symmetry; fragments of friezes and mouldings being often used in the

* Two of these are represented in the second number of my folio work upon Venice.

same manner; so that the mode of their original employment can only be seen in St. Mark's, the Fondaco de' Turchi, Braided House, and one or two others. The most remarkable point about them is, that the groups of beasts or birds on each side of the small pillars bear the closest possible resemblance to the group of Lions over the gate of Mycenæ; and the whole of the ornamentation of that gate, as far as I can judge of it from drawings, is so like Byzantine sculpture, that I cannot help sometimes suspecting the original conjecture of the French antiquarians, that it was a work of the middle ages, to be not altogether indefensible. By far the best among the sculptures at Venice are those consisting of groups thus arranged; the first figure in Plate XI. is one of those used on St. Mark's, and, with its chain of wreathen work round it, is very characteristic of the finest kind, except that the immediate trunk or pillar often branches into luxuriant leafage, usually of the vine, so that the whole ornament seems almost composed from the words of Ezekiel. "A great eagle with great wings, long-winged, full of feathers, which had divers colors, came into Lebanon, and took the highest branch of the cedar: He cropped off the top of his young twigs; and *carried it into a city of traffic; he set it in a city of merchants.* He took also of the seed of the land, . . . and it grew, and became a spreading vine of low stature, *whose branches turned towards him, and the roots thereof were under him.*"

§ XXVIII. The groups of contending and devouring animals are always much ruder in cutting, and take somewhat the place in Byzantine sculpture which the lower grotesques do in the Gothic; true, though clumsy, grotesques being sometime mingled among them, as four bodies joined to one head in the centre*; but never showing any attempt at variety of

---

* The absence of the true grotesque spirit in Byzantine work will be examined in the third chapter of the third volume.

invention, except only in the effective disposition of the light
and shade, and in the vigor and thoughtfulness of the touches
which indicate the plumes of the birds or foldings of the
leaves.   Care, however, is always taken to secure variety
enough to keep the eye entertained, no two sides of these
Byzantine ornaments being in all respects the same: for
instance, in the chainwork round the first figure in Plate XI.
there are two circles enclosing squares on the left-hand side
of the arch at the top, but two smaller circles and a diamond
on the other, enclosing one square, and two small circular
spots or bosses; and in the line of chain at the bottom there
is a circle on the right, and a diamond on the left, and so
down to the working of the smallest details.   I have represented this upper sculpture as dark, in order to give some idea
of the general effect of these ornaments when seen in shadow
against light; an effect much calculated upon by the designer,
and obtained by the use of a golden ground formed of glass
mosaic inserted in the hollows of the marble.   Each square
of glass has the leaf gold upon its surface protected by another
thin film of glass above it, so that no time or weather can
affect its lustre, until the pieces of glass are bodily torn from
their setting.   The smooth glazed surface of the golden ground
is washed by every shower of rain, but the marble usually
darkens into an amber color in process of time; and when the
whole ornament is cast into shadow, the golden surface, being
perfectly reflective, refuses the darkness, and shows itself in
bright and burnished light behind the dark traceries of the
ornament.   Where the marble has retained its perfect white-
ness, on the other hand, and is seen in sunshine, it is shown
as a snowy tracery on a golden ground; and the alternations
and intermingling of these two effects form one of the chief
enchantments of Byzantine ornamentation.

§ XXIX. How far the system of grounding with gold and
color, universal in St. Mark's, was carried out in the sculptures

of the private palaces, it is now impossible to say. The wrecks of them which remain, as above noticed, show few of their ornamental sculptures in their original position; and from those marbles which were employed in succeeding buildings, during the Gothic period, the fragments of their mosaic grounds would naturally rather have been removed than restored. Mosaic, while the most secure of all decorations if carefully watched and refastened when it loosens, may, if neglected and exposed to weather, in process of time disappear so as to leave no vestige of its existence. However this may have been, the assured facts are, that both the shafts of the pillars and the facing of the whole building were of veined or variously colored marble: the capitals and sculptures were either, as they now appear, of pure white marble, relieved upon the veined ground; or, which is infinitely the more probable, grounded in the richer palaces with mosaic of gold, in the inferior ones with blue color; and only the leaves and edges of the sculpture gilded. These brighter hues were opposed by bands of deeper color, generally alternate russet and green, in the archivolts,—bands which still remain in the Casa Loredan and Fondaco de' Turchi, and in a house in the Corte del Remer near the Rialto, as well as in St. Mark's; and by circular disks of green serpentine and porphyry, which, together with the circular sculptures, appear to have been an ornament peculiarly grateful to the Eastern mind, derived probably in the first instance from the suspension of shields upon the wall, as in the majesty of ancient Tyre. "The men of Arvad with thine army were upon thy walls round about, and the Gammadims were in thy towers: they hanged their shields upon thy walls round about; they have made thy beauty perfect."* The sweet and solemn harmony of purple with various green (the same, by the by, to which the hills of Scotland owe their best loveliness) remained a favorite chord

* Ezekiel, xxvii. 11.

of color with the Venetians, and was constantly used even in the later palaces; but never could have been seen in so great perfection as when opposed to the pale and delicate sculpture of the Byzantine time.

§ xxx. Such, then, was that first and fairest Venice which rose out of the barrenness of the lagoon, and the sorrow of her people; a city of graceful arcades and gleaming walls, veined with azure and warm with gold, and fretted with white sculpture like frost upon forest branches turned to marble. And yet, in this beauty of her youth, she was no city of thoughtless pleasure. There was still a sadness of heart upon her, and a depth of devotion, in which lay all her strength. I do not insist upon the probable religious signification of many of the sculptures which are now difficult of interpretation; but the temper which made the cross the principal ornament of every building is not to be misunderstood, nor can we fail to perceive, in many of the minor sculptural subjects, meanings perfectly familiar to the mind of early Christianity. The peacock, used in preference to every other bird, is the well-known symbol of the resurrection; and when drinking from a fountain (Plate XI. fig. 1.) or from a font (Plate XI. fig. 5.), is, I doubt not, also a type of the new life received in faithful baptism. The vine, used in preference to all other trees, was equally recognised as, in all cases, a type either of Christ himself* or of those who were in a state of visible or professed union with him. The dove, at its foot, represents the coming of the Comforter; and even the groups of contending animals had, probably, a distinct and universally apprehended reference to the powers of evil. But I lay no stress on these more occult meanings. The principal circumstance which marks the seriousness of the early Venetian

---

* Perhaps this type is in no place of Scripture more touchingly used than in Lamentations, i. 12., where the word "afflicted" is rendered in the Vulgate "vindemiavit," "vintaged."

mind is perhaps the last in which the reader would suppose it was traceable;—that love of bright and pure color which, in a modified form, was afterwards the root of all the triumph of the Venetian schools of painting, but which, in its utmost simplicity, was characteristic of the Byzantine period only; and of which, therefore, in the close of our review of that period, it will be well that we should truly estimate the significance. The fact is, we none of us enough appreciate the nobleness and sacredness of color. Nothing is more common than to hear it spoken of as a subordinate beauty,— nay, even as the mere source of a sensual pleasure; and we might almost believe that we were daily among men who

> "Could strip, for aught the prospect yields
> To them, their verdure from the fields;
> And take the radiance from the clouds
> With which the sun his setting shrouds."

But it is not so. Such expressions are used for the most part in thoughtlessness; and if the speakers would only take the pains to imagine what the world and their own existence would become, if the blue were taken from the sky, and the gold from the sunshine, and the verdure from the leaves, and the crimson from the blood which is the life of man, the flush from the cheek, the darkness from the eye, the radiance from the hair,—if they could but see for an instant, white human creatures living in a white world,—they would soon feel what they owe to color. The fact is, that, of all God's gifts to the sight of man, color is the holiest, the most divine, the most solemn. We speak rashly of gay color, and sad color, for color cannot at once be good and gay. All good color is in some degree pensive, the loveliest is melancholy, and the purest and most thoughtful minds are those which love color the most.

§ XXXI. I know that this will sound strange in many ears,

and will be especially startling to those who have considered the subject chiefly with reference to painting; for the great Venetian schools of color are not usually understood to be either pure or pensive, and the idea of its preeminence is associated in nearly every mind with the coarseness of Rubens, and the sensualities of Correggio and Titian. But a more comprehensive view of art will soon correct this impression. It will be discovered, in the first place, that the more faithful and earnest the religion of the painter, the more pure and prevalent is the system of his color. It will be found, in the second place, that where color becomes a primal intention with a painter otherwise mean or sensual, it instantly elevates him, and becomes the one sacred and saving element in his work. The very depth of the stoop to which the Venetian painters and Rubens sometimes condescend, is a consequence of their feeling confidence in the power of their color to keep them from falling. They hold on by it, as by a chain let down from heaven, with one hand, though they may sometimes seem to gather dust and ashes with the other. And, in the last place, it will be found that so surely as a painter is irreligious, thoughtless, or obscene in disposition, so surely is his coloring cold, gloomy, and valueless. The opposite poles of art in this respect are Frà Angelico and Salvator Rosa; of whom the one was a man who smiled seldom, wept often, prayed constantly, and never harbored an impure thought. His pictures are simply so many pieces of jewellery, the colors of the draperies being perfectly pure, as various as those of a painted window, chastened only by paleness, and relieved upon a gold ground. Salvator was a dissipated jester and satirist, a man who spent his life in masquing and revelry. But his pictures are full of horror, and their color is for the most part gloomy grey. Truly it would seem as if art had so much of eternity in it, that it must take its dye from the close rather than the course of life:—"In such laughter the heart of man is sorrowful, and the end of that mirth is heaviness."

§ xxxii. These are no singular instances. I know no law more severely without exception than this of the connexion of pure color with profound and noble thought. The late Flemish pictures, shallow in conception and obscene in subject, are always sober in color. But the early religious painting of the Flemings is as brilliant in hue as it is holy in thought. The Bellinis, Francias, Peruginos painted in crimson, and blue, and gold. The Caraccis, Guidos, and Rembrandts in brown and grey. The builders of our great cathedrals veiled their casements and wrapped their pillars with one robe of purple splendor. The builders of the luxurious Renaissance left their palaces filled only with cold white light, and in the paleness of their native stone.*

§ xxxiii. Nor does it seem difficult to discern a noble reason for this universal law. In that heavenly circle which binds the statutes of color upon the front of the sky, when it became the sign of the covenant of peace, the pure hues of divided light were sanctified to the human heart for ever; nor this, it would seem, by mere arbitrary appointment, but in consequence of the fore-ordained and marvellous constitution of those hues into a sevenfold, or, more strictly still, a threefold order, typical of the Divine nature itself. Observe also, the name Shem, or Splendor, given to that son of Noah in whom this covenant with mankind was to be fulfilled, and see how that name was justified by every one of the Asiatic races which descended from him. Not without meaning was the love of Israel to his chosen son expressed by the coat " of many colors;" not without deep sense of the sacredness of that symbol of purity, did the lost daughter of David tear it from her breast:—" With such robes were the king's

* Appendix 12.: " Modern Painting on Glass."

daughters that were virgins apparelled."* We know it to have been by Divine command that the Israelite, rescued from servitude, veiled the tabernacle with its rain of purple and scarlet, while the under sunshine flashed through the fall of the color from its tenons of gold : but was it less by Divine guidance that the Mede, as he struggled out of anarchy, encompassed his king with the sevenfold burning of the battlements of Ecbatana?—of which one circle was golden like the sun, and another silver like the moon; and then came the great sacred chord of color, blue, purple, and scarlet ; and then a circle white like the day, and another dark, like night; so that the city rose like a great mural rainbow, a sign of peace amidst the contending of lawless races, and guarded, with color and shadow, that seemed to symbolize the great order which rules over Day, and Night, and Time, the first organization of the mighty statutes,—the law of the Medes and Persians, that altereth not.

§ XXXIV. Let us not dream that it is owing to the accidents of tradition or education that those races possess the supremacy over color which has always been felt, though but lately acknowledged among men. However their dominion might be broken, their virtue extinguished, or their religion defiled, they retained alike the instinct and the power : the instinct which made even their idolatry more glorious than that of others, bursting forth in fire-worship from pyramid, cave, and mountain, taking the stars for the rulers of its fortune, and the sun for the God of its life; the power which so dazzled and subdued the rough crusader into forgetfulness of sorrow and of shame, that Europe put on the splendor which she had learnt of the Saracen, as her sackcloth of mourning for what she suffered from his sword ;—the power which she confesses to this day, in the utmost thoughtlessness of her pride, or her beauty, as it treads the costly carpet, or veils itself with

* 2 Samuel, xiii. 18.

the variegated Cachemire; and in the emulation of the concourse of her workmen, who, but a few months back, perceived, or at least admitted, for the first time, the pre-eminence which has been determined from the birth of mankind, and on whose charter Nature herself has set a mysterious seal, granting to the Western races, descended from that son of Noah whose name was Extension, the treasures of the sullen rock, and stubborn ore, and gnarled forest, which were to accomplish their destiny across all distance of earth and depth of sea, while she matured the jewel in the sand, and rounded the pearl in the shell, to adorn the diadem of him whose name was Splendor.

§ xxxv. And observe, farther, how in the Oriental mind a peculiar seriousness is associated with this attribute of the love of color; a seriousness rising out of repose, and out of the depth and breadth of the imagination, as contrasted with the activity, and consequent capability of surprise, and of laughter, characteristic of the Western mind: as a man on a journey must look to his steps always, and view things narrowly and quickly; while one at rest may command a wider view, though an unchanging one, from which the pleasure he receives must be one of contemplation, rather than of amusement or surprise. Wherever the pure Oriental spirit manifests itself definitely, I believe its work is serious; and the meeting of the influences of the Eastern and Western races is perhaps marked in Europe more by the dying away of the grotesque laughter of the Goth than by any other sign. I shall have more to say on this head in other places of this volume; but the point I wish at present to impress upon the reader is, that the bright hues of the early architecture of Venice were no sign of gaiety of heart, and that the investiture with the mantle of many colors by which she is known above all other cities of Italy and of Europe, was not granted to her in the fever of her festivity, but in the solemnity of her early and earnest religion. She became in after times the revel of the earth, the masque of Italy; and *therefore* is she now desolate: but her glorious robe of gold and purple was given her when first she rose a vestal from the sea, not when she became drunk with the wine of her fornication.

§ XXXVI. And we have never yet looked with enough reverence upon the separate gift which was thus bestowed upon her; we have never enough considered what an inheritance she has left us, in the works of those mighty painters who were the chief of her children. That inheritance is indeed less than it ought to have been, and other than it ought to have been; for before Titian and Tintoret arose,—the men in whom her work and her glory should have been together consummated,—she had already ceased to lead her sons in the way of truth and life, and they erred much, and fell short of that which was appointed for them. There is no subject of thought more melancholy, more wonderful, than the way in which God permits so often His best gifts to be trodden under foot of men, His richest treasures to be wasted by the moth, and the mightiest influences of His Spirit, given but once in the world's history, to be quenched and shortened by miseries of chance and guilt. I do not wonder at what men Suffer, but I wonder often at what they Lose. We may see how good rises out of pain and evil; but the dead, naked, eyeless loss, what good comes of that? The fruit struck to the earth before its ripeness; the glowing life and goodly purpose dissolved away in sudden death; the words, half spoken, choked upon the lips with clay for ever; or, stranger than all, the whole majesty of humanity raised to its fulness, and every gift and power necessary for a given purpose, at a given moment, centred in one man, and all this perfected blessing permitted to be refused, perverted, crushed, cast aside by those who need it most,—the city which is Not set on a hill, the candle that giveth light to None that are in the house:—

these are the heaviest mysteries of this strange world, and, it seems to me, those which mark its curse the most. And it is true that the power with which this Venice had been entrusted, was perverted, when at its highest, in a thousand miserable ways; still, it was possessed by her alone; to her all hearts have turned which could be moved by its manifestation, and none without being made stronger and nobler by what her hand had wrought. That mighty Landscape, of dark mountains that guard the horizon with their purple towers, and solemn forests, that gather their weight of leaves, bronzed with sunshine, not with age, into those gloomy masses fixed in heaven, which storm and frost have power no more to shake, or shed;—that mighty Humanity, so perfect and so proud, that hides no weakness beneath the mantle, and gains no greatness from the diadem; the majesty of thoughtful form, on which the dust of gold and flame of jewels are dashed as the sea-spray upon the rock, and still the great Manhood seems to stand bare against the blue sky;—that mighty Mythology, which fills the daily walks of men with spiritual companionship, and beholds the protecting angels break with their burning presence through the arrow-flights of battle:—measure the compass of that field of creation, weigh the value of the inheritance that Venice thus left to the nations of Europe, and then judge if so vast, so beneficent a power could indeed have been rooted in dissipation or decay. It was when she wore the ephod of the priest, not the motley of the masquer, that the fire fell upon her from heaven; and she saw the first rays of it through the rain of her own tears, when, as the barbaric deluge ebbed from the hills of Italy, the circuit of her palaces, and the orb of her fortunes, rose together, like the Iris, painted upon the Cloud.

SECOND, OR GOTHIC, PERIOD.

CHAPTER VI.

THE NATURE OF GOTHIC.

§ 1. IF the reader will look back to the division of our subject which was made in the first chapter of the first volume, he will find that we are now about to enter upon the examination of that school of Venetian architecture which forms an intermediate step between the Byzantine and Gothic forms; but which I find may be conveniently considered in its connexion with the latter style. In order that we may discern the tendency of each step of this change, it will be wise in the outset to endeavor to form some general idea of its final result. We know already what the Byzantine architecture is from which the transition was made, but we ought to know something of the Gothic architecture into which it led. I shall endeavor therefore to give the reader in this chapter an idea, at once broad and definite, of the true nature of *Gothic* architecture, properly so called; not of that of Venice only, but of universal Gothic: for it will be one of the most interesting parts of our subsequent inquiry, to find out how far Venetian architecture reached the universal or perfect type of Gothic, and how far it either fell short of it, or assumed foreign and independent forms.

§ II. The principal difficulty in doing this arises from the fact that every building of the Gothic period differs in some important respect from every other; and many include features which, if they occurred in other buildings, would not be considered Gothic at all; so that all we have to reason upon is merely, if I may be allowed so to express it, a greater or less degree of *Gothicness* in each building we examine. And it is this Gothicness,—the character which, according as it is found more or less in a building, makes it more or less Gothic, —of which I want to define the nature; and I feel the same kind of difficulty in doing so which would be encountered by any one who undertook to explain, for instance, the nature of Redness, without any actual red thing to point to, but only orange and purple things. Suppose he had only a piece of heather and a dead oak-leaf to do it with. He might say, the color which is mixed with the yellow in this oak-leaf, and with the blue in this heather, would be red, if you had it separate; but it would be difficult, nevertheless, to make the abstraction perfectly intelligible: and it is so in a far greater degree to make the abstraction of the Gothic character intelligible, because that character itself is made up of many mingled ideas, and can consist only in their union. That is to say, pointed arches do not constitute Gothic, nor vaulted roofs, nor flying buttresses, nor grotesque sculptures; but all or some of these things, and many other things with them, when they come together so as to have life.

§ III. Observe also, that, in the definition proposed, I shall only endeavor to analyze the idea which I suppose already to exist in the reader's mind. We all have some notion, most of us a very determined one, of the meaning of the term Gothic; but I know that many persons have this idea in their minds without being able to define it: that is to say, understanding generally that Westminster Abbey is Gothic, and St. Paul's is not, that Strasburg Cathedral is Gothic, and St.

Peter's is not, they have, nevertheless, no clear notion of what it is that they recognize in the one or miss in the other, such as would enable them to say how far the work at Westminster or Strasburg is good and pure of its kind : still less to say of any nondescript building, like St. James's Palace or Windsor Castle, how much right Gothic element there is in it, and how much wanting.   And I believe this inquiry to be a pleasant and profitable one ; and that there will be found something more than usually interesting in tracing out this grey, shadowy, many-pinnacled image of the Gothic spirit within us ; and discerning what fellowship there is between it and our Northern hearts.   And if, at any point of the inquiry, I should interfere with any of the reader's previously formed conceptions, and use the term Gothic in any sense which he would not willingly attach to it, I do not ask him to accept, but only to examine and understand, my interpretation, as necessary to the intelligibility of what follows in the rest of the work.

§ IV. We have, then, the Gothic character submitted to our analysis, just as the rough mineral is submitted to that of the chemist, entangled with many other foreign substances, itself perhaps in no place pure, or ever to be obtained or seen in purity for more than an instant ; but nevertheless a thing of definite and separate nature, however inextricable or confused in appearance.   Now observe : the chemist defines his mineral by two separate kinds of character ; one external, its crystalline form, hardness, lustre, &c. ; the other internal, the proportions and nature of its constituent atoms.   Exactly in the same manner, we shall find that Gothic architecture has external forms, and internal elements.   Its elements are certain mental tendencies of the builders, legibly expressed in it ; as fancifulness, love of variety, love of richness, and such others.   Its external forms are pointed arches, vaulted roofs, &c.   And unless both the elements and the forms are there,

8

we have no right to call the style Gothic. It is not enough that it has the Form, if it have not also the power and life. It is not enough that it has the Power, if it have not the form. We must therefore inquire into each of these characters successively; and determine first, what is the Mental Expression, and secondly, what the Material Form, of Gothic architecture, properly so called.

1st. Mental Power or Expression. What characters, we have to discover, did the Gothic builders love, or instinctively express in their work, as distinguished from all other builders?

§ v. Let us go back for a moment to our chemistry, and note that, in defining a mineral by its constituent parts, it is not one nor another of them, that can make up the mineral, but the union of all: for instance, it is neither in charcoal, nor in oxygen, nor in lime, that there is the making of chalk, but in the combination of all three in certain measures; they are all found in very different things from chalk, and there is nothing like chalk either in charcoal or in oxygen, but they are nevertheless necessary to its existence.

So in the various mental characters which make up the soul of Gothic. It is not one nor another that produces it; but their union in certain measures. Each one of them is found in many other architectures besides Gothic; but Gothic cannot exist where they are not found, or, at least, where their place is not in some way supplied. Only there is this great difference between the composition of the mineral, and of the architectural style, that if we withdraw one of its elements from the stone, its form is utterly changed, and its existence as such and such a mineral is destroyed; but if we withdraw one of its mental elements from the Gothic style, it is only a little less Gothic than it was before, and the union of two or three of its elements is enough already to bestow a certain Gothicness of character, which gains in intensity as we add the others, and loses as we again withdraw them.

§ VI. I believe, then, that the characteristic or moral elements of Gothic are the following, placed in the order of their importance:

1. Savageness.
2. Changefulness.
3. Naturalism.
4. Grotesqueness.
5. Rigidity.
6. Redundance.

These characters are here expressed as belonging to the building; as belonging to the builder, they would be expressed thus:— 1. Savageness, or Rudeness. 2. Love of Change. 3. Love of Nature. 4. Disturbed Imagination. 5. Obstinacy. 6. Generosity. And I repeat, that the withdrawal of any one, or any two, will not at once destroy the Gothic character of a building, but the removal of a majority of them will. I shall proceed to examine them in their order.

§ VII. 1. SAVAGENESS. I am not sure when the word "Gothic" was first generically applied to the architecture of the North; but I presume that, whatever the date of its original usage, it was intended to imply reproach, and express the barbaric character of the nations among whom that architecture arose. It never implied that they were literally of Gothic lineage, far less that their architecture had been originally invented by the Goths themselves; but it did imply that they and their buildings together exhibited a degree of sternness and rudeness, which, in contradistinction to the character of Southern and Eastern nations, appeared like a perpetual reflection of the contrast between the Goth and the Roman in their first encounter. And when that fallen Roman, in the utmost impotence of his luxury, and insolence of his guilt, became the model for the imitation of civilized Europe, at the close of the so-called Dark ages, the word Gothic became a term of unmitigated contempt, not unmixed with aversion. From that contempt, by the exertion of the antiquaries and architects of this century, Gothic architecture has been sufficiently vindicated; and perhaps some among us, in our admiration of the magnificent science of its structure, and sacredness of its expression, might desire that the term of ancient reproach should be withdrawn, and some other, of more apparent honorableness, adopted in its place. There is no chance, as there is no need, of such a substitution. As far as the epithet was used scornfully, it was used falsely; but there is no reproach in the word, rightly understood; on the contrary, there is a profound truth, which the instinct of mankind almost unconsciously recognizes. It is true, greatly and deeply true, that the architecture of the North is rude and wild; but it is not true, that, for this reason, we are to condemn it, or despise. Far otherwise: I believe it is in this very character that it deserves our profoundest reverence.

§ VIII. The charts of the world which have been drawn up by modern science have thrown into a narrow space the expression of a vast amount of knowledge, but I have never yet seen any one pictorial enough to enable the spectator to imagine the kind of contrast in physical character which exists between Northern and Southern countries. We know the differences in detail, but we have not that broad glance and grasp which would enable us to feel them in their fulness. We know that gentians grow on the Alps, and olives on the Apennines; but we do not enough conceive for ourselves that variegated mosaic of the world's surface which a bird sees in its migration, that difference between the district of the gentian and of the olive which the stork and the swallow see far off, as they lean upon the sirocco wind. Let us, for a moment, try to raise ourselves even above the level of their flight, and imagine the Mediterranean lying beneath us like an irregular lake, and all its ancient promontories sleeping in

the sun : here and there an angry spot of thunder, a grey
stain of storm, moving upon the burning field ; and here and
there a fixed wreath of white volcano smoke, surrounded by
its circle of ashes ; but for the most part a great peacefulness
of light, Syria and Greece, Italy and Spain, laid like pieces
of a golden pavement into the sea-blue, chased, as we stoop
nearer to them, with bossy beaten work of mountain chains,
and glowing softly with terraced gardens, and flowers heavy
with frankincense, mixed among masses of laurel, and orange
and plumy palm, that abate with their grey-green shadows
the burning of the marble rocks, and of the ledges of porphyry sloping under lucent sand. Then let us pass farther
towards the north, until we see the orient colors change
gradually into a vast belt of rainy green, where the pastures
of Switzerland, and poplar valleys of France, and dark forests
of the Danube and Carpathians stretch from the mouths of
the Loire to those of the Volga, seen through clefts in grey
swirls of rain-cloud and flaky veils of the mist of the brooks,
spreading low along the pasture lands : and then, farther
north still, to see the earth heave into mighty masses of leaden
rock and heathy moor, bordering with a broad waste of
gloomy purple that belt of field and wood, and splintering
into irregular and grisly islands amidst the northern seas,
beaten by storm and chilled by ice-drift, and tormented by
furious pulses of contending tide, until the roots of the last
forests fail from among the hill ravines, and the hunger of the
north wind bites their peaks into barrenness ; and, at last, the
wall of ice, durable like iron, sets, deathlike, its white teeth
against us out of the polar twilight. And, having once
traversed in thought this gradation of the zoned iris of the
earth in all its material vastness, let us go down nearer to it,
and watch the parallel change in the belt of animal life : the
multitudes of swift and brilliant creatures that glance in the
air and sea, or tread the sands of the southern zone ; striped

zebras and spotted leopards, glistening serpents, and birds
arrayed in purple and scarlet. Let us contrast their delicacy
and brilliancy of color, and swiftness of motion, with the
frost-cramped strength, and shaggy covering, and dusky plumage of the northern tribes; contrast the Arabian horse
with the Shetland, the tiger and leopard with the wolf and
bear, the antelope with the elk, the bird of paradise with the
osprey : and then, submissively acknowledging the great laws
by which the earth and all that it bears are ruled throughout
their being, let us not condemn, but rejoice at the expression
by man of his own rest in the statutes of the lands that gave
him birth. Let us watch him with reverence as he sets side
by side the burning gems, and smoothes with soft sculpture
the jasper pillars, that are to reflect a ceaseless sunshine, and
rise into a cloudless sky : but not with less reverence let us
stand by him, when, with rough strength and hurried stroke,
he smites an uncouth animation out of the rocks which he
has torn from among the moss of the moorland, and heaves
into the darkened air the pile of iron buttress and rugged
wall, instinct with work of an imagination as wild and way-
ward as the northern sea; creations of ungainly shape and
rigid limb, but full of wolfish life; fierce as the winds that
beat, and changeful as the clouds that shade them.

There is, I repeat, no degradation, no reproach in this, but
all dignity and honorableness; and we should err grievously
in refusing either to recognise as an essential character of the
existing architecture of the North, or to admit as a desirable
character in that which it yet may be, this wildness of thought,
and roughness of work; this look of mountain brotherhood
between the cathedral and the Alp; this magnificence of
sturdy power, put forth only the more energetically because
the fine finger-touch was chilled away by the frosty wind, and
the eye dimmed by the moor-mist, or blinded by the hail;
this outspeaking of the strong spirit of men who may not

gather redundant fruitage from the earth, nor bask in dreamy benignity of sunshine, but must break the rock for bread, and cleave the forest for fire, and show, even in what they did for their delight, some of the hard habits of the arm and heart that grew on them as they swung the axe or pressed the plough.

§ IX. If, however, the savageness of Gothic architecture, merely as an expression of its origin among Northern nations, may be considered, in some sort, a noble character, it possesses a higher nobility still, when considered as an index, not of climate, but of religious principle.

In the 13th and 14th paragraphs of Chapter XXI. of the first volume of this work, it was noticed that the systems of architectural ornament, properly so called, might be divided into three:—1. Servile ornament, in which the execution or power of the inferior workman is entirely subjected to the intellect of the higher :—2. Constitutional ornament, in which the executive inferior power is, to a certain point, emancipated and independent, having a will of its own, yet confessing its inferiority and rendering obedience to higher powers ;—and 3. Revolutionary ornament, in which no executive inferiority is admitted at all. I must here explain the nature of these divisions at somewhat greater length.

Of Servile ornament, the principal schools are the Greek, Ninevite, and Egyptian; but their servility is of different kinds. The Greek master-workman was far advanced in knowledge and power above the Assyrian or Egyptian. Neither he nor those for whom he worked could endure the appearance of imperfection in anything ; and, therefore, what ornament he appointed to be done by those beneath him was composed of mere geometrical forms,—balls, ridges, and perfectly symmetrical foliage,—which could be executed with absolute precision by line and rule, and were as perfect in their way when completed, as his own figure sculpture. The

Assyrian and Egyptian, on the contrary, less cognizant of accurate form in anything, were content to allow their figure sculpture to be executed by inferior workmen, but lowered the method of its treatment to a standard which every work-man could reach, and then trained him by discipline so rigid, that there was no chance of his falling beneath the standard appointed. The Greek gave to the lower workman no sub-ject which he could not perfectly execute. The Assyrian gave him subjects which he could only execute imperfectly, but fixed a legal standard for his imperfection. The workman was, in both systems, a slave.*

§ x. But in the mediæval, or especially Christian, system of ornament, this slavery is done away with altogether; Chris-tianity having recognized, in small things as well as great, the individual value of every soul. But it not only recognizes its value; it confesses its imperfection, in only bestowing dignity upon the acknowledgment of unworthiness. That admission of lost power and fallen nature, which the Greek or Ninevite felt to be intensely painful, and, as far as might be, altogether refused, the Christian makes daily and hourly, contemplating the fact of it without fear, as tending, in the end, to God's greater glory. Therefore, to every spirit which Christianity summons to her service, her exhortation is: Do what you can, and confess frankly what you are unable to do; neither let your effort be shortened for fear of failure, nor your confes-sion silenced for fear of shame. And it is, perhaps, the prin-

* The third kind of ornament, the Renaissance, is that in which the infe-rior detail becomes principal, the executor of every minor portion being required to exhibit skill and possess knowledge as great as that which is possessed by the master of the design; and in the endeavor to endow him with this skill and knowledge, his own original power is overwhelmed, and the whole building becomes a wearisome exhibition of well-educated imbe-cility. We must fully inquire into the nature of this form of error, when we arrive at the examination of the Renaissance schools.

cipal admirableness of the Gothic schools of architecture, that they thus receive the results of the labor of inferior minds; and out of fragments full of imperfection, and betraying that imperfection in every touch, indulgently raise up a stately and unaccusable whole.

§ XI. But the modern English mind has this much in common with that of the Greek, that it intensely desires, in all things, the utmost completion or perfection compatible with their nature. This is a noble character in the abstract, but becomes ignoble when it causes us to forget the relative dignities of that nature itself, and to prefer the perfectness of the lower nature to the imperfection of the higher; not considering that as, judged by such a rule, all the brute animals would be preferable to man, because more perfect in their functions and kind, and yet are always held inferior to him, so also in the works of man, those which are more perfect in their kind are always inferior to those which are, in their nature, liable to more faults and shortcomings. For the finer the nature, the more flaws it will show through the clearness of it; and it is a law of this universe, that the best things shall be seldomest seen in their best form. The wild grass grows well and strongly, one year with another; but the wheat is, according to the greater nobleness of its nature, liable to the bitterer blight. And therefore, while in all things that we see, or do, we are to desire perfection, and strive for it, we are nevertheless not to set the meaner thing, in its narrow accomplishment, above the nobler thing, in its mighty progress; not to esteem smooth minuteness above shattered majesty; not to prefer mean victory to honorable defeat; not to lower the level of our aim, that we may the more surely enjoy the complacency of success. But, above all, in our dealings with the souls of other men, we are to take care how we check, by severe requirement or narrow caution, efforts which might otherwise lead to a noble issue;

and, still more, how we withhold our admiration from great excellences, because they are mingled with rough faults. Now, in the make and nature of every man, however rude or simple, whom we employ in manual labor, there are some powers for better things : some tardy imagination, torpid capacity of emotion, tottering steps of thought, there are, even at the worst; and in most cases it is all our own fault that they *are* tardy or torpid. But they cannot be strengthened, unless we are content to take them in their feebleness, and unless we prize and honor them in their imperfection above the best and most perfect manual skill. And this is what we have to do with all our laborers; to look for the *thoughtful* part of them, and get that out of them, whatever we lose for it, whatever faults and errors we are obliged to take with it. For the best that is in them cannot manifest itself, but in company with much error. Understand this clearly : You can teach a man to draw a straight line, and to cut one; to strike a curved line, and to carve it; and to copy and carve any number of given lines or forms, with admirable speed and perfect precision ; and you find his work perfect of its kind : but if you ask him to think about any of those forms, to consider if he cannot find any better in his own head, he stops; his execution becomes hesitating; he thinks, and ten to one he thinks wrong; ten to one he makes a mistake in the first touch he gives to his work as a thinking being. But you have made a man of him for all that. He was only a machine before, an animated tool.

§ xii. And observe, you are put to stern choice in this matter. You must either make a tool of the creature, or a man of him. You cannot make both. Men were not intended to work with the accuracy of tools, to be precise and perfect in all their actions. If you will have that precision out of them, and make their fingers measure degrees like cog-wheels, and their arms strike curves like compasses, you must unhumanize them. All the energy of their spirits must be given to make cogs and compasses of themselves. All their attention and strength must go to the accomplishment of the mean act. The eye of the soul must be bent upon the finger-point, and the soul's force must fill all the invisible nerves that guide it, ten hours a day, that it may not err from its steely precision, and so soul and sight be worn away, and the whole human being be lost at last—a heap of sawdust, so far as its intellectual work in this world is concerned; saved only by its Heart, which cannot go into the form of cogs and compasses, but expands, after the ten hours are over, into fireside humanity. On the other hand, if you will make a man of the working creature, you cannot make a tool. Let him but begin to imagine, to think, to try to do anything worth doing; and the engine-turned precision is lost at once. Out come all his roughness, all his dulness, all his incapability; shame upon shame, failure upon failure, pause after pause: but out comes the whole majesty of him also; and we know the height of it only, when we see the clouds settling upon him. And, whether the clouds be bright or dark, there will be transfiguration behind and within them.

§ XIII. And now, reader, look round this English room of yours, about which you have been proud so often, because the work of it was so good and strong, and the ornaments of it so finished. Examine again all those accurate mouldings, and perfect polishings, and unerring adjustments of the seasoned wood and tempered steel. Many a time you have exulted over them, and thought how great England was, because her slightest work was done so thoroughly. Alas! if read rightly, these perfectnesses are signs of a slavery in our England a thousand times more bitter and more degrading than that of the scourged African, or helot Greek. Men may be beaten, chained, tormented, yoked like cattle, slaughtered like summer flies, and yet remain in one sense, and the best sense, free.

But to smother their souls within them, to blight and hew into rotting pollards the suckling branches of their human intelligence, to make the flesh and skin which, after the worm's work on it, is to see God, into leathern thongs to yoke machinery with,—this it is to be slave-masters indeed; and there might be more freedom in England, though her feudal lords' lightest words were worth men's lives, and though the blood of the vexed husbandman dropped in the furrows of her fields, than there is while the animation of her multitudes is sent like fuel to feed the factory smoke, and the strength of them is given daily to be wasted into the fineness of a web, or racked into the exactness of a line.

§ xiv. And, on the other hand, go forth again to gaze upon the old cathedral front, where you have smiled so often at the fantastic ignorance of the old sculptors: examine once more those ugly goblins, and formless monsters, and stern statues, anatomiless and rigid; but do not mock at them, for they are signs of the life and liberty of every workman who struck the stone; a freedom of thought, and rank in scale of being, such as no laws, no charters, no charities can secure; but which it must be the first aim of all Europe at this day to regain for her children.

§ xv. Let me not be thought to speak wildly or extrava- gantly. It is verily this degradation of the operative into a machine, which, more than any other evil of the times, is lead- ing the mass of the nations everywhere into vain, incoherent, destructive struggling for a freedom of which they cannot explain the nature to themselves. Their universal outcry against wealth, and against nobility, is not forced from them either by the pressure of famine, or the sting of mortified pride. These do much, and have done much in all ages; but the foundations of society were never yet shaken as they are at this day. It is not that men are ill fed, but that they have no pleasure in the work by which they make their bread, and therefore look to wealth as the only means of pleasure.   It is not that men are pained by the scorn of the upper classes, but they cannot endure their own; for they feel that the kind of labor to which they are condemned is verily a degrading one, and makes them less than men.   Never had the upper classes so much sympathy with the lower, or charity for them, as they have at this day, and yet never were they so much hated by them: for, of old, the separation between the noble and the poor was merely a wall built by law; now it is a veritable difference in level of standing, a precipice between upper and lower grounds in the field of humanity, and there is pestilential air at the bottom of it.   I know not if a day is ever to come when the nature of right freedom will be understood, and when men will see that to obey another man, to labor for him, yield reverence to him or to his place, is not slavery.   It is often the best kind of liberty,—liberty from care.   The man who says to one, Go, and he goeth, and to another, Come, and he cometh, has, in most cases, more sense of restraint and difficulty than the man who obeys him.   The movements of the one are hindered by the burden on his shoulder; of the other, by the bridle on his lips: there is no way by which the burden may be lightened; but we need not suffer from the bridle if we do not champ at it.   To yield reverence to another, to hold ourselves and our lives at his disposal, is not slavery; often, it is the noblest state in which a man can live in this world.   There is, indeed, a reverence which is servile, that is to say, irrational or selfish: but there is also noble reverence, that is to say, reasonable and loving; and a man is never so noble as when he is reverent in this kind; nay, even if the feeling pass the bounds of mere reason, so that it be loving, a man is raised by it.   Which had, in reality, most of the serf nature in him,—the Irish peasant who was lying in wait yesterday for his landlord, with his musket muzzle thrust through the ragged hedge; or that old moun tain servant, who, 200 years ago, at Inverkeithing, gave up his own life and the lives of his seven sons for his chief?*— and as each fell, calling forth his brother to the death, "Another for Hector!" And therefore, in all ages and all countries, reverence has been paid and sacrifice made by men to each other, not only without complaint, but rejoicingly; and famine, and peril, and sword, and all evil, and all shame, have been borne willingly in the causes of masters and kings; for all these gifts of the heart ennobled the men who gave, not less than the men who received them, and nature prompted, and God rewarded the sacrifice. But to feel their souls withering within them, unthanked, to find their whole being sunk into an unrecognized abyss, to be counted off into a heap of mechanism, numbered with its wheels, and weighed with its hammer strokes;—this nature bade not,—this God blesses not,—this humanity for no long time is able to endure.

§ XVI. We have much studied and much perfected, of late, the great civilized invention of the division of labor; only we give it a false name. It is not, truly speaking, the labor that is divided; but the men:—Divided into mere segments of men —broken into small fragments and crumbs of life; so that all the little piece of intelligence that is left in a man is not enough to make a pin, or a nail, but exhausts itself in making the point of a pin, or the head of a nail. Now it is a good and desirable thing, truly, to make many pins in a day; but if we could only see with what crystal sand their points were polished,— sand of human soul, much to be magnified before it can be discerned for what it is,—we should think there might be some loss in it also. And the great cry that rises from all our manufacturing cities, louder than their furnace blast, is all in very deed for this,—that we manufacture everything there except men; we blanch cotton, and strengthen steel, and refine sugar, and shape pottery; but to brighten, to strengthen, to

* Vide Preface to "Fair Maid of Perth."

refine, or to form a single living spirit, never enters into our estimate of advantages. And all the evil to which that cry is urging our myriads can be met only in one way: not by teaching nor preaching, for to teach them is but to show them their misery, and to preach to them, if we do nothing more than preach, is to mock at it. It can be met only by a right under standing, on the part of all classes, of what kinds of labor are good for men, raising them, and making them happy; by a determined sacrifice of such convenience, or beauty, or cheapness as is to be got only by the degradation of the workman; and by equally determined demand for the products and results of healthy and ennobling labor.

§ XVII. And how, it will be asked, are these products to be recognized, and this demand to be regulated? Easily: by the observance of three broad and simple rules:

1. Never encourage the manufacture of any article not absolutely necessary, in the production of which *Invention* has no share.

2. Never demand an exact finish for its own sake, but only for some practical or noble end.

3. Never encourage imitation or copying of any kind, except for the sake of preserving record of great works.

The second of these principles is the only one which directly rises out of the consideration of our immediate subject; but I shall briefly explain the meaning and extent of the first also, reserving the enforcement of the third for another place.

1. Never encourage the manufacture of anything not necessary, in the production of which invention has no share.

For instance. Glass beads are utterly unnecessary, and there is no design or thought employed in their manufacture. They are formed by first drawing out the glass into rods: these rods are chopped up into fragments of the size of beads by the human hand, and the fragments are then rounded in the furnace. The men who chop up the rods sit at their work all day, their hands vibrating with a perpetual and exquisitely timed palsy, and the beads dropping beneath their vibration like hail. Neither they, nor the men who draw out the rods or fuse the fragments, have the smallest occasion for the use of any single human faculty; and every young lady, therefore, who buys glass beads is engaged in the slave-trade, and in a much more cruel one than that which we have so long been endeavoring to put down.

But glass cups and vessels may become the subjects of exquisite invention; and if in buying these we pay for the invention, that is to say for the beautiful form, or color, or engraving, and not for mere finish of execution, we are doing good to humanity.

§ XVIII. So, again, the cutting of precious stones, in all ordinary cases, requires little exertion of any mental faculty; some tact and judgment in avoiding flaws, and so on, but nothing to bring out the whole mind. Every person who wears cut jewels merely for the sake of their value is, therefore, a slave-driver.

But the working of the goldsmith, and the various designing of grouped jewellery and enamel-work, may become the subject of the most noble human intelligence. Therefore, money spent in the purchase of well-designed plate, of precious engraved vases, cameos, or enamels, does good to humanity; and, in work of this kind, jewels may be employed to heighten its splendor; and their cutting is then a price paid for the attainment of a noble end, and thus perfectly allowable.

§ XIX. I shall perhaps press this law farther elsewhere, but our immediate concern is chiefly with the second, namely, never to demand an exact finish, when it does not lead to a noble end. For observe, I have only dwelt upon the rudeness of Gothic, or any other kind of imperfectness, as admirable, where it was impossible to get design or thought without it. If you are to have the thought of a rough and untaught man, you must have it in a rough and untaught way; but from an educated man, who can without effort express his thoughts in an educated way, take the graceful expression, and be thankful. Only *get* the thought, and do not silence the peasant because he cannot speak good grammar, or until you have taught him his grammar. Grammar and refinement are good things, both, only be sure of the better thing first. And thus in art, delicate finish is desirable from the greatest masters, and is always given by them. In some places Michael Angelo, Leonardo, Phidias, Perugino, Turner, all finished with the most exquisite care; and the finish they give always leads to the fuller accomplishment of their noble purposes. But lower men than these cannot finish, for it requires consummate knowledge to finish consummately, and then we must take their thoughts as they are able to give them. So the rule is simple: Always look for invention first, and after that, for such execution as will help the invention, and as the inventor is capable of without painful effort, and *no more*. Above all, demand no refinement of execution where there is no thought, for that is slaves' work, unredeemed. Rather choose rough work than smooth work, so only that the practical purpose be answered, and never imagine there is reason to be proud of anything that may be accomplished by patience and sand-paper.

§ xx. I shall only give one example, which however will show the reader what I mean, from the manufacture already alluded to, that of glass. Our modern glass is exquisitely clear in its substance, true in its form, accurate in its cutting. We are proud of this. We ought to be ashamed of it. The old Venice glass was muddy, inaccurate in all its forms, and clumsily cut, if at all. And the old Venetian was justly proud of it. For there is this difference between the English and Venetian workman, that the former thinks only of accurately matching his patterns, and getting his curves perfectly true and his edges perfectly sharp, and becomes a mere machine for rounding curves and sharpening edges, while the old Venetian cared not a whit whether his edges were sharp or not, but he invented a new design for every glass that he made, and never moulded a handle or a lip without a new fancy in it. And therefore, though some Venetian glass is ugly and clumsy enough, when made by clumsy and uninventive workmen, other Venetian glass is so lovely in its forms that no price is too great for it; and we never see the same form in it twice. Now you cannot have the finish and the varied form too. If the workman is thinking about his edges, he cannot be thinking of his design; if of his design, he cannot think of his edges. Choose whether you will pay for the lovely form or the perfect finish, and choose at the same moment whether you will make the worker a man or a grindstone.

§ XXI. Nay, but the reader interrupts me,—"If the workman can design beautifully, I would not have him kept at the furnace. Let him be taken away and made a gentleman, and have a studio, and design his glass there, and I will have it blown and cut for him by common workmen, and so I will have my design and my finish too."

All ideas of this kind are founded upon two mistaken suppositions: the first, that one man's thoughts can be, or ought to be, executed by another man's hands; the second, that manual labor is a degradation, when it is governed by intellect.

On a large scale, and in work determinable by line and rule, it is indeed both possible and necessary that the thoughts of one man should be carried out by the labor of others; in this sense I have already defined the best architecture to be the expression of the mind of manhood by the hands of childhood. But on a smaller scale, and in a design which cannot be mathematically defined, one man's thoughts can never be expressed by another : and the difference between the spirit of touch of the man who is inventing, and of the man who is obeying directions, is often all the difference between a great and a common work of art. How wide the separation is between original and second-hand execution, I shall endeavor to show elsewhere; it is not so much to our purpose here as to mark the other and more fatal error of despising manual labor when governed by intellect; for it is no less fatal an error to despise it when thus regulated by intellect, than to value it for its own sake. We are always in these days endeavoring to separate the two; we want one man to be always thinking, and another to be always working, and we call one a gentleman, and the other an operative; whereas the workman ought often to be thinking, and the thinker often to be working, and both should be gentlemen, in the best sense. As it is, we make both ungentle, the one envying, the other despising, his brother; and the mass of society is made up of morbid thinkers, and miserable workers. Now it is only by labor that thought can be made healthy, and only by thought that labor can be made happy, and the two cannot be separated with impunity. It would be well if all of us were good handicraftsmen in some kind, and the dishonor of manual labor done away with altogether; so that though there should still be a trenchant distinction of race between nobles and commoners, there should not, among the latter, be a trenchant distinction of employment, as between idle and working men, or between men of liberal and illiberal professions. All professions should be liberal, and there should be less pride felt in peculiarity of employment, and more in excellence of achievement. And yet more, in each several profession, no master should be too proud to do its hardest work. The painter should grind his own colors; the architect work in the mason's yard with his men; the master-manufacturer be himself a more skilful operative than any man in his mills; and the distinction between one man and another be only in experience and skill, and the authority and wealth which these must naturally and justly obtain.

§ XXII. I should be led far from the matter in hand, if I were to pursue this interesting subject. Enough, I trust, has been said to show the reader that the rudeness or imperfection which at first rendered the term "Gothic" one of reproach is indeed, when rightly understood, one of the most noble characters of Christian architecture, and not only a noble but an *essential* one. It seems a fantastic paradox, but it is nevertheless a most important truth, that no architecture can be truly noble which is *not* imperfect. And this is easily demonstrable. For since the architect, whom we will suppose capable of doing all in perfection, cannot execute the whole with his own hands, he must either make slaves of his workmen in the old Greek, and present English fashion, and level his work to a slave's capacities, which is to degrade it; or else he must take his workmen as he finds them, and let them show their weaknesses together with their strength, which will involve the Gothic imperfection, but render the whole work as noble as the intellect of the age can make it.

§ XXIII. But the principle may be stated more broadly still. I have confined the illustration of it to architecture, but I m st not leave it as if true of architecture only. Hitherto I have used the words imperfect and perfect merely to distinguish between work grossly unskilful, and work executed with average precision and science; and I have been pleading that any degree of unskilfulness should be admitted, so only that the laborer's mind had room for expression. But, accurately speaking, no good work whatever can be perfect, and *the demand for perfection is always a sign of a misunder-standing of the ends of art.*

§ XXIV. This for two reasons, both based on everlasting laws. The first, that no great man ever stops working till he has reached his point of failure; that is to say, his mind is always far in advance of his powers of execution, and the latter will now and then give way in trying to follow it; besides that he will always give to the inferior portions of his work only such inferior attention as they require; and according to his greatness he becomes so accustomed to the feeling of dissatisfaction with the best he can do, that in moments of lassitude or anger with himself he will not care though the beholder be dissatisfied also. I believe there has only been one man who would not acknowledge this necessity, and strove always to reach perfection, Leonardo; the end of his vain effort being merely that he would take ten years to a picture, and leave it unfinished. And therefore, if we are to have great men working at all, or less men doing their best, the work will be imperfect, however beautiful. Of human work none but what is bad can be perfect, in its own bad way.*

§ xxv. The second reason is, that imperfection is in some sort essential to all that we know of life. It is the sign of life in a mortal body, that is to say, of a state of progress and change. Nothing that lives is, or can be, rigidly perfect; part of it is decaying, part nascent. The foxglove blossom,— a third part bud, a third part past, a third part in full bloom, —is a type of the life of this world. And in all things that live there are certain irregularities and deficiencies which are not only signs of life, but sources of beauty. No human face is exactly the same in its lines on each side, no leaf perfect in its lobes, no branch in its symmetry. All admit irregularity as they imply change; and to banish imperfection is to destroy expression, to check exertion, to paralyse vitality. All things

* The Elgin marbles are supposed by many persons to be "perfect." In the most important portions they indeed approach perfection, but only there. The draperies are unfinished, the hair and wool of the animals are unfinished, and the entire bas-reliefs of the frieze are roughly cut.

are literally better, lovelier, and more beloved for the imperfections which have been divinely appointed, that the law of human life may be Effort, and the law of human judgment, Mercy.

Accept this then for a universal law, that neither architecture nor any other noble work of man can be good unless it be imperfect; and let us be prepared for the otherwise strange fact, which we shall discern clearly as we approach the period of the Renaissance, that the first cause of the fall of the arts of Europe was a relentless requirement of perfection, incapable alike either of being silenced by veneration for greatness, or softened into forgiveness of simplicity.

Thus far then of the Rudeness or Savageness, which is the first mental element of Gothic architecture. It is an element in many other healthy architectures also, as in Byzantine and Romanesque; but true Gothic cannot exist without it.

§ XXVI. The second mental element above named was CHANGEFULNESS, or Variety.

I have already enforced the allowing independent operation to the inferior workman, simply as a duty *to him*, and as ennobling the architecture by rendering it more Christian. We have now to consider what reward we obtain for the performance of this duty, namely, the perpetual variety of every feature of the building.

Wherever the workman is utterly enslaved, the parts of the building must of course be absolutely like each other; for the perfection of his execution can only be reached by exercising him in doing one thing, and giving him nothing else to do. The degree in which the workman is degraded may be thus known at a glance, by observing whether the several parts of the building are similar or not; and if, as in Greek work, all the capitals are alike, and all the mouldings unvaried, then the degradation is complete; if, as in Egyptian or Ninevite work, though the manner of executing certain figures is always the same, the order of design is perpetually varied, the degradation is less total; if, as in Gothic work, there is perpetual change both in design and execution, the workman must have been altogether set free.

§ XXVII. How much the beholder gains from the liberty of the laborer may perhaps be questioned in England, where one of the strongest instincts in nearly every mind is that Love of Order which makes us desire that our house windows should pair like our carriage horses, and allows us to yield our faith unhesitatingly to architectural theories which fix a form for everything, and forbid variation from it. I would not impeach love of order: it is one of the most useful elements of the English mind; it helps us in our commerce and in all purely practical matters; and it is in many cases one of the foundation stones of morality. Only do not let us suppose that love of order is love of art. It is true that order, in its highest sense, is one of the necessities of art, just as time is a necessity of music; but love of order has no more to do with our right enjoyment of architecture or painting, than love of punctuality with the appreciation of an opera. Experience, I fear, teaches us that accurate and methodical habits in daily life are seldom characteristic of those who either quickly perceive, or richly possess, the creative powers of art; there is, however, nothing inconsistent between the two instincts, and nothing to hinder us from retaining our business habits, and yet fully allowing and enjoying the noblest gifts of Invention. We already do so, in every other branch of art except architecture, and we only do *not* so there because we have been taught that it would be wrong. Our architects gravely inform us that, as there are four rules of arithmetic, there are five orders of architecture; we, in our simplicity, think that this sounds consistent, and believe them. They inform us also that there is one proper form for Corinthian capitals, another for Doric, and another for Ionic. We, considering that there is also a proper form for the letters A, B, and C, think that this also sounds consistent, and accept the proposition. Understanding, therefore, that one form of the said capitals is proper, and no other, and having a conscientious horror of all impropriety, we allow the architect to provide us with the said capitals, of the proper form, in such and such a quantity, and in all other points to take care that the legal forms are observed; which having done, we rest in forced confidence that we are well housed.

§ XXVIII. But our higher instincts are not deceived. We take no pleasure in the building provided for us, resembling that which we take in a new book or a new picture. We may be proud of its size, complacent in its correctness, and happy in its convenience. We may take the same pleasure in its symmetry and workmanship as in a well-ordered room, or a skilful piece of manufacture. And this we suppose to be all the pleasure that architecture was ever intended to give us. The idea of reading a building as we would read Milton or Dante, and getting the same kind of delight out of the stones as out of the stanzas, never enters our minds for a moment. And for good reason:—There is indeed rhythm in the verses, quite as strict as the symmetries or rhythm of the architecture, and a thousand times more beautiful, but there is something else than rhythm. The verses were neither made to order, nor to match, as the capitals were; and we have therefore a kind of pleasure in them other than a sense of propriety. But it requires a strong effort of common sense to shake ourselves quit of all that we have been taught for the last two centuries, and wake to the perception of a truth just as simple and certain as it is new: that great art, whether expressing itself in words, colors, or stones, does *not* say the same thing over and over again; that the merit of architectural, as of every other art, consists in its saying new and different things; that to repeat itself is no more a cha racteristic of genius in marble than it is of genius in print; and that we may, without offending any laws of good taste, require of an architect, as we do of a novelist, that he should be not only correct, but entertaining.

Yet all this is true, and self-evident; only hidden from us, as many other self-evident things are, by false teaching. Nothing is a great work of art, for the production of which either rules or models can be given. Exactly so far as architecture works on known rules, and from given models, it is not an art, but a manufacture; and it is, of the two procedures, rather less rational (because more easy) to copy capitals or mouldings from Phidias, and call ourselves architects, than to copy heads and hands from Titian, and call ourselves painters.

§ XXIX. Let us then understand at once, that change or variety is as much a necessity to the human heart and brain in buildings as in books; that there is no merit, though there is some occasional use, in monotony; and that we must no more expect to derive either pleasure or profit from an architecture whose ornaments are of one pattern, and whose pillars are of one proportion, than we should out of a universe in which the clouds were all of one shape, and the trees all of one size.

§ XXX. And this we confess in deeds, though not in words. All the pleasure which the people of the nineteenth century take in art, is in pictures, sculpture, minor objects of virtù, or mediæval architecture, which we enjoy under the term picturesque : no pleasure is taken anywhere in modern buildings, and we find all men of true feeling delighting to escape out of modern cities into natural scenery : hence, as I shall hereafter show, that peculiar love of landscape which is characteristic of the age. It would be well, if, in all other matters, we were as ready to put up with what we dislike, for the sake of compliance with established law, as we are in architecture.

§ XXXI. How so debased a law ever came to be established,

we shall see when we come to describe the Renaissance schools:
here we have only to note, as the second most essential element
of the Gothic spirit, that it broke through that law wherever it
found it in existence; it not only dared, but delighted in, the
infringement of every servile principle; and invented a series of
forms of which the merit was, not merely that they were new,
but that they were *capable of perpetual novelty*. The pointed
arch was not merely a bold variation from the round, but it
admitted of millions of variations in itself; for the proportions
of a pointed arch are changeable to infinity, while a circular
arch is always the same. The grouped shaft was not merely
a bold variation from the single one, but it admitted of millions of variations in its grouping, and in the proportions resultant from its grouping. The introduction of tracery was not
only a startling change in the treatment of window lights, but
admitted endless changes in the interlacement of the tracery
bars themselves. So that, while in all living Christian architecture the love of variety exists, the Gothic schools exhibited
that love in culminating energy ; and their influence, wherever
it extended itself, may be sooner and farther traced by this
character than by any other; the tendency to the adoption of
Gothic types being always first shown by greater irregularity
and richer variation in the forms of the architecture it is about
to supersede, long before the appearance of the pointed arch
or of any other recognizable *outward* sign of the Gothic mind.

§ XXXII. We must, however, herein note carefully what
distinction there is between a healthy and a diseased love of
change ; for as it was in healthy love of change that the Gothic
architecture rose, it was partly in consequence of diseased love
of change that it was destroyed. In order to understand this
clearly, it will be necessary to consider the different ways in
which change and monotony are presented to us in nature;
both having their use, like darkness and light, and the one
incapable of being enjoyed without the other : change being

most delightful after some prolongation of monotony, as light appears most brilliant after the eyes have been for some time closed.

§ XXXIII. I believe that the true relations of monotony and change may be most simply understood by observing them in music. We may therein notice, first, that there is a sublimity and majesty in monotony which there is not in rapid or frequent variation. This is true throughout all nature. The greater part of the sublimity of the sea depends on its monotony ; so also that of desolate moor and mountain scenery; and especially the sublimity of motion, as in the quiet, unchanged fall and rise of an engine beam. So also there is sublimity in darkness which there is not in light.

§ XXXIV. Again, monotony after a certain time, or beyond a certain degree, becomes either uninteresting or intolerable, and the musician is obliged to break it in one or two ways: either while the air or passage is perpetually repeated, its notes are variously enriched and harmonized; or else, after a certain number of repeated passages, an entirely new passage is introduced, which is more or less delightful according to the length of the previous monotony. Nature, of course, uses both these kinds of variation perpetually. The sea-waves, resembling each other in general mass, but none like its brother in minor divisions and curves, are a monotony of the first kind ; the great plain, broken by an emergent rock or clump of trees, is a monotony of the second.

§ XXXV. Farther : in order to the enjoyment of the change in either case, a certain degree of patience is required from the hearer or observer. In the first case, he must be satisfied to endure with patience the recurrence of the great masses of sound or form, and to seek for entertainment in a careful watchfulness of the minor details. In the second case, he must bear patiently the infliction of the monotony for some moments, in order to feel the full refreshment of the change. This is true even of the shortest musical passage in which the element of monotony is employed. In cases of more majestic monotony, the patience required is so considerable that it becomes a kind of pain,—a price paid for the future pleasure.

§ xxxvi. Again: the talent of the composer is not in the monotony, but in the changes: he may show feeling and taste by his use of monotony in certain places or degrees; that is to say, by his *various* employment of it; but it is always in the new arrangement or invention that his intellect is shown, and not in the monotony which relieves it.

Lastly: if the pleasure of change be too often repeated, it ceases to be delightful, for then change itself becomes monotonous, and we are driven to seek delight in extreme and fantastic degrees of it. This is the diseased love of change of which we have above spoken.

§ xxxvii. From these facts we may gather generally that monotony is, and ought to be, in itself painful to us, just as darkness is; that an architecture which is altogether monotonous is a dark or dead architecture; and, of those who love it, it may be truly said, "they love darkness rather than light." But monotony in certain measure, used in order to give value to change, and, above all, that *transparent* monotony which, like the shadows of a great painter, suffers all manner of dimly suggested form to be seen through the body of it, is an essential in architectural as in all other composition; and the endurance of monotony has about the same place in a healthy mind that the endurance of darkness has: that is to say, as a strong intellect will have pleasure in the solemnities of storm and twilight, and in the broken and mysterious lights that gleam among them, rather than in mere brilliancy and glare, while a frivolous mind will dread the shadow and the storm; and as a great man will be ready to endure much darkness of fortune in order to reach greater eminence of power or felicity, while an inferior man will not pay the price; exactly in like manner a great mind will accept, or even delight in, monotony which would be wearisome to an inferior intellect, because it has more patience and power of expectation, and is ready to pay the full price for the great future pleasure of change. But in all cases it is not that the noble nature loves monotony, any more than it loves darkness or pain. But it can bear with it, and receives a high pleasure in the endurance or patience, a pleasure necessary to the well-being of this world; while those who will not submit to the temporary sameness, but rush from one change to another, gradually dull the edge of change itself, and bring a shadow and weariness over the whole world from which there is no more escape.

§ XXXVIII. From these general uses of variety in the economy of the world, we may at once understand its use and abuse in architecture. The variety of the Gothic schools is the more healthy and beautiful, because in many cases it is entirely unstudied, and results, not from the mere love of change, but from practical necessities. For in one point of view Gothic is not only the best, but the *only rational* architecture, as being that which can fit itself most easily to all services, vulgar or noble. Undefined in its slope of roof, height of shaft, breadth of arch, or disposition of ground plan, it can shrink into a turret, expand into a hall, coil into a staircase, or spring into a spire, with undegraded grace and unexhausted energy; and whenever it finds occasion for change in its form or purpose, it submits to it without the slightest sense of loss either to its unity or majesty,—subtle and flexible like a fiery serpent, but ever attentive to the voice of the charmer. And it is one of the chief virtues of the Gothic builders, that they never suffered ideas of outside symmetries and consistencies to interfere with the real use and value of what they did. If they wanted a window, they opened one; a room, they added one; a buttress, they built one; utterly regardless of any established conventionalities of external appearance, knowing (as indeed it always happened) that such daring interruptions of the formal plan would rather give additional interest to its symmetry than injure it. So that, in the best times of Gothic, a useless window would rather have been opened in an unexpected place for the sake of the surprise, than a useful one forbidden for the sake of symmetry. Every successive architect, employed upon a great work, built the pieces he added in his own way, utterly regardless of the style adopted by his predecessors; and if two towers were raised in nominal correspondence at the sides of a cathedral front, one was nearly sure to be different from the other, and in each the style at the top to be different from the style at the bottom.*

§ XXXIX. These marked variations were, however, only permitted as part of the great system of perpetual change which ran through every member of Gothic design, and rendered it as endless a field for the beholder's inquiry, as for the builder's imagination : change, which in the best schools is subtle and delicate, and rendered more delightful by intermingling of a noble monotony; in the more barbaric schools is somewhat fantastic and redundant; but, in all, a necessary and constant condition of the life of the school. Sometimes the variety is in one feature, sometimes in another; it may be in the capitals or crockets, in the niches or the traceries, or in all together, but in some one or other of the features it will be found always. If the mouldings are constant, the surface sculpture will change; if the capitals are of a fixed design, the traceries will change; if the traceries are monotonous, the capitals will change; and if even, as in some fine schools, the early English for example, there is the slightest approximation to an unvarying type of mouldings, capitals, and floral decora-

---

* In the eighth chapter we shall see a remarkable instance of this sacrifice of symmetry to convenience in the arrangement of the windows of the Ducal Palace.

tion, the variety is found in the disposition of the masses, and in the figure sculpture.

§ XL. I must now refer for a moment, before we quit the consideration of this, the second mental element of Gothic, to the opening of the third chapter of the "Seven Lamps of Architecture," in which the distinction was drawn (§ 2.) between man gathering and man governing; between his acceptance of the sources of delight from nature, and his developement of authoritative or imaginative power in their arrangement: for the two mental elements, not only of Gothic, but of all good architecture, which we have just been examining, belong to it, and are admirable in it, chiefly as it is, more than any other subject of art, the work of man, and the expression of the average power of man. A picture or poem is often little more than a feeble utterance of man's admiration of something out of himself; but architecture approaches more to a creation of his own, born of his necessities, and expressive of his nature. It is also, in some sort, the work of the whole race, while the picture or statue are the work of one only, in most cases more highly gifted than his fellows. And therefore we may expect that the first two elements of good architecture should be expressive of some great truths commonly belonging to the whole race, and necessary to be understood or felt by them in all their work that they do under the sun. And observe what they are: the confession of Imperfection, and the confession of Desire of Change. The building of the bird and the bee needs not express anything like this. It is perfect and unchanging. But just because we are something better than birds or bees, our building must confess that we have not reached the perfection we can imagine, and cannot rest in the condition we have attained. If we pretend to have reached either perfection or satisfaction, we have degraded ourselves and our work. God's work only may express that; but ours may never have that sentence written upon it,—"And behold,

it was very good." And, observe again, it is not merely as it
renders the edifice a book of various knowledge, or a mine of
precious thought, that variety is essential to its nobleness.
The vital principle is not the love of *Knowledge*, but the love
of *Change*. It is that strange *disquietude* of the Gothic spirit
that is its greatness; that restlessness of the dreaming mind,
that wanders hither and thither among the niches, and flickers
feverishly around the pinnacles, and frets and fades in laby-
rinthine knots and shadows along wall and roof, and yet is
not satisfied, nor shall be satisfied. The Greek could stay in
his triglyph furrow, and be at peace; but the work of the
Gothic heart is fretwork still, and it can neither rest in, nor
from, its labor, but must pass on, sleeplessly, until its love of
change shall be pacified for ever in the change that must come
alike on them that wake and them that sleep.

§ XLI. The third constituent element of the Gothic mind
was stated to be NATURALISM; that is to say, the love of natural objetcs for their own sake, and the effort to represent them
frankly, unconstrained by artistical laws.

This characteristic of the style partly follows in necessary
connexion with those named above. For, so soon as the workman is left free to represent what subjects he chooses, he must
look to the nature that is round him for material, and will
endeavor to represent it as he sees it, with more or less
accuracy according to the skill he possesses, and with much
play of fancy, but with small respect for law. There is, however, a marked distinction between the imaginations of the
Western and Eastern races, even when both are left free;
the Western, or Gothic, delighting most in the representation
of facts, and the Eastern (Arabian, Persian, and Chinese) in
the harmony of colors and forms. Each of these intellectual
dispositions has its particular forms of error and abuse, which,
though I have often before stated, I must here again briefly
explain; and this the rather, because the word Naturalism is,

in one of its senses, justly used as a term of reproach, and the questions respecting the real relations of art and nature are so many and so confused throughout all the schools of Europe at this day, that I cannot clearly enunciate any single truth without appearing to admit, in fellowship with it, some kind of error, unless the reader will bear with me in entering into such an analysis of the subject as will serve us for general guidance.

§ XLII. We are to remember, in the first place, that the arrangement of colors and lines is an art analogous to the composition * of music, and entirely independent of the representation of facts. Good coloring does not necessarily convey the image of anything but itself. It consists in certain proportions and arrangements of rays of light, but not in likenesses to anything. A few touches of certain greys and purples laid by a master's hand on white paper, will be good coloring; as more touches are added beside them, we may find out that they were intended to represent a dove's neck, and we may praise, as the drawing advances, the perfect imitation of the dove's neck. But the good coloring does not consist in that imitation, but in the abstract qualities and relations of the grey and purple.

In like manner, as soon as a great sculptor begins to shape his work out of the block, we shall see that its lines are nobly

---

* I am always afraid to use this word "Composition;" it is so utterly misused in the general parlance respecting art. Nothing is more common than to hear divisions of art into "form, composition, and color," or "light and shade and composition," or "sentiment and composition," or it matters not what else and composition; the speakers in each case attaching a perfectly different meaning to the word, generally an indistinct one, and always a wrong one. Composition is, in plain English, "putting together," and it means the putting together of lines, of forms, of colors, of shades, or of ideas. Painters compose in color, compose in thought, compose in form, and compose in effect: the word being of use merely in order to express a scientific, disciplined, and inventive arrangement of any of these, instead of a merely natural or accidental one.

9*

arranged, and of noble character. We may not have the slightest idea for what the forms are intended, whether they are of man or beast, of vegetation or drapery. Their likeness to anything does not affect their nobleness. They are magnificent forms, and that is all we need care to know of them, in order to say whether the workman is a good or bad sculptor.

§ XLIII. Now the noblest art is an exact unison of the abstract value, with the imitative power, of forms and colors. It is the noblest composition, used to express the noblest facts. But the human mind cannot in general unite the two perfections: it either pursues the fact to the neglect of the composition, or pursues the composition to the neglect of the fact.

§ XLIV. And it is intended by the Deity that it *should* do this; the best art is not always wanted. Facts are often wanted without art, as in a geological diagram ; and art often without facts, as in a Turkey carpet. And most men have been made capable of giving either one or the other, but not both; only one or two, the very highest, can give both.

Observe then. Men are universally divided, as respects their artistical qualifications, into three great classes ; a right, a left, and a centre. On the right side are the men of facts, on the left the men of design,* in the centre the men of both.

The three classes of course pass into each other by imperceptible gradations. The men of facts are hardly ever altogether without powers of design ; the men of design are always in some measure cognizant of facts ; and as each class possesses more or less of the powers of the opposite one, it approaches to the character of the central class. Few men, even in that central rank, are so exactly throned on the summit of the crest that they cannot be perceived to incline

* Design is used in this place as expressive of the power to arrange lines and colors nobly. By facts, I mean facts perceived by the eye and mind, not facts accumulated by knowledge. See the chapter on Roman Renaissance (Vol. III. Chap. II.) for this distinction.

in the least one way or the other, embracing both horizons with their glance. Now each of these classes has, as I above said, a healthy function in the world, and correlative diseases or unhealthy functions; and, when the work of either of them is seen in its morbid condition, we are apt to find fault with the class of workmen, instead of finding fault only with the particular abuse which has perverted their action.

§ XLV. Let us first take an instance of the healthy action of the three classes on a simple subject, so as fully to understand the distinction between them, and then we shall more easily examine the corruptions to which they are liable. Fig. 1. in Plate VI. is a spray of vine with a bough of cherry-tree, which I have outlined from nature as accurately as I could, without in the least endeavoring to compose or arrange the form. It is a simple piece of fact-work, healthy and good as such, and useful to any one who wanted to know plain truths about tendrils of vines, but there is no attempt at design in it. Plate XIX., below, represents a branch of vine used to decorate the angle of the Ducal Palace. It is faithful as a representation of vine, and yet so designed that every leaf serves an architectural purpose, and could not be spared from its place without harm. This is central work; fact and design together. Fig. 2. in Plate VI. is a spandril from St. Mark's, in which the forms of the vine are dimly suggested, the object of the design being merely to obtain graceful lines and well proportioned masses upon the gold ground. There is not the least attempt to inform the spectator of any facts about the growth of the vine; there are no stalks or tendrils,—merely running bands with leaves emergent from them, of which nothing but the outline is taken from the vine, and even that imperfectly. This is design, unregardful of facts.

Now the work is, in all these three cases, perfectly healthy. Fig. 1. is not bad work because it has not design, nor Fig. 2. bad work because it has not facts. The object of the one is

to give pleasure through truth, and of the other to give pleasure through composition.　And both aré right.

What, then, are the diseased operations to which the three
classes of workmen are liable ?

§ XLVI.　Primarily, two ; affecting the two inferior classes :

　1st,　When either of those two classes Despises the other ;

　2nd,　When either of the two classes Envies the other ;
producing, therefore, four forms of dangerous error.

First, when the men of facts despise design.　This is the
error of the common Dutch painters, of merely imitative painters of still life, flowers, &c., and other men who, having either
the gift of accurate imitation or strong sympathies with nature, suppose that all is done when the imitation is perfected
or sympathy expressed.　A large body of English landscapists
come into this class, including most clever sketchers from
nature, who fancy that to get a sky of true tone, and a gleam
of sunshine or sweep of shower faithfully expressed, is all that
can be required of art.　These men are generally themselves
answerable for much of their deadness of feeling to the higher
qualities of composition.　They probably have nôt originally
the high gifts of design, but they lose such powers as they
originally possessed by despising, and refusing to study, the
results of great power of design in others.　Their knowledge,
as far as it goes, being accurate, they are usually presump-
tuous and self-conceited, and gradually become incapable of
admiring anything but what is like their own works.　They see
nothing in the works of great designers but the faults, and
do harm almost incalculable in the European society of the
present day by sneering at the compositions of the greatest
men of the earlier ages,* because they do not absolutely tally
with their own ideas of " Nature."

* " Earlier," that is to say, pre-Raphaelite ages.　Men of this stamp will
praise Claude, and such other comparatively debased artists ; but they cannot
taste the work of the thirteenth century.

§ XLVII. The second form of error is when the men of design despise facts. All noble design must deal with facts to a certain extent, for there is no food for it but in nature. The best colorist invents best by taking hints from natural colors; from birds, skies, or groups of figures. And if, in the delight of inventing fantastic color and form the truths of nature are wilfully neglected, the intellect becomes comparatively decrepit, and that state of art results which we find among the Chinese. The Greek designers delighted in the facts of the human form, and became great in consequence; but the facts of lower nature were disregarded by them, and their inferior ornament became, therefore, dead and valueless.

§ XLVIII. The third form of error is when the men of facts envy design : that is to say, when, having only imitative powers, they refuse to employ those powers upon the visible world around them; but, having been taught that composition is the end of art, strive to obtain the inventive powers which nature has denied them, study nothing but the works of reputed designers, and perish in a fungous growth of plagiarism and laws of art.

Here was the great error of the beginning of this century ; it is the error of the meanest kind of men that employ themselves in painting, and it is the most fatal of all, rendering those who fall into it utterly useless, incapable of helping the world with either truth or fancy, while, in all probability, they deceive it by base resemblances of both, until it hardly recognizes truth or fancy when they really exist.

§ XLIX. The fourth form of error is when the men of design envy facts ; that is to say, when the temptation of closely imitating nature leads them to forget their own proper ornamental function, and when they lose the power of the composition for the sake of graphic truth ; as, for instance, in the hawthorn moulding so often spoken of round the porch of Bourges Cathedral, which, though very lovely, might perhaps, as we saw above, have been better, if the old builder, in his excessive desire to make it look like hawthorn, had not painted it green.

§ L. It is, however, carefully to be noted, that the two morbid conditions to which the men of facts are liable are much more dangerous and harmful than those to which the men of design are liable. The morbid state of men of design injures themselves only; that of the men of facts injures the whole world. The Chinese porcelain-painter is, indeed, not so great a man as he might be, but he does not want to break everything that is not porcelain; but the modern English fact-hunter, despising design, wants to destroy everything that does not agree with his own notions of truth, and becomes the most dangerous and despicable of iconoclasts, excited by egotism instead of religion. Again: the Bourges sculptor, painting his hawthorns green, did indeed somewhat hurt the effect of his own beautiful design, but did not prevent any one from loving hawthorn: but Sir George Beaumont, trying to make Constable paint grass brown *instead* of green, was setting himself between Constable and nature, blinding the painter, and blaspheming the work of God.

§ LI. So much, then, of the diseases of the inferior classes, caused by their envying or despising each other. It is evident that the men of the central class cannot be liable to any morbid operation of this kind, they possessing the powers of both.

But there is another order of diseases which affect all the three classes, considered with respect to their pursuit of facts. For observe, all the three classes are in some degree pursuers of facts; even the men of design not being in any case altogether independent of external truth. Now, considering them *all* as more or less searchers after truth, there is another triple division to be made of them. Everything presented to them in nature has good and evil mingled in it: and artists, considered as searchers after truth, are again to be divided into three great classes, a right, a left, and a centre. Those on the right perceive, and pursue, the good, and leave the evil: those in the centre, the greatest, perceive and pursue the good and evil together, the whole thing as it verily is : those on the left perceive and pursue the evil, and leave the good.

§ LII. The first class, I say, take the good and leave the evil. Out of whatever is presented to them, they gather what it has of grace, and life, and light, and holiness, and leave all, or at least as much as possible, of the rest undrawn. The faces of their figures express no evil passions ; the skies of their landscapes are without storm ; the prevalent character of their color is brightness, and of their chiaroscuro fulness of light. The early Italian and Flemish painters, Angelico and Hemling, Perugino, Francia, Raffaelle in his best time, John Bellini, and our own Stothard, belong eminently to this class.

§ LIII. The second, or greatest class, render all that they see in nature unhesitatingly, with a kind of divine grasp and government of the whole, sympathizing with all the good, and yet confessing, permitting, and bringing good out of the evil also. Their subject is infinite as nature, their color equally balanced between splendor and sadness, reaching occasionally the highest degrees of both, and their chiaroscuro equally balanced between light and shade.

The principal men of this class are Michael Angelo, Leonardo, Giotto, Tintoret, and Turner. Raffaelle in his second time, Titian, and Rubens are transitional ; the first inclining to the eclectic, and the last two to the impure class, Raffaelle rarely giving all the evil, Titian and Rubens rarely all the good.

§ LIV. The last class perceive and imitate evil only. They cannot draw the trunk of a tree without blasting and shattering it, nor a sky except covered with stormy clouds : they delight in the beggary and brutality of the human race ; their color is for the most part subdued or lurid, and the greatest spaces of their pictures are occupied by darkness.

Happily the examples of this class are seldom seen in perfection. Salvator Rosa and Caravaggio are the most characteristic: the other men belonging to it approach towards the central rank by imperceptible gradations, as they perceive and represent more and more of good. But Murillo, Zurbaran, Camillo Procaccini, Rembrandt, and Teniers, all belong naturally to this lower class.

§ LV. Now, observe: the three classes into which artists were previously divided, of men of fact, men of design, and men of both, are all of Divine institution; but of these latter three, the last is in no wise of Divine institution. It is entirely human, and the men who belong to it have sunk into it by their own faults. They are, so far forth, either useless or harmful men. It is indeed good that evil should be occasionally represented, even in its worst forms, but never that it should be taken delight in: and the mighty men of the central class will always give us all that is needful of it; sometimes, as Hogarth did, dwelling upon it bitterly as satirists,—but this with the more effect, because they will neither exaggerate it, nor represent it mercilessly, and without the atoning points that all evil shows to a Divinely guided glance, even at its deepest. So then, though the third class will always, I fear, in some measure exist, the two necessary classes are only the first two; and this is so far acknowledged by the general sense of men, that the basest class has been confounded with the second; and painters have been divided commonly only into two ranks, now known, I believe, throughout Europe by the names which they first received in Italy, "Puristi and Naturalisti." Since, however, in the existing state of things, the degraded or evil-loving class, though less defined than that of the Puristi, is just as vast as it is indistinct, this division has done infinite dishonor to the great faithful painters of nature: and it has long been one of the objects I have had most at heart to show that, in reality, the Purists, in their sanctity, are less separated from these natural painters than the Sensualists in their foulness; and that the difference, though less discernible, is in reality greater, between the man who pursues evil for its own sake, and him who bears with it for the sake of truth, than between this latter and the man who will not endure it at all.

§ LVI. Let us, then, endeavor briefly to mark the real relations of these three vast ranks of men, whom I shall call, for convenience in speaking of them, Purists, Naturalists, and Sensualists; not that these terms express their real characters, but I know no word, and cannot coin a convenient one, which would accurately express the opposite of Purist; and I keep the terms Purist and Naturalist in order to comply, as far as possible, with the established usage of language on the Continent. Now, observe: in saying that nearly everything presented to us in nature has mingling in it of good and evil, I do not mean that nature is conceivably improvable, or that anything that God has made could be called evil, if we could see far enough into its uses, but that, with respect to immediate effects or appearances, it may be so, just as the hard rind or bitter kernel of a fruit may be an evil to the eater, though in the one is the protection of the fruit, and in the other its continuance. The Purist, therefore, does not mend nature, but receives from nature and from God that which is good for him; while the Sensualist fills himself " with the husks that the swine did eat."

The three classes may, therefore, be likened to men reaping wheat, of which the Purists take the fine flour, and the Sensualists the chaff and straw, but the Naturalists take all home, and make their cake of the one, and their couch of the other.

§ LVII. For instance. We know more certainly every day that whatever appears to us harmful in the universe has some beneficent or necessary operation; that the storm which destroys a harvest brightens the sunbeams for harvests yet unsown, and that the volcano which buries a city preserves a

thousand from destruction. But the evil is not for the time
less fearful, because we have learned it to be necessary ; and
we easily understand the timidity or the tenderness of the
spirit which would withdraw itself from the presence of
destruction, and create in its imagination a world of which
the peace should be unbroken, in which the sky should not
darken nor the sea rage, in which the leaf should not change
nor the blossom wither. That man is greater, however, who
contemplates with an equal mind the alternations of terror
and of beauty ; who, not rejoicing less beneath the sunny sky,
can bear also to watch the bars of twilight narrowing on the
horizon ; and, not less sensible to the blessing of the peace of
nature, can rejoice in the magnificence of the ordinances by
which that peace is protected and secured. But separated
from both by an immeasurable distance would be the man
who delighted in convulsion and disease for their own sake ;
who found his daily food in the disorder of nature mingled
with the suffering of humanity ; and watched joyfully at the
right hand of the Angel whose appointed work is to destroy
as well as to accuse, while the corners of the House of feasting
were struck by the wind from the wilderness.

§ LVIII. And far more is this true, when the subject of contemplation is humanity itself. The passions of mankind are
partly protective, partly beneficent, like the chaff and grain
of the corn ; but none without their use, none without nobleness when seen in balanced unity with the rest of the spirit
which they are charged to defend. The passions of which
the end is the continuance of the race ; the indignation which
is to arm it against injustice, or strengthen it to resist wanton
injury ; and the fear * which lies at the root of prudence,
reverence, and awe, are all honorable and beautiful, so long
as man is regarded in his relations to the existing world.

* Not selfish fear, caused by want of trust in God, or of resolution in the
soul.

The religious Purist, striving to conceive him withdrawn from those relations, effaces from the countenance the traces of all transitory passion, illumines it with holy hope and love, and seals it with the serenity of heavenly peace; he conceals the forms of the body by the deep-folded garment, or else represents them under severely chastened types, and would rather paint them emaciated by the fast, or pale from the torture, than strengthened by exertion, or flushed by emotion. But the great Naturalist takes the human being in its wholeness, in its mortal as well as its spiritual strength. Capable of sounding and sympathizing with the whole range of its passions, he brings one majestic harmony out of them all; he represents it fearlessly in all its acts and thoughts, in its haste, its anger, its sensuality, and its pride, as well as in its fortitude or faith, but makes it noble in them all; he casts aside the veil from the body, and beholds the mysteries of its form like an angel looking down on an inferior creature: there is nothing which he is reluctant to behold, nothing that he is ashamed to confess; with all that lives, triumphing, falling, or suffering, he claims kindred, either in majesty or in mercy, yet standing, in a sort, afar off, unmoved even in the deepness of his sympathy; for the spirit within him is too thoughtful to be grieved, too brave to be appalled, and too pure to be polluted.

§ LIX. How far beneath these two ranks of men shall we place, in the scale of being, those whose pleasure is only in sin or in suffering; who habitually contemplate humanity in poverty or decrepitude, fury or sensuality; whose works are either temptations to its weakness, or triumphs over its ruin, and recognize no other subjects for thought or admiration than the subtlety of the robber, the rage of the soldier, or the joy of the Sybarite. It seems strange, when thus definitely stated, that such a school should exist. Yet consider a little what gaps and blanks would disfigure our gallery and chamber

walls, in places that we have long approached with reverence,
if every picture, every statue, were removed from them, of
which the subject was either the vice or the misery of mankind, portrayed without any moral purpose: consider the
innumerable groups having reference merely to various forms
of passion, low or high; drunken revels and brawls among
peasants, gambling or fighting scenes among soldiers, amours
and intrigues among every class, brutal battle pieces, banditti
subjects, gluts of torture and death in famine, wreck, or
slaughter, for the sake merely of the excitement,—that quick-
ening and suppling of the dull spirit that cannot be gained
for it but by bathing it in blood, afterward to wither back into
stained and stiffened apathy; and then that whole vast false
heaven of sensual passion, full of nymphs, satyrs, graces, god-
desses, and I know not what, from its high seventh circle in
Correggio's Antiope, down to the Grecized ballet-dancers and
smirking Cupids of the Parisian upholsterer. Sweep away all
this, remorselessly, and see how much art we should have left.

§ LX. And yet these are only the grossest manifestations of
the tendency of the school. There are subtler, yet not less
certain, signs of it in the works of men who stand high in
the world's list of sacred painters. I doubt not that the
reader was surprised when I named Murillo among the men
of this third rank. Yet, go into the Dulwich Gallery, and
meditate for a little over that much celebrated picture of the
two beggar boys, one eating lying on the ground, the other
standing beside him. We have among our own painters one
who cannot indeed be set beside Murillo as a painter of
Madonnas, for he is a pure Naturalist, and, never having seen
a Madonna, does not paint any; but who, as a painter of
beggar or peasant boys, may be set beside Murillo, or any
one else,—W. Hunt. He loves peasant boys, because he
finds them more roughly and picturesquely dressed, and more
healthily colored, than others. And he paints all that he sees

in them fearlessly; all the health and humor, and freshness, and vitality, together with such awkwardness and stupidity, and what else of negative or positive harm there may be in the creature; but yet so that on the whole we love it, and find it perhaps even beautiful, or if not, at least we see that there is capability of good in it, rather than of evil; and all is lighted up by a sunshine and sweet color that makes the smock frock as precious as cloth of gold. But look at those two ragged and vicious vagrants that Murillo has gathered out of the street. You smile at first, because they are eating so naturally, and their roguery is so complete. But is there anything else than roguery there, or was it well for the painter to give his time to the painting of those repulsive and wicked children? Do you feel moved with any charity towards children as you look at them? Are we the least more likely to take any interest in ragged schools, or to help the next pauper child that comes in our way, because the painter has shown us a cunning beggar feeding greedily. Mark the choice of the act. He might have shown hunger in other ways, and given interest to even this act of eating, by making the face wasted, or the eye wistful. But he did not care to do this. He delighted merely in the disgusting manner of eating, the food filling the cheek; the boy is not hungry, else he would not turn round to talk and grin as he eats.

§ LXI. But observe another point in the lower figure. It lies so that the sole of the foot is turned towards the spectator; not because it would have lain less easily in another attitude, but that the painter may draw, and exhibit, the grey dust engrained in the foot. Do not call this the painting of nature: it is mere delight in foulness. The lesson, if there be any, in the picture, is not one whit the stronger. We all know that a beggar's bare foot cannot be clean; there is no need to thrust its degradation into the light, as if no human imagination were vigorous enough for its conception.

§ LXII. The position of the Sensualists, in treatment of land-scape, is less distinctly marked than in that of the figure: because even the wildest passions of nature are noble: but the inclination is manifested by carelessness in marking generic form in trees and flowers: by their preferring confused and irregular arrangements of foliage or foreground to symmetrical and simple grouping; by their general choice of such pictu-resqueness as results from decay, disorder, and disease, rather than of that which is consistent with the perfection of the things in which it is found; and by their imperfect rendering of the elements of strength and beauty in all things. I propose to work out this subject fully in the last volume of " Modern Painters;" but I trust that enough has been here said to enable the reader to understand the relations of the three great classes of artists, and therefore also the kinds of morbid condition into which the two higher (for the last has no other than a morbid condition) are liable to fall. For, since the function of the Naturalists is to represent, as far as may be, the whole of nature, and of the Purists to represent what is absolutely good for some special purpose or time, it is evident that both are liable to error from shortness of sight, and the last also from weakness of judgment. I say, in the first place, both may err from shortness of sight, from not seeing all that there is in nature; seeing only the outsides of things, or those points of them which bear least on the matter in hand. For instance, a modern continental Naturalist sees the anatomy of a limb tho-roughly, but does not see its color against the sky, which lat-ter fact is to a painter far the more important of the two. And because it is always easier to see the surface than the depth of things, the full sight of them requiring the highest powers of penetration, sympathy, and imagination, the world is full of vulgar Naturalists: not Sensualists, observe, not men who delight in evil; but men who never see the deepest good, and who bring discredit on all painting of Nature by the little that they discover in her. And the Purist, besides being liable to this same shortsightedness, is liable also to fatal errors of judgment; for he may think that good which is not so, and that the highest good which is the least. And thus the world is full of vulgar Purists,* who bring discredit on all selection by the silliness of their choice; and this the more, because the very becoming a Purist is commonly indicative of some slight degree of weakness, readiness to be offended, or narrowness of understanding of the ends of things: the greatest men being, in all times of art, Naturalists, without any exception; and the greatest Purists being those who approach nearest to the Naturalists, as Benozzo Gozzoli and Perugino. Hence there is a tendency in the Naturalists to despise the Purists, and in the Purists to be offended with the Naturalists (not understanding them, and confounding them with the Sensualists); and this is grievously harmful to both.

§ LXIII. Of the various forms of resultant mischief it is not here the place to speak: the reader may already be somewhat wearied with a statement which has led us apparently so far

---

* I reserve for another place the full discussion of this interesting subject, which here would have led me too far; but it must be noted, in passing, that this vulgar Purism, which rejects truth, not because it is vicious, but because it is humble, and consists not in choosing what is good, but in disguising what is rough, extends itself into every species of art. The most definite instance of it is the dressing of characters of peasantry in an opera or ballet scene; and the walls of our exhibitions are full of works of art which "exalt nature " in the same way, not by revealing what is great in the heart, but by smoothing what is coarse in the complexion. There is nothing, I believe, so vulgar, so hopeless, so indicative of an irretrievably base mind, as this species of Purism. Of healthy Purism carried to the utmost endurable length in this direction, exalting the heart first, and the features with it, perhaps the most characteristic instance I can give is Stothard's vignette to "Jorasse," in Rogers's Italy; at least it would be so if it could be seen beside a real group of Swiss girls. The poems of Rogers, compared with those of Crabbe, are admirable instances of the healthiest Purism and healthiest Naturalism in poetry. The first great Naturalists of Christian art were Orcagna and Giotto.

from our immediate subject.   But the digression was necessary, in order that I might clearly define the sense in which I use the word Naturalism when I state it to be the third most essential characteristic of Gothic architecture.   I mean that the Gothic builders belong to the central or greatest rank in *both* the classifications of artists which we have just made; that, considering all artists as either men of design, men of facts, or men of both, the Gothic builders were men of both; and that again, considering all artists as either Purists, Naturalists, or Sensualists, the Gothic builders were Naturalists.

§ LXIV. I say first, that the Gothic builders were of that central class which unites fact with design; but that the part of the work which was more especially their own was the truth-fulness.   Their power of artistical invention or arrangement was not greater than that of Romanesque and Byzantine work-men: by those workmen they were taught the principles, and from them received their models, of design; but to the orna-mental feeling and rich fancy of the Byzantine the Gothic builder added a love of *fact* which is never found in the South. Both Greek and Roman used conventional foliage in their orna-ment, passing into something that was not foliage at all, knot-ting itself into strange cup-like buds or clusters, and growing out of lifeless rods instead of stems; the Gothic sculptor received these types, at first, as things that ought to be, just as we have a second time received them; but he could not rest in them.   He saw there was no veracity in them, no know-ledge, no vitality.   Do what he would, he could not help liking the true leaves better; and cautiously, a little at a time, he put more of nature into his work, until at last it was all true, retaining, nevertheless, every valuable character of the original well-disciplined and designed arrangement.*

* The reader will understand this in a moment by glancing at Plate XX, the last in this volume, where the series 1. to 12. represents the change in one kind of leaf, from the Byzantine to the perfect Gothic.

§ LXV. Nor is it only in external and visible subject that the Gothic workman wrought for truth: he is as firm in his rendering of imaginative as of actual truth; that is to say, when an idea would have been by a Roman, or Byzantine, symbolically represented, the Gothic mind realizes it to the utmost. For instance, the purgatorial fire is represented in the mosaic of Torcello (Romanesque) as a red stream, longitudinally striped like a riband, descending out of the throne of Christ, and gradually extending itself to envelope the wicked. When we are once informed what this means, it is enough for its purpose; but the Gothic inventor does not leave the sign in need of interpretation. He makes the fire as like real fire as he can; and in the porch of St. Maclou at Rouen the sculptured flames burst out of the Hades gate, and flicker up, in writhing tongues of stone, through the interstices of the niches, as if the church itself were on fire. This is an extreme instance, but it is all the more illustrative of the entire difference in temper and thought between the two schools of art, and of the intense love of veracity which influenced the Gothic design.

§ LXVI. I do not say that this love of veracity is always healthy in its operation. I have above noticed the errors into which it falls from despising design; and there is another kind of error noticeable in the instance just given, in which the love of truth is too hasty, and seizes on a surface truth instead of an inner one. For in representing the Hades fire, it is not the mere *form* of the flame which needs most to be told, but its unquenchableness, its Divine ordainment and limitation, and its inner fierceness, not physical and material, but in being the expression of the wrath of God. And these things are not to be told by imitating the fire that flashes out of a bundle of sticks. If we think over his symbol a little, we shall perhaps find that the Romanesque builder told more truth in that likeness of a blood-red stream, flowing between definite shores, and out of God's throne, and expanding, as if

10

fed by a perpetual current, into the lake wherein the wicked are cast, than the Gothic builder in those torch-flickerings about his niches. But this is not to our immediate purpose; I am not at present to insist upon the faults into which the love of truth was led in the later Gothic times, but on the feeling itself, as a glorious and peculiar characteristic of the Northern builders. For, observe, it is not, even in the above instance, love of truth, but want of thought, which *causes* the fault. The love of truth, as such, is good, but when it is misdirected by thoughtlessness or over-excited by vanity, and either seizes on facts of small value, or gathers them chiefly that it may boast of its grasp and apprehension, its work may well become dull or offensive. Yet let us not, therefore, blame the inherent love of facts, but the incautiousness of their selection, and impertinence of their statement.

§ LXVII. I said, in the second place, that Gothic work, when referred to the arrangement of all art, as purist, naturalist, or sensualist, was naturalist. This character follows necessarily on its extreme love of truth, prevailing over the sense of beauty, and causing it to take delight in portraiture of every kind, and to express the various characters of the human countenance and form, as it did the varieties of leaves and the ruggedness of branches. And this tendency is both increased and ennobled by the same Christian humility which we saw expressed in the first character of Gothic work, its rudeness. For as that resulted from a humility which confessed the imperfection of the *workman*, so this naturalist portraiture is rendered more faithful by the humility which confesses the imperfection of the *subject*. The Greek sculptor could neither bear to confess his own feebleness, nor to tell the faults of the forms that he portrayed. But the Christian workman, believing that all is finally to work together for good, freely confesses both, and neither seeks to disguise his own roughness of work, nor his subject's roughness of make. Yet this frankness being joined, for the most part, with depth of religious feeling in other directions, and especially with charity, there is sometimes a tendency to Purism in the best Gothic sculpture; so that it frequently reaches great dignity of form and tenderness of expression, yet never so as to lose the veracity of portraiture, wherever portraiture is possible: not exalting its kings into demi-gods, nor its saints into arch-angels, but giving what kingliness and sanctity was in them, to the full, mixed with due record of their faults; and this in the most part with a great indifference like that of Scripture history, which sets down, with unmoved and unexcusing resoluteness, the virtues and errors of all men of whom it speaks, often leaving the reader to form his own estimate of them, without an indication of the judgment of the historian. And this veracity is carried out by the Gothic sculptors in the minuteness and generality, as well as the equity, of their delineation: for they do not limit their art to the portraiture of saints and kings, but introduce the most familiar scenes and most simple subjects; filling up the backgrounds of Scripture histories with vivid and curious representations of the commonest incidents of daily life, and availing themselves of every occasion in which, either as a symbol, or an explana-tion of a scene or time, the things familiar to the eye of the workman could be introduced and made of account. Hence Gothic sculpture and painting are not only full of valuable portraiture of the greatest men, but copious records of all the domestic customs and inferior arts of the ages in which it flourished.*

---

* The best art either represents the facts of its own day, or, if facts of the past, expresses them with accessaries of the time in which the work was done. All good art, representing past events, is therefore full of the most frank ana-chronism, and always *ought* to be. No painter has any business to be an antiquarian. We do not want his impressions or suppositions respecting things that are past. We want his clear assertions respecting things present

§ LXVIII. There is, however, one direction in which the Natu-ralism of the Gothic workmen is peculiarly manifested; and this direction is even more characteristic of the school than the Naturalism itself; I mean their peculiar fondness for the forms of Vegetation. In rendering the various circumstances of daily life, Egyptian and Ninevite sculpture is as frank and as diffuse as the Gothic. From the highest pomps of state or triumphs of battle, to the most trivial domestic arts and amuse-ments, all is taken advantage of to fill the field of granite with the perpetual interest of a crowded drama; and the early Lombardic and Romanesque sculpture is equally copious in its description of the familiar circumstances of war and the chase. But in all the scenes portrayed by the workmen of these na-tions, vegetation occurs only as an explanatory accessary; the reed is introduced to mark the course of the river, or the tree to mark the covert of the wild beast, or the ambush of the enemy, but there is no especial interest in the forms of the vegetation strong enough to induce them to make it a subject of separate and accurate study. Again, among the nations who followed the arts of design exclusively, the forms of foliage introduced were meagre and general, and their real intricacy and life were neither admired nor expressed. But to the Gothic workman the living foliage became a subject of intense affection, and he struggled to render all its characters with as much accuracy as was compatible with the laws of his design and the nature of his material, not unfrequently tempted in his enthusiasm to transgress the one and disguise the other.

§ LXIX. There is a peculiar significancy in this, indicative both of higher civilization and gentler temperament, than had before been manifested in architecture. Rudeness, and the love of change, which we have insisted upon as the first ele-ments of Gothic, are also elements common to all healthy schools. But here is a softer element mingled with them, peculiar to the Gothic itself. The rudeness or ignorance which would have been painfully exposed in the treatment of the human form, are still not so great as to prevent the successful rendering of the wayside herbage; and the love of change, which becomes morbid and feverish in following the haste of the hunter, and the rage of the combatant, is at once soothed and satisfied as it watches the wandering of the tendril, and the budding of the flower. Nor is this all: the new direction of mental interest marks an infinite change in the means and the habits of life. The nations whose chief support was in the chase, whose chief interest was in the battle, whose chief pleasure was in the banquet, would take small care respecting the shapes of leaves and flowers; and notice little in the forms of the forest trees which sheltered them, except the signs indicative of the wood which would make the toughest lance, the closest roof, or the clearest fire. The affectionate observation of the grace and outward character of vegetation is the sure sign of a more tranquil and gentle existence, sustained by the gifts, and gladdened by the splendor, of the earth. In that careful distinction of species, and richness of delicate and undisturbed organization, which characterize the Gothic design, there is the history of rural and thoughtful life, influenced by habitual tenderness, and devoted to subtle inquiry; and every discriminating and delicate touch of the chisel, as it rounds the petal or guides the branch, is a prophecy of the developement of the entire body of the natural sciences, beginning with that of medicine, of the recovery of literature, and the establishment of the most necessary principles of domestic wisdom and national peace.

§ LXX. I have before alluded to the strange and vain supposition, that the original conception of Gothic architecture had been derived from vegetation,—from the symmetry of avenues, and the interlacing of branches. It is a supposition which never could have existed for a moment in the mind of any person acquainted with early Gothic; but, however idle as a theory, it is most valuable as a testimony to the character of the perfected style. It is precisely because the reverse of this theory is the fact, because the Gothic did not arise out of, but develope itself into, a resemblance to vegetation, that this resemblance is so instructive as an indication of the temper of the builders. It was no chance suggestion of the form of an arch from the bending of a bough, but a gradual and continual discovery of a beauty in natural forms which could be more and more perfectly transferred into those of stone, that influenced at once the heart of the people, and the form of the edifice. The Gothic architecture arose in massy and mountainous strength, axe-hewn, and iron-bound, block heaved upon block by the monk's enthusiasm and the soldier's force; and cramped and stanchioned into such weight of grisly wall, as might bury the anchoret in darkness, and beat back the utmost storm of battle, suffering but by the same narrow crosslet the passing of the sunbeam, or of the arrow. Gradually, as that monkish enthusiasm became more thoughtful, and as the sound of war became more and more intermittent beyond the gates of the convent or the keep, the stony pillar grew slender and the vaulted roof grew light, till they had wreathed themselves into the semblance of the summer woods at their fairest, and of the dead field-flowers, long trodden down in blood, sweet monumental statues were set to bloom for ever, beneath the porch of the temple, or the canopy of the tomb.

§ LXXI. Nor is it only as a sign of greater gentleness or refinement of mind, but as a proof of the best possible direction of this refinement, that the tendency of the Gothic to the expression of vegetative life is to be admired. That sentence of Genesis, "I have given thee every green herb for meat," like all the rest of the book, has a profound symbolical as well as a literal meaning. It is not merely the nourishment of the body, but the food of the soul, that is intended. The green herb is, of all nature, that which is most essential to the healthy spiritual life of man.   Most of us do not need fine scenery; the precipice and the mountain peak are not intended to be seen by all men,—perhaps their power is greatest over those who are unaccustomed to them.   But trees, and fields, and flowers were made for all, and are necessary for all.   God has connected the labor which is essential to the bodily suste- nance, with the pleasures which are healthiest for the heart; and while He made the ground stubborn, He made its herbage fragrant, and its blossoms fair.   The proudest architecture that man can build has no higher honor than to bear the image and recall the memory of that grass of the field which is, at once, the type and the support of his existence; the goodly building is then most glorious when it is sculptured into the likeness of the leaves of Paradise; and the great Gothic spirit, as we showed it to be noble in its disquietude, is also noble in its hold of nature; it is, indeed, like the dove of Noah, in that she found no rest upon the face of the waters,—but like her in this also, "Lo, in her mouth was an olive branch, plucked off."

§ LXXII. The fourth essential element of the Gothic mind was above stated to be the sense of the GROTESQUE; but I shall defer the endeavor to define this most curious and sub- tle character until we have occasion to examine one of the divisions of the Renaissance schools, which was morbidly influenced by it (Vol. III. Chap. III.).   It is the less necessary to insist upon it here, because every reader familiar with Gothic architecture must understand what I mean, and will, I believe, have no hesitation in admitting that the tendency to delight in fantastic and ludicrous, as well as in sublime, images, is a universal instinct of the Gothic imagination.

§ LXXIII. The fifth element above named was RIGIDITY; and this character I must endeavor carefully to define, for neither the word I have used, nor any other that I can think of, will express it accurately.   For I mean, not merely stable, but *active* rigidity; the peculiar energy which gives tension to movement, and stiffness to resistance, which makes the fiercest lightning forked rather than curved, and the stoutest oak-branch angular rather than bending, and is as much seen in the quivering of the lance as in the glittering of the icicle.

§ LXXIV. I have before had occasion (Vol. I. Chap. XIII. § VII.) to note some manifestations of this energy or fixedness; but it must be still more attentively considered here, as it shows itself throughout the whole structure and decoration of Gothic work. Egyptian and Greek buildings stand, for the most part, by their own weight and mass, one stone passively incumbent on another: but in the Gothic vaults and traceries there is a stiffness analogous to that of the bones of a limb, or fibres of a tree; an elastic tension and communication of force from part to part, and also a studious expression of this throughout every visible line of the building. And, in like manner, the Greek and Egyptian ornament is either mere surface engraving, as if the face of the wall had been stamped with a seal, or its lines are flowing, lithe, and luxuriant; in either case, there is no expression of energy in framework of the ornament itself. But the Gothic ornament stands out in prickly independence, and frosty for-titude, jutting into crockets, and freezing into pinnacles; here starting up into a monster, there germinating into a blossom; anon knitting itself into a branch, alternately thorny, bossy, and bristly, or writhed into every form of nervous entanglement; but, even when most graceful, never for an instant languid, always quickset; erring, if at all, ever on the side of brusquerie.

§ LXXV. The feelings or habits in the workman which give rise to this character in the work, are more complicated and various than those indicated by any other sculptural expres-sion hitherto named. There is, first, the habit of hard and rapid working; the industry of the tribes of the North, quickened by the coldness of the climate, and giving an expression of sharp energy to all they do (as above noted, Vol. I. Chap. XIII. § VII.), as opposed to the languor of the Southern tribes, however much of fire there may be in the heart of that languor, for lava itself may flow languidly. There is also the habit of finding enjoyment in the signs of cold, which is never found, I believe, in the inhabitants of countries south of the Alps. Cold is to them an unredeemed evil, to be suffered, and forgotten as soon as may be; but the long winter of the North forces the Goth (I mean the Englishman, Frenchman, Dane, or German), if he would lead a happy life at all, to find sources of happiness in foul weather as well as fair, and to rejoice in the leafless as well as in the shady forest. And this we do with all our hearts; finding perhaps nearly as much contentment by the Christmas fire as in the summer sunshine, and gaining health and strength on the ice-fields of winter, as well as among the meadows of spring. So that there is nothing adverse or painful to our feelings in the cramped and stiffened structure of vegetation checked by cold; and instead of seeking, like the Southern sculptor, to express only the softness of leafage nourished in all tenderness, and tempted into all luxuriance by warm winds and glowing rays, we find pleasure in dwelling upon the crabbed, perverse, and morose animation of plants that have known little kindness from earth or heaven, but, season after season, have had their best efforts palsied by frost, their brightest buds buried under snow, and their goodliest limbs lopped by tempest.

§ LXXVI. There are many subtle sympathies and affections which join to confirm the Gothic mind in this peculiar choice of subject; and when we add to the influence of these, the necessities consequent upon the employment of a rougher material, compelling the workman to seek for vigor of effect, rather than refinement of texture or accuracy of form, we have direct and manifest causes for much of the difference between the northern and southern cast of conception: but there are indirect causes holding a far more important place in the Gothic heart, though less immediate in their influence on design. Strength of will, independence of character, resoluteness of purpose, impatience of undue control, and that general tendency to set the individual reason against authority, and the individual deed against destiny, which, in the Northern tribes, has opposed itself throughout all ages to the languid submission, in the Southern, of thought to tradition, and purpose to fatality, are all more or less traceable in the rigid lines, vigorous and various masses, and daringly projecting and independent structure of the Northern Gothic ornament: while the opposite feelings are in like manner legible in the graceful and softly guided waves and wreathed bands, in which Southern decoration is constantly disposed; in its tendency to lose its independence, and fuse itself into the surface of the masses upon which it is traced; and in the expression seen so often, in the arrangement of those masses themselves, of an abandonment of their strength to an inevitable necessity, or a listless repose.

§ LXXVII. There is virtue in the measure, and error in the excess, of both these characters of mind, and in both of the styles which they have created; the best architecture, and the best temper, are those which unite them both; and this fifth impulse of the Gothic heart is therefore that which needs most caution in its indulgence. It is more definitely Gothic than any other, but the best Gothic building is not that which is *most* Gothic: it can hardly be too frank in its confession of rudeness, hardly too rich in its changefulness, hardly too faithful in its naturalism; but it may go too far in its rigidity, and, like the great Puritan spirit in its extreme, lose itself either in frivolity of division, or perversity of purpose.* It actually

* See the account of the meeting at Talla Linns, in 1682, given in the fourth chapter of the "Heart of Midlothian." At length they arrived at the conclu-

did so in its later times; but it is gladdening to remember that in its utmost nobleness, the very temper which has been thought most adverse to it, the Protestant spirit of self-dependence and inquiry, was expressed in its every line. Faith and aspiration there were, in every Christian ecclesiastical building, from the first century to the fifteenth; but the moral habits to which England in this age owes the kind of greatness that she has,—the habits of philosophical investigation, of accurate thought, of domestic seclusion and independence, of stern self-reliance, and sincere upright searching into religious truth,—were only traceable in the features which were the distinctive creation of the Gothic schools, in the veined foliage, and thorny fret-work, and shadowy niche, and buttressed pier, and fearless height of subtle pinnacle and crested tower, sent like an "unperplexed question up to Heaven."*

§ LXXVIII. Last, because the least essential, of the constituent elements of this noble school, was placed that of REDUN-DANCE,—the uncalculating bestowal of the wealth of its labor. There is, indeed, much Gothic, and that of the best period, in which this element is hardly traceable, and which depends for its effect almost exclusively on loveliness of simple design and grace of uninvolved proportion: still, in the most characteristic buildings, a certain portion of their effect depends upon accumulation of ornament; and many of those which have most influence on the minds of men, have attained it by means of this attribute alone. And although, by careful study of the school, it is possible to arrive at a condition of taste

sion that "they who owned (or allowed) such names as Monday, Tuesday, January, February, and so forth, served themselves heirs to the same if not greater punishment than had been denounced against the idolaters of old."

* See the beautiful description of Florence in Elizabeth Browning's "Casa Guidi Windows," which is not only a noble poem, but the only book I have seen which, favoring the Liberal cause in Italy, gives a just account of the incapacities of the modern Italian.

which shall be better contented by a few perfect lines than by a whole façade covered with fretwork, the building which only satisfies such a taste is not to be considered the best. For the very first requirement of Gothic architecture being, as we saw above, that it shall both admit the aid, and appeal to the admiration, of the rudest as well as the most refined minds, the richness of the work is, paradoxical as the statement may appear, a part of its humility. No architecture is so haughty as that which is simple; which refuses to address the eye, except in a few clear and forceful lines; which implies, in offering so little to our regards, that all it has offered is perfect; and disdains, either by the complexity or the attractiveness of its features, to embarrass our investigation, or betray us into delight. That humility, which is the very life of the Gothic school, is shown not only in the imperfection, but in the accumulation, of ornament. The inferior rank of the workman is often shown as much in the richness, as the roughness, of his work; and if the co-operation of every hand, and the sympathy of every heart, are to be received, we must be content to allow the redundance which disguises the failure of the feeble, and wins the regard of the inattentive. There are, however, far nobler interests mingling, in the Gothic heart, with the rude love of decorative accumulation: a magnificent enthusiasm, which feels as if it never could do enough to reach the fulness of its ideal; an unselfishness of sacrifice, which would rather cast fruitless labor before the altar than stand idle in the market; and, finally, a profound sympathy with the fulness and wealth of the material universe, rising out of that Naturalism whose operation we have already endeavored to define. The sculptor who sought for his models among the forest leaves, could not but quickly and deeply feel that complexity need not involve the loss of grace, nor richness that of repose; and every hour which he spent in the study of the minute and various work of Nature, made him feel more forcibly the barrenness of what was best in that of man : nor is it to be wondered at, that, seeing her perfect and exquisite creations poured forth in a profusion which conception could not grasp nor calculation sum, he should think that it ill became him to be niggardly of his own rude craftsmanship ; and where he saw throughout the universe a faultless beauty lavished on measureless spaces of broidered field and blooming mountain, to grudge his poor and imperfect labor to the few stones that he had raised one upon another, for habitation or memorial. The years of his life passed away before his task was accomplished ; but generation succeeded generation with unwearied enthusiasm, and the cathedral front was at last lost in the tapestry of its traceries, like a rock among the thickets and herbage of spring.

§ LXXIX. We have now, I believe, obtained a view approaching to completeness of the various moral or imaginative elements which composed the inner spirit of Gothic architecture. We have, in the second place, to define its outward form.

Now, as the Gothic spirit is made up of several elements, some of which may, in particular examples, be wanting, so the Gothic form is made up of minor conditions of form, some of which may, in particular examples, be imperfectly developed.

We cannot say, therefore, that a building is either Gothic or not Gothic in form, any more than we can in spirit. We can only say that it is more or less Gothic, in proportion to the number of Gothic forms which it unites.

§ LXXX. There have been made lately many subtle and ingenious endeavors to base the definition of Gothic form entirely upon the roof-vaulting ; endeavors which are both forced and futile : for many of the best Gothic buildings in the world have roofs of timber, which have no more connexion with the main structure of the walls of the edifice than a hat has with that of the head it protects ; and other Gothic buildings are merely enclosures of spaces, as ramparts and walls, or enclo sures of gardens or cloisters, and have no roofs at all, in the sense in which the word "roof" is commonly accepted. But every reader who has ever taken the slightest interest in architecture must know that there is a great popular impression on this matter, which maintains itself stiffly in its old form, in spite of all ratiocination and definition; namely, that a flat lintel from pillar to pillar is Grecian, a round arch Norman or Romanesque, and a pointed arch Gothic.

And the old popular notion, as far as it goes, is perfectly right, and can never be bettered. The most striking outward feature in all Gothic architecture is, that it is composed of pointed arches, as in Romanesque that it is in like manner composed of round; and this distinction would be quite as clear, though the roofs were taken off every cathedral in Europe. And yet, if we examine carefully into the real force and meaning of the term "roof" we shall perhaps be able to retain the old popular idea in a definition of Gothic architecture which shall also express whatever dependence that architecture has upon true forms of roofing.

§ LXXXI. In Chap. XIII. of the first volume, the reader will remember that roofs were considered as generally divided into two parts; the roof proper, that is to say, the shell, vault, or ceiling, internally visible; and the roof-mask, which protects this lower roof from the weather. In some buildings these parts are united in one framework; but, in most, they are more or less independent of each other, and in nearly all Gothic buildings there is considerable interval between them.

Now it will often happen, as above noticed, that owing to the nature of the apartments required, or the materials at hand, the roof proper may be flat, coved, or domed, in buildings which in their walls employ pointed arches, and are, in the straitest sense of the word, Gothic in all other respects Yet so far forth as the roofing alone is concerned, they are not Gothic unless the pointed arch be the principal form adopted either in the stone vaulting or the timbers of the roof proper.

I shall say then, in the first place, that " Gothic architecture is that which uses, if possible, the pointed arch in the roof proper." This is the first step in our definition.

§ LXXXII. Secondly. Although there may be many advisable or necessary forms for the lower roof or ceiling, there is, in cold countries exposed to rain and snow, only one advisable form for the roof-mask, and that is the gable, for this alone will throw off both rain and snow from all parts of its surface as speedily as possible. Snow can lodge on the top of a dome, not on the ridge of a gable. And thus, as far as roofing is concerned, the gable is a far more essential feature of Northern architecture than the pointed vault, for the one is a thorough necessity, the other often a graceful conventionality : the gable occurs in the timber roof of every dwelling-house and every cottage, but not the vault ; and the gable built on a polygonal or circular plan, is the origin of the turret and spire ; * and all the so-called aspiration of Gothic architecture is, as above noticed (Vol. I. Chap. XII. § VI.), nothing more than its development. So that we must add to our definition another clause, which will be, at present, by far the most important, and it will stand thus : " Gothic architecture is that which uses the pointed arch for the roof proper, and the gable for the roof-mask."

§ LXXXIII. And here, in passing, let us notice a principle as true in architecture as in morals. It is not the *compelled*, but the *wilful*, transgression of law which corrupts the character. Sin is not in the act, but in the choice. It is a law for Gothic architecture, that it shall use the pointed arch for its roof proper ; but because, in many cases of domestic building, this becomes impossible for want of room (the whole height of the apartment being required every where), or in various other

* Salisbury spire is only a tower with a polygonal gabled roof of stone, and so also the celebrated spires of Caen and Coutances.

ways inconvenient, flat ceilings may be used, and yet the Gothic shall not lose its purity. But in the roof-mask, there can be no necessity nor reason for a change of form : the gable is the best ; and if any other—dome, or bulging crown, or whatso. ever else—be employed at all, it must be in pure caprice, and wilful transgression of law. And wherever, therefore, this is done, the Gothic has lost its character ; it is pure Gothic no more.

§ LXXXIV. And this last clause of the definition is to be more strongly insisted upon, because it includes multitudes of buildings, especially domestic, which are Gothic in spirit, but which we are not in the habit of embracing in our general conception of Gothic architecture ; multitudes of street dwelling-houses and straggling country farm-houses, built with little care for beauty, or observance of Gothic laws in vaults or windows, and yet maintaining their character by the sharp and quaint gables of the roofs. And, for the reason just given, a house is far more Gothic which has square windows, and a boldly gabled roof, than the one which has pointed arches for the windows, and a domed or flat roof. For it often happened in the best Gothic times, as it must in all times, that it was more easy and convenient to make a window square than pointed ; not but that, as above emphatically stated, the richness of church architecture was also found in domestic ; and systematically "when the pointed arch was used in the church it was used in the street," only in all times there were cases

Fig. VIII.

in which men could not build as they would, and were obliged to construct their doors or win dows in the readiest way ; and this readiest way was then, in small work, as it will be to the end of time, to put a flat stone for a lintel and build the windows as in Fig. VIII.; and the occurrence of such windows in a building or a street will not un-Gothicize them, so long as the bold gable roof be retained, and the spirit of the work be visibly Gothic in other respects. But if the roof be wilfully and conspicuously of any other form than the gable,—if it be domed, or Turkish, or Chinese, —the building has positive corruption mingled with its Gothic elements, in proportion to the conspicuousness of the roof; and, if not absolutely un-Gothicized, can maintain its character only by such vigor of vital Gothic energy in other parts as shall cause the roof to be forgotten, thrown off like an eschar from the living frame. Nevertheless, we must always admit that it *may* be forgotten, and that if the Gothic seal be indeed set firmly on the walls, we are not to cavil at the forms reserved for the tiles and leads. For, observe, as our definition at present stands, being understood of large roofs only, it will allow a conical glass-furnace to be a Gothic building, but will *not* allow so much, either of the Duomo of Florence, or the Baptistery of Pisa. We must either mend it, therefore, or understand it in some broader sense.

§ LXXXV. And now, if the reader will look back to the fifth paragraph of Chap. III. Vol. I., he will find that I carefully extended my definition of a roof so as to include more than is usually understood by the term. It was there said to be the covering of a space, *narrow or wide*. It does not in the least signify, with respect to the real nature of the covering, whether the space protected be two feet wide, or ten; though in the one case we call the protection an arch, in the other a vault or roof. But the real point to be considered is, the manner in which this protection stands, and not whether it is narrow or broad. We call the vaulting of a bridge "an arch," because it is narrow with respect to the river it crosses; but if it were built above us on the ground, we should call it a waggon vault, because then we should feel the breadth of it. The real question is the nature of the curve, not the extent of space over which it is carried: and this is more the case with respect to

Gothic than to any other architecture; for, in the greater number of instances, the form of the roof is entirely dependent on the ribs; the domical shells being constructed in all kinds of inclinations, quite undeterminable by the eye, and all that is definite in their character being fixed by the curves of the ribs.

§ LXXXVI. Let us then consider our definition as including the narrowest arch, or tracery bar, as well as the broadest roof, and it will be nearly a perfect one. For the fact is, that all good Gothic is nothing more than the development, in various ways, and on every conceivable scale, of the group formed by the *pointed arch for the bearing line* below, and *the gable for the protecting line* above; and from the huge, gray, shaly slope of the cathedral roof, with its elastic pointed vaults beneath, to the slight crown-like points that enrich the smallest niche of its doorway, one law and one expression will be found in all. The modes of support and of decoration are infinitely various, but the real Fig. IX. character of the building, in all good Gothic, depends upon the single lines of the gable over the pointed arch, Fig. IX., endlessly rearranged or repeated. The larger woodcut, Fig. X. on the next page, represents three characteristic conditions of the treatment of the group: *a*, from a tomb at Verona (1328); *b*, one of the lateral porches at Abbeville; *c*, one of the uppermost points of the great western façade of Rouen Cathedral; both these last being, I believe, early work of the fifteenth century. The forms of the pure early English and French Gothic are too well known to need any notice; my reason will appear presently for choosing, by way of example, these somewhat rare conditions.

§ LXXXVII. But, first, let us try whether we cannot get the forms of the other great architectures of the world broadly expressed by relations of the same lines into which we have

compressed the Gothic. We may easily do this if the reader
will first allow me to remind him of the true nature of the

Fig. X.

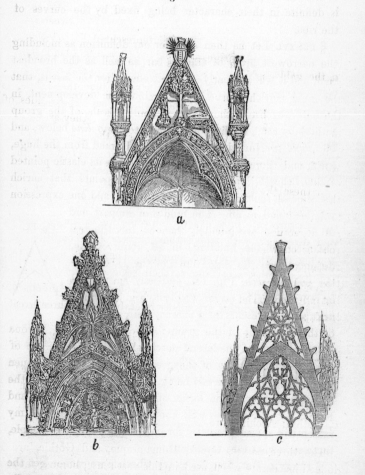

a

b   *c*

pointed arch, as it was expressed in § x. Chap. X. of the first
volume. It was said there, that it ought to be called a

" curved gable," for, strictly speaking, an " arch " cannot be
" pointed." The so-called pointed arch ought always to be
considered as a gable, with its sides curved in order to enable
them to bear pressure from without. Thus considering it,
there are but three ways in which an interval between piers
can be bridged,—the three ways represented by A B and C,
Fig. XI.,* on this page,—A, the lintel; B, the round arch;
C, the gable. All the architects in the world will never discover any other ways of bridging a space than these three;
they may vary the curve of the arch, or curve the sides of
the gable, or break them; but in doing this they are merely
modifying or subdividing, not adding to the generic forms.

§ LXXXVIII. Now there are three good architectures in the
world, and there never can be more, correspondent to each
of these three simple ways of covering in a space, which is
the original function of all architectures. And those three
architectures are *pure* exactly in proportion to the simplicity
and directness with which they express the condition of
roofing on which they are founded. They have many interesting varieties, according to their scale, manner of decoration, and character of the nations by whom they are practised,
but all their varieties are finally referable to the three great
heads :—

Fig. XI.

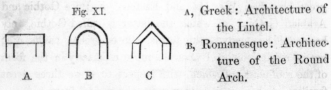

A   B   C

A, Greek : Architecture of
the Lintel.

B, Romanesque : Architec-
ture of the Round
Arch.

C, Gothic : Architecture of the Gable

The three names, Greek, Romanesque, and Gothic, are
indeed inaccurate when used in this vast sense, because they
imply national limitations; but the three architectures may

* Or by the shaded portions of Fig. XXIX. Vol. I.

nevertheless not unfitly receive their names from those nations by whom they were carried to the highest perfections. We may thus briefly state their existing varieties.

§ LXXXIX. A. GREEK: Lintel Architecture. The worst of the three; and, considered with reference to stone construction, always in some measure barbarous. Its simplest type is Stonehenge; its most refined, the Parthenon; its noblest, the Temple of Karnak.

In the hands of the Egyptian, it is sublime; in those of the Greek, pure; in those of the Roman, rich; and in those of the Renaissance builder, effeminate.

B. ROMANESQUE: Round-arch Architecture. Never thoroughly developed until Christian times. It falls into two great branches, Eastern and Western, or Byzantine and Lombardic; changing respectively in process of time, with certain helps from each other, into Arabian Gothic, and Teutonic Gothic. Its most perfect Lombardic type is the Duomo of Pisa; its most perfect Byzantine type (I believe), St. Mark's at Venice. Its highest glory is, that it has no corruption. It perishes in giving birth to another architecture as noble as itself.

C. GOTHIC: Architecture of the Gable. The daughter of the Romanesque; and, like the Romanesque, divided into two great branches, Western and Eastern, or Pure Gothic and Arabian Gothic; of which the latter is called Gothic, only because it has many Gothic forms, pointed arches, vaults, &c., but its spirit remains Byzantine, more especially in the form of the roof-mask, of which, with respect to these three great families, we have next to determine the typical form.

§ XC. For, observe, the distinctions we have hitherto been stating, depend on the form of the stones first laid from pier to pier; that is to say, of the simplest condition of roofs proper. Adding the relations of the roof-mask to these lines, we shall have the perfect type of form for each school.

In the Greek, the Western Romanesque, and Western Gothic, the roof-mask is the gable: in the Eastern Roman-

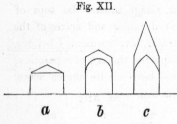

Fig. XII.

esque, and Eastern Goth-ic, it is the dome: but I have not studied the roof-ing of either of these last two groups, and shall not venture to generalize them in a diagram. But

a   b   c

the three groups, in the hands of the Western builders, may be thus simply repre-sented: *a*, Fig. XII., Greek;* *b*, Western Romanesque; *c*, Western, or true, Gothic.

Now, observe, first, that the relation of the roof-mask to the roof proper, in the Greek type, forms that pediment which gives its most striking character to the temple, and is the principal recipient of its sculptural decoration. The relation of these lines, therefore, is just as important in the Greek as in the Gothic schools.

§ XCI. Secondly, the reader must observe the difference of steepness in the Romanesque and Gothic gables. This is not an unimportant distinction, nor an undecided one. The Romanesque gable does not pass gradually into the more ele-vated form; there is a great gulf between the two; the

---

* The reader is not to suppose that Greek architecture had always, or often, flat ceilings, because I call its lintel the roof proper. He must remember I always use these terms of the first simple arrangements of materials that bridge a space; bringing in the real roof afterwards, if I can. In the case of Greek temples it would be vain to refer their structure to the real roof, for many were hypæthral, and without a roof at all. I am unfortunately more ignorant of Egyptian roofing than even of Arabian, so that I cannot bring this school into the diagram; but the gable appears to have been magnifi-cently used for a bearing roof. Vide Mr. Fergusson's section of the Pyramid of Geezeh, "Principles of Beauty in Art," Plate I., and his expressions of admiration of Egyptian roof masonry, page 201.

whole effect of all Southern architecture being dependent upon the use of the flat gable, and of all Northern upon that of the acute. I need not here dwell upon the difference between the lines of an Italian village, or the flat tops of most Italian towers, and the peaked gables and spires of the North, attaining their most fantastic developement, I believe, in Belgium: but it may be well to state the law of separation, namely, that a Gothic gable *must* have all its angles acute, and a Romanesque one *must*

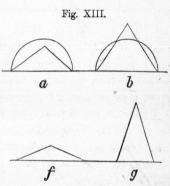

Fig. XIII.

have the upper one obtuse: or, to give the reader a simple practical rule, take any gable, *a* or *b*, Fig. XIII., and strike a semicircle on its base; if its top rises above the semicircle, as at *b*, it is a Gothic gable; if it falls beneath it, a Romanesque one; but the best forms in each group are those which are distinctly steep, or distinctly low. In the figure *f* is, perhaps, the average of Romanesque slope, and *g* of Gothic.

§ xcii. But although we do not find a transition from one school into the other in the slope of the gables, there is often a confusion between the two schools in the association of the gable with the arch below it. It has just been stated that the pure Romanesque condition is the round arch under the low gable, *a*, Fig. XIV. on next page, and the pure Gothic condition is the pointed arch under the high gable, *b*. But in the passage from one style to the other, we sometimes find the two conditions reversed; the pointed arch under a low gable, as *d*, or the round arch under a high gable, as *c*. The form *d* occurs in the tombs of Verona, and *c* in the doors of Venice.

Fig. XIV.

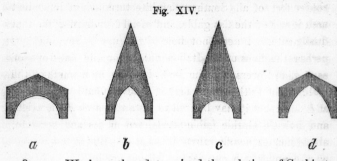

a   *b*   *c*   *d*

§ XCIII. We have thus determined the relation of Gothic to the other architectures of the world, as far as regards the main lines of its construction; but there is still one word which needs to be added to our definition of its form, with respect to a part of its decoration, which rises out of that construction. We have seen that the first condition of its

Fig. XV.

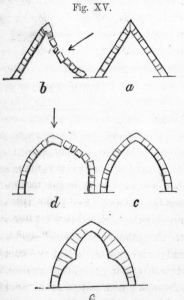

form is, that it shall have pointed arches. When Gothic is perfect, therefore, it will follow that the pointed arches must be built in the strongest possible manner.

Now, if the reader will look back to Chapter XI. of Vol. I., he will find the subject of the masonry of the pointed arch discussed at length, and the conclusion deduced, that of all possible forms of the pointed arch (a certain weight of material being given), that generically represented at *e*, Fig. XV., is the strongest. In fact, the

reader can see in a moment that the weakness of the pointed
arch is in its flanks, and that by merely thickening them gradually at this point all chance of fracture is removed. Or,
perhaps, more simply still:—Suppose a gable built of stone,
as at *a*, and pressed upon from without by a weight in the
direction of the arrow, clearly it would be liable to fall in, as
at *b*. To prevent this, we make a pointed arch of it, as at *c ;*
and now it cannot fall inwards, but if pressed upon from
above may give way outwards, as at *d*. But at last we build
as at *e*, and now it can neither fall out nor in.

§ xciv. The forms of arch thus obtained, with a pointed
projection called a cusp on each side, must for ever be delightful to the human mind, as being expressive of the utmost
strength and permanency obtainable with a given mass of
material. But it was not by any such process of reasoning,
nor with any reference to laws of construction, that the cusp
was originally invented. It is merely the special application
to the arch of the great ornamental system of FOLIATION ; or

Fig. XVI.

the adaptation of the forms of leafage which has been above insisted
upon as the principal characteristic
of Gothic Naturalism. This love of
foliage was exactly proportioned,
in its intensity, to the increase of
strength in the Gothic spirit : in
the Southern Gothic it is *soft* leafage
that is most loved ; in the Northern
thorny leafage. And if we take up
any Northern illuminated manuscript
of the great Gothic time, we shall
find every one of its leaf ornaments
surrounded by a thorny structure laid round it in gold or in
color ; sometimes apparently copied faithfully from the prickly
development of the root of the leaf in the thistle, running

11

along the stems and branches exactly as the thistle leaf does along its own stem, and with sharp spines proceeding from the points, as in Fig. XVI. At other times, and for the most part in work in the thirteenth century, the golden ground takes the form of pure and severe cusps, sometimes enclosing the leaves, sometimes filling up the forks of the branches (as in the example fig. 1. Plate I. Vol. III.), passing imperceptibly from the

Fgi. XVII.

distinctly vegetable condition (in which it is just as certainly representative of the thorn, as other parts of the design are of the bud, leaf, and fruit) into the crests on the necks, or the membranous sails of the wings, of serpents, dragons, and other grotesques, as in Fig. XVII., and into rich and vague fantasies of curvature; among which, however, the pure cusped system of the pointed arch is continually discernible, not accidentally, but designedly indicated, and connecting itself with the literally architectural portions of the design.

§ xcv. The system, then, of what is called Foliation, whether simple, as in the cusped arch, or complicated, as in tracery, rose out of this love of leafage; not that the form of the arch is intended to *imitate* a leaf, but *to be invested with the same characters of beauty which the designer had discovered in the leaf.* Observe, there is a wide difference between these two intentions. The idea that large Gothic structure, in arches and roofs, was intended to imitate vegetation is, as above noticed, untenable for an instant in the front of facts. But the Gothic builder perceived that, in the leaves which he copied for his minor decorations, there was a peculiar beauty, arising from certain characters of curvature in outline, and certain methods of subdivision and of radiation in structure. On a small scale, in his sculptures and his missal-painting, he copied the leaf or thorn itself; on a large scale he adopted from it its abstract sources of beauty, and gave the same kinds of curvatures and the same species of subdivision to the outline of his arches, so far as was consistent with their strength, never, in any single instance, suggesting the resemblance to leafage by *irregularity* of outline, but keeping the structure perfectly simple, and, as we have seen, so consistent with the best principles of masonry, that in the finest Gothic designs of arches, which are always *single* cusped (the cinquefoiled arch being licentious, though in early work often very lovely), it is literally impossible, without consulting the context of the building, to say whether the cusps have been added for the sake of beauty or of strength; nor, though in mediæval architecture they were, I believe, assuredly first employed in mere love of their picturesque form, am I absolutely certain that their earliest invention was not a structural effort. For the earliest cusps with which I am acquainted are those used in the vaults of the great galleries of the Serapeum, discovered in 1850 by M. Maniette at Memphis, and described by Colonel Hamilton in a paper read in February last before the Royal Society of Literature.* The roofs of its galleries were admirably shown in Colonel Hamilton's drawings made to scale upon the spot, and their profile is a cusped round arch, perfectly pure and simple; but whether thrown into this form for the sake of strength or of grace, I am unable to say.

§ xcvi. It is evident, however, that the structural advantage of the cusp is available only in the case of arches on a comparatively small scale. If the arch becomes very large, the projections under the flanks must become too ponderous to be secure; the suspended weight of stone would be liable

See ' Athenæum," March 5th, 1853.

to break off, and such arches are therefore never constructed with heavy cusps, but rendered secure by general mass of masonry; and what additional *appearance* of support may be thought necessary (sometimes a considerable degree of *actual* support) is given by means of tracery.

§ xcvii. Of what I stated in the second chapter of the "Seven Lamps" respecting the nature of tracery, I need repeat here only this much, that it began in the use of penetrations through the stone work of windows or walls, cut into forms which looked like stars when seen from within, and like leaves when seen from without: the name foil or feuille being universally applied to the separate lobes of their extremities, and the pleasure received from them being the same as that

Fig. XVIII.

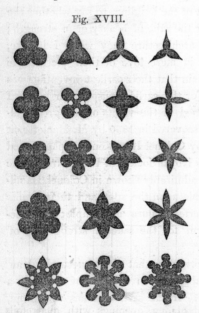

which we feel in the triple, quadruple, or other radiated leaves of vegetation, joined with the perception of a severely geometrical order and symmetry. A few of the most common forms are represented, unconfused by exterior mouldings, in Fig. XVIII., and the best traceries are nothing more than close clusters of such forms, with mouldings following their outlines.

§ xcviii. The term "foliated," therefore, is equally descriptive of the most perfect conditions both of the simple arch and of the traceries by which, in later

* See "Athenæum," March 5th, 1853.

Gothic, it is filled; and this foliation is an essential character of the style. No Gothic is either good or characteristic which is not foliated either in its arches or apertures. Sometimes the bearing arches are foliated, and the ornamentation above composed of figure sculpture; sometimes the bearing arches are plain, and the ornamentation above them is composed of foliated apertures. But the element of foliation *must* enter somewhere, or the style is imperfect. And our final definition of Gothic will, therefore, stand thus :—

"*Foliated* Architecture, which uses the pointed arch for the roof proper, and the gable for the roof-mask."

§ xcix. And now there is but one point more to be examined, and we have done.

Foliation, while it is the most distinctive and peculiar, is also the easiest method of decoration which Gothic architecture possesses; and, although in the disposition of the proportions and forms of foils, the most noble imagination may be shown, yet a builder without imagination at all, or any other faculty of design, can produce some effect upon the mass of his work by merely covering it with foolish foliation. Throw any number of crossing lines together at random, as in Fig. XIX.,

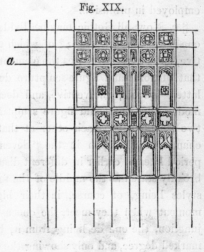

Fig. XIX.

and fill their squares and oblong openings with quatrefoils and cinquefoils, and you will immediately have what will stand, with most people, for very satisfactory Gothic. The slightest possible acquaintance with existing forms will enable any architect to vary his patterns of foliation with as much ease as he would those of a kaleidoscope, and to produce a building which the present European public will think magnificent, though there may not be, from foundation to coping, one ray of invention, or any other intellectual merit, in the whole mass of it. But floral decoration, and the disposition of mouldings, require some skill and thought; and, if they are to be agreeable at all, must be verily invented, or accurately copied. They cannot be drawn altogether at random, without becoming so commonplace as to involve detection: and although, as I have just said, the noblest imagination may be shown in the dispositions of traceries, there is far more room for its play and power when those traceries are associated with floral or animal ornament; and it is probable, *à priori*, that, wherever true invention exists, such ornament will be employed in profusion.

§ c. Now, all Gothic may be divided into two vast schools, one early, the other late;* of which the former, noble, inventive, and progressive, uses the element of foliation moderately, that of floral and figure-sculpture decoration profusely; the latter, ignoble, uninventive, and declining, uses foliation immoderately, floral and figure sculpture subordinately. The two schools touch each other at that instant of momentous change, dwelt upon in the "Seven Lamps," chap. ii., a period later or earlier in different districts, but which may be broadly stated as the middle of the fourteenth century; both styles being, of course, in their highest excellence at the moment when they meet, the one ascending to the point of junction, the one declining from it, but, at first, not in any marked degree, and only showing the characters which justify

---

* Late, and chiefly confined to Northern countries, so that the two schools may be opposed either as Early and Late Gothic, or (in the fourteenth century) as Southern and Northern Gothic.

its being above called, generically, ignoble, as its declension reaches steeper slope.

§ CI. Of these two great schools, the first uses foliation only in large and simple masses, and covers the minor members, cusps, &c., of that foliation, with various sculpture. The latter decorates foliation itself with minor foliation, and breaks its traceries into endless and lace-like subdivision of tracery.

A few instances will explain the difference clearly. Fig. 2. Plate XII. represents half of an eight-foiled aperture from Salisbury; where the element of foliation is employed in the larger disposition of the starry form; but in the decoration of the cusp it has entirely disappeared, and the ornament is floral.

But in fig. 1., which is part of a fringe round one of the later windows in Rouen Cathedral, the foliation is first carried boldly round the arch, and then each cusp of it divided into other forms of foliation. The two larger canopies of niches below, figs. 5. and 6., are respectively those seen at the flanks of the two uppermost examples of gabled Gothic in Fig. X. p. 235. Those examples were there chosen in order also to illustrate the distinction in the character of ornamentation which we are at present examining; and if the reader will look back to them, and compare their methods of treatment, he will at once be enabled to fix that distinction clearly in his mind. He will observe that in the uppermost the element of foliation is scrupulously confined to the bearing arches of the gable, and of the lateral niches, so that, on any given side of the monument, only three foliated arches are discernible. All the rest of the ornamentation is " bossy sculpture," set on the broad marble surface. On the point of the gable are set the shield and dog-crest of the Scalas, with its bronze wings, as of a dragon, thrown out from it on either side; below, an admirably sculptured oak-tree fills the centre of the field; beneath it is the death of Abel, Abel lying dead upon his face

on one side, Cain opposite, looking up to heaven in terror: the
border of the arch is formed of various leafage, alternating
with the scala shield; and the cusps are each filled by one
flower, and two broad flowing leaves. The whole is exquisitely relieved by color; the ground being of pale red
Verona marble, and the statues and foliage of white Carrara
marble, inlaid.

§ CII. The figure below it, *b*, represents the southern lateral
door of the principal church in Abbeville: the smallness of
the scale compelled me to make it somewhat heavier in the
lines of its traceries than it is in reality, but the door itself is
one of the most exquisite pieces of flamboyant Gothic in the
world; and it is interesting to see the shield introduced here,
at the point of the gable, in exactly the same manner as in the
upper example, and with precisely the same purpose,—to stay
the eye in its ascent, and to keep it from being offended by
the sharp point of the gable, the reversed angle of the shield
being so energetic as completely to balance the upward tendency of the great convergent lines. It will be seen, however,
as this example is studied, that its other decorations are altogether different from those of the Veronese tomb; that, here,
the whole effect is dependent on mere multiplications of similar
lines of tracery, sculpture being hardly introduced except in
the seated statue under the central niche, and, formerly, in
groups filling the shadowy hollows under the small niches in
the archivolt, but broken away in the Revolution. And if now
we turn to Plate XII., just passed, and examine the heads of
the two lateral niches there given from each of these monuments on a larger scale, the contrast will be yet more apparent.
The one from Abbeville (fig. 5.), though it contains much
floral work of the crisp Northern kind in its finial and crockets,
yet depends for all its effect on the various patterns of
foliation with which its spaces are filled; and it is so cut
through and through that it is hardly stronger than a piece

of lace: whereas the pinnacle from Verona depends for its effect on one broad mass of shadow, boldly shaped into the trefoil in its bearing arch; and there is no other trefoil on that side of the niche. All the rest of its decoration is floral, or by almonds and bosses; and its surface of stone is unpierced, and kept in broad light, and the mass of it thick and strong enough to stand for as many more centuries as it has already stood, scatheless, in the open street of Verona. The figures 3. and 4., above each niche, show how the same principles are carried out into the smallest details of the two edifices, 3. being the moulding which borders the gable at Abbeville, and 4. that in the same position at Verona; and as thus in all cases the distinction in their treatment remains the same, the one attracting the eye to broad sculptured *surfaces*, the other to involutions of intricate *lines*, I shall hereafter characterize the two schools, whenever I have occasion to refer to them, the one as Surface-Gothic, the other as Linear-Gothic.

§ CIII. Now observe: it is not, at present, the question, whether the form of the Veronese niche, and the design of its flower-work, be as good as they might have been; but simply, which of the two architectural principles is the greater and better. And this we cannot hesitate for an instant in deciding. The Veronese Gothic is strong in its masonry, simple in its masses, but perpetual in its variety. The late French Gothic is weak in masonry, broken in mass, and repeats the same idea continually. It is very beautiful, but the Italian Gothic is the nobler style.

§ CIV. Yet, in saying that the French Gothic repeats one idea, I mean merely that it depends too much upon the foliation of its traceries. The disposition of the traceries themselves is endlessly varied and inventive; and indeed, the mind of the French workman was, perhaps, even richer in fancy than that of the Italian, only he had been taught a less noble style. This is especially to be remembered with respect to the subor

11*

dir.ation of figure sculpture above noticed as characteristic of the later Gothic.

It is not that such sculpture is wanting; on the contrary, it is often worked into richer groups, and carried out with a perfection of execution, far greater than those which adorn the earlier buildings: but, in the early work, it is vigorous, prominent, and essential to the beauty of the whole; in the late work it is enfeebled, and shrouded in the veil of tracery, from which it may often be removed with little harm to the general effect. *

§ cv. Now the reader may rest assured that no principle of art is more absolute than this,—that a composition from which anything can be removed without doing mischief is always so far forth inferior. On this ground, therefore, if on no other, there can be no question, for a moment, which of the two schools is the greater; although there are many most noble works in the French traceried Gothic, having a sublimity of their own dependent on their extreme richness and grace of line, and for which we may be most grateful to their builders. And, indeed, the superiority of the Surface-Gothic cannot be completely felt, until we compare it with the more degraded Linear schools, as, for instance, with our own English Perpendicular. The ornaments of the Veronese niche, which we have used for our example, are by no means among the best of their school, yet they will serve our purpose for such a comparison. That of its pinnacle is composed of a single upright flowering plant, of which the stem shoots up through the centres of the leaves, and bears a pendent blossom, somewhat like that

* In many of the best French Gothic churches, the groups of figures have been all broken away at the Revolution, without much harm to the picturesqueness, though with grievous loss to the historical value of the architecture: whereas, if from the niche at Verona we were to remove its floral ornaments, and the statue beneath it, nothing would remain but a rude square trefoiled shell, utterly valueless, or even ugly.

of the imperial lily. The leaves are thrown back from the stem with singular grace and freedom, and foreshortened, as if by a skilful painter, in the shallow marble relief. Their arrangement is roughly shown in the little woodcut at the side (Fig. XX.); and if the reader will simply try the experiment for himself, — first, of covering a piece of paper with crossed lines, as if for accounts, and filling all the interstices with any foliation that comes into his head, as in Figure XIX. above; and then, of trying to fill the point of a gable with a piece of leafage like that in Figure XX., putting the figure itself aside, — he will presently find that more thought and invention are required to design this single minute pinnacle, than to cover acres of ground with English perpendicular.

Fig XX.

§ cvi. We have now, I believe, obtained a sufficiently accurate knowledge both of the spirit and form of Gothic architecture; but it may, perhaps, be useful to the general reader, if, in conclusion, I set down a few plain and practical rules for determining, in every instance, whether a given building be good Gothic or not, and, if not Gothic, whether its architecture is of a kind which will probably reward the pains of careful examination.

§ cvii. First. Look if the roof rises in a steep gable, high above the walls. If it does not do this, there is something wrong; the building is not quite pure Gothic, or has been altered.

§ cviii. Secondly. Look if the principal windows and doors have pointed arches with gables over them. If not pointed arches, the building is not Gothic; if they have not any gables over them, it is either not pure, or not first-rate.

If, however, it has the steep roof, the pointed arch, and gable all united, it is nearly certain to be a Gothic building of a very fine time.

§ CIX. Thirdly. Look if the arches are cusped, or apertures foliated. If the building has met the first two conditions, it is sure to be foliated somewhere; but, if not everywhere, the parts which are unfoliated are imperfect, unless they are large bearing arches, or small and sharp arches in groups, forming a kind of foliation by their own multiplicity, and relieved by sculpture and rich mouldings. The upper windows, for instance, in the east end of Westminster Abbey are imperfect for want of foliation. If there be no foliation anywhere, the building is assuredly imperfect Gothic.

§ CX. Fourthly. If the building meets all the first three conditions, look if its arches in general, whether of windows and doors, or of minor ornamentation, are carried on *true shafts with bases and capitals*. If they are, then the building is assuredly of the finest Gothic style. It may still, perhaps, be an imitation, a feeble copy, or a bad example of a noble style; but the manner of it, having met all these four conditions, is assuredly first-rate.

If its apertures have not shafts and capitals, look if they are plain openings in the walls, studiously simple, and unmoulded at the sides; as, for instance, the arch in Plate XIX. Vol. I. If so, the building may still be of the finest Gothic, adapted to some domestic or military service. But if the sides of the window be moulded, and yet there are no capitals at the spring of the arch, it is assuredly of an inferior school.

This is all that is necessary to determine whether the building be of a fine Gothic style. The next tests to be applied are in order to discover whether it be good architecture or not : for it may be very impure Gothic, and yet very noble architecture ; or it may be very pure Gothic, and yet, if a copy, or originally raised by an ungifted builder, very bad architecture.

If it belong to any of the great schools of color, its criticism becomes as complicated, and needs as much care, as that of a piece of music, and no general rules for it can be given ; but if not—

§ cxi. First. See if it looks as if it had been built by strong men ; if it has the sort of roughness, and largeness, and non-chalance, mixed in places with the exquisite tenderness which seems always to be the sign-manual of the broad vision, and massy power of men who can see *past* the work they are doing, and betray here and there something like disdain for it. If the building has this character, it is much already in its favor ; it will go hard but it proves a noble one. If it has not this, but is altogether accurate, minute, and scrupulous in its workmanship, it must belong to either the very best or the very worst of schools: the very best, in which exquisite design is wrought out with untiring and conscientious care, as in the Giottesque Gothic ; or the very worst, in which mechanism has taken the place of design. It is more likely, in general, that it should belong to the worst than the best : so that, on the whole, very accurate workmanship is to be esteemed a bad sign ; and if there is nothing remarkable about the building but its precision, it may be passed at once with contempt.

§ cxii. Secondly. Observe if it be irregular, its different parts fitting themselves to different purposes, no one caring what becomes of them, so that they do their work. If one part always answers accurately to another part, it is sure to be a bad building ; and the greater and more conspicuous the irregularities, the greater the chances are that it is a good one. For instance, in the Ducal Palace, of which a rough woodcut is given in Chap. VIII., the general idea is sternly symmetrical; but two windows are lower than the rest of the six; and if the reader will count the arches of the small arcade as far as to the great balcony, he will find it is not in the centre, but set to the right-hand side by the whole width of one of those arches. We may be pretty sure that the building is a good one; none but a master of his craft would have ventured to do this.

§ CXIII. Thirdly. Observe if all the traceries, capitals, and other ornaments are of perpetually varied design. If not, the work is assuredly bad.

§ CXIV. Lastly. *Read* the sculpture. Preparatory to reading it, you will have to discover whether it is legible (and, if legible, it is nearly certain to be worth reading). On a good building, the sculpture is *always* so set, and on such a scale, that at the ordinary distance from which the edifice is seen, the sculpture shall be thoroughly intelligible and interesting. In order to accomplish this, the uppermost statues will be ten or twelve feet high, and the upper ornamentation will be colossal, increasing in fineness as it descends, till on the foundation it will often be wrought as if for a precious cabinet in a king's chamber; but the spectator will not notice that the upper sculptures are colossal. He will merely feel that he can see them plainly, and make them all out at his ease.

And, having ascertained this, let him set himself to read them. Thenceforward the criticism of the building is to be conducted precisely on the same principles as that of a book; and it must depend on the knowledge, feeling, and not a little on the industry and perseverance of the reader, whether, even in the case of the best works, he either perceive them to be great, or feel them to be entertaining.

CHAPTER VII.

GOTHIC PALACES.

§ I. THE buildings out of the remnants of which we have
endeavored to recover some conception of the appearance of
Venice during the Byzantine period, contribute hardly anything at this day to the effect of the streets of the city.
They are too few and too much defaced to attract the eye or
influence the feelings. The charm which Venice still possesses, and which for the last fifty years has rendered it the
favorite haunt of all the painters of picturesque subject, is
owing to the effect of the palaces belonging to the period we
have now to examine, mingled with those of the Renaissance.

This effect is produced in two different ways. The Renaissance palaces are not more picturesque in themselves than the
club-houses of Pall Mall; but they become delightful by the
contrast of their severity and refinement with the rich and
rude confusion of the sea life beneath them, and of their
white and solid masonry with the green waves. Remove
from beneath them the orange sails of the fishing boats, the
black gliding of the gondolas, the cumbered decks and rough
crews of the barges of traffic, and the fretfulness of the green
water along their foundations, and the Renaissance palaces
possess no more interest than those of London or Paris. But
the Gothic palaces are picturesque in themselves, and wield
over us an independent power. Sea and sky, and every other
accessory might be taken away from them, and still they

would be beautiful and strange. They are not less striking in the loneliest streets of Padua and Vicenza (where many were built during the period of the Venetian authority in those cities) than in the most crowded thoroughfares of Venice itself; and if they could be transported into the midst of London, they would still not altogether lose their power over the feelings.

§ II. The best proof of this is in the perpetual attractiveness of all pictures, however poor in skill, which have taken for their subject the principal of these Gothic buildings, the Ducal palace. In spite of all architectural theories and teachings, the paintings of this building are always felt to be delightful; we cannot be wearied by them, though often sorely tried; but we are not put to the same trial in the case of the palaces of the Renaissance. They are never drawn singly, or as the principal subject, nor can they be. The building which faces the Ducal Palace on the opposite side of the Piazzetta is cele-brated among architects, but it is not familiar to our eyes; it is painted only incidentally, for the completion, not the sub-ject, of a Venetian scene; and even the Renaissance arcades of St. Mark's Place, though frequently painted, are always treated as a mere avenue to its Byzantine church and colossal tower. And the Ducal Palace itself owes the peculiar charm which we have hitherto felt, not so much to its greater size as compared with other Gothic buildings, or nobler design (for it never yet has been rightly drawn), as to its comparative iso-lation. The other Gothic structures are as much injured by the continual juxtaposition of the Renaissance palaces, as the latter are aided by it; they exhaust their own life by breath-ing it into the Renaissance coldness: but the Ducal Palace stands comparatively alone, and fully expresses the Gothic power.

§ III. And it is just that it should be so seen, for it is the original of nearly all the rest. It is not the elaborate and more

studied developement of a national style, but the great and
sudden invention of one man, instantly forming a national
style, and becoming the model for the imitation of every
architect in Venice for upwards of a century. It was the
determination of this one fact which occupied me the greater
part of the time I spent in Venice. It had always appeared
to me most strange that there should be in no part of the city
any incipient or imperfect types of the form of the Ducal
Palace; it was difficult to believe that so mighty a building
had been the conception of one man, not only in disposition
and detail, but in style; and yet impossible, had it been otherwise, but that some early examples of approximate Gothic
form must exist. There is not one. The palaces built between
the final cessation of the Byzantine style, about 1300, and the
date of the Ducal Palace (1320—1350), are all completely
distinct in character, so distinct that I at first intended the
account of them to form a separate section of this volume;
and there is literally *no* transitional form between them and
the perfection of the Ducal Palace. Every Gothic building in
Venice which resembles the latter is a copy of it. I do not
mean that there was no Gothic in Venice before the Ducal
Palace, but that the mode of its application to domestic architecture had not been determined. The real root of the Ducal
Palace is the apse of the church of the Frari. The traceries
of that apse, though earlier and ruder in workmanship, are
nearly the same in mouldings, and precisely the same in treatment (especially in the placing of the lions' heads), as those
of the great Ducal Arcade; and the originality of thought in
the architect of the Ducal Palace consists in his having adapted
those traceries, in a more highly developed and finished form,
to civil uses. In the apse of the church they form narrow and
tall window lights, somewhat more massive than those of
Northern Gothic, but similar in application: the thing to be
done was to adapt these traceries to the forms of domestic

building necessitated by national usage. The early palaces
consisted, as we have seen, of arcades sustaining walls faced
with marble, rather broad and long than elevated. This form
was kept for the Ducal Palace; but instead of round arches
from shaft to shaft, the Frari traceries were substituted, with
two essential modifica-
tions. Besides being enormously increased in scale
and thickness, that they
might better bear the su-
perincumbent weight, the
quatrefoil, which in the
Frari windows is above
the arch, as at *a*, Fig.

Fig. XXI.

a   *b*

XXI., was, in the Ducal Palace, put between the arches, as at
b ; the main reason for this alteration being that the bearing
power of the arches, which was now to be trusted with the
weight of a wall forty feet high,* was thus
thrown *between* the quatrefoils, instead of
under them, and thereby applied at far better advantage. And, in the second place,
the joints of the masonry were changed. In
the Frari (as often also in St. John and St.
Paul's) the tracery is formed of two simple
cross bars or slabs of stone, pierced into
the requisite forms, and separated by a horizontal joint, just on a level with the lowest
cusp of the quatrefoils, as seen in Fig. XXI. *a.* But at the
Ducal Palace the horizontal joint is in the centre of the quatrefoils, and two others are introduced beneath it at right angles

Fig. XXII.

a

b

---

* 38 ft. 2 in., without its cornice, which is 10 inches deep, and st stains
pinnacles of stone 7 feet high. I was enabled to get the measures by a scaf
folding erected in 1851 to repair the front.

to the run of the mouldings, as seen in Fig. XXI. *b*.* The Ducal Palace builder was sternly resolute in carrying out this rule of masonry. In the traceries of the large upper windows, where the cusps are cut through as in the quatrefoil Fig. XXII., the lower cusp is left partly solid, as at *a*, merely that the joint *a b* may have its right place and direction.

§ IV. The ascertaining the formation of the Ducal Palace traceries from those of the Frari, and its priority to all other buildings which resemble it in Venice, rewarded me for a great deal of uninteresting labor in the examination of mouldings and other minor features of the Gothic palaces, in which alone the internal evidence of their date was to be discovered, there being no historical records whatever respecting them. But the accumulation of details on which the complete proof of the fact depends, could not either be brought within the compass of this volume, or be made in anywise interesting to the general reader. I shall therefore, without involving myself in any discussion, give a brief account of the developement of Gothic design in Venice, as I believe it to have taken place. I shall possibly be able at some future period so to compress the evidence on which my conviction rests, as to render it intelligible to the public, while, in the meantime, some of the more essential points of it are thrown together in the Appendix, and in the history of the Ducal Palace given in the next chapter.

§ V. According, then, to the statement just made, the Gothic architecture of Venice is divided into two great periods: one, in which, while various irregular Gothic tendencies are exhibited, no consistent type of domestic building was developed; the other, in which a formed and consistent school of domestic architecture resulted from the direct imitation of the

---

* I believe the necessary upper joint is vertical, through the uppermost lobe of the quatrefoil, as in the figure; but I have lost my memorandum of this joint.

great design of the Ducal Palace. We must deal with these two periods separately; the first of them being that which has been often above alluded to, under the name of the transitional period.

We shall consider in succession the general form, the windows, doors, balconies, and parapets, of the Gothic palaces belonging to each of these periods.

§ VI. First. General Form.

We have seen that the wrecks of the Byzantine palaces consisted merely of upper and lower arcades surrounding cortiles; the disposition of the interiors being now entirely changed, and their original condition untraceable. The entrances to these early buildings are, for the most part, merely large circular arches, the central features of their continuous arcades: they do not present us with definitely separated windows and doors.

But a great change takes place in the Gothic period. These long arcades break, as it were, into pieces, and coagulate into central and lateral windows, and small arched doors, pierced in great surfaces of brick wall. The sea story of a Byzantine palace consists of seven, nine, or more arches in a continuous line; but the sea story of a Gothic palace consists of a door and one or two windows on each side, as in a modern house. The first story of a Byzantine palace consists of, perhaps, eighteen or twenty arches, reaching from one side of the house to the other; the first story of a Gothic palace consists of a window of four or five lights in the centre, and one or two single windows on each side. The germ, however, of the Gothic arrangement is already found in the Byzantine, where, as we have seen, the arcades, though continuous, are always composed of a central mass and two wings of smaller arches. The central group becomes the door or the middle light of the Gothic palace, and the wings break into its lateral windows.

§ VII. But the most essential difference in the entire arrangement, is the loss of the unity of conception which regulated Byzantine composition. How subtle the sense of gradation which disposed the magnitudes of the early palaces we have seen already, but I have not hitherto noticed that the Byzantine work was centralized in its ornamentation as much as in its proportions. Not only were the lateral capitals and archivolts kept comparatively plain, while the central ones were sculptured, but the midmost piece of sculpture, whatever it might be,—capital, inlaid circle, or architrave,—was always made superior to the rest. In the Fondaco de' Turchi, for instance, the midmost capital of the upper arcade is the key to the whole group, larger and more studied than all the rest; and the lateral ones are so disposed as to answer each other on the opposite sides, thus, A being put for the central one,

F E B C **A** C B E F,

a sudden break of the system being admitted in one unique capital at the extremity of the series.

§ VIII. Now, long after the Byzantine arcades had been contracted into windows, this system of centralization was more or less maintained; and in all the early groups of windows of five lights the midmost capital is different from the two on each side of it, which always correspond. So strictly is this the case, that whenever the capitals of any group of windows are not centralized in this manner, but are either entirely like each other, or all different, so as to show no correspondence, it is a certain proof, even if no other should exist, of the comparative lateness of the building.

In every group of windows in Venice which I was able to examine, and which were centralized in this manner, I found evidence in their mouldings of their being *anterior* to the Ducal Palace. That palace did away with the subtle proportion and centralization of the Byzantine. Its arches are of equa.

width, and its capitals are all different and ungrouped; some, indeed, are larger than the rest, but this is not for the sake of proportion, only for particular service when more weight is to be borne. But, among other evidences of the early date of the sea façade of that building, is one subtle and delicate concession to the system of centralization which is finally closed. The capitals of the upper arcade are, as I said, all different, and show no arranged correspondence with each other; but *the central one is of pure Parian marble*, while all the others are of Istrian stone.

The bold decoration of the central window and balcony above, in the Ducal Palace, is only a peculiar expression of the principality of the central window, which was characteristic of the Gothic period not less than of the Byzantine. In the private palaces the central windows become of importance by their number of lights; in the Ducal Palace such an arrangement was, for various reasons, inconvenient, and the central window, which, so far from being more important than the others, is every way inferior in design to the two at the eastern extremity of the façade, was nevertheless made the leading feature by its noble canopy and balcony.

§ ix. Such being the principal differences in the general conception of the Byzantine and Gothic palaces, the particulars in the treatment of the latter are easily stated. The marble facings are gradually removed from the walls; and the bare brick either stands forth confessed boldly, contrasted with the marble shafts and archivolts of the windows, or it is covered with stucco painted in fresco, of which more hereafter. The Ducal Palace, as in all other respects, is an exact expression of the middle point in the change. It still retains marble facing; but instead of being disposed in slabs as in the Byzantine times, it is applied in solid bricks or blocks of marble, $11\frac{1}{2}$ inches long, by 6 inches high.

The stories of the Gothic palaces are divided by string

courses, considerably bolder in projection than those of the Byzantines, and more highly decorated; and while the angles of the Byzantine palaces are quite sharp and pure, those of the Gothic palaces are wrought into a chamfer, filled by small twisted shafts which have capitals under the cornice of each story.

§ x. These capitals are little observed in the general effect, but the shafts are of essential importance in giving an aspect of firmness to the angle; a point of peculiar necessity in Venice, where, owing to the various convolutions of the canals, the angles of the palaces are not only frequent, but often necessarily *acute*, every inch of ground being valuable. In other cities, the appearance as well as the assurance of stability can always be secured by the use of massy stones, as in the fortress palaces of Florence; but it must have been always desirable at Venice to build as lightly as possible, in consequence of the comparative insecurity of the foundations. The early palaces were, as we have seen, perfect models of grace and lightness, and the Gothic, which followed, though much more massive in the style of its details, never admitted more weight into its structure than was absolutely necessary for its strength. Hence, every Gothic palace has the appearance of enclosing as many rooms, and attaining as much strength, as is possible, with a minimum quantity of brick and stone. The traceries of the windows, which in Northern Gothic only support the *glass*, at Venice support the *building ;* and thus the greater ponderousness of the *traceries* is only an indication of the greater lightness of the *structure.* Hence, when the Renaissance architects give their opinions as to the stability of the Ducal Palace when injured by fire, one of them, Christofore Sorte, says, that he thinks it by no means laudable that the " Serenissimo Dominio " of the Venetian senate "should live in a palace built in the air."* And again, Andrea della

* "Dice, che non lauda per alcun modo di metter questo Serenissimo

Valle says, that* "the wall of the saloon is thicker by fifteen inches than the shafts below it, projecting nine inches within, and six without, *standing as if in the air,* above the piazza;† and yet this wall is so nobly and strongly knit together, that Rusconi, though himself altogether devoted to the Renaissance school, declares that the fire which had destroyed the whole interior of the palace had done this wall no more harm than the bite of a fly to an elephant. "Troveremo che el danno che ha patito queste muraglie sarà conforme alla beccatura d' una mosca fatta ad un elefante."‡

§ XI. And so in all the other palaces built at the time, consummate strength was joined with a lightness of form and sparingness of material which rendered it eminently desirable that the eye should be convinced, by every possible expedient, of the stability of the building; and these twisted pillars at the angles are not among the least important means adopted for this purpose, for they seem to bind the walls together as a cable binds a chest. In the Ducal Palace, where they are carried up the angle of an unbroken wall forty feet high, they are divided into portions, gradually diminishing in length towards the top, by circular bands or rings, set with the nail-head or dog-tooth ornament, vigorously projecting, and giving the column nearly the aspect of the stalk of a reed; its diminishing proportions being exactly arranged as they are by Nature in all jointed plants. At the top of the palace, like the wheat-stalk branching into the ear of corn, it expands

Dominio in tanto pericolo d' habitar un palazzo fabricato in aria."—*Pareri di XV. Architetti, con illustrazioni dell' Abbate Giuseppe Cadorin,* (Venice, 1838) p. 104.

* "Il muro della sala è più grosso delle colonne sott' esso piedi uno e onze tre, et posto in modo che onze sei sta come in aere sopra la piazza, et onze nove dentro."—*Pareri di XV. Architetti,* p. 47.

† Compare "Seven Lamps," chap. iii. § 7.

‡ Pareri, above quoted, p. 21.

into a small niche with a pointed canopy, which joins with
the fantastic parapet in at once relieving, and yet making
more notable by its contrast, the weight of massy wall below.
The arrangement is seen in the woodcut, Chap. VIII.; the
angle shafts being slightly exaggerated in thickness, together
with their joints, as otherwise they would hardly have been
intelligible on so small a scale.

The Ducal Palace is peculiar in these niches at the angles,
which throughout the rest of the city appear on churches
only; but some may perhaps have been removed by restorations, together with the parapets with which they were
associated.

§ XII. Of these roof parapets of Venice, it has been already
noticed that the examples which remain differ from those of
all other cities of Italy in their purely ornamental character.
(Chap. I. § XII.) They are not battlements, properly so-called;
still less machicolated cornices, such as crown the fortress
palaces of the great mainland nobles; but merely adaptations
of the light and crown-like ornaments which crest the walls
of the Arabian mosque. Nor are even these generally used

Fig. XXIII.

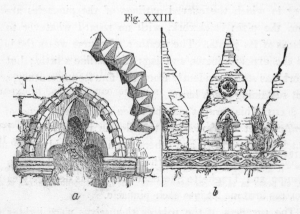

a   b

on the main walls of the palaces themselves. They occur on
12

the Ducal Palace, on the Casa d' Oro, and, some years back, were still standing on the Fondaco de' Turchi; but the majority of the Gothic Palaces have the plain dog-tooth cornice under the tiled projecting roof (Vol. I. Chap. XIV. § IV.); and the highly decorated parapet is employed only on the tops of walls which surround courts or gardens, and which, without such decoration, would have been utterly devoid of interest. Fig. XXIII. represents, at *b*, part of a parapet of this kind which surrounds the court-yard of a palace in the Calle del Bagatin, between San G. Grisostomo, and San Canzian: the whole is of brick, and the mouldings peculiarly sharp and varied; the height of each separate pinnacle being about four feet, crowning a wall twelve or fifteen feet high: a piece of the moulding which surrounds the quatrefoil is given larger in the figure at *a*, together with the top of the small arch below, having the common Venetian dentil round it, and a delicate little moulding with dog-tooth ornament to carry the flanks of the arch. The moulding of the brick is throughout sharp and beautiful in the highest degree. One of the most curious points about it is the careless way in which the curved outlines of the pinnacles are cut into the plain brickwork, with no regard whatever to the places of its joints. The weather of course wears the bricks at the exposed joints, and jags the outline a little; but the work has stood, evidently from the fourteenth century, without sustaining much harm.

§ XIII. This parapet may be taken as a general type of the *wall*-parapet of Venice in the Gothic period; some being much less decorated, and others much more richly: the most beautiful in Venice is in the little Calle, opening on the Campo and Traghetto San Samuele; it has delicately carved devices in stone let into each pinnacle.

The parapets of the palaces themselves were lighter and more fantastic, consisting of narrow lance-like spires of marble, set between the broader pinnacles, which were in such cases generally carved into the form of a fleur-de-lis : the French word gives the reader the best idea of the form, though he must remember that this use of the lily for the parapets has nothing to do with France, but is the carrying out of the Byzantine system of floral ornamentation, which introduced the outline of the lily everywhere; so that I have found it convenient to call its most beautiful capitals, the *lily* capitals of St. Mark's. But the occurrence of this flower, more distinctly than usual, on the battlements of the Ducal Palace, was the cause of some curious political speculation in the year 1511, when a piece of one of these battlements was shaken down by the great earthquake of that year. Sanuto notes in his diary that "the piece that fell was just that which bore the lily," and records sundry sinister anticipations, founded on this important omen, of impending danger to the adverse French power. As there happens, in the Ducal Palace, to be a joint in the pinnacles which exactly separates the "part which bears the lily" from that which is fastened to the cornice, it is no wonder that the omen proved fallacious.

§ XIV. The decorations of the parapet were completed by attaching gilded balls of metal to the extremities of the leaves of the lilies, and of the intermediate spires, so as literally to form for the wall a diadem of silver touched upon the points with gold ; the image being rendered still more distinct in the Casa d' Oro, by variation in the height of the pinnacles, the highest being in the centre of the front.

Very few of these light roof parapets now remain; they are, of course, the part of the building which dilapidation first renders it necessary to remove. That of the Ducal Palace, however, though often, I doubt not, restored, retains much of the ancient form, and is exceedingly beautiful, though it has no appearance from below of being intended for pro-tection, but serves only, by its extreme lightness, to relieve

the eye when wearied by the breadth of wall beneath; it is
nevertheless a most serviceable defence for any person walking
along the edge of the roof. It has some appearance of
insecurity, owing to the entire independence of the pieces of
stone composing it, which, though of course fastened by iron,
look as if they stood balanced on the cornice like the pillars
of Stonehenge; but I have never heard of its having been
disturbed by anything short of an earthquake; and, as we
have seen, even the great earthquake of 1511, though it much
injured the Gorne, or battlements of the Casa d' Oro, and
threw down several statues at St. Mark's,* only shook one lily
from the brow of the Ducal Palace.

§ xv. Although, however, these light and fantastic forms
appear to have been universal in the battlements meant primarily for decoration, there was another condition of parapet
altogether constructed for the protection of persons walking
on the roofs or in the galleries of the churches, and from these
more substantial and simple defences, the BALCONIES, to which
the Gothic palaces owe half of their picturesque effect, were
immediately derived; the balcony being, in fact, nothing more
than a portion of such roof parapets arranged round a projecting window-sill sustained on brackets, as in the central
example of the annexed figure. We must, therefore, examine

---

* It is a curious proof how completely, even so early as the beginning of
the sixteenth century, the Venetians had lost the habit of *reading* the
religious art of their ancient churches, that Sanuto, describing this injury,
says, that "four of the *Kings* in marble fell from their pinnacles above the
front, at St. Mark's church;" and presently afterwards corrects his mistake,
and apologises for it thus: "These were four saints, St. Constantine, St. De-
metrius, St. George, and St. Theodore, all Greek saints. *They look like Kings.*"
Observe the perfect, because unintentional, praise given to the old sculptor.

I quote the passage from the translation of these precious diaries of Sanuto,
by my friend Mr. Rawdon Brown, a translation which I hope will some day
become a standard book in English libraries.

these defensive balustrades and the derivative balconies consecutively.

§ XVI. Obviously, a parapet
with an unbroken edge, upon
which the arm may rest (a
condition above noticed, Vol.
I. p. 157., as essential to the
proper performance of its
duty), can be constructed only
in one of three ways. It must
either be (1.) of solid stone,
decorated, if at all, by mere
surface sculpture, as in the
uppermost example in the annexed figure; or (2.) pierced
into some kind of tracery, as in
the second; or (3.) composed
of small pillars carrying a level
bar of stone, as in the third;
this last condition being, in a
diseased and swollen form,
familiar to us in the balustrades of our bridges.*

Fig. XXIV.

§ XVII. (1.) Of these three kinds, the first, which is employed for the pulpit at Torcello and in the nave of St. Mark's,
whence the uppermost example is taken, is beautiful when
sculpture so rich can be employed upon it; but it is liable to
objection, first, because it is heavy and unlike a parapet when
seen from below; and, secondly, because it is inconvenient in
use. The position of leaning over a balcony becomes cramped
and painful if long continued, unless the foot can be sometimes
advanced *beneath* the ledge on which the arm leans, i. e.
between the balusters or traceries, which of course cannot be
done in the solid parapet: it is also more agreeable to be able

* I am not speaking here of iron balconies. See below, § XXII.

to see partially down through the penetrations, than to be obliged to lean far over the edge. The solid parapet was rarely used in Venice after the earlier ages.

§ XVIII. (2.) The Traceried Parapet is chiefly used in the Gothic of the North, from which the above example, in the Casa Contarini Fasan, is directly derived. It is, when well designed, the richest and most beautiful of all forms, and many of the best buildings of France and Germany are dependent for half their effect upon it; its only fault being a slight tendency to fantasticism. It was never frankly received in Venice, where the architects had unfortunately returned to the Renaissance forms before the flamboyant parapets were fully developed in the North; but, in the early stage of the Renaissance, a kind of pierced parapet was employed, founded

Fig. XXV.

on the old Byzantine interwoven traceries; that is to say, the slab of stone was pierced here and there with holes, and then an interwoven pattern traced on the surface round them. The difference in system will be understood in a moment by comparing the uppermost example in the figure at the side, which is a Northern parapet from the Cathedral of Abbeville, with the lowest, from a secret chamber in the Casa Foscari. It will be seen that the Venetian one is far more simple and severe, yet singularly piquant, the black penetrations telling sharply on the plain broad surface. Far inferior in beauty, it has yet one point of superiority to that of Abbeville, that it proclaims itself more definitely to be stone. The other has rather the look of lace.

The intermediate figure is a panel of the main balcony of the Ducal Palace, and is introduced here as being an exactly transitional condition between the Northern and Venetian types. It was built when the German Gothic workmen were exercising considerable influence over those in Venice, and there was some chance of the Northern parapet introducing itself. It actually did so, as above shown, in the Casa Contarini Fasan, but was for the most part stoutly resisted and kept at bay by the Byzantine form, the lowest in the last figure, until that form itself was displaced by the common, vulgar, Renaissance baluster; a grievous loss, for the severe pierced type was capable of a variety as endless as the fantasticism of our own Anglo-Saxon manuscript ornamentation.

§ XIX. (3.) The Baluster Parapet. Long before the idea of tracery had suggested itself to the minds either of Venetian or any other architects, it had, of course, been necessary to provide protection for galleries, edges of roofs, &c.; and the most natural form in which such protection could be obtained was that of a horizontal bar or hand-rail, sustained upon short shafts or balusters, as in Fig. XXIV. p. 269. This form was, above all others, likely to be adopted where variations of Greek or Roman pillared architecture were universal in the larger masses of the building; the parapet became itself a small series of columns, with capitals and architraves; and whether the cross-bar laid upon them should be simply horizontal, and in contact with their capitals, or sustained by mimic arches, round or pointed, depended entirely on the system adopted in the rest of the work. Where the large arches were round, the small balustrade arches would be so likewise; where those were pointed, these would become so in sympathy with them.

§ XX. Unfortunately, wherever a balcony or parapet is used in an inhabited house, it is, of course, the part of the structure which first suffers from dilapidation, as well as that of which the security is most anxiously cared for. The main pillars of a casement may stand for centuries unshaken under the steady weight of the superincumbent wall, but the cement and various insetting of the balconies are sure to be disturbed by the irregular pressures and impulses of the persons leaning on them; while, whatever extremity of decay may be allowed in other parts of the building, the balcony, as soon as it seems dangerous, will assuredly be removed or restored. The reader will not, if he considers this, be surprised to hear that, among all the remnants of the Venetian domestic architecture of the eleventh, twelfth, and thirteenth centuries, there is not a single instance of the original balconies being preserved. The palace mentioned below (§ XXXII.), in the piazza of the Rialto, has, indeed, solid slabs of stone between its shafts, but I cannot be certain that they are of the same period; if they are, this is the only existing example of the form of protection employed for casements during this transitional period, and it cannot be reasoned from as being the general one.

§ XXI. It is only, therefore, in the churches of Torcello, Murano, and St. Mark's, that the ancient forms of gallery defence may still be seen. At Murano, between the pillars of the apse, a beautiful balustrade is employed, of which a single arch is given in the Plate opposite, fig. 4., with its section, fig. 5.; and at St. Mark's, a noble round-arched parapet, with small pillars of precisely the same form as those of Murano, but shorter, and bound at the angles into groups of four by the serpentine knot so often occurring in Lombardic work, runs round the whole exterior of the lower story of the church, and round great part of its interior galleries, alternating with the more fantastic form, fig. 6. In domestic architecture, the remains of the original balconies begin to occur first in the beginning of the fourteenth century, when the round arch had entirely disappeared; and the parapet consists, almost without exception, of a series of small trefoiled arches, cut boldly through a bar of stone which rests upon the shafts, at first very simple, and generally adorned with a cross at the point of each arch, as in fig. 7. in the last Plate, which gives the angle of such a balcony on a large scale; but soon enriched into the beautiful conditions, figs. 2 and 3., and sustained on brackets formed of lions' heads, as seen in the central example of their entire effect, fig. 1.

§ XXII. In later periods, the round arches return; then the interwoven Byzantine form; and finally, as above noticed, the common English or classical balustrade; of which, however, exquisite examples, for grace and variety of outline, are found designed in the backgrounds of Paul Veronese. I could willingly follow out this subject fully, but it is impossible to do so without leaving Venice; for the chief city of Italy, as far as regards the strict effect of the balcony, is Verona; and if we were once to lose ourselves among the sweet shadows of its lonely streets, where the falling branches of the flowers stream like fountains through the pierced traceries of the marble, there is no saying whether we might soon be able to return to our immediate work. Yet before leaving the subject of the balcony * altogether, I must allude, for a moment, to the peculiar treatment of the iron-work out of which it is frequently wrought on the mainland of Italy — never in Venice. The iron is always wrought, not cast, beaten first into thin leaves, and then cut either into strips or bands, two or three inches broad, which are bent into various curves to form the sides of the balcony, or else into actual leafage, sweeping and free, like the leaves of nature, with which it is richly decorated. There is no end to the variety of design, no limit to the lightness and flow of the forms, which the workman can produce out of iron treated in this manner; and it is very nearly as

* Some details respecting the mechanical structure of the Venetian balcony are given in the final Appendix.

12*

impossible for any metal-work, so handled, to be poor, or igno
ble in effect, as it is for cast metal-work to be otherwise.

§ XXIII. We have next to examine those features of the
Gothic palaces in which the transitions of their architecture
are most distinctly traceable; namely, the arches of the windows and doors.

It has already been repeatedly stated, that the Gothic style
had formed itself completely on the mainland, while the
Byzantines still retained their influence at Venice; and that
the history of early Venetian Gothic is therefore not that of
a school taking new forms independently of external influence,
but the history of the struggle of the Byzantine manner with
a contemporary style quite as perfectly organized as itself, and
far more energetic. And this struggle is exhibited partly in
the gradual change of the Byzantine architecture into other
forms, and partly by isolated examples of genuine Gothic taken
prisoner, as it were, in the contest; or rather entangled among
the enemy's forces, and maintaining their ground till their
friends came up to sustain them. Let us first follow the steps
of the gradual change, and then give some brief account of
the various advanced guards and forlorn hopes of the Gothic
attacking force.

§ XXIV. The uppermost shaded series of six forms of windows
in Plate XIV. opposite, represents, at a glance, the modifications of this feature in Venetian palaces, from the eleventh to
the fifteenth century. Fig. 1. is Byzantine, of the eleventh
and twelfth centuries; figs. 2 and 3. transitional, of the thirteenth and early fourteenth centuries; figs. 4 and 5. pure
Gothic, of the thirteenth, fourteenth and early fifteenth; and
fig. 6. late Gothic, of the fifteenth century, distinguished by
its added finial. Fig. 4. is the longest-lived of all these forms:
it occurs first in the thirteenth century; and, sustaining modifications only in its mouldings, is found also in the middle of
the fifteenth.

I shall call these the six orders* of Venetian windows, and when I speak of a window of the fourth, second, or sixth order, the reader will only have to refer to the numerals at the top of Plate XIV.

Then the series below shows the principal forms found in each period, belonging to each several order; except 1 *b* to 1 *c*, and the two lower series, numbered 7 to 16, which are types of Venetian doors.

§ xxv. We shall now be able, without any difficulty, to follow the course of transition, beginning with the first order, 1 and 1 *a*, in the second row. The horse-shoe arch, 1 *b*, is the door-head commonly associated with it, and the other three in the same row occur in St. Mark's exclusively; 1 *c* being used in the nave, in order to give a greater appearance of lightness to its great lateral arcades, which at first the spectator supposes to be round-arched, but he is struck by a peculiar grace and elasticity in the curves for which he is unable to account, until he ascends into the galleries whence the true form of the arch is discernible. The other two— 1 *d*, from the door of the southern transept, and 1 *c*, from that of the treasury,—sufficiently represent a group of fantastic forms derived from the Arabs, and of which the exquisite decoration is one of the most important features in St. Mark's. Their form is indeed permitted merely to obtain more fantasy

---

* I found it convenient in my own memoranda to express them simply as fourths, seconds, &c. But "order" is an excellent word for any known group of forms, whether of windows, capitals, bases, mouldings, or any other architectural feature, provided always that it be not understood in any wise to imply preeminence or isolation in these groups. Thus I may rationally speak of the six orders of Venetian windows, provided I am ready to allow a French architect to speak of the six or seven, or eight, or seventy or eighty, orders of Norman windows, if so many are distinguishable; and so also we may rationally speak, for the sake of intelligibility, of the five orders of Greek pillars, provided only we understand that there may be five millions of orders as good or better, of pillars *not* Greek.

in the curves of this decoration.* The reader can see in a moment, that, as pieces of masonry, or bearing arches, they are infirm or useless, and therefore never could be employed in any building in which dignity of structure was the primal object. It is just because structure is *not* the primal object in St. Mark's, because it has no severe weights to bear, and much loveliness of marble and sculpture to exhibit, that they are therein allowable. They are of course, like the rest of the building, built of brick and faced with marble, and their inner masonry, which must be very ingenious, is therefore not discernible. They have settled a little, as might have been expected, and the consequence is, that there is in every one of them, except the upright arch of the treasury, a small fissure across the marble of the flanks.

§ XXVI. Though, however, the Venetian builders adopted these Arabian forms of arch where grace of ornamentation was their only purpose, they saw that such arrangements were unfit for ordinary work; and there is no instance, I believe,

Fig. XXVI.

in Venice, of their having used any of them for a dwelling-house in the truly Byzantine period. But so soon as the

---

* Or in their own curves; as, on a small scale, in the balustrade Fig. 6. Plate XIII. above.

Gothic influence began to be felt, and the pointed arch forced itself upon them, their first concession to its attack was the adoption, in preference to the round arch, of the form 3 *a* (Plate XIV. above); the point of the Gothic arch forcing itself up, as it were, through the top of the semicircle which it was soon to supersede.

§ xxvii. The woodcut above, Fig. XXVI., represents the door and two of the lateral windows of a house in the Corte del Remer, facing the Grand Canal, in the parish of the Apostoli. It is remarkable as having its great entrance on the first floor, attained by a bold flight of steps, sustained on pure *pointed* arches wrought in brick. I cannot tell if these arches are contemporary with the building, though it must always have had an access of the kind. The rest of its aspect is Byzantine, except only that the rich sculptures of its archivolt show in combats of animals, beneath the soffit, a beginning of the Gothic fire and energy. The moulding of its plinth is of a Gothic profile,* and the windows are pointed, not with a reversed curve, but in a pure straight gable, very curiously contrasted with the delicate bending of the pieces

Fig XXVII.

of marble armor cut for the shoulders of each arch. There is a two-lighted window, such as that seen in the vignette, on each side of the door, sustained in the centre by a basket-worked Byzantine capital: the mode of covering the brick archivolt with marble, both in the windows and doorway, is precisely like that of the true Byzantine palaces.

§ xxviii. But as, even on a small scale, these arches are weak, if executed in brickwork, the appearance of this sharp

* For all details of this kind, the reader is referred to the final Appendix in Vol. III.

point in the outline was rapidly accompanied by a parallel
change in the method of building; and instead of constructing
the arch of brick and coating it with marble, the builders
formed it of three pieces of hewn stone inserted in the wall,
as in Fig. XXVII.   Not, however, at first in this perfect
form.   The endeavor to reconcile the grace of the reversed
arch with the strength of the round one, and still to build in
brick, ended at first in conditions such as that represented at

Fig. XXVIII.

a   *b*

a, Fig. XXVIII., which is a window in the Calle del Pistor,
close to the church of the Apostoli, a very interesting and
perfect example.   Here, observe, the poor round arch is still
kept to do all the hard work, and the fantastic ogee takes its
pleasure above, in the form of a moulding merely, a chain of
bricks cast to the required curve.   And this condition, translated into stone-work, becomes a window of the second order
(*b*, Fig. XXVIII., or 2. in Plate XIV.); a form perfectly
strong and serviceable, and of immense importance in the
transitional architecture of Venice.

§ xxix. At *b*, Fig. XXVIII. as above, is given one of the
earliest and simplest occurrences of the second order window
(in a double group, exactly like the brick transitional form *a*),
from a most important fragment of a defaced house in the

Salizzada San Lio, close to the Merceria. It is associated with a fine *pointed* brick arch, indisputably of contemporary work, towards the close of the thirteenth century, and it is shown to be later than the previous example, *a*, by the greater developement of its mouldings. The archivolt profile, indeed, is the simpler of the two, not having the sub-arch; as in the brick example; but the other mouldings are far more developed. Fig. XXIX. shows at 1 the arch profiles, at 2 the capital profiles, at 3 the basic-plinth profiles, of each window, *a* and *b*.

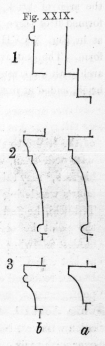

Fig. XXIX.

§ xxx. But the second order window soon attained nobler developement. At once simple, graceful, and strong, it was received into all the architecture of the period, and there is hardly a street in Venice which does not exhibit some important remains of palaces built with this form of window in many stories, and in numerous groups. The most extensive and perfect is one upon the Grand Canal in the parish of the Apostoli, near the Rialto, covered with rich decoration, in the Byzantine manner, between the windows of its first story; but not completely characteristic of the transitional period, because still retaining the dentil in the arch mouldings, while the transitional houses all have the simple roll. Of the fully established type, one of the most extensive and perfect examples is in a court in the Calle di Rimedio, close to the Ponte dell' Angelo, near St. Mark's Place. Another looks out upon a small square garden, one of the few visible in the centre of Venice, close by the Corte Salviati (the latter being known to every cicerone as that from which

Bianca Capello fled). But, on the whole, the most interesting to the traveller is that of which I have given a vignette opposite.

But for this range of windows, the little piazza SS. Apostoli would be one of the least picturesque in Venice; to those, however, who seek it on foot, it becomes geographically interesting from the extraordinary involution of the alleys leading to it from the Rialto. In Venice, the straight road is usually by water, and the long road by land; but the difference of distance appears, in this case, altogether inexplicable. Twenty or thirty strokes of the oar will bring a gondola from the foot of the Rialto to that of the Ponte SS. Apostoli; but the unwise pedestrian, who has not noticed the white clue beneath his feet,* may think himself fortunate, if, after a quarter of an hour's wandering among the houses behind the Fondaco de' Tedeschi, he find himself anywhere in the neighborhood of the point he seeks. With much patience, however, and modest following of the guidance of the marble thread, he will at last emerge over a steep bridge into the open space of the Piazza, rendered cheerful in autumn by a perpetual market of pomegranates, and purple gourds, like enormous black figs; while the canal, at its extremity, is half-blocked up by barges laden with vast baskets of grapes as black as charcoal, thatched over with their own leaves.

Looking back, on the other side of this canal, he will see the windows represented in Plate XV., which, with the arcade of pointed arches beneath them, are the remains of the palace once belonging to the unhappy doge, Marino Faliero.

* Two threads of white marble, each about an inch wide, inlaid in the dark grey pavement, indicate the road to the Rialto from the farthest extremity of the north quarter of Venice. The peasant or traveller, lost in the intricacy of the pathway in this portion of the city, cannot fail, after a few experimental traverses, to cross these white ines, which thenceforward he has nothing to do but to follow, though their capricious sinuosities will try his patience not a little.

The balcony is, of course, modern, and the series of windows has been of greater extent, once terminated by a pilaster on the left hand, as well as on the right; but the terminal arches have been walled up. What remains, however, is enough, with its sculptured birds and dragons, to give the reader a very distinct idea of the second order window in its perfect form. The details of the capitals, and other minor portions, if these interest him, he will find given in the final Appendix.

§ XXXI. The advance of the Gothic spirit was, for a few years, checked by this compromise between the round and pointed arch. The truce, however, was at last broken, in consequence of the discovery that the key-stone would do duty quite as well in the form *b* as in the form *a*, Fig. XXX., and the substitution of *b*, at the head of the arch, gives us the window of the third order, 3 *b*, 3 *d*, and 3 *e*, in Plate XIV. The forms 3 *a* and 3 *c* are exceptional; the first occurring, as we have seen, in the Corte del Remer, and in one other palace on the Grand Canal, close to the Church of St. Eustachio; the second only, as far as I know, in one house on the Canna-Reggio, belonging to the true Gothic period. The other three examples, 3 *b*, 3 *d*, 3 *e*, are generally characteristic of the third order; and it will be observed that they differ not merely in mouldings, but in slope of sides, and this latter difference is by far the most material. For in the example 3 *b* there is hardly any true Gothic expression; it is still the pure Byzantine arch, with a point thrust up through it: but the moment the flanks slope, as in 3 *d*, the Gothic expression is definite, and the entire school of the architecture is changed.

Fig. XXX.

a   *b*

This slope of the flanks occurs, first, in so slight a degree as to be hardly preceptible, and gradually increases until, reaching the form 3 *e* at the close of the thirteenth century the window is perfectly prepared for a transition into the fifth order

§ XXXII. The most perfect examples of the third order in
Venice are the windows of the ruined palace of Marco Querini,
the father-in-law of Bajamonte Tiepolo, in consequence of
whose conspiracy against the government this palace was
ordered to be razed in 1310; but it was only partially ruined,
and was afterwards used as the common shambles. The
Venetians have now made a poultry market of the lower story
(the shambles being removed to a suburb), and a prison of
the upper, though it is one of the most important and interesting monuments in the city, and especially valuable as giving
us a secure date for the central form of these very rare transitional windows. For, as it was the palace of the father-in-
law of Bajamonte, and the latter was old enough to assume
the leadership of a political faction in 1280,* the date of the
accession to the throne of the Doge Pietro Gradenigo, we are
secure of this palace having been built not later than the
middle of the thirteenth century. Another example, less
refined in workmanship, but, if possible, still more interesting,

Fig. XXXI.

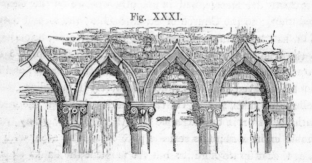

owing to the variety of its capitals, remains in the little piazza
opening to the Rialto, on the St. Mark's side of the Grand
Canal. The house faces the bridge, and its second story has

* An account of the conspiracy of Bajamonte may be found in almost any
Venetian history; the reader may consult Mutinelli, Annali Urbani, lib. iii.

been built in the thirteenth century, above a still earlier
Byzantine cornice remaining, or perhaps introduced from
some other ruined edifice, in the walls of the first floor. The
windows of the second story are of pure third order; four of
them are represented above, with their flanking pilaster, and
capitals varying constantly in the form of the flower or leaf
introduced between their volutes.

§ XXXIII. Another most important example exists in the
lower story of the Casa Sagredo, on the Grand Canal, remarkable as having the early upright form (3. *b*, Plate XIV.) with
a somewhat late moulding. Many others occur in the fragmentary ruins in the streets: but the two boldest conditions
which I found in Venice are those of the Chapter-House of
the Frari, in which the Doge Francesco Dandolo was buried
circa 1339; and those of the flank of the Ducal Palace itself
absolutely corresponding with those of the Frari, and therefore of inestimable value in determining the date of the
palace. Of these more hereafter.

§ XXXIV. Contemporarily with these windows of the second
and third orders, those of the fourth (4. *a*, and 4. *b*, in Plate
XIV.) occur, at first in pairs, and with simple mouldings,
precisely similar to those of the second order, but much more
rare, as in the example at the
side, Fig. XXXII., from the
Salizada San Liò; and then,
enriching their mouldings as
shown in the continuous series
4. *c*, 4. *d*, of Plate XIV., asso-
ciate themselves with the fifth
order windows of the perfect
Gothic period. There is hardly
a palace in Venice without
some example, either early or

Fig. XXXII.

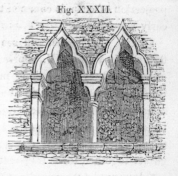

late, of these fourth order windows; but the Plate opposite

(XVI.) represents one of their purest groups at the close of the thirteenth century, from a house on the Grand Canal, nearly opposite the Church of the Scalzi. I have drawn it from the side, in order that the great depth of the arches may be seen, and the clear detaching of the shafts from the sheets of glass behind. The latter, as well as the balcony, are comparatively modern; but there is no doubt that if glass were used in the old window, it was set behind the shafts, at the same depth. The entire modification of the interiors of all the Venetian houses by recent work has however prevented me from entering into any inquiry as to the manner in which the ancient glazing was attached to the interiors of the windows.

The fourth order window is found in great richness and beauty at Verona, down to the latest Gothic times, as well as in the earliest, being then more frequent than any other form. It occurs, on a grand scale, in the old palace of the Scaligers, and profusely throughout the streets of the city. The series 4. *a* to 4. *e*, Plate XIV., shows its most ordinary conditions and changes of arch-line: 4. *a* and 4. *b* are the early Venetian forms; 4. *c*, later, is general at Venice; 4. *d*, the best and most piquant condition, owing to its fantastic and bold projection of cusp, is common to Venice and Verona; 4. *e*, is early Veronese.

§ xxxv. The reader will see at once, in descending to the fifth row in Plate XIV., representing the windows of the fifth order, that they are nothing more than a combination of the third and fourth. By this union they become the nearest approximation to a perfect Gothic form which occurs characteristically at Venice; and we shall therefore pause on the threshold of this final change, to glance back upon, and gather together, those fragments of purer pointed architecture which were above noticed as the forlorn hopes of the Gothic assault.

The little Campiello San Rocco is entered by a sotto-portico behind the church of the Frari. Looking back, the upper traceries of the magnificent apse are seen towering above the irregular roofs and chimneys of the little square; and our lost Prout was enabled to bring the whole subject into an exquisitely picturesque composition, by the fortunate occurrence of four quaint trefoiled windows in one of the houses on the right. Those trefoils are among the most ancient efforts of Gothic art in Venice. I have given a rude sketch of them in Fig. XXXIII. They are built entirely of brick, except the central shaft and capital, which are of Istrian stone. Their structure is the simplest possible; the trefoils being cut

Fig. XXXIII.

out of the radiating bricks which form the pointed arch, and the edge or upper limit of that pointed arch indicated by a roll moulding formed of cast bricks, in length of about a foot, and ground at the bottom so as to meet in one, as in Fig. XXXIV. The capital of the shaft is one of the earliest transitional forms;* and observe the curious following out, even in this minor instance, of the great law of centralization above explained with respect to the Byzantine palaces. There is a central shaft, a pilaster on each side, and then the wall. The pilaster has, by way of capital, a square flat brick, projecting a little, and

Fig. XXXIV.

---

* See account of series of capitals in final Appendix.

cast, at the edge, into the form of the first type of all
cornices (a, p. 63. Vol. I.; the reader ought to glance back
at this passage, if he has forgotten it) ; and the shafts and
pilasters all stand, without any added bases, on a projecting
plinth of the same simple profile. These windows have been
much defaced; but I have not the least doubt that their
plinths are the original ones : and the whole group is one of
the most valuable in Venice, as showing the way in which
the humblest houses, in the noble times, followed out the
system of the larger palaces, as far as they could, in their
rude materials. It is not often that the dwellings of the
lower orders are preserved to us from the thirteenth century.

§ XXXVI. In the two upper lines of the opposite Plate
(XVII.), I have arranged some of the more delicate and
finished examples of Gothic work of this period. Of these,
fig. 4. is taken from the outer arcade of San Fermo of Verona,
to show the condition of mainland architecture, from which
all these Venetian types were borrowed. This arch, together
with the rest of the arcade, is wrought in fine stone, with a
band of inlaid red brick, the whole chiselled and fitted with
exquisite precision, all Venetian work being coarse in comparison. Throughout the streets of Verona, arches and windows of the thirteenth century are of continual occurrence,
wrought, in this manner, with brick and stone; sometimes
the brick alternating with the stones of the arch, as in the
finished example given in Plate XIX. of the first volume, and
there selected in preference to other examples of archivolt
decoration, because furnishing a complete type of the master
school from which the Venetian Gothic is derived.

§ XXXVII. The arch from St. Fermo, however, fig. 4. Plate
XVII., corresponds more closely, in its entire simplicity, with
the little windows from the Campiello San Rocco; and with
the type 5. set beside it in Plate XVII., from a very ancient
house in the Corte del Forno at Santa Marina (all in brick);

while the upper examples, 1. and 2., show the use of the flat but highly enriched architrave, for the connexion of which with Byzantine work see the final Appendix, Vol. III., under the head "Archivolt." These windows (figs. 1. and 2. Plate XVII.) are from a narrow alley in a part of Venice now exclusively inhabited by the lower orders, close to the arsenal;* they are entirely wrought in brick, with exquisite mouldings, not cast, but *moulded in the clay by the hand*, so that there is not one piece of the arch like another ; the pilasters and shafts being, as usual, of stone.

§ XXXVIII. And here let me pause for a moment, to note what one should have thought was well enough known in England,—yet I could not perhaps touch upon anything less considered,—the real use of brick. Our fields of good clay were never given us to be made into oblong morsels of one size. They were given us that we might play with them, and that men who could not handle a chisel, might knead out of them some expression of human thought. In the ancient architecture of the clay districts of Italy, every possible adaptation of the material is found exemplified : from the coarsest and most brittle kinds, used in the mass of the structure, to bricks for arches and plinths, cast in the most perfect curves, and of almost every size, strength, and hardness; and moulded bricks, wrought into flower-work and tracery as fine as raised patterns upon china. And, just as many of the finest works of the Italian sculptors were executed in porcelain, many of the best thoughts of their architects are expressed in brick, or in the softer material of terra cotta ; and if this were so in

* If the traveller desire to find them (and they are worth seeking), let him row from the Fondamenta S. Biagio down the Rio della Tana ; and look, on his right, for a low house with windows in it like those in the woodcut No. XXXI., above, p. 282. Let him go in at the door of the portico in the middle of this house, and he will find himself in a small alley, with the windows in question on each side of him.

Italy, where there is not one city from whose towers we may not descry the blue outline of Alp or Apennine, everlasting quarries of granite or marble, how much more ought it to be so among the fields of England! I believe that the best academy for her architects, for some half century to come, would be the brick-field; for of this they may rest assured, that till they know how to use clay, they will never know how to use marble.

§ xxxix. And now observe, as we pass from fig. 2. to fig. 3., and from fig. 5. to fig. 6., in Plate XVII., a most interesting step of transition. As we saw above, § xiv., the round arch yielding to the Gothic, by allowing a point to emerge at its summit, so here we have the Gothic conceding something to the form which had been assumed by the round; and itself slightly altering its outline so as to meet the condescension of the round arch half way. At page 137. of the first volume, I have drawn to scale one of these minute concessions of the pointed arch, granted at Verona out of pure courtesy to the Venetian forms, by one of the purest Gothic ornaments in the world; and the small window here, fig. 6., is a similar example at Venice itself, from the Campo Santa Maria Mater Domini, where the reversed curve at the head of the pointed arch is just perceptible and no more. The other examples, figs. 3. and 7., the first from a small but very noble house in the Merceria, the second from an isolated palace at Murano, show more advanced conditions of the reversed curve, which, though still employing the broad decorated architrave of the earlier examples, are in all other respects prepared for the transition to the simple window of the fifth order.

§ xl. The next example, the uppermost of the three lower series in Plate XVII., shows this order in its early purity; associated with intermediate decorations like those of the Byzantines, from a palace once belonging to the Erizzo family, near the Arsenal. The ornaments appear to be actually of

Greek workmanship (except, perhaps, the two birds over the central arch, which are bolder, and more free in treatment), and built into the Gothic fronts; showing, however, the early date of the whole by the manner of their insertion, corresponding exactly with that employed in the Byzantine palaces, and by the covering of the intermediate spaces with sheets of marble, which, however, instead of being laid over the entire wall, are now confined to the immediate spaces between and above the windows, and are bounded by a dentil moulding.

In the example below this the Byzantine ornamentation has vanished, and the fifth order window is seen in its generic form, as commonly employed throughout the early Gothic period. Such arcades are of perpetual occurrence; the one in the Plate was taken from a small palace on the Grand Canal, nearly opposite the Casa Foscari. One point in it deserves especial notice, the increased size of the lateral window as compared with the rest: a circumstance which occurs in a great number of the groups of windows belonging to this period, and for which I have never been able to account.

§ XLI. Both these figures have been most carefully engraved; and the uppermost will give the reader a perfectly faithful idea of the general effect of the Byzantine sculptures, and of the varied alabaster among which they are inlaid, as well as of the manner in which these pieces are set together, every joint having been drawn on the spot: and the transition from the embroidered and silvery richness of this architecture, in which the Byzantine ornamentation was associated with the Gothic form of arch, to the simplicity of the pure Gothic arcade as seen in the lower figure, is one of the most remarkable phenomena in the history of Venetian art. If it had occurred suddenly, and at an earlier period, it might have been traced partly to the hatred of the Greeks, consequent upon

13

the treachery of Manuel Comnenus,* and the fatal war to which it led; but the change takes place gradually, and not till a much later period. I hoped to have been able to make some careful inquiries into the habits of domestic life of the Venetians before and after the dissolution of their friendly relations with Constantinople; but the labor necessary for the execution of my more immediate task has entirely prevented this: and I must be content to lay the succession of the architectural styles plainly before the reader, and leave the collateral questions to the investigation of others; merely noting this one assured fact, that *the root of all that is greatest in Christian art is struck in the thirteenth century;* that the temper of that century is the life-blood of all manly work thenceforward in Europe; and I suppose that one of its peculiar characteristics was elsewhere, as assuredly in Florence, a singular simplicity in domestic life ·

> "I saw Bellincion Berti walk abroad
> In leathern girdle, and a clasp of bone;
> And, with no artful coloring on her cheeks,
> His lady leave the glass. The sons I saw
> Of Verli and of Vecchio, well content
> With unrobed jerkin, and their good dames handling
> The spindle and the flax.   .   .   .

* The bitterness of feeling with which the Venetians must have remembered this, was probably the cause of their magnificent heroism in the final siege of the city under Dandolo, and, partly, of the excesses which disgraced their victory. The conduct of the allied army of the Crusaders on this occasion cannot, however, be brought in evidence of general barbarism in the thirteenth century: first, because the masses of the crusading armies were in great part composed of the refuse of the nations of Europe; and secondly, because such a mode of argument might lead us to inconvenient conclusions respecting ourselves, so long as the horses of the Austrian cavalry are stabled in the cloister of the convent which contains the Last Supper of Leonardo da Vinci. See Appendix 3. Vol. III.: "Austrian Government in Italy."

> One waked to tend the cradle, hushing it
> With sounds that lulled the parents' infancy.
> Another, with her maidens, drawing off
> The tresses from the distaff, lectured them
> Old tales of Troy, and Fesole, and Rome."*

§ XLII. Such, then, is the simple fact at Venice, that from the beginning of the thirteenth century there is found a singular increase of simplicity in all architectural ornamentation; the rich Byzantine capitals giving place to a pure and severe type hereafter to be described,† and the rich sculptures vanishing from the walls, nothing but the marble facing remaining. One of the most interesting examples of this transitional state is a palace at San Severo, just behind the Casa Zorzi. This latter is a Renaissance building, utterly worthless in every respect, but known to the Venetian Ciceroni; and by inquiring for it, and passing a little beyond it down the Fondamenta San Severo, the traveller will see, on the other side of the canal, a palace which the Ciceroni never notice, but which is unique in Venice for the magnificence of the veined purple alabasters with which it has been decorated, and for the manly simplicity of the foliage of its capitals. Except in these, it has no sculpture whatever, and its effect is dependent

---

* It is generally better to read ten lines of any poet in the original language, however painfully, than ten cantos of a translation. But an exception may be made in favor of Cary's Dante. If no poet ever was liable to lose more in translation, none was ever so carefully translated; and I hardly know whether most to admire the rigid fidelity, or the sweet and solemn harmony, of Cary's verse. There is hardly a fault in the fragment quoted above, except the word "lectured," for Dante's beautiful "favoleggiava;" and even in this case, joining the first words of the following line, the translation is strictly literal. It is true that the conciseness and the rivulet-like melody of Dante must continually be lost; but if I could only read English, and had to choose, for a library narrowed by poverty, between Cary's Dante and our own original Milton, I should choose Cary without an instant's pause.

† See final Appendix, Vol. III., under head "Capitals."

entirely on color. Disks of green serpentine are inlaid on the
field of purple alabaster; and the pillars are alternately of red
marble with white capitals, and of white marble with red capitals. Its windows appear of the third order; and the back
of the palace, in a small and most picturesque court, shows a
group of windows which are, perhaps, the most superb examples of that order in Venice. But the windows to the front
have, I think, been of the fifth order, and their cusps have
been cut away.

§ XLIII. When the Gothic feeling began more decidedly to
establish itself, it evidently became a question with the
Venetian builders, how the intervals between the arches, now
left blank by the abandonment of the Byzantine sculptures,
should be enriched in accordance with the principles of the
new school. Two most important examples are left of the
experiments made at this period: one at the Ponte del Forner,
at San Cassano, a noble house in which the spandrils of the
windows are filled by the emblems of the four Evangelists,
sculptured in deep relief, and touching the edges of the arches
with their expanded wings; the other now known as the
Palazzo Cicogna, near the church of San Sebastiano, in the
quarter called "of the Archangel Raphael," in which a large
space of wall above the windows is occupied by an intricate
but rude tracery of involved quatrefoils. Of both these
palaces I purposed to give drawings in my folio work; but I
shall probably be saved the trouble by the publication of the
beautiful calotypes lately made at Venice of both; and it is
unnecessary to represent them here, as they are unique in
Venetian architecture, with the single exception of an unimportant imitation of the first of them in a little by-street close
to the Campo Sta. Maria Formosa. For the question as to
the mode of decorating the interval between the arches was
suddenly and irrevocably determined by the builder of the
Ducal Palace, who, as we have seen, taking his first idea from

the traceries of the Frari, and arranging those traceries as best fitted his own purpose, designed the great arcade (the lowest of the three in Plate XVII.,) which thenceforward became the established model for every work of importance in Venice. The palaces built on this model, however, most of them not till the beginning of the fifteenth century, belong properly to the time of the Renaissance; and what little we have to note respecting them may be more clearly stated in connexion with other facts characteristic of that period.

§ XLIV. As the examples in Plate XVII. are necessarily confined to the upper parts of the windows, I have given in the Plate opposite (XVIII.*) examples of the fifth order window, both in its earliest and in its fully developed form, completed from base to keystone. The upper example is a beautiful group from a small house, never of any size or pretension, and now inhabited only by the poor, in the Campiello della Strope, close to the Church of San Giacomo de Lorio. It is remarkable for its excessive purity of curve, and is of very early date, its mouldings being simpler than usual.† The lower example is from the second story of a palace belonging to the Priuli family, near San Lorenzo, and shows one feature to which our attention has not hitherto been directed, namely, the penetration of the cusp, leaving only a silver thread of stone traced on the darkness of the window. I need not say that, in this condition, the cusp ceases to have any constructive use, and is merely decorative, but often exceedingly beautiful. The steps of transition from the early solid cusp to this slender thread are noticed in the final Appendix, under the head "Tracery bars;" the commencement of the change being in the thinning of the stone, which is not cut through until it is thoroughly emaciated. Generally speaking, the condition in

---

* This Plate is not from a drawing of mine. It has been engraved by Mr Armytage, with great skill, from two daguerreotypes.

† Vide final Appendix, under head "Archivolt."

which the cusp is found is a useful test of age, when compared with other points; the more solid it is, the more ancient: but the massive form is often found associated with the perforated, as late as the beginning of the fourteenth century. In the Ducal Palace, the lower or bearing traceries have the solid cusp, and the upper traceries of the windows, which are merely decorative, have the perforated cusp, both with exquisite effect.

§ XLV. The smaller balconies between the great shafts in the lower example in Plate XVIII. are original and characteristic: not so the lateral one of the detached window, which has been restored; but by imagining it to be like that represented in fig. 1. Plate XIII. above, which is a perfect window of the finest time of the fifth order, the reader will be enabled to form a complete idea of the external appearance of the principal apartments in the house of a noble of Venice, at the beginning of the fourteenth century.

§ XLVI. Whether noble, or merchant, or, as frequently happened, both, every Venetian appears, at this time, to have raised his palace or dwelling-house upon one type. Under every condition of importance, through every variation of size, the forms and mode of decoration of all the features were universally alike; not servilely alike, but fraternally; not with the sameness of coins cast from one mould, but with the likeness of the members of one family. No fragment of the period is preserved, in which the windows, be they few or many, a group of three or an arcade of thirty, have not the noble cusped arch of the fifth order. And they are especially to be noted by us at this day, because these refined and richly ornamented forms were used in the habitations of a nation as laborious, as practical, as brave, and as prudent as ourselves; and they were built at a time when that nation was struggling with calamities and changes threatening its existence almost every hour. And, farther, they are interesting because perfectly applicable to modern habitation. The refinement of domestic life appears to have been far advanced in Venice from her earliest days; and the remains of her Gothic palaces are, at this day, the most delightful residences in the city, having undergone no change in external form, and probably having been rather injured than rendered more convenient by the modifications which poverty and Renaissance taste, contending with the ravages of time, have introduced in the interiors. So that, in Venice and the cities grouped around it, Vicenza, Padua, and Verona, the traveller may ascertain, by actual experience, the effect which would be produced upon the comfort or luxury of daily life by the revival of the Gothic school of architecture. He can still stand upon the marble balcony in the soft summer air, and feel its smooth surface warm from the noontide as he leans on it in the twilight; he can still see the strong sweep of the unruined traceries drawn on the deep serenity of the starry sky, and watch the fantastic shadows of the clustered arches shorten in the moonlight on the chequered floor; or he may close the casements fitted to their unshaken shafts against such wintry winds as would have made an English house vibrate to its foundation, and, in either case, compare their influence on his daily home feeling with that of the square openings in his English wall.

§ XLVII. And let him be assured, if he find there is more to be enjoyed in the Gothic window, there is also more to be trusted. It is the best and strongest building, as it is the most beautiful. I am not now speaking of the particular form of Venetian Gothic, but of the general strength of the pointed arch as opposed to that of the level lintel of the square window; and I plead for the introduction of the Gothic form into our domestic architecture, not merely because it is lovely, but because it is the only form of faithful, strong, enduring, and honorable building, in such materials as come

daily to our hands. By increase of scale and cost, it is possible to build, in any style, what will last for ages; but only in
the Gothic is it possible to give security and dignity to work
wrought with imperfect means and materials. And I trust
that there will come a time when the English people may see
the folly of building basely and insecurely. It is common
with those architects against whose practice my writings
have hitherto been directed, to call them merely theoretical
and imaginative. I answer, that there is not a single principle
asserted either in the "Seven Lamps" or here, but is of the
simplest, sternest veracity, and the easiest practicability; that
buildings, raised as I would have them, would stand unshaken
for a thousand years; and the buildings raised by the architects who oppose them will not stand for one hundred and
fifty, they sometimes do not stand for an hour. There is
hardly a week passes without some catastrophe brought about
by the base principles of modern building; some vaultless
floor that drops the staggering crowd through the jagged
rents of its rotten timbers; some baseless bridge that is
washed away by the first wave of a summer flood; some
fungous wall of nascent rottenness that a thunder-shower
soaks down with its workmen into a heap of slime and death.*
These we hear of, day by day: yet these indicate but the
thousandth part of the evil. The portion of the national
income sacrificed in mere bad building, in the perpetual

---

* "On Thursday, the 20th, the front walls of two of the new houses now
building in Victoria Street, Westminster, fell to the ground. . . . The
roof was on, *and a massive compo cornice* was put up at top, as well as dress-
ings to the upper windows. The roof is formed by girders and 4½-brick
arches in cement, covered with asphalte to form a flat. The failure is attributed *to the quantity of rain which has fallen.* Others suppose that some of
the girders were defective, and gave way, carrying the walls with them."—
Builder, for January 29th, 1853. The rest of this volume might be filled
with such notices, if we sought for them.

repairs, and swift condemnation and pulling down of ill-built shells of houses, passes all calculation. And the weight of the penalty is not yet felt; it will tell upon our children some fifty years hence, when the cheap work, and contract work, and stucco and plaster work, and bad iron work, and all the other expedients of modern rivalry, vanity, and dishonesty, begin to show themselves for what they are.

§ XLVIII. Indeed, dishonesty and false economy will no more build safely in Gothic than in any other style: but of all forms which we could possibly employ, to be framed hastily and out of bad materials, the common square win- dow is the worst; and its level head of brickwork (*a*, Fig. XXXV.) is the weakest way of covering a space. Indeed, in the hastily heaped shells of modern houses, there may be seen often even a worse manner of placing the bricks, as at *b*, sup- porting them by a bit of lath till the mortar dries; but even when worked with the utmost care, and having every brick tapered into the form of a voussoir and accurately fitted, I have seen such a window- head give way, and a wide fissure torn through all the brick- work above it, two years after it was built; while the pointed arch of the Veronese Gothic, wrought in brick also, occurs at every corner of the streets of the city, untouched since the thirteenth century, and without a single flaw.

Fig. XXXV.

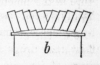

§ XLIX. Neither can the objection, so often raised against the pointed arch, that it will not admit the convenient adjust- ment of modern sashes and glass, hold for an instant. There is not the smallest necessity, because the arch is pointed, that the aperture should be so. The work of the arch is to sustain the building above; when this is once done securely, the pointed head of it may be filled in any way we choose. In the best cathedral doors it is always filled by a shield of solid stone; in many early windows of the best Gothic it is filled in the same manner, the introduced slab of stone becoming a field for rich decoration; and there is not the smallest reason why lancet windows, used in bold groups, with each pointed arch filled by a sculptured tympanum, should not allow as much light to enter, and in as convenient a way, as the most luxuriously glazed square windows of our brick houses. Give the groups of associated lights bold gabled canopies; charge the gables with sculpture and color; and instead of the base and almost useless Greek portico, letting the rain and wind enter it at will, build the steeply vaulted and completely sheltered Gothic porch; and on all these fields for rich decoration let the common workman carve what he pleases, to the best of his power, and we may have a school of domestic architecture in the nineteenth century, which will make our children grateful to us, and proud of us, till the thirtieth.

§ L. There remains only one important feature to be examined, the entrance gate or door. We have already observed that the one seems to pass into the other, a sign of increased love of privacy rather than of increased humility, as the Gothic palaces assume their perfect form. In the Byzantine palaces the entrances appear always to have been rather great gates than doors, magnificent semicircular arches opening to the water, and surrounded by rich sculpture in the archivolts. One of these entrances is seen in the small woodcut above, Fig. XXV., and another has been given carefully in my folio work: their sculpture is generally of grotesque animals scattered among leafage, without any definite meaning; but the great outer entrance of St. Mark's, which appears to have been completed some time after the rest of the fabric, differs from all others in presenting a series of subjects altogether Gothic in feeling, selection, and vitality of execution, and which show the occult entrance of the Gothic spirit before it had yet succeeded in effecting any modification of the Byzantine forms. These sculptures represent the months of the year employed in the avocations usually attributed to them throughout the whole compass of the middle ages, in Northern architecture and manuscript calendars, and at last exquisitely versified by Spenser. For the sake of the traveller in Venice, who should examine this archivolt carefully, I shall enumerate these sculptures in their order, noting such parallel representations as I remember in other work.

§ LI. There are four successive archivolts, one within the other, forming the great central entrance of St. Mark's. The first is a magnificent external arch, formed of obscure figures mingled among masses of leafage, as in ordinary Byzantine work; within this there is a hemispherical dome, covered with modern mosaic; and at the back of this recess the other three archivolts follow consecutively, two sculptured, one plain; the one with which we are concerned is the outermost.

It is carved both on its front and under-surface or soffit; on the front are seventeen female figures bearing scrolls, from which the legends are unfortunately effaced. These figures were once gilded on a dark blue ground, as may still be seen in Gentile Bellini's picture of St. Mark's in the Accademia delle Belle Arti. The sculptures of the months are on the under-surface, beginning at the bottom on the left hand of the spectator as he enters, and following in succession round the archivolt; separated, however, into two groups, at its centre, by a beautiful figure of the youthful Christ, sitting in the midst of a slightly hollowed sphere covered with stars to represent the firmament, and with the attendant sun and moon, set one on each side, to rule over the day and over the night

§ LII. The months are personified as follows: —

1. JANUARY. *Carrying home a noble tree on his shoulders, the leafage of which nods forwards, and falls nearly to his feet.* Superbly cut. This is a rare representation of him. More frequently he is represented as the two-headed Janus,

sitting at a table, drinking at one mouth and eating at the other. Sometimes as an old man, warming his feet at a fire, and drinking from a bowl; though this type is generally reserved for February. Spenser, however, gives the same symbol as that on St. Mark's:

> " Numbd with holding all the day
> An hatchet keene, with which he felled wood."

His sign, Aquarius, is obscurely indicated in the archivolt by some wavy lines representing water, unless the figure has been broken away.

2. FEBRUARY. *Sitting in a carved chair, warming his bare feet at a blazing fire.* Generally, when he is thus represented, there is a pot hung over the fire, from the top of the chimney. Sometimes he is pruning trees, as in Spenser:

> " Yet had he by his side
> His plough and harnesse fit to till the ground,
> And tooles to prune the trees."

Not unfrequently, in the calendars, this month is represented by a female figure carrying candles, in honor of the Purification of the Virgin.

His sign, Pisces, is prominently carved above him.

3. MARCH. Here, as almost always in Italy, *a warrior:* the Mars of the Latins being of course, in mediæval work, made representative of the military power of the place and period; and thus, at Venice, having the winged Lion painted upon his shield. In Northern work, however, I think March is commonly employed in pruning trees; or, at least, he is so when that occupation is left free for him by February's being engaged with the ceremonies of Candlemas. Sometimes, also, he is reaping a low and scattered kind of grain; and by Spenser, who exactly marks the junction of mediæval and classical feeling, his military and agricultural functions are united, while also, in the Latin manner, he is made the first of the months:

"First sturdy March, with brows full sternly bent,
   And armèd strongly, rode upon a Ram,
   The same which over Hellespontus swam;
   Yet in his hand a spade he also hent,
   And in a bag all sorts of seeds ysame,*
   Which on the earth he strowed as he went."

His sign, the Ram, is very superbly carved above him in the archivolt.

4. APRIL. Here, *carrying a sheep upon his shoulder.* A rare representation of him. In Northern work he is almost universally gathering flowers, or holding them triumphantly in each hand. The Spenserian mingling of this mediæval image with that of his being wet with showers, and wanton with love, by turning his zodiacal sign, Taurus, into the bull of Europa, is altogether exquisite.

"Upon a Bull he rode, the same which led
   Europa floting through the Argolick fluds:
   His horns were gilden all with golden studs,
   And garnishèd with garlonds goodly dight
   Of all the fairest flowres and freshest buds
   Which th' earth brings forth; and *wet he seemed in sight
   With waves, through which he waded for his love's delight.*"

5. MAY *is seated, while two young maidens crown him with flowers.* A very unusual representation, even in Italy; where, as in the North, he is almost always riding out hunting or hawking, sometimes playing on a musical instrument. In Spenser, this month is personified as "the fayrest mayd on ground," borne on the shoulders of the Twins.

In this archivolt there are only two heads to represent the zodiacal sign.

The summer and autumnal months are always represented in a series of agricultural occupations, which, of course, vary

* "Ysame," collected together.

with the locality in which they occur; but generally in their order only. Thus, if June is mowing, July is reaping; if July is mowing, August is reaping; and so on. I shall give a parallel view of some of these varieties presently; but, meantime, we had better follow the St. Mark's series, as it is peculiar in some respects.

6. JUNE. *Reaping.* The corn and sickle sculptured with singular care and precision, in bold relief, and the zodiacal sign, the Crab, above, also worked with great spirit. Spenser puts plough irons into his hand. Sometimes he is sheep-shearing; and, in English and northern French manuscripts, carrying a kind of fagot or barrel, of the meaning of which I am not certain.

7. JULY. *Mowing.* A very interesting piece of sculpture, owing to the care with which the flowers are wrought out among the long grass. I do not remember ever finding July but either reaping or mowing. Spenser works him hard, and puts him to both labors:

> " Behinde his backe a sithe, and by his side
> Under his belt he bore a sickle circling wide."

8. AUGUST. Peculiarly represented in this archivolt, *sitting in a chair, with his head upon his hand, as if asleep; the Virgin* (the zodiacal sign) *above him, lifting up her hand.* This appears to be a peculiarly Italian version of the proper employment of August. In Northern countries he is generally threshing, or gathering grapes. Spenser merely clothes him with gold, and makes him lead forth

> "the righteous Virgin, which of old
> Lived here on earth, and plenty made abound."

9. SEPTEMBER. *Bearing home grapes in a basket.* Almost always sowing, in Northern work. By Spenser, with his

usual exquisite ingenuity, employed in gathering in the general harvest, and *portioning it out with the Scales*, his zodiacal sign.

10. OCTOBER. *Wearing a conical hat, and digging busily with a long spade.* In Northern work he is sometimes a vintager, sometimes beating the acorns out of an oak to feed swine. When September is vintaging, October is generally sowing. Spenser employs him in the harvest both of vine and olive.

11. NOVEMBER. *Seems to be catching small birds in a net.* I do not remember him so employed elsewhere. He is nearly always killing pigs; sometimes beating the oak for them; with Spenser, fatting them.

12. DECEMBER. *Killing swine.* It is hardly ever that this employment is not given to one or other of the terminal months of the year. If not so engaged, December is usually putting new loaves into the oven; sometimes killing oxen. Spenser properly makes him feasting and drinking instead of January.

§ LIII. On the next page I have given a parallel view of the employment of the months from some Northern manuscripts, in order that they may be more conveniently compared with the sculptures of St. Mark's, in their expression of the varieties of climate and agricultural system. Observe that the letter (f.) in some of the columns, opposite the month of May, means that he has a falcon on his fist; being, in those cases, represented as riding out, in high exultation, on a caparisoned white horse. A series nearly similar to that of St. Mark's occurs on the door of the Cathedral of Lucca, and on that of the Baptistery of Pisa; in which, however, if I recollect rightly, February is fishing, and May has something resembling an umbrella in his hand, instead of a hawk. But, in all cases, the figures are treated with the peculiar spirit of the Gothic sculptors; and this archivolt is the first expression of that spirit which is to be found in Venice.

	St. Mark's.	MS. French. Late 18th Century.	MS. French. Late 18th Century.	MS. French. Late 18th Century.	MS. French. Early 14th Century.	MS. English. Early 14th Century.	MS. Flemish. 15th Century.
JANUARY.	Carrying wood.	Janus feasting.	Janus feasting.	Drinking and stirring fire.	Warming feet.	Janus feasting.	Feasting.
FEBRUARY.	Warming feet.	Warming feet.	Warming feet.	Pruning.	Bearing candles.	Warming feet.	Warming hands.
MARCH.	Going to war.	Pruning.	Pruning.	Striking with axe.	Pruning.	Carrying candles.	Reaping.
APRIL.	Carrying sheep.	Gathering flowers.	Gathering flowers.	Gathering flowers.	Gathering flowers.	Pruning.	Gathering flowers.
MAY.	Crowned with flowers.	Riding (f.).	Riding (f.).	Playing on violin.	Riding (f.).	Riding (f.).	Riding with lady on pillion.
JUNE.	Reaping.	Mowing.	Mowing.	Gathering large red flowers.	Carrying (fagots?)	Carrying fagots.	Sheep-shearing.
JULY.	Mowing.	Reaping.	Reaping.	Mowing.	Mowing.	Mowing.	Mowing.
AUGUST.	Asleep.	Threshing.	Reaping.	Reaping.	Reaping.	Reaping.	Reaping.
SEPTEMBER.	Carrying grapes.	Sowing.	Gathering grapes.	Drinking wine.	Threshing.	Threshing.	Sowing.
OCTOBER.	Digging.	Gathering grapes.	Sowing.	Sowing.	Sowing.	Sowing.	Beating oak.
NOVEMBER.	Catching birds.	Beating oak.	Killing swine.	Killing swine.	Killing swine.	Killing swine.	Pressing (grapes?)
DECEMBER.	Killing swine.	Killing swine.	Baking.	Killing oxen.	Baking.	Baking.	Killing swine.

§ LIV. In the private palaces, the entrances soon admitted some concession to the Gothic form also. They pass through nearly the same conditions of change as the windows, with these three differences : first, that no arches of the fantastic fourth order occur in any doorways; secondly, that the pure pointed arch occurs earlier, and much oftener, in doorways than in window-heads; lastly, that the entrance itself, if small, is nearly always square-headed in the earliest examples, without any arch above, but afterwards the arch is thrown across above the lintel. The interval between the two, or tympanum, is filled with sculpture, or closed by iron bars, with sometimes a projecting gable, to form a porch, thrown over the whole, as in the perfect example, 7. *a*, Plate XIV. above. The other examples in the two lower lines 6. and 7. of that Plate are each characteristic of an enormous number of doors, variously decorated, from the thirteenth to the close of the fifteenth century. The particulars of their mouldings are given in the final Appendix.

§ LV. It was useless, on the small scale of this Plate, to attempt any delineation of the richer sculptures with which the arches are filled; so that I have chosen for it the simplest examples I could find of the forms to be illustrated: but, in all the more important instances, the door-head is charged either with delicate ornaments and inlaid patterns in variously colored brick, or with sculptures, consisting always of the shield or crest of the family, protected by an angel. Of these more perfect doorways I have given three examples carefully, in my folio work; but I must repeat here one part of the ccount of their subjects given in its text, for the convenience of those to whom the larger work may not be accessible.

§ LVI. "In the earlier ages, all agree thus far, that the name of the family is told, and together with it there is always an intimation that they have placed their defence and their prosperity in God's hands; frequently accompanied with some general expression of benediction to the person passing over the threshold. This is the general theory of an old Venetian doorway;—the theory of modern doorways remains to be explained: it may be studied to advantage in our rows of new-built houses, or rather of new-built house, changeless for miles together, from which, to each inhabitant, we allot his proper quantity of windows, and a Doric portico. The Venetian carried out his theory very simply. In the centre of the archivolt we find almost invariably, in the older work, the hand between the sun and moon in the attitude of blessing, expressing the general power and presence of God, the source of light. On the tympanum is the shield of the family. Venetian heraldry requires no beasts for supporters, but usually prefers angels, neither the supporters nor crests forming any necessary part of Venetian bearings. Sometimes, however, human figures, or grotesques, are substituted; but, in that case, an angel is almost always introduced above the shield, bearing a globe in his left hand, and therefore clearly intended for the 'Angel of the Lord,' or, as it is expressed elsewhere, the ' Angel of His Presence.' Where elaborate sculpture of this kind is inadmissible, the shield is merely represented as suspended by a leather thong ; and a cross is introduced above the archivolt. The Renaissance architects perceived the irrationality of all this, cut away both crosses and angels, and substituted heads of satyrs, which were the proper presiding deities of Venice in the Renaissance periods, and which in our own domestic institutions, we have ever since, with much piety and sagacity, retained."

§ LVII. The habit of employing some religious symbol, or writing some religious legend, over the door of the house, does not entirely disappear until far into the period of the Renaissance. The words " Peace be to this house " occur on one side of a Veronese gateway, with the appropriate and veracious inscription S. P. Q. R., on a Roman standard, on the other; and "Blessed is he that cometh in the name of the Lord," is written on one of the doorways of a building added at the flank of the Casa Barbarigo, in the sixteenth or seventeenth century. It seems to be only modern Protestantism which is entirely ashamed of *all* symbols and words that appear in anywise like a confession of faith.

§ LVIII. This peculiar feeling is well worthy of attentive analysis. It indeed, in most cases, hardly deserves the name of a feeling; for the meaningless doorway is merely an ignorant copy of heathen models: but yet, if it were at this moment proposed to any of us, by our architects, to remove the grinning head of a satyr, or other classical or Palladian ornament, from the keystone of the door, and to substitute for it a cross, and an inscription testifying our faith, I believe that most persons would shrink from the proposal with an obscure and yet overwhelming sense that things would be sometimes done, and thought, within the house which would make the inscription on its gate a base hypocrisy. And if so, let us look to it, whether that strong reluctance to utter a definite religious profession, which so many of us feel, and which, not very carefully examining into its dim nature, we conclude to be modesty, or fear of hypocrisy, or other such form of amiableness, be not, in very deed, neither less nor more than Infidelity; whether Peter's "I know not the man" be not the sum and substance of all these misgivings and hesitations; and whether the shamefacedness which we attribute to sincerity and reverence, be not such shamefacedness as may at last put us among those of whom the Son of Man shall be ashamed.

§ LIX. Such are the principal circumstances to be noted in the external form and details of the Gothic palaces; of their interior arrangements there is little left unaltered. The gateways which we have been examining almost universally lead, in the earlier palaces, into a long interior court, round which

the mass of the palace is built; and in which its first story is
reached by a superb external staircase, sustained on four or
five pointed arches gradually increasing as they ascend, both
in height and span,—this change in their size being, so far as
I remember, peculiar to Venice, and visibly a consequence of
the habitual admission of arches of different sizes in the Byzantine façades. These staircases are protected by exquisitely
carved parapets, like those of the outer balconies, with lions
or grotesque heads set on the angles, and with true projecting
balconies on their landing-places. In the centre of the court
there is always a marble well; and these wells furnish some
of the most superb examples of Venetian sculpture. I am
aware only of one remaining from the Byzantine period; it is
octagonal, and treated like the richest of our Norman fonts:
but the Gothic wells of every date, from the thirteenth century
downwards, are innumerable, and full of beauty, though their
form is little varied; they being, in almost every case, treated
like colossal capitals of pillars, with foliage at the angles, and
the shield of the family upon their sides.

§ LX. The interior apartments always consist of one noble
hall on the first story, often on the second also, extending
across the entire depth of the house, and lighted in front by
the principal groups of its windows, while smaller apartments
open from it on either side. The ceilings, where they remain
untouched, are of bold horizontal beams, richly carved and
gilded; but few of these are left from the true Gothic times,
the Venetian interiors having, in almost every case, been re-
modelled by the Renaissance architects. This change, however, for once, we cannot regret, as the walls and ceilings,
when so altered, were covered with the noblest works of Veronese, Titian, and Tintoret; nor the interior walls only, but, as
before noticed, often the exteriors also. Of the color decorations of the Gothic exteriors I have, therefore, at present taken
no notice, as it will be more convenient to embrace this subject

ın one general view of the systems of coloring of the Venetian palaces, when we arrive at the period of its richest developement. * The details, also, of most interest, respecting the forms and transitional decoration of their capitals, will be given in the final Appendix to the next volume, where we shall be able to include in our inquiry the whole extent of the Gothic period; and it remains for us, therefore, at present, only to review the history, fix the date, and note the most important particulars in the structure of the building which at once consummates and embodies the entire system of the Gothic architecture of Venice, — the DUCAL PALACE.

* Vol. III. Chap. I. I have had considerable difficulty in the arrangement of these volumes, so as to get the points bearing upon each other grouped in consecutive and intelligible order.

CHAPTER VIII.

THE DUCAL PALACE.

§ I. It was stated in the commencement of the preceding chapter that the Gothic art of Venice was separated by the building of the Ducal Palace into two distinct periods; and that in all the domestic edifices which were raised for half a century after its completion, their characteristic and chiefly effective portions were more or less directly copied from it. The fact is, that the Ducal Palace was the great work of Venice at this period, itself the principal effort of her imagination, employing her best architects in its masonry, and her best painters in its decoration, for a long series of years; and we must receive it as a remarkable testimony to the influence which it possessed over the minds of those who saw it in its progress, that, while in the other cities of Italy every palace and church was rising in some original and daily more daring form, the majesty of this single building was able to give pause to the Gothic imagination in its full career; stayed the restlessness of innovation in an instant, and forbade the powers which had created it thenceforth to exert themselves in new directions, or endeavor to summon an image more attractive.

§ II. The reader will hardly believe that while the architectural invention of the Venetians was thus lost, Narcissus-like, in self-contemplation, the various accounts of the progress of the building thus admired and beloved are so confused as frequently to leave it doubtful to what portion of the palace they refer; and that there is actually, at the time being, a dispute between the best Venetian antiquaries, whether the main façade of the palace be of the fourteenth or fifteenth century. The determination of this question is of course necessary before we proceed to draw any conclusions from the style of the work; and it cannot be determined without a careful review of the entire history of the palace, and of all the documents relating to it. I trust that this review may not be found tedious,—assuredly it will not be fruitless,— bringing many facts before us, singularly illustrative of the Venetian character.

§ III. Before, however, the reader can enter upon any inquiry into the history of this building, it is necessary that he should be thoroughly familiar with the arrangement and names of its principal parts, as it at present stands; otherwise he cannot comprehend so much as a single sentence of any of the documents referring to it. I must do what I can, by the help of a rough plan and bird's-eye view, to give him the necessary topographical knowledge:

Fig. XXXVI. opposite is a rude ground plan of the buildings round St. Mark's Place; and the following references will clearly explain their relative positions:

A. St. Mark's Place.

B. Piazzetta.

P. V. Procuratie Vecchie.

P. N. (opposite) Procuratie Nuove.

P. L. Libreria Vecchia.

1. Piazzetta de' Leoni.

T. Tower of St. Mark.

F F. Great Façade of St. Mark's Church.

M. St. Mark's. (It is so united with the Ducal Palace, that the separation cannot be indicated in the plan, unless all the walls had been marked, which would have confused the whole.)

D D D. Ducal Palace.   g s. Giant's stair.

C. Court of Ducal Palace.   J. Judgment angle.
c   Porta della Carta.   a. Figtree angle.
p p. Ponte della Paglia (Bridge of Straw).
S. Ponte de' Sospiri (Bridge of Sighs).
R R. Riva de' Schiavoni.

The reader will observe that the Ducal Palace is arranged somewhat in the form of a hollow square, of which one side faces the Piazzetta, B, and another the quay called the Riva de' Schiavoni, R R; the third is on the dark canal called the "Rio del Palazzo," and the fourth joins the Church of St. Mark.

Of this fourth side, therefore, nothing can be seen. Of the other three sides we shall have to speak constantly; and they will be respectively called, that towards the Piazzetta, the "Piazzetta Façade;" that towards the Riva de' Schiavoni, the "Sea Façade;" and that towards the Rio del Palazzo, the "Rio Façade." This Rio, or canal, is usually looked upon by the traveller with great respect, or even horror, because it passes under the Bridge of Sighs. It is, however, one of the principal thoroughfares of the city; and the bridge and its canal together occupy, in the mind of a Venetian, very much the position of Fleet Street and Temple Bar in that of a Londoner,—at least, at the time when Temple Bar was occasionally decorated with human heads. The two buildings closely resemble each other in form.

§ IV. We must now proceed to obtain some rough idea of the appearance and distribution of the palace itself; but its arrangement will be better understood by supposing ourselves raised some hundred and fifty feet above the point in the lagoon in front of it, so as to get a general view of the Sea Façade and Rio Façade (the latter in very steep perspective), and to look down into its interior court. Fig. XXXVII. roughly represents such a view, omitting all details on the roofs, in order to avoid confusion. In this drawing we have merely to notice that, of the two bridges seen on the right, the uppermost, above the black canal, is the Bridge of Sighs; the lower one is the Ponte della Paglia, the regular thoroughfare from quay to quay, and, I believe, called the Bridge of Straw, because the boats which brought straw from the mainland used to sell it at this place. The corner of the palace, rising above this bridge, and formed by the meeting of the Sea Façade and Rio Façade, will always be called the Vine angle, because it is decorated by a sculpture of the drunkenness of Noah. The angle opposite will be called the Fig-tree angle, because it is decorated by a sculpture of the Fall of Man. The long and narrow range of building, of which the roof is seen in perspective behind this angle, is the part of the palace fronting the Piazzetta; and the angle under the pinnacle most to the left of the two which terminate it will be called, for a reason presently to be stated, the Judgment angle. Within the square formed by the building is seen its interior court (with one of its wells), terminated by small and fantastic buildings of the Renaissance period, which face the Giant's Stair, of which the extremity is seen sloping down on the left.

§ v. The great façade which fronts the spectator looks southward. Hence the two traceried windows lower than the rest, and to the right of the spectator, may be conveniently distinguished as the "Eastern Windows." There are two others like them, filled with tracery, and at the same level, which look upon the narrow canal between the Ponte della Paglia and the Bridge of Sighs: these we may conveniently call the "Canal Windows." The reader will observe a vertical line in this dark side of the palace, separating its nearer and plainer wall from a long four-storied range of rich architecture. This more distant range is entirely Renaissance: its extremity is not indicated, because I have no accurate sketch of the small buildings and bridges beyond it, and we shall have nothing whatever to do with this part of the palace in our

14

present inquiry. The nearer and undecorated wall is part of

Fig. XXXVIII.

the older palace, though much defaced by
modern opening of common windows, re-
fittings of the brickwork, &c.

§ VI. It will be observed that the façade
is composed of a smooth mass of wall, sustained on two tiers of pillars, one above
the other. The manner in which these
support the whole fabric will be understood at once by the rough section, Fig.
XXXVIII., which is supposed to be taken right through the
palace to the interior court, from near the middle of the Sea
Façade. Here *a* and *d* are the rows of shafts, both in the
inner court and on the Façade, which carry the main walls;
b, *c* are solid walls variously strengthened with pilasters. A,
B, C are the three stories of the interior of the palace.

The reader sees that it is impossible for any plan to be more
simple, and that if the inner floors and walls of the stories A,
B were removed, there would be left merely the form of a
basilica,—two high walls, carried on ranges of shafts, and
roofed by a low gable.

The stories A, B are entirely modernized, and divided into
confused ranges of small apartments, among which what
vestiges remain of ancient masonry are entirely undecipherable, except by investigations such as I have had neither the
time nor, as in most cases they would involve the removal of
modern plastering, the opportunity, to make. With the sub-
divisions of this story, therefore, I shall not trouble the
reader; but those of the great upper story, C, are highly
important.

§ VII. In the bird's-eye view above, fig. XXXVII., it will
be noticed that the two windows on the right are lower than
the other four of the façade. In this arrangement there is
one of the most remarkable instances I know of the daring

sacrifice of symmetry to convenience, which was noticed in Chap. VII. as one of the chief noblenesses of the Gothic schools.

The part of the palace in which the two lower windows occur, we shall find, was first built, and arranged in four stories in order to obtain the necessary number of apartments. Owing to circumstances, of which we shall presently give an account, it became necessary, in the beginning of the fourteenth century, to provide another large and magnificent chamber for the meeting of the senate. That chamber was added at the side of the older building; but, as only one room was wanted, there was no need to divide the added portion into two stories. The entire height was given to the single chamber, being indeed not too great for just harmony with its enormous length and breadth. And then came the question how to place the windows, whether on a line with the two others, or above them.

The ceiling of the new room was to be adorned by the paintings of the best masters in Venice, and it became of great importance to raise the light near that gorgeous roof, as well as to keep the tone of illumination in the Council Chamber serene; and therefore to introduce light rather in simple masses than in many broken streams. A modern architect, terrified at the idea of violating external symmetry, would have sacrificed both the pictures and the peace of the council. He would have placed the larger windows at the same level with the other two, and have introduced above them smaller windows, like those of the upper story in the older building, as if that upper story had been continued along the façade. But the old Venetian thought of the honor of the paintings, and the comfort of the senate, before his own reputation. He unhesitatingly raised the large windows to their proper position with reference to the interior of the chamber, and suffered the external appearance to take care of itself. And I believe the whole pile rather gains than loses in effect by the variation thus obtained in the spaces of wall above and below the windows.

§ VIII. On the party wall, between the second and third windows, which faces the eastern extremity of the Great Council Chamber, is painted the Paradise of Tintoret; and this wall will therefore be hereafter called the "Wall of the Paradise."

In nearly the centre of the Sea Façade, and between the first and second windows of the Great Council Chamber, is a large window to the ground, opening on a balcony, which is one of the chief ornaments of the palace, and will be called in future the "Sea Balcony."

The façade which looks on the Piazzetta is very nearly like this to the Sea, but the greater part of it was built in the fifteenth century, when people had become studious of their symmetries. Its side windows are all on the same level. Two light the west end of the Great Council Chamber, one lights a small room anciently called the Quarantia Civil Nuova; the other three, and the central one, with a balcony like that to the Sea, light another large chamber, called Sala del Scrutinio, or "Hall of Enquiry," which extends to the extremity of the palace above the Porta della Carta.

§ IX. The reader is now well enough acquainted with the topography of the existing building, to be able to follow the accounts of its history.

We have seen above, that there were three principal styles of Venetian architecture ; Byzantine, Gothic, and Renaissance.

The Ducal Palace, which was the great work of Venice, was built successively in the three styles. There was a Byzantine Ducal Palace, a Gothic Ducal Palace, and a Renaissance Ducal Palace. The second superseded the first totally ; a few stones of it (if indeed so much) are all that is left. But the third superseded the second in part only, and the existing building is formed by the union of the two.

We shall review the history of each in succession.*

1st. The BYZANTINE PALACE.

In the year of the death of Charlemagne, 813†, the Venetians determined to make the island of Rialto the seat of the government and capital of their state. Their Doge, Angelo or Agnello Participazio, instantly took vigorous means for the enlargement of the small group of buildings which were to be the nucleus of the future Venice. He appointed persons to superintend the raising of the banks of sand, so as to form more secure foundations, and to build wooden bridges over the canals. For the offices of religion, he built the Church of St. Mark; and on, or near, the spot where the Ducal Palace now stands, he built a palace for the administration of the government.‡

* The reader will find it convenient to note the following editions of the printed books which have been principally consulted in the following inquiry. The numbers of the manuscripts referred to in the Marcian Library are given with the quotations.

    Sansovino. Venetia Descritta. 4to, Venice, 1663.

    Sansovino. Lettera intorno al Palazzo Ducale. 8vo, Venice, 1829.

    Temanza. Antica Pianta di Venezia, with text. Venice, 1780.

    Cadorin. Pareri di XV. Architetti. 8vo, Venice, 1838.

    Filiasi. Memorie storiche. 8vo, Padua, 1811.

    Bettio. Lettera discorsiva del Palazzo Ducale. 8vo, Venice, 1837.

    Selvatico. Architettura di Venezia. 8vo, Venice, 1847.

† The year commonly given is 810, as in the Savina Chronicle (Cod. Marcianus), p. 13. "Del 810 fece principiar el pallazzo Ducal nel luogo ditto Bruolo in confin di S. Moisè, et fece riedificar la isola di Eraclia." The Sagornin Chronicle gives 804; and Filiasi, vol. vi. chap. 1., corrects this date to 813.

‡ "Ampliò la città, fornilla di casamenti, *e per il culto d' Iddio e l' amministrazione della giustizia* eresse la cappella di S. Marco, e il palazzo di sua residenza."—Pareri, p. 120. Observe, that piety towards God, and justice towards man, have been at least the nominal purposes of every act and institution of ancient Venice. Compare also Temanza, p. 24. "Quello che abbiamo di certo si è che il suddetto Agnello lo incominciò da fondamenti, e così pure la cappella ducale di S. Marco."

The history of the Ducal Palace therefore begins with the birth of Venice, and to what remains of it, at this day, is entrusted the last representation of her power.

§ x Of the exact position and form of this palace of Participazio little is ascertained. Sansovino says that it was "built near the Ponte della Paglia, and answeringly on the Grand Canal," * towards San Giorgio; that is to say, in the place now occupied by the Sea Façade; but this was merely the popular report of his day. We know, however, positively, that it was somewhere upon the site of the existing palace; and that it had an important front towards the Piazzetta, with which, as we shall see hereafter, the present palace at one period was incorporated. We know, also, that it was a pile of some magnificence, from the account given by Sagornino of the visit paid by the Emperor Otho the Great, to the Doge Pietro Orseolo II. The chronicler says that the Emperor "beheld carefully all the beauty of the palace;" † and the Venetian historians express pride in the building's being worthy of an emperor's examination. This was after the palace had been much injured by fire in the revolt against Candiano

---

* What I call the Sea, was called "the Grand Canal" by the Venetians, as well as the great water street of the city; but I prefer calling it "the Sea," in order to distinguish between that street and the broad water in front of the Ducal Palace, which, interrupted only by the island of San Giorgio, stretches for many miles to the south, and for more than two to the boundary of the Lido. It was the deeper channel, just in front of the Ducal Palace, continuing the line of the great water street itself, which the Venetians spoke of as "the Grand Canal." The words of Sansovino are: "Fu cominciato dove si vede, vicino al ponte della paglia, et rispondente sul canal grande." Filiasi says simply: "The palace was built where it now is." "Il palazio fu fatto dove ora pure esiste."—Vol. iii. chap. 27. The Savina Chronicle, already quoted, says; "in the place called the Bruolo (or Broglio), that is to say, on the Piazzetta."

† "Omni decoritate illius perlustrata."—Sagornino, quoted by Cadorin and Temanza.

IV.,* and just repaired, and richly adorned by Orseolo him-self, who is spoken of by Sagornino as having also "adorned the chapel of the Ducal Palace" (St. Mark's) with ornaments of marble and gold.† There can be no doubt whatever that the palace at this period resembled and impressed the other Byzantine edifices of the city, such as the Fondaco de Turchi &c., whose remains have been already described; and that, like them, it was covered with sculpture, and richly adorned with gold and color.

§ XI. In the year 1106, it was for the second time injured by fire,‡ but repaired before 1116, when it received another emperor, Henry V. (of Germany), and was again honored by imperial praise.§ Between 1173 and the close of the century, it seems to have been again repaired and much enlarged by the Doge Sebastian Ziani. Sansovino says that this Doge not only repaired it, but "enlarged it in every direction;" ‖ and,

* There is an interesting account of this revolt in Monaci, p. 68. Some historians speak of the palace as having been destroyed entirely; but, that it did not even need important restorations, appears from Sagornino's expression, quoted by Cadorin and Temanza. Speaking of the Doge Participazio, he says: "Qui Palatii hucusque manentis fuerit fabricator." The reparations of the palace are usually attributed to the successor of Candiano, Pietro Orseolo I.; but the legend, under the picture of that Doge in the Council Chamber, speaks only of his rebuilding St. Mark's, and "performing many miracles." His whole mind seems to have been occupied with ecclesiastical affairs; and his piety was finally manifested in a way somewhat startling to the state, by his absconding with a French priest to St. Michael's, in Gascony, and there becoming a monk. What repairs, therefore, were necessary to the Ducal Palace, were left to be undertaken by his son, Orseolo II., above named.

† "Quam non modo marmoreo, verum aureo compsit ornamento."— *Temanza*, p. 25.

‡ "L' anno 1106, uscito fuoco d' una casa privata, arse parte del palazzo."—*Sansovino.* Of the beneficial effect of these fires, vide Cadorin, p. 121. 123

§ "Urbis situm, ædificiorum decorem, et regiminis æquitatem multipliciter commendavit."—*Cronaca Dandolo*, quoted by Cadorin.

‖ "Non solamente rinovò il palazzo, ma lo aggrandì per ogni verso."—*Sansovino.* Zanotto quotes the Altinat Chronicle for account of these repairs.

after this enlargement, the palace seems to have remained
untouched for a hundred years, until, in the commencement
of the fourteenth century, the works of the Gothic Palace
were begun. As, therefore, the old Byzantine building was,
at the time when those works first interfered with it, in the
form given to it by Ziani, I shall hereafter always speak of it
as the *Ziani* Palace; and this the rather, because the only
chronicler whose words are perfectly clear respecting the
existence of part of this palace so late as the year 1422, speaks
of it as built by Ziani. The old " palace, of which half remains
to this day, was built, as we now see it, by Sebastian Ziani." *

So far, then, of the Byzantine Palace.

§ xii. 2nd. The GOTHIC PALACE. The reader, doubtless,
recollects that the important change in the Venetian government which gave stability to the aristocratic power took place
about the year 1297,† under the Doge Pietro Gradenigo, a man
thus characterized by Sansovino:—"A prompt and prudent
man, of unconquerable determination and great eloquence,
who laid, so to speak, the foundations of the eternity of this
republic, by the admirable regulations which he introduced
into the government."

We may now, with some reason, doubt of their admirableness; but their importance, and the vigorous will and intellect
of the Doge, are not to be disputed. Venice was in the zenith
of her strength, and the heroism of her citizens was displaying
itself in every quarter of the world.‡   The acquiescence in the
secure establishment of the aristocratic power was an expres-

---

* "El palazzo che anco di mezzo se vede vecchio, per M. Sebastian Ziani
fu fatto compir, come el se vede."—*Chronicle of Pietro Dolfino*, Cod. Ven. p.
47. This Chronicle is spoken of by Sansovino as "molto particolare e dis-
tinta."—*Sansovino, Venezia descritta*, p. 593.—It terminates in the year 1422.

† See Vol. I. Appendix 3.

‡ Vide Sansovino's enumeration of those who flourished in the reign of
Gradenigo, p. 564.

sion, by the people, of respect for the families which had been chiefly instrumental in raising the commonwealth to such a height of prosperity.

The Serrar del Consiglio fixed the numbers of the Senate within certain limits, and it conferred upon them a dignity greater than they had ever before possessed. It was natural that the alteration in the character of the assembly should be attended by some change in the size, arrangement, or decoration of the chamber in which they sat.

We accordingly find it recorded by Sansovino, that " in 1301 another saloon was begun on the Rio del Palazzo, *under the Doge Gradenigo*, and finished in 1309, *in which year the Grand Council first sat in it*." * In the first year, therefore, of the fourteenth century, the Gothic Ducal Palace of Venice was begun; and as the Byzantine Palace was, in its foundation, coeval with that of the state, so the Gothic Palace was, in its foundation, coeval with that of the aristocratic power. Considered as the principal representation of the Venetian school of architecture, the Ducal Palace is the Parthenon of Venice, and Gradenigo its Pericles.

§ XIII. Sansovino, with a caution very frequent among Venetian historians, when alluding to events connected with the Serrar del Consiglio, does not specially mention the cause for the requirement of the new chamber; but the Sivos Chronicle is a little more distinct in expression. " In 1301, it was determined to build a great saloon *for the assembling* of the Great Council, and the room was built which is *now* called the Sala del Scrutinio." † *Now*, that is to say, at the time when the

* Sansovino, 324. 1.

† " 1301 fu presa parte di fare una sala grande per la riduzione del gran consiglio, e fu fatta quella che ora si chiama dello Scrutinio."— *Cronaca Sivos*, quoted by Cadorin. There is another most interesting entry in the Chronicle of Magno, relating to this event; but the passage is so ill written, that I am not sure if I have deciphered it correctly :—" Del 1301 fu preso de fabrichar

Sivos Chronicle was written; the room has long ago been destroyed, and its name given to another chamber on the opposite side of the palace: but I wish the reader to remember the date 1301, as marking the commencement of a great architectural epoch, in which took place the first appliance of the energy of the aristocratic power, and of the Gothic style, to the works of the Ducal Palace. The operations then begun were continued, with hardly an interruption, during the whole period of the prosperity of Venice. We shall see the new buildings consume, and take the place of, the Ziani Palace, piece by piece: and when the Ziani Palace was destroyed, they fed upon themselves; being continued round the square, until, in the sixteenth century, they reached the point where they had been begun in the fourteenth, and pursued the track they had then followed some distance beyond the junction; destroying or hiding their own commencement, as the serpent, which is the type of eternity, conceals its tail in its jaws.

§ xiv. We cannot, therefore, *see* the extremity, wherein lay the sting and force of the whole creature,—the chamber, namely, built by the Doge Gradenigo; but the reader must keep that commencement and the date of it carefully in his mind. The body of the Palace Serpent will soon become visible to us.

The Gradenigo Chamber was somewhere on the Rio Façade, behind the present position of the Bridge of Sighs; i.e. about the point marked on the roof by the dotted lines in the woodcut; it is not known whether low or high, but probably on a first story. The great façade of the Ziani Palace being, as

la sala fo ruina e fu fata (fatta) quella se adoperava a far el pregadi e fu adopera per far el Gran Consegio fin 1423, che fu anni 122." This last sentence, which is of great importance, is luckily unmistakable:—" The room was used for the meetings of the Great Council until 1423, that is to say, for 122 years." —*Cod. Ven.* tom. i. p. 126. The Chronicle extends from 1253 to 1454.

above mentioned, on the Piazzetta, this chamber was as far back and out of the way as possible; secrecy and security being obviously the points first considered.

§ xv. But the newly constituted Senate had need of other additions to the ancient palace besides the Council Chamber. A short, but most significant, sentence is added to Sansovino's account of the construction of that room. "There were, *near it,*" he says, "the Cancellaria, and the *Gheba* or *Gabbia,* afterwards called the Little Tower."*

Gabbia means a "cage;" and there can be no question that certain apartments were at this time added at the top of the palace and on the Rio Façade, which were to be used as prisons. Whether any portion of the old Torresella still remains is a doubtful question; but the apartments at the top of the palace, in its fourth story, were still used for prisons as late as the beginning of the seventeenth century.† I wish the reader especially to notice that a separate tower or range of apartments was built for this purpose, in order to clear the government of the accusations so constantly made against them, by ignorant or partial historians, of wanton cruelty to prisoners. The stories commonly told respecting the "piombi" of the Ducal Palace are utterly false. Instead of being, as usually reported, small furnaces under the leads of the palace, they were comfortable rooms, with good flat roofs of larch, and carefully ventilated.‡ The new chamber, then, and the prisons,

---

* "Vi era appresso la Cancellaria, e la Gheba o Gabbia, chiamata poi Torresella."—P. 324. A small square tower is seen above the Vine angle in the view of Venice dated 1500, and attributed to Albert Durer. It appears about 25 feet square, and is very probably the Torresella in question.

† Vide Bettio, Lettera, p. 23.

‡ Bettio, Lettera, p 20. "Those who wrote without having seen them described them as covered with lead; and those who have seen them know that, between their flat timber roofs and the sloping leaden roof of the palace, the interval is five metres where it is least, and nine where it is greatest."

being built, the Great Council first sat in their retired cham
ber on the Rio in the year 1309.

§ XVI. Now, observe the significant progress of events.
They had no sooner thus established themselves in power than
they were disturbed by the conspiracy of the Tiepolos, in the
year 1310. In consequence of that conspiracy the Council
of Ten was created, still under the Doge Gradenigo; who,
having finished his work and left the aristocracy of Venice
armed with this terrible power, died in the year 1312, some
say by poison. He was succeeded by the Doge Marino Giorgio, who reigned only one year; and then followed the pros-
perous government of John Soranzo. There is no mention
of any additions to the Ducal Palace during his reign, but he
was succeeded by that Francesco Dandolo, the sculptures on
whose tomb, still existing in the cloisters of the Salute, may
be compared by any traveller with those of the Ducal Palace.
Of him it is recorded in the Savina Chronicle: "This Doge
also had the great gate built which is at the entry of the
palace, above which is his statue kneeling, with the gonfalon
in hand, before the feet of the Lion of St. Mark's." *

§ XVII. It appears, then, that after the Senate had completed
their Council Chamber and the prisons, they required a nobler
door than that of the old Ziani Palace for their Magnificences
to enter by. This door is twice spoken of in the government
accounts of expenses, which are fortunately preserved,† in the
following terms:—

"1335, June 1. We, Andrew Dandolo and Mark Loredano,
        procurators of St. Mark's, have paid to Martin the stone-

---

* "Questo Dose anche fese far la porta granda che se al intrar del Palazzo, in su la qual vi e la sua statua che sta in zenocchioni con lo confalon
in man, davanti li pie de lo Lion S Marco."—*Savin Chronicle*, Cod. Ven. p.
120.

† These documents I have not examined myself, being satisfied of the
accuracy of Cadorin, from whom I take the passages quoted.

cutter and his associates * . . . . for a stone of which
the lion is made which is put over the gate of the
palace."

"1344, November 4. We have paid thirty-five golden ducats
for making gold leaf, to gild the lion which is over the
door of the palace stairs."

The position of this door is disputed, and is of no consequence to the reader, the door itself having long ago disappeared, and been replaced by the Porta della Carta.

§ XVIII. But before it was finished, occasion had been discovered for farther improvements. The Senate found their
new Council Chamber inconveniently small, and, about thirty
years after its completion, began to consider where a larger
and more magnificent one might be built. The government
was now thoroughly established, and it was probably felt that
there was some meanness in the retired position, as well as
insufficiency in the size, of the Council Chamber on the Rio.
The first definite account which I find of their proceedings,
under these circumstances, is in the Caroldo Chronicle : †

"1340. On the 28th of December, in the preceding year,
Master Marco Erizzo, Nicolo Soranzo, and Thomas Gradenigo,
were chosen to examine where a new saloon might be built
in order to assemble therein the Greater Council. . . . . On
the 3rd of June, 1341, the Great Council elected two procu-
rators of the work of this saloon, with a salary of eighty
ducats a year."

It appears from the entry still preserved in the Archivio,
and quoted by Cadorin, that it was on the 28th of December,
1340, that the commissioners appointed to decide on this
important matter gave in their report to the Grand Council,

* "Libras tres, soldos 15 grossorum."—*Cadorin,* 189. 1.

† Cod. Ven., No. CXLI. p 365.

and that the decree passed thereupon for the commencement
of a new Council Chamber on the Grand Canal.*

The room then begun is the one now in existence, and its
building involved the building of all that is best and most
beautiful in the present Ducal Palace, the rich arcades of the
lower stories being all prepared for sustaining this Sala del
Gran Consiglio.

§ XIX. In saying that it is the same now in existence, I do
not mean that it has undergone no alterations; as we shall
see hereafter, it has been refitted again and again, and some
portions of its walls rebuilt; but in the place and form in
which it first stood, it still stands; and by a glance at the
position which its windows occupy, as shown in Fig.
XXXVII. above, the reader will see at once that whatever
can be known respecting the design of the Sea Façade, must
be gleaned out of the entries which refer to the building of
this Great Council Chamber.

Cadorin quotes two of great importance, to which we shall
return in due time, made during the progress of the work in
1342 and 1344; then one of 1349, resolving that the works
at the Ducal Palace, which had been discontinued during the
plague, should be resumed; and finally one in 1362, which
speaks of the Great Council Chamber as having been neglected
and suffered to fall into " great desolation," and resolves that
it shall be forthwith completed. †

The interruption had not been caused by the plague only,

---

* Sansovino is more explicit than usual in his reference to this decree:
"For it having appeared that the place (the first Council Chamber) was not
capacious enough, the saloon on the Grand Canal was ordered."　" Per cio
parendo che il luogo non fosse capace, fu ordinata la Sala sul Canal Grande."
—P. 324.

† Cadorin, 185. 2.　The decree of 1342 is falsely given as of 1345 by the
Sivos Chronicle, and by Magno; while Sanuto gives the decree to its right
year, 1342, but speaks of the Council Chamber as only begun in 1345.

but by the conspiracy of Faliero, and the violent death of the master builder.* The work was resumed in 1362, and completed within the next three years, at least so far as that Guariento was enabled to paint his Paradise on the walls†; so that the building must, at any rate, have been roofed by this time. Its decorations and fittings, however, were long in completion; the paintings on the roof being only executed in 1400.‡ They represented the heavens covered with stars,§ this being, says Sansovino, the bearings of the Doge Steno. Almost all ceilings and vaults were at this time in Venice covered with stars, without any reference to armorial bearings; but Steno claims, under his noble title of Stellifer, an important share in completing the chamber, in an inscription upon two square tablets, now inlaid in the walls on each side of the great window towards the sea:

" MILLE QUADRINGENTI CURREBANT QUATUOR ANNI
HOC OPUS ILLUSTRIS MICHAEL DUX STELLIFER AUXIT."

And in fact it is to this Doge that we owe the beautiful balcony of that window, though the work above it is partly of more recent date; and I think the tablets bearing this important inscription have been taken out and reinserted in the newer masonry. The labor of these final decorations occupied a total period of sixty years. The Grand Council sat in the finished chamber for the first time in 1423. In that year

---

* Calendario. See Appendix 1. Vol. III.

† "Il primo che vi colorisse fu Guariento, il quale l' anno 1365 vi fece il Paradiso in testa della sala."—*Sansovino.*

‡ "L' an poi 1400 vi fece il cielo compartita a quadretti d' oro, ripieni di stelle, ch' era la insegna del Doge Steno."—*Sansovino,* lib. VIII.

§ "In questi tempi si messe in oro il cielo della sala del Gran Consiglio et si fece il pergolo del finestra grande chi guarda sul canale, adornato l' uno e l' altro di stelle, ch' erano l' insegne del Doge."—*Sansovino,* lib. XIII. Compare also Pareri, p. 129.

the Gothic Ducal Palace of Venice was completed. It had taken, to build it, the energies of the entire period which I have above described as the central one of her life.

§ xx. 3rd. The RENAISSANCE PALACE. I must go back a step or two, in order to be certain that the reader understands clearly the state of the palace in 1423. The works of addition or renovation had now been proceeding, at intervals, during a space of a hundred and twenty-three years. Three generations at least had been accustomed to witness the gradual advancement of the form of the Ducal Palace into more stately symmetry, and to contrast the works of sculpture and painting with which it was decorated,—full of the life, knowledge, and hope of the fourteenth century,—with the rude Byzantine chiselling of the palace of the Doge Ziani. The magnificent fabric just completed, of which the new Council Chamber was the nucleus, was now habitually known in Venice as the "Palazzo Nuovo;" and the old Byzantine edifice, now ruinous, and more manifest in its decay by its contrast with the goodly stones of the building which had been raised at its side, was of course known as the "Palazzo Vecchio."* That fabric, however, still occupied the principal position in Venice. The new Council Chamber had been erected by the side of it towards the Sea; but there was not then the wide quay in front, the Riva dei Schiavoni, which now renders the Sea Façade as important as that to the Piazzetta. There was only a narrow walk between the pillars and the water; and the *old* palace of Ziani still faced the Piazzetta, and interrupted, by its decrepitude, the magnificence of the square where the nobles daily met. Every increase of the beauty of the new palace rendered the discrepancy between it and the companion building more painful;

---

* Baseggio (Pareri, p. 127.) is called the Proto of the *New* Palace. Farther notes will be found in Appendix 1, Vol. III.

and then began to arise in the minds of all men a vague idea
of the necessity of destroying the old palace, and completing
the front of the Piazzetta with the same splendor as the Sea
Façade. But no such sweeping measure of renovation had
been contemplated by the Senate when they first formed the
plan of their new Council Chamber. First a single additional
room, then a gateway, then a larger room; but all considered
merely as necessary additions to the palace, not as involving
the entire reconstruction of the ancient edifice. The ex-
haustion of the treasury, and the shadows upon the political
horizon, rendered it more than imprudent to incur the vast
additional expense which such a project involved; and the
Senate, fearful of itself, and desirous to guard against the
weakness of its own enthusiasm, passed a decree, like the
effort of a man fearful of some strong temptation to keep his
thoughts averted from the point of danger. It was a decree,
not merely that the old palace should not be rebuilt, but that
no one should *propose* rebuilding it. The feeling of the
desirableness of doing so was too strong to permit fair
discussion, and the Senate knew that to bring forward such a
motion was to carry it.

§ XXI. The decree, thus passed in order to guard against
their own weakness, forbade any one to speak of rebuilding
the old palace under the penalty of a thousand ducats. But
they had rated their own enthusiasm too low : there was a
man among them whom the loss of a thousand ducats could
not deter from proposing what he believed to be for the good
of the state.

Some excuse was given him for bringing forward the motion,
by a fire which occurred in 1419, and which injured both
the church of St. Mark's, and part of the old palace fronting
the Piazzetta. What followed, I shall relate in the words of
Sanuto.*

* Cronaca Sanudo, No. CXXV. in the Marcian Library, p. 568.

§ XXII. "Therefore they set themselves with all diligence
and care to repair and adorn sumptuously, first God's house;
but in the Prince's house things went on more slowly, *for it
did not please the Doge* to restore it in the form in which it
was before;* and they could not rebuild it altogether in a
better manner, so great was the parsimony of these old
fathers; because it was forbidden by laws, which condemned
in a penalty of a thousand ducats any one who should propose
to throw down the *old* palace, and to rebuild it more richly
and with greater expense. But the Doge, who was magna-
nimous, and who desired above all things what was honorable
to the city, had the thousand ducats carried into the Senate
Chamber, and then proposed that the palace should be rebuilt;
saying: that, 'since the late fire had ruined in great part the
Ducal habitation (not only his own private palace, but all the
places used for public business) this occasion was to be taken
for an admonishment sent from God, that they ought to
rebuild the palace more nobly, and in a way more befitting the
greatness to which, by God's grace, their dominions had
reached; and that his motive in proposing this was neither
ambition, nor selfish interest: that, as for ambition, they
might have seen in the whole course of his life, through so
many years, that he had never done anything for ambition,
either in the city, or in foreign business; but in all his actions
had kept justice first in his thoughts, and then the advantage
of the state, and the honor of the Venetian name: and that,
as far as regarded his private interest, if it had not been for
this accident of the fire, he would never have thought of
changing anything in the palace into either a more sumptuous
or a more honorable form; and that during the many years
in which he had lived in it, he had never endeavored to make
any change, but had always been content with it, as his predecessors had left it; and that he knew well that, if they took

* Tomaso Mocenigo.

in hand to build it as he exhorted and besought them, being now very old, and broken down with many toils, God would call him to another life before the walls were raised a pace from the ground. And that therefore they might perceive that he did not advise them to raise this building for his own convenience, but only for the honor of the city and its Dukedom; and that the good of it would never be felt by him, but by his successors.' Then he said, that 'in order, as he had always done, to observe the laws, . . . he had brought with him the thousand ducats which had been appointed as the penalty for proposing such a measure, so that he might prove openly to all men that it was not his own advantage that he sought, but the dignity of the state.'" There was no one (Sanuto goes on to tell us) who ventured, or desired, to oppose the wishes of the Doge; and the thousand ducats were unanimously devoted to the expenses of the work. "And they set themselves with much diligence to the work; and the palace was begun in the form and manner in which it is at present seen; but, as Mocenigo had prophesied, not long after, he ended his life, and not only did not see the work brought to a close, but hardly even begun."

§ XXIII. There are one or two expressions in the above extracts which, if they stood alone, might lead the reader to suppose that the whole palace had been thrown down and rebuilt. We must however remember, that, at this time, the new Council Chamber, which had been one hundred years in building, was actually unfinished, the council had not yet sat in it; and it was just as likely that the Doge should then propose to destroy and rebuild it, as in this year, 1853, it is that any one should propose in our House of Commons to throw down the new Houses of Parliament, under the title of the "old palace," and rebuild *them*.

§ XXIV. The manner in which Sanuto expresses himself will at once be seen to be perfectly natural, when it is remembered that although we now speak of the whole building as the "Ducal Palace," it consisted, in the minds of the old Venetians, of four distinct buildings. There were in it the palace, the state prisons, the senate-house, and the offices of public business; in other words, it was Buckingham Palace, the Tower of olden days, the Houses of Parliament, and Downing Street, all in one; and any of these four portions might be spoken of, without involving an allusion to any other. "Il Palazzo" was the Ducal residence, which, with most of the public offices, Mocenigo *did* propose to pull down and rebuild, and which was actually pulled down and rebuilt. But the new Council Chamber, of which the whole façade to the Sea consisted, never entered into either his or Sanuto's mind for an instant, as necessarily connected with the Ducal residence.

I said that the new Council Chamber, at the time when Mocenigo brought forward his measure, had never yet been used. It was in the year 1422* that the decree passed to rebuild the palace: Mocenigo died in the following year,† and Francesco Foscari was elected in his room. The Great Council Chamber was used for the first time on the day when Foscari entered the Senate as Doge,—the 3rd of April, 1423, according to the Caroldo Chronicle;‡ the 23rd, which is probably correct, by an anonymous MS., No. 60., in the Correr Museum;§—and, the following year, on the 27th of March,

* Vide notes in Appendix.

† On the 4th of April, 1423, according to the copy of the Zancarol Chronicle in the Marcian Library, but previously, according to the Caroldo Chronicle, which makes Foscari enter the Senate as Doge on the 3rd of April.

‡ "Nella quale (the Sala del Gran Consiglio) non si fece Gran Consiglio salvo nell' anno 1423, alli 3 April, et fu il primo giorno che il Duce Foscari venisse in Gran Consiglio dopo la sua creatione."—Copy in Marcian Library, p. 365.

§ "E a di 23 April (1423, by the context) sequente fo fatto Gran Conseio in la salla nuovo dovi avanti non esta piu fatto Gran Conseio si che el primo Gran Conseio dopo la sua (Foscari's) creation fo fatto in la salla nuova, nel qual conseio fu el Marchese di Mantoa," &c. p. 426.

the first hammer was lifted up against the old palace of Ziani.*

§ xxv. That hammer stroke was the first act of the period properly called the "Renaissance." It was the knell of the architecture of Venice,—and of Venice herself.

The central epoch of her life was past; the decay had already begun: I dated its commencement above (Ch. I. Vol. I.) from the death of Mocenigo. A year had not yet elapsed since that great Doge had been called to his account: his patriotism, always sincere, had been in this instance mistaken; in his zeal for the honor of future Venice, he had forgotten what was due to the Venice of long ago. A thousand palaces might be built upon her burdened islands, but none of them could take the place, or recall the memory, of that which was first built upon her unfrequented shore. It fell; and, as if it had been the talisman of her fortunes, the city never flourished again.

§ xxvi. I have no intention of following out, in their intricate details, the operations which were begun under Foscari and continued under succeeding Doges till the palace assumed its present form, for I am not in this work concerned, except by occasional reference, with the architecture of the fifteenth century: but the main facts are the following. The palace of Ziani was destroyed; the existing façade to the Piazzetta built, so as both to continue and to resemble, in most particulars, the work of the Great Council Chamber. It was carried back from the Sea as far as the Judgment angle; beyond which is the Porta della Carta, begun in 1439, and finished in two years, under the Doge Foscari;† the interior buildings connected with it were added by the Doge Christopher Moro (the Othello of Shakspeare)‡ in 1462.

* Compare Appendix 1. Vol. III.

† "Tutte queste fatture si compirono sotto il dogado del Foscari, nel 1441." —*Pareri*, p. 131.

‡ This indentification has been accomplished, and I think conclusively, by

§ xxvII. By reference to the figure the reader will see that we have now gone the round of the palace, and that the new work of 1462 was close upon the first piece of the Gothic palace, the *new* Council Chamber of 1301. Some remnants of the Ziani Palace were perhaps still left between the two extremities of the Gothic Palace; or, as is more probable, the last stones of it may have been swept away after the fire of 1419, and replaced by new apartments for the Doge. But whatever buildings, old or new, stood on this spot at the time of the completion of the Porta della Carta were destroyed by another great fire in 1479, together with so much of the palace on the Rio that, though the saloon of Gradenigo, then known as the Sala de' Pregadi, was not destroyed, it became necessary to reconstruct the entire façades of the portion of the palace behind the Bridge of Sighs, both towards the court and canal. This work was entrusted to the best Renaissance architects of the close of the fifteenth and opening of the sixteenth centuries; Antonio Ricci executing the Giant's staircase, and on his absconding with a large sum of the public money, Pietro Lombardo taking his place. The whole work must have been completed towards the middle of the sixteenth century. The architects of the palace, advancing round the square and led by fire, had more than reached the point from which they had set out; and the work of 1560 was joined to the work of 1301—1340, at the point marked by the conspicuous vertical line in Fig. XXXVII. on the Rio Façade.

§ xxvIII. But the palace was not long permitted to remain in this finished form. Another terrific fire, commonly called

my friend Mr. Rawdon Brown, who has devoted all the leisure which, during the last twenty years, his manifold offices of kindness to almost every English visitant of Venice have left him, in discovering and translating the passages of the Venetian records which bear upon English history and literature. I shall have occasion to take advantage hereafter of a portion of his labors which I trust will shortly be made public.

the great fire, burst out in 1574, and destroyed the inner fittings and all the precious pictures of the Great Council Chamber, and of all the upper rooms on the Sea Façade, and most of those on the Rio Façade, leaving the building a mere shell, shaken and blasted by the flames. It was debated in the Great Council whether the ruin should not be thrown down, and an entirely new palace built in its stead. The opinions of all the leading architects of Venice were taken, respecting the safety of the walls, or the possibility of repairing them as they stood. These opinions, given in writing, have been preserved, and published by the Abbé Cadorin, in the work already so often referred to; and they form one of the most important series of documents connected with the Ducal Palace.

I cannot help feeling some childish pleasure in the accidental resemblance to my own name in that of the architect whose opinion was first given in favor of the ancient fabric, Giovanni Rusconi. Others, especially Palladio, wanted to pull down the old palace, and execute designs of their own; but the best architects in Venice, and to his immortal honor, chiefly Francesco Sansovino, energetically pleaded for the Gothic pile, and prevailed. It was successfully repaired, and Tintoret painted his noblest picture on the wall from which the Paradise of Guariento had withered before the flames.

§ XXIX. The repairs necessarily undertaken at this time were however extensive, and interfere in many directions with the earlier work of the palace: still the only serious alteration in its form was the transposition of the prisons, formerly at the top of the palace, to the other side of the Rio del Palazzo; and the building of the Bridge of Sighs, to connect them with the palace, by Antonio da Ponte. The completion of this work brought the whole edifice into its present form; with the exception of alterations in doors, partitions, and staircases among the inner apartments, not worth noticing, and such

barbarisms and defacements as have been suffered within the
last fifty years, by, I suppose, nearly every building of importance in Italy.

§ xxx. Now, therefore, we are at liberty to examine some
of the details of the Ducal Palace, without any doubt about
their dates. I shall not, however, give any elaborate illustrations of them here, because I could not do them justice on the
scale of the page of this volume, or by means of line engraving.
I believe a new era is opening to us in the art of illustration, *
and that I shall be able to give large figures of the details of
the Ducal Palace at a price which will enable every person
who is interested in the subject to possess them; so that the
cost and labor of multiplying illustrations here would be altogether wasted. I shall therefore direct the reader's attention
only to such points of interest as can be explained in the text.

§ xxxi. First, then, looking back to the woodcut at the
beginning of this chapter, the reader will observe that, as the
building was very nearly square on the ground plan, a peculiar
prominence and importance were given to its angles, which
rendered it necessary that they should be enriched and softened
by sculpture. I do not suppose that the fitness of this arrangement will be questioned; but if the reader will take the pains to
glance over any series of engravings of church towers or other
four-square buildings in which great refinement of form has
been attained, he will at once observe how their effect depends
on some modification of the sharpness of the angle, either by
groups of buttresses, or by turrets and niches rich in sculpture.
It is to be noted also that this principle of breaking the angle
is peculiarly Gothic, arising partly out of the necessity of
strengthening the flanks of enormous buildings, where composed of imperfect materials, by buttresses or pinnacles; partly
out of the conditions of Gothic warfare, which generally required a tower at the angle; partly out of the natural dislike

* See the last chapter of the third volume.

of the meagreness of effect in buildings which admitted large surfaces of wall, if the angle were entirely unrelieved. The Ducal Palace, in its acknowledgment of this principle, makes a more definite concession to the Gothic spirit than any of the previous architecture of Venice. No angle, up to the time of its erection, had been otherwise decorated than by a narrow fluted pilaster of red marble, and the sculpture was reserved always, as in Greek and Roman work, for the plane surfaces of the building, with, as far as I recollect, two exceptions only, both in St. Mark's; namely, the bold and grotesque gargoyle on its north-west angle, and the angels which project from the four inner angles under the main cupola; both of these arrangements being plainly made under Lombardic influence. And if any other instances occur, which I may have at present forgotten, I am very sure the Northern influence will always be distinctly traceable in them.

§ XXXII. The Ducal Palace, however, accepts the principle in its completeness, and throws the main decoration upon its angles. The central window, which looks rich and important in the woodcut, was entirely restored in the Renaissance time, as we have seen, under the Doge Steno; so that we have no traces of its early treatment; and the principal interest of the older palace is concentrated in the angle sculpture, which is arranged in the following manner. The pillars of the two bearing arcades are much enlarged in thickness at the angles, and their capitals increased in depth, breadth, and fulness of subject; above each capital, on the angle of the wall, a sculptural subject is introduced, consisting, in the great lower arcade, of two or more figures of the size of life; in the upper arcade, of a single angel holding a scroll: above these angels rise the twisted pillars with their crowning niches, already noticed in the account of parapets in the seventh chapter; thus forming an unbroken line of decoration from the ground to the top of the angle.

15

§ XXXIII. It was before noticed that one of the corners of the palace joins the irregular outer buildings connected with St. Mark's, and is not generally seen. There remain, therefore, to be decorated, only the three angles, above distinguished as the Vine angle, the Fig-tree angle, and the Judgment angle; and at these we have, according to the arrangement just explained,—

First, Three great bearing capitals (lower arcade).

Secondly, Three figure subjects of sculpture above them (lower arcade).

Thirdly, Three smaller bearing capitals (upper arcade).

Fourthly, Three angels above them (upper arcade).

Fifthly, Three spiral shafts with niches.

§ XXXIV. I shall describe the bearing capitals hereafter, in their order, with the others of the arcade; for the first point to which the reader's attention ought to be directed is the choice of subject in the great figure sculptures above them. These, observe, are the very corner stones of the edifice, and in them we may expect to find the most important evidences of the feeling, as well as of the skill, of the builder. If he has anything to say to us of the purpose with which he built the palace, it is sure to be said here; if there was any lesson which he wished principally to teach to those for whom he built, here it is sure to be inculcated; if there was any sentiment which they themselves desired to have expressed in the principal edifice of their city, this is the place in which we may be secure of finding it legibly inscribed.

§ XXXV. Now the first two angles, of the Vine and Fig-tree, belong to the old, or true Gothic, Palace; the third angle belongs to the Renaissance imitation of it: therefore, at the first two angles, it is the Gothic spirit which is going to speak to us; and, at the third, the Renaissance spirit.

The reader remembers, I trust, that the most characteristic sentiment of all that we traced in the working of the Gothic heart, was the frank confession of its own weakness; and I must anticipate, for a moment, the results of our inquiry in subsequent chapters, so far as to state that the principal element in the Renaissance spirit, is its firm confidence in its own wisdom.

Hear, then, the two spirits speak for themselves.

The first main sculpture of the Gothic Palace is on what I have called the angle of the Fig-tree:

Its subject is the FALL OF MAN.

The second sculpture is on the angle of the Vine:

Its subject is the DRUNKENNESS OF NOAH.

The Renaissance sculpture is on the Judgment angle:

Its subject is the JUDGMENT OF SOLOMON.

It is impossible to overstate, or to regard with too much admiration, the significance of this single fact. It is as if the palace had been built at various epochs, and preserved uninjured to this day, for the sole purpose of teaching us the difference in the temper of the two schools.

§ XXXVI. I have called the sculpture on the Fig-tree angle the principal one; because it is at the central bend of the palace, where it turns to the Piazzetta (the façade upon the Piazzetta being, as we saw above, the more important one in ancient times). The great capital, which sustains this Fig-tree angle, is also by far more elaborate than the head of the pilaster under the Vine angle, marking the preeminence of the former in the architect's mind. It is impossible to say which was first executed, but that of the Fig-tree angle is somewhat rougher in execution, and more stiff in the design of the figures, so that I rather suppose it to have been the earliest completed.

§ XXXVII. In both the subjects, of the Fall and the Drunkenness, the tree, which forms the chiefly decorative portion of the sculpture,—fig in the one case, vine in the other,—was a necessary adjunct. Its trunk, in both sculptures, forms the true outer angle of the palace; boldly cut separate from the stonework behind, and branching out above the figures so as to enwrap each side of the angle, for several feet, with its deep foliage. Nothing can be more masterly or superb than the sweep of this foliage on the Fig-tree angle; the broad leaves lapping round the budding fruit, and sheltering from sight, beneath their shadows, birds of the most graceful form and delicate plumage. The branches are, however, so strong, and the masses of stone hewn into leafage so large, that, notwithstanding the depth of the undercutting, the work remains nearly uninjured; not so at the vine angle, where the natural delicacy of the vine-leaf and tendril having tempted the sculptor to greater effort, he has passed the proper limits of his art, and cut the upper stems so delicately that half of them have been broken away by the casualties to which the situation of the sculpture necessarily exposes it. What remains is, however, so interesting in its extreme refinement, that I have chosen it for the subject of the opposite illustration rather than the nobler masses of the fig-tree, which ought to be rendered on a larger scale. Although half of the beauty of the composition is destroyed by the breaking away of its central masses, there is still enough in the distribution of the variously bending leaves, and in the placing of the birds on the lighter branches, to prove to us the power of the designer. I have already referred to this Plate as a remarkable instance of the Gothic Naturalism; and, indeed, it is almost impossible for the copying of nature to be carried farther than in the fibres of the marble branches, and the careful finishing of the tendrils: note especially the peculiar expression of the knotty joints of the vine in the light branch which rises highest. Yet only half the finish of the work can be seen in the Plate: for, in several cases, the sculptor has shown the under sides of the leaves turned boldly to the light, and has literally *carved every rib and vein upon them, in relief;* not merely the main ribs which sustain the lobes of the leaf, and actually project in nature, but the irregular and sinuous veins which chequer the membranous tissues between them, and which the sculptor has represented conventionally as relieved like the others, in order to give the vine leaf its peculiar tessellated effect upon the eye.

§ XXXVIII. As must always be the case in early sculpture, the figures are much inferior to the leafage; yet so skilful in many respects, that it was a long time before I could persuade myself that they had indeed been wrought in the first half of the fourteenth century. Fortunately, the date is inscribed upon a monument in the Church of San Simeon Grande, bearing a recumbent statue of the saint, of far finer workmanship, in every respect, than those figures of the Ducal Palace, yet so like them, that I think there can be no question that the head of Noah was wrought by the sculptor of the palace in emulation of that of the statue of St. Simeon. In this latter sculpture, the face is represented in death; the mouth partly open, the lips thin and sharp, the teeth carefully sculptured beneath; the face full of quietness and majesty, though very ghastly; the hair and beard flowing in luxuriant wreaths, disposed with the most masterly freedom, yet severity, of design, far down upon the shoulders; the hands crossed upon the body, carefully studied, and the veins and sinews perfectly and easily expressed, yet without any attempt at extreme finish or display of technical skill. This monument bears date 1317,* and its sculptor was justly proud of it; thus recording his name:

" CELAVIT MARCUS OPUS HOC INSIGNE ROMANIS,
      LAUDIBUS NON PARCUS EST SUA DIGNA MANUS."

* "IN XRI—NOIE AMEN ANNINCARNATIONIS MCCCXVII. INESETBR." "In the name of Christ, Amen, in the year of the incarnation, 1317, in the month of September," &c.

§ xxxix. The head of the Noah on the Ducal Palace, evidently worked in emulation of this statue, has the same profusion of flowing hair and beard, but wrought in smaller and harder curls; and the veins on the arms and breast are more sharply drawn, the sculptor being evidently more practised in keen and fine lines of vegetation than in those of the figure; so that, which is most remarkable in a workman of this early period, he has failed in telling his story plainly, regret and wonder being so equally marked on the features of all the three brothers that it is impossible to say which is intended for Ham. Two of the heads of the brothers are seen in the Plate; the third figure is not with the rest of the group, but set at a distance of about twelve feet, on the other side of the arch which springs from the angle capital.

§ xl. It may be observed, as a farther evidence of the date of the group, that, in the figures of all the three youths, the feet are protected simply by a bandage arranged in crossed folds round the ankle and lower part of the limb; a feature of dress which will be found in nearly every piece of figure sculpture in Venice, from the year 1300 to 1380, and of which the traveller may see an example within three hundred yards of this very group, in the bas-reliefs on the tomb of the Doge Andrea Dandolo (in St. Mark's), who died in 1354.

§ xli. The figures of Adam and Eve, sculptured on each side of the Fig-tree angle, are more stiff than those of Noah and his sons, but are better fitted for their architectural service; and the trunk of the tree, with the angular body of the serpent writhed around it, is more nobly treated as a terminal group of lines than that of the vine.

The Renaissance sculptor of the figures of the Judgment of Solomon has very nearly copied the fig-tree from this angle, placing its trunk between the executioner and the mother, who leans forward to stay his hand. But, though the whole group is much more free in design than those of the earlier palace, and in many ways excellent in itself, so that it always strikes the eye of a careless observer more than the others, it is of immeasurably inferior spirit in the workman-ship; the leaves of the tree, though far more studiously varied in flow than those of the fig-tree from which they are partially copied, have none of its truth to nature; they are ill set on the stems, bluntly defined on the edges, and their curves are not those of growing leaves, but of wrinkled drapery.

§ XLII. Above these three sculptures are set, in the upper arcade, the statues of the archangels Raphael, Michael, and Gabriel: their positions will be understood by reference to the lowest figure in Plate XVII., where that of Raphael above the Vine angle is seen on the right. A diminutive figure of Tobit follows at his feet, and he bears in his hand a scroll with this inscription:

EFICE Q̄

SOFRE

TŪR AFA

EL REVE

RENDE

QUIETŪ

i. e. Effice (quæso?) fretum, Raphael reverende, quietum.* I could not decipher the inscription on the scroll borne by the angel Michael; and the figure of Gabriel, which is by much the most beautiful feature of the Renaissance portion of the palace, has only in its hand the Annunciation lily.

---

* "Oh, venerable Raphael, make thou the gulf calm, we beseech thee." The peculiar office of the angel Raphael is, in general, according to tradition, the restraining the harmful influences of evil spirits. Sir Charles Eastlake told me. that sometimes in this office he is represented bearing the gall of the fish caught by Tobit; and reminded me of the peculiar superstitions of the Venetians respecting the raising of storms by fiends, as embodied in the well-known tale of the Fisherman and St. Mark's ring.

§ XLIII. Such are the subjects of the main sculptures deco
rating the angles of the palace; notable, observe, for their
simple expression of two feelings, the consciousness of human
frailty, and the dependence upon Divine guidance and pro
tection: this being, of course, the general purpose of the
introduction of the figures of the angels; and, I imagine,
intended to be more particularly conveyed by the manner in
which the small figure of Tobit follows the steps of Raphael,
just touching the hem of his garment. We have next to
examine the course of divinity and of natural history embodied by the old sculpture in the great series of capitals which
support the lower arcade of the palace; and which, being at
a height of little more than eight feet above the eye, might
be read, like the pages of a book, by those (the noblest men
in Venice) who habitually walked beneath the shadow of this
great arcade at the time of their first meeting each other for
morning converse.

§ XLIV. The principal sculptures of the capitals consist of
personifications of the Virtues and Vices, the favorite subjects
of decorative art, at this period, in all the cities of Italy; and
there is so much that is significant in the various modes of
their distinction and general representation, more especially
with reference to their occurrence as expressions of praise to
the dead in sepulchral architecture, hereafter to be examined,
that I believe the reader may both happily and profitably rest
for a little while beneath the first vault of the arcade, to
review the manner in which these symbols of the virtues were
first invented by the Christian imagination, and the evidence
they generally furnish of the state of religious feeling in those
by whom they were recognised.

§ XLV. In the early ages of Christianity, there was little
care taken to analyze character. One momentous question
was heard over the whole world,—Dost thou believe in the
Lord with all thine heart? There was but one division

among men,—the great unatoneable division between the disciple and adversary. The love of Christ was all, and in all;
and in proportion to the nearness of their memory of His
person and teaching, men understood the infinity of the
requirements of the moral law, and the manner in which it
alone could be fulfilled. The early Christians felt that virtue,
like sin, was a subtle universal thing, entering into every act
and thought, appearing outwardly in ten thousand diverse
ways, diverse according to the separate framework of every
heart in which it dwelt; but one and the same always in its
proceeding from the love of God, as sin is one and the same
in proceeding from hatred of God. And in their pure, early,
and practical piety, they saw there was no need for codes of
morality, or systems of metaphysics. Their virtue comprehended everything, entered into everything; it was too vast
and too spiritual to be defined; but there was no need of its
definition. For through faith, working by love, they knew
that all human excellence would be developed in due order;
but that, without faith, neither reason could define, nor effort
reach, the lowest phase of Christian virtue. And therefore,
when any of the Apostles have occasion to describe or enumerate any forms of vice or virtue by name, there is no
attempt at system in their words. They use them hurriedly
and energetically, heaping the thoughts one upon another,
in order as far as possible to fill the reader's mind with a sense
of the infinity both of crime and of righteousness. Hear St.
Paul describe sin: "Being filled with all unrighteousness,
fornication, wickedness, covetousness, maliciousness; full of
envy, murder, debate, deceit, malignity; whisperers, back-
biters, haters of God, despiteful, proud, boasters, inventors of
evil things, disobedient to parents, without understanding,
covenant breakers, without natural affection, implacable,
unmerciful." There is evidently here an intense feeling of
the universality of sin; and in order to express it, the Apostle

15*

hurries his words confusedly together, little caring about their order, as knowing all the vices to be indissolubly connected one with another. It would be utterly vain to endeavor to arrange his expressions as if they had been intended for the ground of any system, or to give any philosophical definition of the vices.* So also hear him speaking of virtue: "Rejoice in the Lord. Let your moderation be known unto all men. Be careful for nothing, but in everything let your requests be made known unto God; and whatsoever things are honest, whatsoever things are just, whatsoever things are pure, what-soever things are lovely, whatsoever things are of good report, if there be any virtue, and if there be any praise, think on these things." Observe, he gives up all attempt at definition; he leaves the definition to every man's heart, though he writes so as to mark the overflowing fulness of his own vision of virtue. And so it is in all writings of the Apostles; their manner of exhortation, and the kind of conduct they press, vary according to the persons they address, and the feeling of the moment at which they write, and never show any attempt at logical precision. And, although the words of their Master are not thus irregularly uttered, but are weighed like fine gold, yet, even in His teaching, there is no detailed or organized system of morality; but the command only of that faith and love which were to embrace the whole being of man: "On these two commandments hang all the law and the prophets." Here and there an incidental warning against this or that more dangerous form of vice or error, "Take heed and beware of covetousness," "Beware of the leaven of the Pharisees;" here and there a plain example of the meaning of

---

* In the original, the succession of words is evidently suggested partly by similarity of sound; and the sentence is made weighty by an alliteration which is quite lost in our translation; but the very allowance of influence to these minor considerations is a proof how little any metaphysical order or system was considered necessary in the statement.

Christian love, as in the parables of the Samaritan and the Prodigal, and His own perpetual example: these were the elements of Christ's constant teaching; for the Beatitudes, which are the only approximation to anything like a systematic statement, belong to different conditions and characters of individual men, not to abstract virtues. And all early Christians taught in the same manner. They never cared to expound the nature of this or that virtue; for they knew that the believer who had Christ, had all. Did he need fortitude? Christ was his rock: Equity? Christ was his righteousness: Holiness? Christ was his sanctification: Liberty? Christ was his redemption: Temperance? Christ was his ruler: Wisdom? Christ was his light: Truthfulness? Christ was the truth: Charity? Christ was love.

§ XLVI. Now, exactly in proportion as the Christian religion became less vital, and as the various corruptions which time and Satan brought into it were able to manifest themselves, the person and offices of Christ were less dwelt upon, and the virtues of Christians more. The Life of the Believer became in some degree separated from the Life of Christ; and his virtue, instead of being a stream flowing forth from the throne of God, and descending upon the earth, began to be regarded by him as a pyramid upon earth, which he had to build up, step by step, that from the top of it he might reach the Heavens. It was not possible to measure the waves of the water of life, but it was perfectly possible to measure the bricks of the Tower of Babel; and gradually, as the thoughts of men were withdrawn from their Redeemer, and fixed upon themselves, the virtues began to be squared, and counted, and classified, and put into separate heaps of firsts and seconds; some things being virtuous cardinally, and other things virtuous only north-north-west. It is very curious to put in close juxtaposition the words of the Apostles and of some of the writers of the fifteenth century touching sanctification. For instance, hear first St. Paul to the Thessalonians: "The very God of peace sanctify you wholly; and I pray God your whole spirit and soul and body be preserved blameless unto the coming of our Lord Jesus Christ. Faithful is he that calleth you, who also will do it." And then the following part of a prayer which I translate from a MS. of the fifteenth century: "May He (the Holy Spirit) govern the five Senses of my body; may He cause me to embrace the Seven Works of Mercy, and firmly to believe and observe the Twelve Articles of the Faith and the Ten Commandments of the Law, and defend me from the Seven Mortal Sins, even to the end."

§ XLVII. I do not mean that this quaint passage is generally characteristic of the devotion of the fifteenth century: the very prayer out of which it is taken is in other parts exceedingly beautiful:* but the passage is strikingly illustrative of the tendency of the later Romish Church, more especially in its most corrupt condition, just before the Reformation, to

* It occurs in a prayer for the influence of the Holy Spirit, "That He may keep my soul, and direct my way; compose my bearing, and form my thoughts in holiness; may He govern my body, and protect my mind; strengthen me in action, approve my vows, and accomplish my desires; cause me to lead an honest and honorable life, and give me good hope, charity and chastity, humility and patience: may He govern the Five Senses of my body," &c. The following prayer is also very characteristic of this period. It opens with a beautiful address to Christ upon the cross; then proceeds thus: "Grant to us, O Lord, we beseech thee, this day and ever, the use of penitence, of abstinence, of humility, and chastity; and grant to us light, judgment, understanding, and true knowledge, even to the end. One thing I note in comparing old prayers with modern ones, that however quaint, or however erring, they are always tenfold more condensed, comprehensive, and to their purpose, whatever that may be. There is no dilution in them, no vain or monotonous phraseology. They ask for what is desired plainly and earnestly, and never could be shortened by a syllable. The following series of ejaculations are deep in spirituality, and curiously to our present purpose in the philological quaintness of being built upon prepositions:—

throw all religion into forms and ciphers; which tendency, as it affected Christian ethics, was confirmed by the Renaissance enthusiasm for the works of Aristotle and Cicero, from whom the code of the fifteenth century virtues was borrowed, and whose authority was then infinitely more revered by all the Doctors of the Church than that either of St. Paul or St. Peter.

§ XLVIII. Although, however, this change in the tone of the Christian mind was most distinctly manifested when the revival of literature rendered the works of the heathen philosophers the leading study of all the greatest scholars of the period, it had been, as I said before, taking place gradually from the earliest ages. It is, as far as I know, that root of the Renaissance poison-tree, which, of all others, is deepest struck ; showing itself in various measures through the writings of all the Fathers, of course exactly in proportion to the respect which they paid to classical authors, especially to Plato, Aristotle, and Cicero. The mode in which the pestilent study of that literature affected them may be well illustrated by the examination of a single passage from the works of one of the best of them, St. Ambrose, and of the mode in which that passage was then amplified and formulized by later writers.

§ XLIX. Plato, indeed, studied alone, would have done no one any harm. He is profoundly spiritual and capacious in all his views, and embraces the small systems of Aristotle and

" Domine Jesu Christe, sancta cruce tua apud me sis, ut me defendas.
Domine Jesu Christe, pro veneranda cruce tua post me sis, ut me gubernes.
Domine Jesu Christe, pro benedicta cruce tua intra me sis, ut me reficeas.
Domine Jesu Christe, pro benedicta cruce tua circa me sis, ut me conserves.
Domine Jesu Christe, pro gloriosa cruce tua ante me sis, ut me deduces.
Domine Jesu Christe, pro laudanda cruce tua super me sis, ut benedicas.
Domine Jesu Christe, pro magnifica cruce tua in me sis, ut me ad regnum tuum perducas, per D. N. J. C. Amen."

Cicero, as the solar system does the Earth. He seems to me especially remarkable for the sense of the great Christian virtue of Holiness, or sanctification; and for the sense of the presence of the Deity in all things, great or small, which always runs in a solemn undercurrent beneath his exquisite playfulness and irony; while all the merely moral virtues may be found in his writings defined in the most noble manner, as a great painter defines his figures, *without outlines*. But the imperfect scholarship of later ages seems to have gone to Plato, only to find in him the system of Cicero; which indeed was very definitely expressed by him. For it having been quickly felt by all men who strove, unhelped by Christian faith, to enter at the strait gate into the paths of virtue, that there were four characters of mind which were protective or preservative of all that was best in man, namely, Prudence, Justice, Courage, and Temperance,* these were afterwards with most illogical inaccuracy, called cardinal *virtues*, Prudence being evidently no virtue, but an intellectual gift : but this inaccuracy arose partly from the ambiguous sense of the Latin word "virtutes," which sometimes, in mediæval language, signifies virtues, sometimes powers (being occasionally used in the Vulgate for the word "hosts," as in Psalm ciii. 21., cxlviii. 2., &c., while "fortitudines" and "exercitus" are used for the same word in other places), so that Prudence might properly be styled a power, though not properly a virtue; and partly from the confusion of Prudence with Heavenly Wisdom. The real rank of these four virtues, if so they are to be called, is however properly expressed by the term "cardinal." They are virtues of the compass, those by which all others are directed and strengthened ; they are not the greatest virtues, but the

---

* This arrangement of the cardinal virtues is said to have been first made by Archytas. See D'Ancarville's illustration of the three figures of Prudence, Fortitude, and Charity, in Selvatico's "Cappellina degli Scrovegni," Padua, 1836.

restraining or modifying virtues, thus Prudence restrains zeal, Justice restrains mercy, Fortitude and Temperance guide the entire system of the passions; and, thus understood, these virtues properly assumed their peculiar leading or guiding position in the system of Christian ethics. But in Pagan ethics, they were not only guiding, but comprehensive. They meant a great deal more on the lips of the ancients, than they now express to the Christian mind. Cicero's Justice includes charity, beneficence, and benignity, truth, and faith in the sense of trustworthiness. His Fortitude includes courage, self-command, the scorn of fortune and of all temporary felicities. His Temperance includes courtesy and modesty. So also, in Plato, these four virtues constitute the sum of education. I do not remember any more simple or perfect expression of the idea, than in the account given by Socrates, in the " Alcibiades I.," of the education of the Persian kings, for whom, in their youth, there are chosen, he says, four tutors from among the Persian nobles; namely, the Wisest, the most Just, the most Temperate, and the most Brave of them. Then each has a distinct duty : " The Wisest teaches the young king the worship of the gods, and the duties of a king (something more here, observe, than our ' Prudence!') ; the most Just teaches him to speak all truth, and to act out all truth, through the whole course of his life; the most Temperate teaches him to allow no pleasure to have the mastery of him, so that he may be truly free, and indeed a king; and the most Brave makes him fearless of all things, showing him that the moment he fears anything, he becomes a slave."

§ L. All this is exceedingly beautiful, so far as it reaches; but the Christian divines were grievously led astray by their endeavors to reconcile this system with the nobler law of love. At first, as in the passage I am just going to quote from St. Ambrose, they tried to graft the Christian system on the four branches of the Pagan one; but finding that the tree would not grow, they planted the Pagan and Christian branches side by side; adding, to the four cardinal virtues, the three called by the schoolmen theological, namely, Faith, Hope, and Charity: the one series considered as attainable by the Heathen, but the other by the Christian only. Thus Virgil to Sordello:

> "Loco e laggiù, non tristo da martiri
> Ma di tenebre solo, ove i lamenti
> Non suonan come guai, ma son sospiri:
>
> .   .   .   .   .
>
> Quivi sto io, con quei che le tre sante
> Virtù non si vestiro, e senza vizio
> Conobber l' altre, e seguir, tutte quante."

> .   .   .   .   .   "There I with those abide
> Who the Three Holy Virtues put not on,
> But understood the rest, and without blame
> Followed them all."
>
> CARY.

§ LI. This arrangement of the virtues was, however, productive of infinite confusion and error: in the first place, because Faith is classed with its own fruits,—the gift of God, which is the root of the virtues, classed simply as one of them; in the second, because the words used by the ancients to express the several virtues had always a different meaning from the same expressions in the Bible, sometimes a more extended, sometimes a more limited one. Imagine, for instance, the confusion which must have been introduced into the ideas of a student who read St. Paul and Aristotle alternately; considering that the word which the Greek writer uses for Justice, means, with St. Paul, Righteousness. And lastly, it is impossible to overrate the mischief produced in former days, as well as in our own, by the mere habit of reading Aristotle, whose system is so false, so forced, and so confused, that the study of it at our universities is quite enough to occasion the utter want of accurate habits of thought which so often disgraces men otherwise well-educated. In a word, Aristotle mistakes the Prudence or Temperance which must regulate the operation of the virtues, for the essence of the virtues themselves; and, striving to show that all virtues are means between two opposite vices, torments his wit to discover and distinguish as many pairs of vices as are necessary to the completion of his system, not disdaining to employ sophistry where invention fails him.

And, indeed, the study of classical literature, in general, not only fostered in the Christian writers the unfortunate love of systematizing, which gradually degenerated into every species of contemptible formulism, but it accustomed them to work out their systems by the help of any logical quibble, or verbal subtlety, which could be made available for their purpose, and this not with any dishonest intention, but in a sincere desire to arrange their ideas in systematical groups, while yet their powers of thought were not accurate enough, nor their common sense stern enough, to detect the fallacy, or disdain the finesse, by which these arrangements were frequently accomplished.

§ LII. Thus St. Ambrose, in his commentary on Luke vi. 20., is resolved to transform the four Beatitudes there described into rewards of the four cardinal Virtues, and sets himself thus ingeniously to the task :

" 'Blessed be ye poor.' Here you have Temperance. 'Blessed are ye that hunger now.' He who hungers, pities those who are an-hungered; in pitying, he gives to them, and in giving he becomes just (largiendo fit justus). 'Blessed are ye that weep now, for ye shall laugh.' Here you have Prudence, whose part it is to weep, so far as present things are concerned, and to seek things which are eternal. 'Blessed are ye when men shall hate you.' Here you have Fortitude."

§ LIII. As a preparation for this profitable exercise of wit, we have also a reconciliation of the Beatitudes as stated by

St. Matthew, with those of St. Luke, on the ground that "in those eight are these four, and in these four are those eight;" with sundry remarks on the mystical value of the number eight, with which I need not trouble the reader. With St. Ambrose, however, this puerile systematization is quite subordinate to a very forcible and truthful exposition of the real nature of the Christian life. But the classification he employs furnishes ground for farther subtleties to future divines; and in a MS. of the thirteenth century I find some expressions in this commentary on St. Luke, and in the treatise on the duties of bishops, amplified into a treatise on the "Steps of the Virtues: by which every one who perseveres may, by a straight path, attain to the heavenly country of the Angels." ("Liber de Gradibus Virtutum: quibus ad patriam angelorum supernam itinere recto ascenditur ab omni perseverante.") These Steps are thirty in number (one expressly for each day of the month), and the curious mode of their association renders the list well worth quoting:—

§ LIV.	Primus gradus est	Fides Recta.	Unerring faith.
	Secundus ,,	Spes firma.	Firm hope.
	Tertius ,,	Caritas perfecta.	Perfect charity.
	4. ,,	Patientia vera.	True patience.
	5. ,,	Humilitas sancta.	Holy humility.
	6. ,,	Mansuetudo.	Meekness.
	7. ,,	Intelligentia.	Understanding.
	8. ,,	Compunctio cordis.	Contrition of heart.
	9. ,,	Oratio.	Prayer.
	10. ,,	Confessio pura.	Pure confession.
	11. ,,	Penitentia digna.	Fitting penance.*
	12. ,,	Abstinentia.	Abstinence (fasting).
	13. ,,	Timor Dei.	Fear of God.
	14. ,,	Virginitas.	Virginity.

* Or Penitence: but I rather think this is understood only in Compunctio cordis.

15.	gradus est	Justicia.	Justice.
16.	„	Misericordia.	Mercy.
17.	„	Elemosina.	Almsgiving.
18.	„	Hospitalitas.	Hospitality.
19.	„	Honor parentum.	Honoring of parents.
20.	„	Silencium.	Silence.
21.	„	Consilium bonum.	Good counsel.
22.	„	Judicium rectum.	Right judgment.
23.	„	Exemplum bonum.	Good example.
24.	„	Visitatio infirmorum.	Visitation of the sick.
25.	„	Frequentatio sanctorum.	Companying with saints.
26.	„	Oblatio justa.	Just oblations.
27.	„	Decimas Deo solvere.	Paying tithes to God
28.	„	Sapientia.	Wisdom.
29.	„	Voluntas bona.	Goodwill.
30.	„	Perseverantia.	Perseverance.

§ LV The reader will note that the general idea of Christian virtue embodied in this list is true, exalted, and beautiful; the points of weakness being the confusion of duties with virtues, and the vain endeavor to enumerate the various offices of charity as so many separate virtues; more frequently arranged as seven distinct works of mercy. This general tendency to a morbid accuracy of classification was associated, in later times, with another very important element of the Renaissance mind, the love of personification; which appears to have reached its greatest vigor in the course of the sixteenth century, and is expressed to all future ages, in a consummate manner, in the poem of Spenser. It is to be noted that personification is, in some sort, the reverse of symbolism, and is far less noble Symbolism is the setting forth of a great truth by an imperfect and inferior sign (as, for instance, of the hope of the resurrection by the form of the phœnix); and it is almost always employed by men in their most serious moods of faith, rarely in recreation. Men who use symbolism forcibly are almost always true believers in what they symbolize. But Personification is the bestowing of a human or living form upon an abstract idea: it is, in most cases, a mere recreation of the fancy, and is apt to disturb the belief in the reality of the thing personified. Thus symbolism constituted the entire system of the Mosaic dispensation: it occurs in every word of Christ's teaching; it attaches perpetual mystery to the last and most solemn act of His life. But I do not recollect a single instance of personification in any of His words. And as we watch, thenceforward, the history of the Church, we shall find the declension of its faith exactly marked by the abandonment of symbolism,* and the profuse employment of personification,— even to such an extent that the virtues came, at last, to be confused with the saints; and we find in the later Litanies, St. Faith, St. Hope, St. Charity, and St. Chastity, invoked immediately after St. Clara and St. Bridget.

§ LVI. Nevertheless, in the hands of its early and earnest masters, in whom fancy could not overthow the foundations of faith, personification is often thoroughly noble and lovely; the earlier conditions of it being just as much more spiritual and vital than the later ones, as the still earlier symbolism was more spiritual than they. Compare, for instance, Dante's burning Charity, running and returning at the wheels of the chariot of God,—

> "So ruddy, that her form had scarce
> Been known within a furnace of clear flame,"

with Reynolds's Charity, a nurse in a white dress, climbed upon by three children.† And not only so, but the number

---

* The transformation of a symbol into a reality, observe, as in transubstantiation, is as much an abandonment of symbolism as the forgetfulness of symbolic meaning altogether.

† On the window of New College, Oxford.

and nature of the virtues differ considerably in the statements of different poets and painters, according to their own views of religion, or to the manner of life they had it in mind to illustrate. Giotto, for instance, arranges his system altogether differently at Assisi, where he is setting forth the monkish life, and in the Arena Chapel, where he treats of that of mankind in general, and where, therefore, he gives only the so-called theological and cardinal virtues; while, at Assisi, the three principal virtues are those which are reported to have appeared in vision to St. Francis, Chastity, Obedience and Poverty: Chastity being attended by Fortitude, Purity, and Penance; Obedience by Prudence and Humility; Poverty by Hope and Charity. The systems vary with almost every writer, and in almost every important work of art which embodies them, being more or less spiritual according to the power of intellect by which they were conceived. The most noble in literature are, I suppose, those of Dante and Spenser: and with these we may compare five of the most interesting series in the early art of Italy; namely, those of Orcagna, Giotto, and Simon Memmi, at Florence and Padua, and those of St. Mark's and the Ducal Palace at Venice. Of course, in the richest of these series, the vices are personified together with the virtues, as in the Ducal Palace; and by the form or name of opposed vice, we may often ascertain, with much greater accuracy than would otherwise be possible, the particular idea of the contrary virtue in the mind of the writer or painter. Thus, when opposed to Prudence, or Prudentia, on the one side, we find Folly, or Stultitia, on the other, it shows that the virtue understood by Prudence, is not the mere guiding or cardinal virtue, but the Heavenly Wisdom,* opposed to that folly which "hath said in its heart, there is

---

* Uniting the three ideas expressed by the Greek philosophers under the terms φρόνησ ι , σοφία, and ἐπιστήμη; and part of the idea of σωφροσύνη.

no God;" and of which it is said, "the thought of foolishness is sin;" and again, "Such as be foolish shall not stand in thy sight." This folly is personified, in early painting and illumination, by a half-naked man, greedily eating an apple or other fruit, and brandishing a club; showing that sensuality and violence are the two principal characteristics of Foolishness, and lead into atheism. The figure, in early Psalters, always forms the letter D, which commences the fifty-third Psalm, "*Dixit insipiens.*"

§ LVII. In reading Dante, this mode of reasoning from contraries is a great help, for his philosophy of the vices is the only one which admits of classification; his descriptions of virtue, while they include the ordinary formal divisions, are far too profound and extended to be brought under definition. Every line of the "Paradise" is full of the most exquisite and spiritual expressions of Christian truth; and that poem is only less read than the "Inferno" because it requires far greater attention, and, perhaps, for its full enjoyment, a holier heart.

§ LVIII. His system in the "Inferno" is briefly this. The whole nether world is divided into seven circles, deep within deep, in each of which, according to its depth, severer punishment is inflicted. These seven circles, reckoning them downwards, are thus allotted:

1. To those who have lived virtuously, but knew not Christ.
2. To Lust.
3. To Gluttony.
4. To Avarice and Extravagance.
5. To Anger and *Sorrow*.
6. To Heresy.
7. To Violence and Fraud.

This seventh circle is divided into two parts; of which the first, reserved for those who have been guilty of Violence, is again divided into three, apportioned severally to those who have committed, or desired to commit, violence against their neighbors, against themselves, or against God.

The lowest hell, reserved for the punishment of Fraud, is itself divided into ten circles, wherein are severally punished the sins of,—

1. Betraying women.
2. Flattery.
3. Simony.
4. False prophecy.
5. Peculation.
6. Hypocrisy.
7. Theft.
8. False counsel.
9. Schism and Imposture.
10. Treachery to those who repose entire trust in the traitor.

LIX. There is, perhaps, nothing more notable in this most interesting system than the profound truth couched under the attachment of so terrible a penalty to sadness or sorrow. It is true that Idleness does not elsewhere appear in the scheme, and is evidently intended to be included in the guilt of sadness by the word "accidioso;" but the main meaning of the poet is to mark the duty of rejoicing in God, according both to St. Paul's command, and Isaiah's promise, "Thou meetest him that rejoiceth and worketh righteousness."* I do not know words that might with more benefit be borne with us, and set in our hearts momentarily against the minor regrets and rebelliousnesses of life, than these simple ones:

> " Tristi fummo
> Nel aer dolce, che del sol s' allegra,
> Or ci attristiam, nella belletta negra."

* Isa. lxiv. 5.

> "We once were sad,
> In the sweet air, made gladsome by the sun.
> Now in these murky settlings are we sad."*   CARY.

The virtue usually opposed to this vice of sullenness is Alacritas, uniting the sense of activity and cheerfulness. Spenser has cheerfulness simply, in his description, never enough to be loved or praised, of the virtues of Womanhood; first, feminineness or womanhood in specialty; then,—

> "Next to her sate goodly Shamefastnesse,
> Ne ever durst her eyes from ground upreare,
> Ne ever once did looke up from her desse,*
> As if some blame of evill she did feare
> That in her cheekes made roses oft appeare:
> And her against sweet Cherefulnesse was placed,
> Whose eyes, like twinkling stars in evening cleare,
> Were deckt with smyles that all sad humours chaced.

> "And next to her sate sober Modestie,
> Holding her hand upon her gentle hart;
> And her against, sate comely Curtesie,
> *That unto every person knew her part;*
> And her before was seated overthwart
> Soft Silence, and submisse Obedience,
> Both linckt together never to dispart."

§ LX. Another notable point in Dante's system is the intensity of uttermost punishment given to treason, the peculiar sin of Italy, and that to which, at this day, she attributes her own misery with her own lips. An Italian, questioned as to the

---

* I can hardly think it necessary to point out to the reader the association between sacred cheerfulness and solemn thought, or to explain any appearance of contradiction between passages in which (as above in Chap. V.) I have had to oppose sacred pensiveness to unholy mirth, and those in which I have to oppose sacred cheerfulness to unholy sorrow.

† "Desse," seat.

causes of the failure of the campaign of 1848, always makes one answer, "We were betrayed;" and the most melancholy feature of the present state of Italy is principally this, that she does not see that, of all causes to which failure might be attributed, this is at once the most disgraceful, and the most hopeless. In fact, Dante seems to me to have written almost prophetically, for the instruction of modern Italy, and chiefly so in the sixth canto of the "Purgatorio."

§ LXI. Hitherto we have been considering the system of the "Inferno" only. That of the "Purgatorio" is much simpler, it being divided into seven districts, in which the souls are severally purified from the sins of Pride, Envy, Wrath, Indifference, Avarice, Gluttony, and Lust; the poet thus implying in opposition, and describing in various instances, the seven virtues of Humility, Kindness,* Patience, Zeal, Poverty, Abstinence, and Chastity, as adjuncts of the Christian character, in which it may occasionally fail, while the essential group of the three theological and four cardinal virtues are represented as in direct attendance on the chariot of the Deity; and all the sins of Christians are in the seventeenth canto traced to the deficiency or aberration of Affection.

§ LXII. The system of Spenser is unfinished, and exceedingly complicated, the same vices and virtues occurring under different forms in different places, in order to show their different relations to each other. I shall not therefore give any general sketch of it, but only refer to the particular personification of each virtue in order to compare it with that of the Ducal

---

* Usually called Charity: but this virtue in its full sense is one of the attendant spirits by the Throne; the Kindness here meant is Charity with a special object; or Friendship and Kindness, as opposed to Envy, which has always, in like manner, a special object. Hence the love of Orestes and Pylades is given as an instance of the virtue of Friendship; and the Virgin's, "They have no wine," at Cana, of general kindness and sympathy with others pleasure.

Palace.* The peculiar superiority of his system is in its exquisite setting forth of Chastity under the figure of Britomart; not monkish chastity, but that of the purest Love. In completeness of personification no one can approach him; not even in Dante do I remember anything quite so great as the description of the Captain of the Lusts of the Flesh:

> "As pale and wan as ashes was his looke;
> His body lean and meagre as a rake;
> And skin all withered like a dryed rooke;
> Thereto as cold and drery as a snake;
> That seemd to tremble evermore, and quake:
> *All in a canvas thin he was bedight,*
> *And girded with a belt of twisted brake:*
> Upon his head he wore an helmet light,
> Made of a dead mans skull."

He rides upon a tiger, and in his hand is a bow, bent;

> "And many arrows under his right side,
> Headed with flint, and fethers bloody dide."

The horror and the truth of this are beyond everything that I know, out of the pages of Inspiration. Note the heading of the arrows with flint, because sharper and more subtle in the edge than steel, and because steel might consume away with rust, but flint not; and consider in the whole description how the wasting away of body and soul together, and the *coldness* of the heart, which unholy fire has consumed into ashes, and the loss of all power, and the kindling of all terrible impatience,

---

* The "Faerie Queen," like Dante's "Paradise," is only half estimated, because few persons take the pains to think out its meaning. I have put a brief analysis of the first book in Appendix 2. Vol. III.; which may perhaps induce the reader to follow out the subject for himself. No time devoted to profane literature will be better rewarded than that spent *earnestly* on Spenser.

and the implanting of thorny and inextricable griefs, are set forth by the various images, the belt of brake, the tiger steed, and the *light* helmet, girding the head with death.

§ LXIII. Perhaps the most interesting series of the Virtues expressed in Italian art are those above mentioned of Simon Memmi in the Spanish chapel at Florence, of Ambrogio di Lorenzo in the Palazzo Publico of Pisa, of Orcagna in Or San Michele at Florence, of Giotto at Padua and Assisi, in mosaic on the central cupola of St. Mark's, and in sculpture on the pillars of the Ducal Palace. The first two series are carefully described by Lord Lindsay; both are too complicated for comparison with the more simple series of the Ducal Palace. the other four of course agree in giving first the cardinal and evangelical virtues; their variations in the statement of the rest will be best understood by putting them in a parallel arrangement.

St. Mark's.	Orcagna.	Giotto.	Ducal Palace.
Constancy.	Perseverance.		Constancy.
Modesty.			Modesty.
Chastity.	Virginity.	Chastity.	Chastity.
Patience.	Patience.		Patience.
Mercy.			
Abstinence.			Abstinence?
Piety.*	Devotion.		
Benignity.			
Humility.	Humility.	Humility.	Humility.
	Obedience.	Obedience	Obedience.
	Docility.		
	Caution.		
		Poverty.	*Honesty.*
			Liberality.
			Alacrity.

* Inscribed, I believe, Pietas, meaning general reverence and godly fear.

§ LXIV. It is curious, that in none of these lists do we find either *Honesty* or *Industry* ranked as a virtue, except in the Venetian one, where the latter is implied in Alacritas, and opposed not only by "Accidia" or sloth, but by a whole series of eight sculptures on another capital, illustrative, as I believe, of the temptations to idleness; while various other capitals, as we shall see presently, are devoted to the representation of the active trades. Industry, in Northern art and Northern morality, assumes a very principal place. I have seen in French manuscripts the virtues reduced to these seven, Charity, Chastity, Patience, Abstinence, Humility, Liberality, and Industry: and I doubt whether, if we were but to add Honesty (or Truth), a wiser or shorter list could be made out.

§ LXV. We will now take the pillars of the Ducal Palace in their order. It has already been mentioned (Vol. I. Chap. I. § XLVI.) that there are, in all, thirty-six great pillars supporting the lower story; and that these are to be counted from right to left, because then the more ancient of them come first: and that, thus arranged, the first, which is not a shaft, but a pilaster, will be the support of the Vine angle; the eighteenth will be the great shaft of the Fig-tree angle; and the thirty-sixth, that of the Judgment angle.

§ LXVI. All their capitals, except that of the first, are octagonal, and are decorated by sixteen leaves, differently enriched in every capital, but arranged in the same way; eight of them rising to the angles, and there forming volutes; the eight others set between them, on the sides, rising half-way up the bell of the capital; there nodding forward, and showing above them, rising out of their luxuriance, the groups or single figures which we have to examine.* In some instances, the

---

* I have given one of these capitals carefully already in my folio work, and hope to give most of the others in due time. It was of no use to draw them here, as the scale would have been too small to allow me to show the expression of the figures.

intermediate or lower leaves are reduced to eight sprays of foliage; and the capital is left dependent for its effect on the bold position of the figures. In referring to the figures on the octagonal capitals, I shall call the outer side, fronting either the Sea or the Piazzetta, the first side; and so count round from left to right; the fourth side being thus, of course, the innermost. As, however, the first five arches were walled up after the great fire, only three sides of their capitals are left visible, which we may describe as the front and the eastern and western sides of each.

§ LXVII. FIRST CAPITAL: i. e. of the pilaster at the Vine angle.

In front, towards the Sea. A child holding a bird before him, with its wings expanded, covering his breast.

On its eastern side. Children's heads among leaves.

On its western side. A child carrying in one hand a comb; in the other, a pair of scissors.

It appears curious, that this, the principal pilaster of the façade, should have been decorated only by these graceful grotesques, for I can hardly suppose them anything more. There may be meaning in them, but I will not venture to conjecture any, except the very plain and practical meaning conveyed by the last figure to all Venetian children, which it would be well if they would act upon. For the rest, I have seen the comb introduced in grotesque work as early as the thirteenth century, but generally for the purpose of ridiculing too great care in dressing the hair, which assuredly is not its purpose here. The children's heads are very sweet and full of life, but the eyes sharp and small.

§ LXVIII. SECOND CAPITAL. Only three sides of the original work are left unburied by the mass of added wall. Each side has a bird, one web-footed, with a fish, one clawed, with a serpent, which opens its jaws, and darts its tongue at the bird's breast; the third pluming itself, with a feather between the mandibles of its bill. It is by far the most beautiful of the three capitals decorated with birds.

THIRD CAPITAL. Also has three sides only left. They have three heads, large, and very ill cut; one female, and crowned.

FOURTH CAPITAL. Has three children. The eastern one is defaced: the one in front holds a small bird, whose plumage is beautifully indicated, in its right hand; and with its left holds up half a walnut, showing the nut inside: the third holds a fresh fig, cut through, showing the seeds.

The hair of all the three children is differently worked: the first has luxuriant flowing hair, and a double chin; the second, light flowing hair falling in pointed locks on the forehead; the third, crisp curling hair, deep cut with drill holes.

This capital has been copied on the Renaissance side of the palace, only with such changes in the ideal of the children as the workman thought expedient and natural. It is highly interesting to compare the child of the fourteenth with the child of the fifteenth century. The early heads are full of youthful life, playful, humane, affectionate, beaming with sensation and vivacity, but with much manliness and firmness, also, not a little cunning, and some cruelty perhaps, beneath all; the features small and hard, and the eyes keen. There is the making of rough and great men in them. But the children of the fifteenth century are dull smooth-faced dunces, without a single meaning line in the fatness of their stolid cheeks; and, although, in the vulgar sense, as handsome as the other children are ugly, capable of becoming nothing but perfumed coxcombs.

FIFTH CAPITAL. Still three sides only left, bearing three half-length statues of kings; this is the first capital which bears any inscription. In front, a king with a sword in his right hand points to a handkerchief embroidered and fringed, with a head on it, carved on the cavetto of the abacus. His name is written above, "TITUS VESPASIAN IMPERATOR" (contracted IPAT.).

On eastern side, "TRAJANUS IMPERATOR." Crowned, a sword in right hand, and sceptre in left.

On western, "(OCT)AVIANUS AUGUSTUS IMPERATOR." Th "OCT" is broken away. He bears a globe in his right hand, with "MUNDUS PACIS" upon it; a sceptre in his left, which I think has terminated in a human figure. He has a flowing beard, and a singularly high crown; the face is much injured, but has once been very noble in expression.

SIXTH CAPITAL. Has large male and female heads, very coarsely cut, hard, and bad.

§ LXIX. SEVENTH CAPITAL. This is the first of the series which is complete; the first open arch of the lower arcade being between it and the sixth. It begins the representation of the Virtues.

First side. Largitas, or Liberality: always distinguished from the higher Charity. A male figure, with his lap full of money, which he pours out of his hand. The coins are plain, circular, and smooth; there is no attempt to mark device upon them. The inscription above is, "LARGITAS ME ONORAT."

In the copy of this design on the twenty-fifth capital, instead of showering out the gold from his open hand, the figure holds it in a plate or salver, introduced for the sake of disguising the direct imitation. The changes thus made in the Renais-sance pillars are always injuries.

This virtue is the proper opponent of Avarice; though it does not occur in the systems of Orcagna or Giotto, being included in Charity. It was a leading virtue with Aristotle and the other ancients.

§ LXX. *Second side.* Constancy; not very characteristic. An armed man with a sword in his hand, inscribed, "CON STANTIA SUM, NIL TIMENS."

This virtue is one of the forms of fortitude, and Giotto therefore sets as the vice opponent to Fortitude, "Inconstantia," represented as a woman in loose drapery, falling from a rolling globe. The vision seen in the interpreter's house in the Pilgrim's Progress, of the man with a very bold countenance, who says to him who has the writer's ink-horn by his side, "Set down my name," is the best personification of the Venetian "Constantia" of which I am aware in literature. It would be well for us all to consider whether we have yet given the order to the man with the ink-horn, "Set down my name."

§ LXXI. *Third side.* Discord; holding up her finger, but needing the inscription above to assure us of her meaning, "DISCORDIA SUM, DISCORDANS." In the Renaissance copy she is a meek and nun-like person with a veil.

She is the Atë of Spenser; "mother of debate," thus described in the fourth book:

> "Her face most fowle and filthy was to see,
>   With squinted eyes contrarie wayes intended;
>   And loathly mouth, unmeete a mouth to bee,
>   That nought but gall and venim comprehended,
>   And wicked wordes that God and man offended:
>   Her lying tongue was in two parts divided,
>   And both the parts did speake, and both contended;
>   And as her tongue, so was her hart discided,
>   That never thoght one thing, but doubly stil was guided."

Note the fine old meaning of "discided," cut in two; it is a great pity we have lost this powerful expression. We might keep "determined" for the other sense of the word.

§ LXXII. *Fourth side.* Patience. A female figure, very expressive and lovely, in a hood, with her right hand on her breast, the left extended, inscribed "PATIENTIA MANET MECUM."

She is one of the principal virtues in all the Christian systems: a masculine virtue in Spenser, and beautifully placed as the *Physician* in the House of Holinesse. The opponent vice, Impatience, is one of the hags who attend the Captain of the Lusts of the Flesh; the other being Impotence. In like manner, in the "Pilgrim's Progress," the opposite of Patience is Passion; but Spenser's thought is farther carried. His two hags, Impatience and Impotence, as attendant upon the evil spirit of Passion, embrace all the phenomena of human conduct, down even to the smallest matters, according to the adage, "More haste, worse speed."

§ LXXIII. *Fifth side*. Despair. A female figure thrusting a dagger into her throat, and tearing her long hair, which flows down among the leaves of the capital below her knees. One of the finest figures of the series; inscribed "DESPERACIO MÔS (mortis?) CRUDELIS." In the Renaissance copy she is totally devoid of expression, and appears, instead of tearing her hair, to be dividing it into long curls on each side.

This vice is the proper opposite of Hope. By Giotto she is represented as a woman hanging herself, a fiend coming for her soul. Spenser's vision of Despair is well known, it being indeed currently reported that this part of the Faerie Queen was the first which drew to it the attention of Sir Philip Sidney.

§ LXXIV. *Sixth side*. Obedience: with her arms folded; meek, but rude and commonplace, looking at a little dog standing on its hind legs and begging, with a collar round its neck. Inscribed "OBEDIENTI * *;" the rest of the sentence is much defaced, but looks like *ſⲟꙇoⲉ̄ⲕⲓ𝔟ⲉ̄ⲟ*. 1 suppose the note of contraction above the final A has disappeared and that the inscription was "Obedientiam domino exhibeo."

This virtue is, of course, a principal one in the monkish systems; represented by Giotto at Assisi as "an angel robed in black, placing the finger of his left hand on his mouth, and passing the yoke over the head of a Franciscan monk kneeling at his feet."*

Obedience holds a less principal place in Spenser. We have seen her above associated with the other peculiar virtues of womanhood.

§ LXXV. *Seventh side.* Infidelity. A man in a turban, with a small image in his hand, or the image of a child. Of the inscription nothing but " INFIDELITATE * * * " and some fragmentary letters, " ILI, CERO," remain.

By Giotto Infidelity is most nobly symbolized as a woman helmeted, the helmet having a broad rim which keeps the light from her eyes. She is covered with heavy drapery, stands infirmly as if about to fall, is *bound by a cord round her neck to an image* which she carries in her hand, and has flames bursting forth at her feet.

In Spenser, Infidelity is the Saracen knight Sans Foy,—

> " Full large of limbe and every joint
> He was, and carèd not for God or man a point."

For the part which he sustains in the contest with Godly Fear, or the Red-cross knight, see Appendix 2. Vol. III.

§ LXXVI. *Eighth side.* Modesty; bearing a pitcher. (In the Renaissance copy, a vase like a coffee-pot.) Inscribed " MODESTIA

ᚱOᛒᚢOᛒᛏᛁᚾᚩO."

I do not find this virtue in any of the Italian series, except that of Venice. In Spenser she is of course one of those attendant on Womanhood, but occurs as one of the tenants of the Heart of Man, thus portrayed in the second book,

> "Straunge was her tyre, and all her garment blew,
>   Close rownd about her tuckt with many a plight:
>   Upon her fist the bird which shonneth vew.

* * * * * * * *

---

* Lord Lindsay, vol. ii. p. 226.

> And ever and anone with rosy red
> The bashfull blood her snowy cheekes did dye,
> That her became, as polisht yvory
> Which cunning craftesman hand hath overlayd
> With fayre vermilion or pure castory."

§ LXXVII. EIGHTH CAPITAL. It has no inscriptions, and its subjects are not, by themselves, intelligible; but they appear to be typical of the degradation of human instincts.

First side. A caricature of Arion on his dolphin; he wears a cap ending in a long proboscis-like horn, and plays a violin with a curious twitch of the bow and wag of the head, very graphically expressed, but still without anything approaching to the power of Northern grotesque. His dolphin has a goodly row of teeth, and the waves beat over his back.

Second side. A human figure, with curly hair and the legs of a bear; the paws laid, with great sculptural skill, upon the foliage. It plays a violin, shaped like a guitar, with a bent double-stringed bow.

Third side. A figure with a serpent's tail and a monstrous head, founded on a Negro type, hollow-cheeked, large-lipped, and wearing a cap made of a serpent's skin, holding a fir-cone in its hand.

Fourth side. A monstrous figure, terminating below in a tortoise. It is devouring a gourd, which it grasps greedily with both hands; it wears a cap ending in a hoofed leg.

Fifth side. A centaur wearing a crested helmet, and holding a curved sword.

Sixth side. A knight, riding a headless horse, and wearing chain armor, with a triangular shield flung behind his back, and a two-edged sword.

Seventh side. A figure like that on the fifth, wearing a round helmet, and with the legs and tail of a horse. He bears a long mace with a top like a fir-cone.

Eighth side. A figure with curly hair, and an acorn in its hand, ending below in a fish.

§ LXVIII. NINTH CAPITAL. *First side.* Faith. She has her left hand on her breast, and the cross on her right. Inscribed "FIDES OPTIMA IN DEO." The Faith of Giotto holds the cross in her right hand; in her left, a scroll with the Apostles' Creed. She treads upon cabalistic books, and has a key suspended to her waist. Spenser's Faith (Fidelia) is still more spiritual and noble:

> "She was araied all in lilly white,
> And in her right hand bore a cup of gold,
> With wine and water fild up to the hight,
> In which a serpent did himselfe enfold,
> That horrour made to all that did behold;
> But she no whitt did chaunge her constant mood:
> And in her other hand she fast did hold
> A booke, that was both signd and seald with blood;
> Wherein darke things were writt, hard to be understood."

§ LXXIX. *Second side.* Fortitude. A long-bearded man [Samson?] tearing open a lion's jaw. The inscription is illegible, and the somewhat vulgar personification appears to belong rather to Courage than Fortitude. On the Renaissance copy it is inscribed "FORTITUDO SUM VIRILIS." The Latin word has, perhaps, been received by the sculptor as merely signifying "Strength," the rest of the perfect idea of this virtue having been given in "Constantia" previously. But both these Venetian symbols together do not at all approach the idea of Fortitude as given generally by Giotto and the Pisan sculptors; clothed with a lion's skin, knotted about her neck, and falling to her feet in deep folds; drawing back her right hand, with the sword pointed towards her enemy; and slightly retired behind her immovable shield, which, with Giotto, is square, and rested on the ground like a tower, covering her up to above her shoulders; bearing on it a lion, and with broken heads of javelins deeply infixed.

Among the Greeks, this is, of course, one of the principal virtues; apt, however, in their ordinary conception of it to degenerate into mere manliness or courage.

§ LXXX. *Third side.* Temperance; bearing a pitcher of water and a cup. Inscription, illegible here, and on the Renaissance copy nearly so, "TEMPERANTIA SUM" (INOM' Lˢ)? only left. In this somewhat vulgar and most frequent conception of this virtue (afterwards continually repeated, as by Sir Joshua in his window at New College) temperance is confused with mere abstinence, the opposite of Gula, or gluttony; whereas the Greek Temperance, a truly cardinal virtue, is the moderator of *all* the passions, and so represented by Giotto, who has placed a bridle upon her lips, and a sword in her hand, the hilt of which she is binding to the scabbard. In his system, she is opposed among the vices, not by Gula or Gluttony, but by Ira, Anger. So also the Temperance of Spencer, or Sir Guyon, but with mingling of much sternness:

> "A goodly knight, all armd in harnesse meete,
> That from his head no place appeared to his feete,
> His carriage was full comely and upright;
> His countenance demure and temperate;
> But yett so sterne and terrible in sight,
> That cheard his friendes, and did his foes amate."

The Temperance of the Greeks, σωφροσύνη, involves the idea of Prudence, and is a most noble virtue, yet properly marked by Plato as inferior to sacred enthusiasm, though necessary for its government. He opposes it, under the name "Mortal Temperance" or "the Temperance which is of men," to divine madness, μανία, or inspiration; but he most justly and nobly expresses the general idea of it under the term ὕβρις, which, in the "Phædrus," is divided into various intemperances with respect to various objects, and set forth under the image of a black, vicious, diseased and furious horse, yoked by the side of Prudence or Wisdom (set forth under the figure of a white horse with a crested and noble head, like that which we have among the Elgin Marbles) to the chariot of the Soul. The system of Aristotle, as above stated, is throughout a mere complicated blunder, supported by sophistry, the laboriously developed mistake of Temperance for the essence of the virtues which it guides. Temperance in the mediæval systems is generally opposed by Anger, or by Folly, or Gluttony: but her proper opposite is Spenser's Acrasia, the principal enemy of Sir Guyon, at whose gates we find the subordinate vice "Excesse," as the introduction to Intemperance; a graceful and feminine image, necessary to illustrate the more dangerous forms of subtle intemperance, as opposed to the brutal "Gluttony" in the first book. She presses grapes into a cup, because of the words of St. Paul, "Be not drunk with wine, wherein is excess;" but always delicately,

> " Into her cup she scruzd with daintie breach
>   Of her fine fingers, without fowle empeach,
>   That so faire winepresse made the wine more **sweet**."

The reader will, I trust, pardon these frequent extracts from Spenser, for it is nearly as necessary to point out the profound divinity and philosophy of our great English poet, as the beauty of the Ducal Palace.

§ LXXXI. *Fourth side.* Humility; with a veil upon her head, carrying a lamp in her lap. Inscribed in the copy, " HUMILI-TAS HABITAT IN ME."

This virtue is of course a peculiarly Christian one, hardly recognized in the Pagan systems, though carefully impressed upon the Greeks in early life in a manner which at this day it would be well if we were to imitate, and, together with an almost feminine modesty, giving an exquisite grace to the conduct and bearing of the well-educated Greek youth. It is, of course, one of the leading virtues in all the monkish systems, but I have not any notes of the manner of its representation.

§ LXXXII. *Fifth side.* Charity. A woman with her lap full of loaves (?), giving one to a child, who stretches his arm out for it across a broad gap in the leafage of the capital.

Again very far inferior to the Giottesque rendering of this virtue. In the Arena Chapel she is distinguished from all the other virtues by having a circular glory round her head, and a cross of fire; she is crowned with flowers, presents with her right hand a vase of corn and fruit, and with her left receives treasure from Christ, who appears above her, to provide her with the means of continual offices of beneficence, while she tramples under foot the treasures of the earth.

The peculiar beauty of most of the Italian conceptions of Charity, is in the subjection of mere munificence to the glowing of her love, always represented by flames; here in the form of a cross round her head; in Orcagna's shrine at Florence, issuing from a censer in her hand; and, with Dante, inflaming her whole form, so that, in a furnace of clear fire, she could not have been discerned.

Spenser represents her as a mother surrounded by happy children, an idea afterwards grievously hackneyed and vulgarized by English painters and sculptors.

§ LXXXIII. *Sixth side.* Justice. Crowned, and with sword. Inscribed in the copy, " REX SUM JUSTICIE."

This idea was afterwards much amplified and adorned in the only good capital of the Renaissance series, under the Judgment angle. Giotto has also given his whole strength to the painting of this virtue, representing her as enthroned under a noble Gothic canopy, holding scales, not by the beam, but one in each hand; a beautiful idea, showing that the equality of the scales of Justice is not owing to natural laws, but to her own immediate weighing the opposed causes in her own hands. In one scale is an executioner beheading a criminal; in the other an angel crowning a man who seems (in Selvatico's plate) to have been working at a desk or table.

Beneath her feet is a small predella, representing various persons riding securely in the woods, and others dancing to the sound of music.

Spenser's Justice, Sir Artegall, is the hero of an entire book, and the betrothed knight of Britomart, or chastity.

§ LXXXIV. *Seventh side.* Prudence. A man with a book and a pair of compasses, wearing the noble cap, hanging down towards the shoulder, and bound in a fillet round the brow, which occurs so frequently during the fourteenth century in Italy in the portraits of men occupied in any civil capacity.

This virtue is, as we have seen, conceived under very different degrees of dignity, from mere worldly prudence up to heavenly wisdom, being opposed sometimes by Stultitia, sometimes by Ignorantia. I do not find, in any of the representations of her, that her truly distinctive character, namely, *forethought*, is enough insisted upon: Giotto expresses her vigilance and just measurement or estimate of all things by painting her as Janus-headed, and gazing into a convex mirror, with compasses in her right hand; the convex mirror showing her power of looking at many things in small compass. But forethought or anticipation, by which, independently of greater or less natural capacities, one man becomes more *prudent* than another, is never enough considered or symbolized.

The idea of this virtue oscillates, in the Greek systems, between Temperance and Heavenly Wisdom.

§ LXXXV. *Eighth side.* Hope. A figure full of devotional expression, holding up its hands as in prayer, and looking to a hand which is extended towards it out of sunbeams. In the Renaissance copy this hand does not appear.

Of all the virtues, this is the most distinctively Christian (it could not, of course, enter definitely into any Pagan scheme) ; and above all others, it seems to me the *testing* virtue,—that by the possession of which we may most certainly determine whether we are Christians or not ; for many men have charity, that is to say, general kindness of heart, or even a kind of faith, who have not any habitual *hope* of, or longing for, heaven. The Hope of Giotto is represented as winged, rising in the air, while an angel holds a crown before her. I do not know if Spenser was the first to introduce our marine virtue, leaning on an anchor, a symbol as inaccurate as it is vulgar : for, in the first place, anchors are not for men, but for ships ; and in the second, anchorage is the characteristic not of Hope, but of Faith. Faith is dependent, but Hope is aspirant. Spenser, however, introduces Hope twice,—the first time as the Virtue with the anchor ; but afterwards fallacious Hope, far more beautifully, in the Masque of Cupid :

> "She always smyld, and in her hand did hold
> An holy-water sprinckle, dipt in deowe."

§ LXXXVI. TENTH CAPITAL. *First side.* Luxury (the opposite of chastity, as above explained). A woman with a jewelled chain across her forehead, smiling as she looks into a mirror, exposing her breast by drawing down her dress with one hand. Inscribed " LUXURIA SUM IMENSA."

These subordinate forms of vice are not met with so frequently in art as those of the opposite virtues, but in Spenser we find them all. His Luxury rides upon a goat :

> "In a greene gowne he clothed was full faire,
> Which underneath did hide his filthinesse,
> And in his hand a burning hart he bare."

But, in fact, the proper and comprehensive expression of this vice is the Cupid of the ancients ; and there is not any minor circumstance more indicative of the *intense* difference between the mediæval and the Renaissance spirit, than the mode in which this god is represented.

I have above said, that all great European art is rooted in the thirteenth century; and it seems to me that there is a kind of central year about which we may consider the energy of the middle ages to be gathered; a kind of focus of time, which, by what is to my mind a most touching and impressive Divine appointment, has been marked for us by the greatest writer of the middle ages, in the first words he utters; namely, the year 1300, the "mezzo del cammin" of the life of Dante. Now, therefore, to Giotto, the contemporary of Dante, and who drew Dante's still existing portrait in this very year, 1300, we may always look for the central mediæval idea in any subject: and observe how he represents Cupid; as one of three, a terrible trinity, his companions being Satan and Death; and he himself "a lean scarecrow, with bow, quiver, and fillet, and feet ending in claws,"[*] thrust down into Hell by Penance, from the presence of Purity and Fortitude. Spenser, who has been so often noticed as furnishing the exactly intermediate type of conception between the mediæval and the Renaissance, indeed represents Cupid under the form of a beautiful winged god, and riding on a lion, but still no plaything of the Graces, but full of terror:

> "With that the darts which his right hand did straine
> Full dreadfully he shooke, that all did quake,
> And clapt on hye his coloured wingës twaine,
> That all his many it afraide did make."

His *many*, that is to say, his company; and observe what a company it is. Before him go Fancy, Desire, Doubt, Danger, Fear, Fallacious Hope, Dissemblance, Suspicion, Grief, Fury,

[*] Lord Lindsay, vol. ii. letter iv.

Displeasure, Despite, and Cruelty. After him, Reproach, Repentance, Shame,

> " Unquiet Care, and fond Unthriftyhead,
>   Lewd Losse of Time, and Sorrow seeming dead,
>   Inconstant Chaᵜnge, and false Disloyalty,
>   Consuming Riotise, and guilty Dread
>   Of heavenly vengeaunce ; faint Infirmity,
>   Vile Poverty, and lastly Death with infamy."

Compare these two pictures of Cupid with the Love-god of the Renaissance, as he is represented to this day, confused with angels, in every faded form of ornament and allegory, in our furniture, our literature, and our minds.

§ LXXXVII. *Second side.* Gluttony. A woman in a turban, with a jewelled cup in her right hand. In her left, the clawed limb of a bird, which she is gnawing. Inscribed " GULA SINE ORDINE SUM."

Spenser's Gluttony is more than usually fine :

> " His belly was upblowne with luxury,
>   And eke with fatnesse swollen were his eyne,
>   And like a crane his necke was long and fyne,
>   Wherewith he swallowed up excessive feast,
>   For want whereof poore people oft did pyne."

He rides upon a swine, and is clad in vine-leaves, with a garland of ivy. Compare the account of Excesse, above, as opposed to Temperance.

§ LXXXVIII. *Third side.* Pride. A knight, with a heavy and stupid face, holding a sword with three edges : his armor covered with ornaments in the form of roses, and with two ears attached to his helmet. The inscription indecipherable, all but " SUPERBIA."

Spenser has analyzed this vice with great care. He first

represents it as the Pride of life; that is to say, the pride which runs in a deep under current through all the thoughts and acts of men. As such, it is a feminine vice, directly opposed to Holiness, and mistress of a castle called the House of Pryde, and her chariot is driven by Satan, with a team of beasts, ridden by the mortal sins. In the throne chamber of her palace she is thus described:

> "So proud she shyned in her princely state,
> Looking to Heaven, for Earth she did disdayne;
> And sitting high, for lowly she did hate:
> Lo, underneath her scornefull feete was layne
> A dreadfull dragon with an hideous trayne;
> And in her hand she held a mirrhour bright,
> Wherein her face she often vewed fayne."

The giant Orgoglio is a baser species of pride, born of the Earth and Eolus; that is to say, of sensual and vain conceits. His foster-father and the keeper of his castle is Ignorance. (Book I. canto VIII.)

Finally, Disdain is introduced, in other places, as the form of pride which vents itself in insult to others.

§ LXXXIX. *Fourth side.* Anger. A woman tearing her dress open at her breast. Inscription here undecipherable; but in the Renaissance copy it is "IRA CRUDELIS EST IN ME."

Giotto represents this vice under the same symbol; but it is the weakest of all the figures in the Arena Chapel. The "Wrath" of Spenser rides upon a lion, brandishing a fire-brand, his garments stained with blood. Rage, or Furor, occurs subordinately in other places. It appears to me very strange that neither Giotto nor Spenser should have given any representation of the *restrained* Anger, which is infinitely the most terrible; both of them make him violent.

§ XC. *Fifth side.* Avarice. An old woman with a veil over her forehead, and a bag of money in each hand. A figure very marvellous for power of expression. The throat is all made up of sinews with skinny channels deep between them, strained as by anxiety, and wasted by famine; the features hunger-bitten, the eyes hollow, the look glaring and intense, yet without the slightest caricature. Inscribed in the Renaissance copy, " AVARITIA IMPLETOR."

Spenser's Avarice (the vice) is much feebler than this; but the god Mammon and his kingdom have been described by him with his usual power. Note the position of the house of Richesse:

> " Betwixt them both was but a little stride,
> That did the House of Richesse from Hell-mouth divide."

It is curious that most moralists confuse avarice with covetousness, although they are vices totally different in their operation on the human heart, and on the frame of society. The love of money, the sin of Judas and Ananias, is indeed the root of all evil in the hardening of the heart; but " covetousness, which is idolatry," the sin of Ahab, that is, the inordinate desire of some seen or recognized good,—thus destroying peace of mind,—is probably productive of much more misery in heart, and error in conduct, than avarice itself, only covetousness is not so inconsistent with Christianity : for covetousness may partly proceed from vividness of the affections and hopes, as in David, and be consistent with much charity; not so avarice.

§ XCI. *Sixth side.* Idleness. Accidia. A figure much broken away, having had its arms round two branches of trees.

I do not know why Idleness should be represented as among trees, unless, in the Italy of the fourteenth century, forest country was considered as desert, and therefore the domain of Idleness. Spenser fastens this vice especially upon the clergy,—

> " Upon a slouthfull asse he chose to ryde,
> Arayd in habit blacke, and amis thin,

> Like to an holy monck, the service to begin.
> And in his hand his portesse still be bare,
> That much was worne, but therein little redd."

And he properly makes him the leader of the train of the vices

> May seem the wayne was very evil ledd,
> When such an one had guiding of the way."

Observe that subtle touch of truth in the "wearing" of the portesse, indicating the abuse of books by idle readers, so thoroughly characteristic of unwilling studentship from the schoolboy upwards.

§ XCII. *Seventh side.* Vanity. She is smiling complacently as she looks into a mirror in her lap. Her robe is embroidered with roses, and roses form her crown. Undecipherable.

There is some confusion in the expression of this vice, between pride in the personal appearance and lightness of purpose. The word Vanitas generally, I think, bears, in the mediæval period, the sense given it in Scripture. "Let not him that is deceived trust in Vanity, for Vanity shall be his recompense." "Vanity of Vanities." "The Lord knoweth the thoughts of the wise, that they are vain." It is difficult to find this sin,—which, after Pride, is the most universal, perhaps the most fatal, of all, fretting the whole depth of our humanity into storm "to waft a feather or to drown a fly,"— definitely expressed in art. Even Spenser, I think, has only partially expressed it under the figure of Phædria, more properly Idle Mirth, in the second book. The idea is, however, entirely worked out in the Vanity Fair of the "Pilgrim's Progress."

§ XCIII. *Eighth side.* Envy. One of the noblest pieces of expression in the series. She is pointing malignantly with her finger; a serpent is wreathed about her head like a cap, another forms the girdle of her waist, and a dragon rests in her lap.

Giotto has, however, represented her, with still greate·

subtlety, as having her fingers terminating in claws, and raising her right hand with an expression partly of impotent
regret, partly of involuntary grasping; a serpent, issuing
from her mouth, is about to bite her between the eyes; she
has long membranous ears, horns on her head, and flames con-
suming her body. The Envy of Spenser is only inferior to
that of Giotto, because the idea of folly and quickness of
hearing is not suggested by the size of the ear: in other respects it is even finer, joining the idea of fury, in the wolf on
which he rides, with that of corruption on his lips, and of dis-
coloration or distortion in the whole mind:

> "Malicious Envy rode
> Upon a ravenous wolfe, and still did chaw
> Between his cankred teeth a venemous tode,
> That all the poison ran about his jaw.
> *All in a kirtle of discolourd say*
> *He clothed was, ypaynted full of eies,*
> And in his bosome secretly there lay
> An hatefull snake, the which his taile uptyes
> in many folds, and mortall sting implyes."

He has developed the idea in more detail, and still more
loathsomely, in the twelfth canto of the fifth book.

§ xciv. ELEVENTH CAPITAL. Its decoration is composed
of eight birds, arranged as shown in Plate V. of the "Seven
Lamps," which, however, was sketched from the Renaissance
copy. These birds are all varied in form and action, but not
so as to require special description.

§ xcv. TWELFTH CAPITAL. This has been very interesting,
but is grievously defaced, four of its figures being entirely
broken away, and the character of two others quite undecipherable. It is fortunate that it has been copied in the thirty-
third capital of the Renaissance series, from which we are
able to identify the lost figures.

First side. Misery. A man with a wan face, seemingly

pleading with a child who has its hands crossed on its breast There is a buckle at his own breast in the shape of a cloven heart. Inscribed " MISERIA."

The intention of this figure is not altogether apparent, as it is by no means treated as a vice; the distress seeming real, and like that of a parent in poverty mourning over his child. Yet it seems placed here as in direct opposition to the virtue of Cheerfulness, which follows next in order; rather, however, I believe, with the intention of illustrating human life, than the character of the vice which, as we have seen, Dante placed in the circle of hell. The word in that case would, I think, have been "Tristitia," the "unholy Griefe" of Spenser—

> " All in sable sorrowfully clad,
> Downe hanging his dull head with heavy chere:
>
> .   .   .   .
>
> A pair of pincers in his hand he had,
> With which he pinched people to the heart."

He has farther amplified the idea under another figure in the fifth canto of the fourth book:

> " His name was Care; a blacksmith by his trade,
>   That neither day nor night from working spared;
>   But to small purpose yron wedges made:
>   Those be unquiet thoughts that carefull minds invade.
>   Rude was his garment, and to rags all rent,
>   Ne better had he, ne for better cared;
>   With blistered hands among the cinders brent."

It is to be noticed, however, that in the Renaissance copy this figure is stated to be, not Miseria, but "Misericordia." The contraction is a very moderate one, Misericordia being in old MS. written always as " Mia." If this reading be right, the figure is placed here rather as the companion, than the opposite, of Cheerfulness; unless, indeed, it is intended to unite the idea of Mercy and Compassion with that of Sacred Sorrow.

§ xcvi. *Second side*. Cheerfulness. A woman with long flowing hair, crowned with roses, playing on a tambourine, and with open lips, as singing. Inscribed " ALACRITAS."

We have already met with this virtue among those especially set by Spenser to attend on Womanhood. It is inscribed in the Renaissance copy, " ALACHRITAS CHANIT MECUM." Note the gutturals of the rich and fully developed Venetian dialect now affecting the Latin, which is free from them in the earlier capitals.

§ xcvii. *Third side*. Destroyed ; but, from the copy, we find it has been Stultitia, Folly ; and it is there represented simply as a man *riding*, a sculpture worth the consideration of the English residents who bring their horses to Venice. Giotto gives Stultitia a feather, cap, and club. In early manuscripts he is always eating with one hand, and striking with the other ; in later ones he has a cap and bells, or cap crested with a cock's head, whence the word " coxcomb."

§ xcviii. *Fourth side*. Destroyed, all but a book, which identifies it with the " Celestial Chastity " of the Renaissance copy ; there represented as a woman pointing to a book (connecting the convent life with the pursuit of literature ?).

Spenser's Chastity, Britomart, is the most exquisitely wrought of all his characters ; but, as before noticed, she is not the Chastity of the convent, but of wedded life.

§ xcix. *Fifth side*. Only a scroll is left; but, from the copy, we find it has been Honesty or Truth. Inscribed " HONESTA-TEM DILIGO." It is very curious, that among all the Christian systems of the virtues which we have examined, we should find this one in Venice only.

The Truth of Spenser, Una, is, after Chastity, the most exquisite character in the " Faerie Queen."

§ c. *Sixth side*. Falsehood. An old woman leaning on a

crutch; and inscribed in the copy, "FALSITAS IN ME SEMPER
EST." The Fidessa of Spenser, the great enemy of Una, or
Truth, is far more subtly conceived, probably not without
special reference to the Papal deceits. In her true form she
is a loathsome hag, but in her outward aspect,

> " A goodly lady, clad in scarlot red,
>   Purfled with gold and pearle; . . .
>   Her wanton palfrey all was overspred
>   With tinsell trappings, woven like a wave,
>   Whose bridle rung with golden bels and bosses brave."

Dante's Fraud, Geryon, is the finest personification of all,
but the description (Inferno, canto XVII.) is too long to be
quoted.

§ CI. *Seventh side.* Injustice. An armed figure holding a
halbert; so also in the copy. The figure used by Giotto with
the particular intention of representing unjust government, is
represented at the gate of an embattled castle in a forest, between rocks, while various deeds of violence are committed at
his feet. Spenser's "Adicia" is a furious hag, at last transformed into a tiger.

Eighth side. A man with a dagger looking sorrowfully at
a child, who turns its back to him. I cannot understand this
figure. It is inscribed in the copy, "ASTINECIA (Abstinentia?)
OPITIMA?"

§ CII. THIRTEENTH CAPITAL. It has lions' heads all round,
coarsely cut.

FOURTEENTH CAPITAL. It has various animals, each sitting
on its haunches. Three dogs, one a greyhound, one long-
haired, one short-haired with bells about its neck; two
monkeys, one with fan-shaped hair projecting on each side
of its face; a noble boar, with its tusks, hoofs, and bristles
sharply cut; and a lion and lioness.

§ CIII. FIFTEENTH CAPITAL. The pillar to which it belongs

is thicker than the rest, as well as the one over it in the upper arcade.

The sculpture of this capital is also much coarser, and seems to me later than that of the rest; and it has no inscription, which is embarrassing, as its subjects have had much meaning; but I believe Selvatico is right in supposing it to have been intended for a general illustration of Idleness.

First side. A woman with a distaff; her girdle richly decorated, and fastened by a buckle.

Second side. A youth in a long mantle, with a rose in his hand.

Third side. A woman in a turban stroking a puppy, which she holds by the haunches.

Fourth side. A man with a parrot.

Fifth side. A woman in very rich costume, with braided hair, and dress thrown into minute folds, holding a rosary (?) in her left hand, her right on her breast.

Sixth side. A man with a very thoughtful face, laying his hand upon the leaves of the capital.

Seventh side. A crowned lady, with a rose in her hand.

Eighth side. A boy with a ball in his left hand, and his right laid on his breast.

§ CIV. SIXTEENTH CAPITAL. It is decorated with eight large heads, partly intended to be grotesque,* and very coarse and bad, except only that in the sixth side, which is totally different from all the rest, and looks like a portrait. It is thin, thoughtful, and dignified; thoroughly fine in every way. It wears a cap surmounted by two winged lions; and, therefore, I think Selvatico must have inaccurately written the list given in the note, for this head is certainly meant to express the

---

* Selvatico states that these are intended to be representative of eight nations, Latins, Tartars, Turks, Hungarians, Greeks Goths, Egyptians, and Persians. Either the inscriptions are now defaced or I have carelessly omitted to note them.

superiority of the Venetian character over that of other nations. Nothing is more remarkable in all early sculpture, than its appreciation of the signs of dignity of character in the features, and the way in which it can exalt the principal figure in any subject by a few touches.

§ CV. SEVENTEENTH CAPITAL. This has been so destroyed by the sea wind, which sweeps at this point of the arcade round the angle of the palace, that its inscriptions are no longer legible, and great part of its figures are gone. Selvatico states them as follows: Solomon, the wise; Priscian, the grammarian; Aristotle, the logician; Tully, the orator; Pythagoras, the philosopher; Archimedes, the mechanic; Orpheus, the musician; Ptolemy, the astronomer. The fragments actually remaining are the following:

First side. A figure with two books, in a robe richly decorated with circles of roses. Inscribed " SALOMON (SAP) IENS."

Second side. A man with one book, poring over it: he has had a long stick or reed in his hand. Of inscription only the letters " GRAMMATIC" remain.

Third side. "ARISTOTLE:" so inscribed. He has a peaked double beard and a flat cap, from under which his long hair falls down his back.

Fourth side. Destroyed.

Fifth side. Destroyed, all but a board with three (counters?) on it.

Sixth side. A figure with compasses. Inscribed " GEO-MET * * "

Seventh side. Nothing is left but a guitar with its handle wrought into a lion's head.

Eighth side. Destroyed.

§ CVI. We have now arrived at the EIGHTEENTH CAPITAL, the most interesting and beautiful of the palace. It represents the planets, and the sun and moon, in those divisions of the zodiac known to astrologers as their "houses;" and perhaps indicates, by the position in which they are placed, the period of the year at which this great corner-stone was laid. The inscriptions above have been in quaint Latin rhyme, but are now decipherable only in fragments, and that with the more difficulty because the rusty iron bar that binds the abacus has broken away, in its expansion, nearly all the upper portions of the stone, and with them the signs of contraction, which are of great importance. I shall give the fragments of them that I could decipher; first as the letters actually stand (putting those of which I am doubtful in brackets, with a note of interrogation), and then as I would read them.

§ CVII. It should be premised that, in modern astrology, the houses of the planets are thus arranged:

The house of the	Sun,	is	Leo.
	Moon,	„	Cancer.
„ of	Mars,	„	Aries and Scorpio.
„	Venus,	„	Taurus and Libra.
„	Mercury,	„	Gemini and Virgo.
„	Jupiter,	„	Sagittarius and Pisces.
„	Saturn,	„	Capricorn.
„	Herschel,	„	Aquarius.

The Herschel planet being of course unknown to the old astrologers, we have only the other six planetary powers, together with the sun; and Aquarius is assigned to Saturn as his house. I could not find Capricorn at all; but this sign may have been broken away, as the whole capital is grievously defaced. The eighth side of the capital, which the Herschel planet would now have occupied, bears a sculpture of the Creation of Man: it is the most conspicuous side, the one set diagonally across the angle; or the eighth in our usual mode of reading the capitals, from which I shall not depart.

§ CVIII. *The first side*, then, or that towards the Sea, has Aquarius, as the house of Saturn, represented as a seated figure beautifully draped, pouring a stream of water out of an amphora over the leaves of the capital. His inscription is :

"ET SATURNE DOMUS (ECLOCERUNT ?) 1ˢ 7BRE."

§ CIX. *Second side*. Jupiter, in his houses Sagittarius and Pisces, represented throned, with an upper dress disposed in radiating folds about his neck, and hanging down upon his breast, ornamented by small pendent trefoiled studs or bosses. He wears the drooping bonnet and long gloves; but the folds about the neck, shot forth to express the rays of the star, are the most remarkable characteristic of the figure. He raises his sceptre in his left hand over Sagittarius, represented as the centaur Chiron ; and holds two thunnies in his right. Something rough, like a third fish, has been broken away below them; the more easily because this part of the group is entirely undercut, and the two fish glitter in the light, relieved on the deep gloom below the leaves. The inscription is :

"INDE JOVI'† DONA PISES SIMUL ATQˢ CIRONA."

Or,

"Inde Jovis dona
Pisces simul atque Chirona."

Domus is, I suppose, to be understood before Jovis : "Then the house of Jupiter gives (or governs ?) the fishes and Chiron."

§ CX. *Third side*. Mars, in his houses Aries and Scorpio. Represented as a very ugly knight in chain mail, seated sideways on the ram, whose horns are broken away, and having a

† The comma in these inscriptions stands for a small cuneiform mark, I believe of contraction, and the small ˢ for a zigzag mark of the same kind. The dots or periods are similarly marked on the stone.

large scorpion in his left hand, whose tail is broken also, to
the infinite injury of the group, for it seems to have curled
across to the angle leaf, and formed a bright line of light, like
the fish in the hand of Jupiter. The knight carries a shield,
on which fire and water are sculptured, and bears a banner
upon his lance, with the word "DEFEROSUM" which puzzled
me for some time. It should be read, I believe, "De ferro
sum;" which would be good *Venetian* Latin for "I am of
iron."

§ CXI. *Fourth side.* The Sun, in his house Leo. Represented under the figure of Apollo, sitting on the Lion, with
rays shooting from his head, and the world in his hand.
The inscription :

"TU ES DOMU' SOLIS (QUO * ?) SIGNE LEONI."

I believe the first phrase is, "Tunc est Domus solis;" but
there is a letter gone after the "quo," and I have no idea
what case of signum "signe" stands for.

CXII. *Fifth side.* Venus, in her houses Taurus and Libra.
The most beautiful figure of the series. She sits upon the
bull, who is deep in the dewlap, and better cut than most of
the animals, holding a mirror in her right hand, and the scales
in her left. Her breast is very nobly and tenderly indicated
under the folds of her drapery, which is exquisitely studied in
its fall. What is left of the inscription, runs :

"LIBRA CUM TAURO DOMUS * * * PURIOR AUR*."

§ CXIII. *Sixth side.* Mercury, represented as wearing a
pendent cap, and holding a book : he is supported by three
children in reclining attitudes, representing his houses Gemini
and Virgo. But I cannot understand the inscription, though
more than usually legible.

"OCCUPAT ERIGONE STIBONS GEMINUQ' LACONE."

§ CXIV. *Seventh side.* The Moon, in her house Cancer. This sculpture, which is turned towards the Piazzetta, is the most picturesque of the series. The moon is represented as a woman in a boat, upon the sea, who raises the crescent in her right hand, and with her left draws a crab out of the waves, up the boat's side. The moon was, I believe, represented in Egyptian sculptures as in a boat; but I rather think the Venetian was not aware of this, and that he meant to express the peculiar sweetness of the moonlight at Venice, as seen across the lagoons. Whether this was intended by putting the planet in the boat, may be questionable, but assuredly the idea was meant to be conveyed by the dress of the figure. For all the draperies of the other figures on this capital, as well as on the rest of the façade, are disposed in severe but full folds, showing little of the forms beneath them; but the moon's drapery *ripples* down to her feet, so as exactly to suggest the trembling of the moonlight on the waves. This beautiful idea is highly characteristic of the thoughtfulness of the early sculptors: five hundred men may be now found who could have cut the drapery, as such, far better, for one who would have disposed its folds with this intention. The inscription is:

"LUNE CANCER DOMU T. PBET IORBE SIGNORU."

§ CXV. *Eighth side.* God creating Man. Represented as a throned figure, with a glory round the head, laying his left hand on the head of a naked youth, and sustaining him with his right hand. The inscription puzzled me for a long time; but except the lost r and m of "formavit," and a letter quite undefaced, but to me unintelligible, before the word Eva, in the shape of a figure of 7, I have safely ascertained the rest.

"DELIMO DSADA DECO STAFO * * AVITTEVA."

Or

" De limo Dominus Adam, de costa fo(rm)avit Evam ;"

From the dust the Lord made Adam, and from the rib Eve.

I imagine the whole of this capital, therefore—the principal one of the old palace,—to have been intended to signify, first, the formation of the planets for the service of man upon the earth ; secondly, the entire subjection of the fates and fortune of man to the will of God, as determined from the time when the earth and stars were made, and, in fact, written in the volume of the stars themselves.

Thus interpreted, the doctrines of judicial astrology were not only consistent with, but an aid to, the most spiritual and humble Christianity.

In the workmanship and grouping of its foliage, this capital is, on the whole, the finest I know in Europe. The sculptor has put his whole strength into it. I trust that it will appear among the other Venetian casts lately taken for the Crystal Palace; but if not, I have myself cast all its figures, and two of its leaves, and I intend to give drawings of them on a large scale in my folio work.

§ CXVI. NINETEENTH CAPITAL. This is, of course, the second counting from the Sea, on the Piazzetta side of the palace, calling that of the Fig-tree angle the first.

It is the most important capital, as a piece of evidence in point of dates, in the whole palace. Great pains have been taken with it, and in some portion of the accompanying fur- niture or ornaments of each of its figures a small piece of colored marble has been inlaid, with peculiar significance : for the capital represents the *arts of sculpture and architec- ture ;* and the inlaying of the colored stones (which are far too small to be effective at a distance, and are found in this one capital only of the whole series) is merely an expression

17*

of the architect's feeling of the essential importance of this art of inlaying, and of the value of color generally in his own art.

§ CXVII. *First side.* "ST. SIMPLICIUS": so inscribed. A figure working with a pointed chisel on a small oblong block of green serpentine, about four inches long by one wide, inlaid in the capital. The chisel is, of course, in the left hand, but the right is held up open, with the palm outwards.

Second side. A crowned figure, carving the image of a child on a small statue, with a ground of red marble. The sculptured figure is highly finished, and is in type of head much like the Ham or Japheth at the Vine angle. Inscription effaced.

Third side. An old man, uncrowned, but with curling hair, at work on a small column, with its capital complete, and a little shaft of dark red marble, spotted with paler red. The capital is precisely of the form of that found in the palace of the Tiepolos and the other thirteenth century work of Venice. This one figure would be quite enough, without any other evidence whatever, to determine the date of this flank of the Ducal Palace as not later, at all events, than the first half of the fourteenth century. Its inscription is broken away, all but "DISIPULO."

Fourth side. A crowned figure; but the object on which it has been working is broken away, and all the inscription except "ST. E(N?)AS."

Fifth side. A man with a turban, and a sharp chisel, at work on a kind of panel or niche, the back of which is of red marble.

Sixth side. A crowned figure, with hammer and chisel, employed *on a little range of windows of the fifth order*, having roses set, instead of orbicular ornaments, between the spandrils, with a rich cornice, and a band of marble inserted above. This sculpture assures us of the date of the fifth order window, which it shows to have been universal in the early fourteenth century.

There are also five arches in the block on which the sculptor is working, marking the frequency of the number five in the window groups of the time.

Seventh side. A figure at work on a pilaster, with Lombardic thirteenth century capital (for account of the series of forms in Venetian capitals, see the final Appendix of the next volume), the shaft of dark red spotted marble.

Eighth side. A figure with a rich open crown, working on a delicate recumbent statue, the head of which is laid on a pillow covered with a rich chequer pattern; the whole supported on a block of dark red marble. Inscription broken away, all but "ST. SYM. (Symmachus?) TV * * ANVS." There appear, therefore, altogether to have been five saints, two of them popes, if Simplicius is the pope of that name (three in front, two on the fourth and sixth sides), alternating with the three uncrowned workmen in the manual labor of sculpture. I did not, therefore, insult our present architects in saying above that they "ought to work in the mason's yard with their men." It would be difficult to find a more interesting expression of the devotional spirit in which all great work was undertaken at this time.

§ CXVLI. TWENTIETH CAPITAL. It is adorned with heads of animals, and is the finest of the whole series in the broad massiveness of its effect; so simply characteristic, indeed, of the grandeur of style in the entire building, that I chose it for the first Plate in my folio work. In spite of the sternness of its plan, however, it is wrought with great care in surface detail; and the ornamental value of the minute chasing obtained by the delicate plumage of the birds, and the clustered bees on the honeycomb in the bear's mouth, opposed to the strong simplicity of its general form, cannot be too much admired. There are also more grace, life, and variety in the sprays of foliage on each side of it, and under the heads, than in any other capital of the series, though the earliness of the workmanship is marked by considerable hardness and coldness in the larger heads. A Northern Gothic workman, better acquainted with bears and wolves than it was possible to become in St. Mark's Place, would have put far more life into these heads, but he could not have composed them more skilfully.

§ cxix. *First side.* A lion with a stag's haunch in his mouth. Those readers who have the folio plate, should observe the peculiar way in which the ear is cut into the shape of a ring, jagged or furrowed on the edge; an archaic mode of treatment peculiar, in the Ducal Palace, to the lions' heads of the fourteenth century. The moment we reach the Renaissance work, the lions' ears are smooth. Inscribed simply, "LEO."

Second side. A wolf with a dead bird in his mouth, its body wonderfully true in expression of the passiveness of death. The feathers are each wrought with a central quill and radiating filaments. Inscribed "LUPUS."

Third side. A fox, not at all like one, with a dead cock in his mouth, its comb and pendent neck admirably designed so as to fall across the great angle leaf of the capital, its tail hanging down on the other side, its long straight feathers exquisitely cut. Inscribed "(VULP ?)IS."

Fourth side. Entirely broken away.

Fifth side. "APER." Well tusked, with a head of maize in his mouth; at least I suppose it to be maize, though shaped like a pine-cone.

Sixth side. "CHANIS." With a bone, very ill cut; and a bald-headed species of dog, with ugly flap ears.

Seventh side. "MUSCIPULUS." With a rat (?) in his mouth.

Eighth side. "URSUS." With a honeycomb, covered with large bees.

§ CXX. TWENTY-FIRST CAPITAL. Represents the principal inferior professions.

First side. An old man, with his brow deeply wrinkled, and very expressive features, beating in a kind of mortar with a hammer. Inscribed "LAPICIDA SUM."

Second side. I believe, a goldsmith; he is striking a small flat bowl or patera, on a pointed anvil, with a light hammer. The inscription is gone.

Third side. A shoemaker with a shoe in his hand, and an instrument for cutting leather suspended beside him. Inscription undecipherable.

Fourth side. Much broken. A carpenter planing a beam resting on two horizontal logs. Inscribed "CARPENTARIUS SUM."

Fifth side. A figure shovelling fruit into a tub; the latter very carefully carved from what appears to have been an excellent piece of cooperage. Two thin laths cross each other over the top of it. The inscription, now lost, was, according to Selvatico, "MENSURATOR"?

Sixth side. A man, with a large hoe, breaking the ground, which lies in irregular furrows and clods before him. Now undecipherable, but according to Selvatico, "AGRICHOLA."

Seventh side. A man, in a pendent cap, writing on a large scroll which falls over his knee. Inscribed "NOTARIUS SUM."

Eighth side. A man forging a sword, or scythe-blade: he wears a large skull-cap; beats with a large hammer on a solid anvil; and is inscribed "FABER SUM."

§ CXXI. TWENTY-SECOND CAPITAL. The Ages of Man; and the influence of the planets on human life.

First side. The moon, governing infancy for four years, according to Selvatico. I have no note of this side, having, I suppose, been prevented from raising the ladder against it by some fruit-stall or other impediment in the regular course of my examination; and then forgotten to return to it.

Second side. A child with a tablet, and an alphabet inscribed on it. The legend above is

" M̄ECUREUˢ D̄N̄T. PUERICIE. PAN. X."

Or, " Mercurius dominatur pueritiæ per annos X." (Selvatico reads VII.) " Mercury governs boyhood for ten (or seven) years."

Third side. An older youth, with another tablet, but broken. Inscribed

" ADOLOSCENCIE * * * P. AN. VII."

Selvatico misses this side altogether, as I did the first, so that the lost planet is irrecoverable, as the inscription is now defaced. Note the o for e in adolescentia; so also we constantly find u for o; showing, together with much other incontestable evidence of the same kind, how full and deep the old pronunciation of Latin always remained, and how ridiculous our English mincing of the vowels would have sounded to a Roman ear.

Fourth side. A youth with a hawk on his fist.

" IUVENTUTI D̄N̄T SOL. P. AN. XIX."
The sun governs youth for nineteen years.

Fifth side. A man sitting, helmed, with a sword over his shoulder. Inscribed

" SENECTUTI D̄N̄T MARS. P. AN. XV."
Mars governs manhood for fifteen years.

Sixth side. A very graceful and serene figure, in the pendent cap, reading.

" SENICIE D̄N̄T JUPITER, P. ANN. XII."
Jupiter governs age for twelve years.

Seventh side.   An old man in a skull-cap, praying.

"DECREPITE DNT SATN UQ^S ADMOTE."   (Saturnus usque ad mortem.)
       Saturn governs decrepitude until death.

Eighth side.   The dead body lying on a mattress.

"ULTIMA EST MORS PENA PECCATI."
     Last comes death, the penalty of sin.

§ CXXII. Shakspeare's Seven Ages are of course merely the
expression of this early and well known system. He has deprived the dotage of its devotion; but I think wisely, as the
Italian system would imply that devotion was, or should be,
always delayed until dotage.

TWENTY-THIRD CAPITAL. I agree with Selvatico in thinking
this has been restored. It is decorated with large and vulgar
heads.

§ CXXIII. TWENTY-FOURTH CAPITAL. This belongs to the
large shaft which sustains the great party wall of the Sala del
Gran Consiglio. The shaft is thicker than the rest; but the
capital, though ancient, is coarse and somewhat inferior in
design to the others of the series. It represents the history
of marriage: the lover first seeing his mistress at a window,
then addressing her, bringing her presents; then the bridal,
the birth and the death of a child. But I have not been able
to examine these sculptures properly, because the pillar is
encumbered by the railing which surrounds the two guns set
before the Austrian guard-house.

§ CXXIV. TWENTY-FIFTH CAPITAL. We have here the em
ployments of the months, with which we are already tolerably
acquainted. There are, however, one or two varieties worth
noticing in this series.

First side. March. Sitting triumphantly in a rich dress, as
the beginning of the year.

Second side. April and May. April with a lamb : May with a feather fan in her hand.

Third side. June. Carrying cherries in a basket.

I did not give this series with the others in the previous chapter, because this representation of June is peculiarly Venetian. It is called "the month of cherries," mese delle ceriese, in the popular rhyme on the conspiracy of Tiepolo, quoted above, Vol. I.

The cherries principally grown near Venice are of a deep red colour, and large, but not of high flavour, though refreshing. They are carved upon the pillar with great care, all their stalks undercut.

Fourth side. July and August. The first reaping; the *leaves* of the straw being given, shooting out from the tubular stalk. August, opposite, beats (the grain?) in a basket.

Fifth side. September. A woman standing in a wine-tub, and holding a branch of vine. Very beautiful.

Sixth side. October and November. I could not make out their occupation; they seem to be roasting or boiling some root over a fire.

Seventh side. December. Killing pigs, as usual.

Eighth side. January warming his feet, and February frying fish. This last employment is again as characteristic of the Venetian winter as the cherries are of the Venetian summer.

The inscriptions are undecipherable, except a few letters here and there, and the words MARCIUS, APRILIS, and FEBRUARIUS.

This is the last of the capitals of the early palace ; the next, or twenty-sixth capital, is the first of those executed in the fifteenth century under Foscari ; and hence to the Judgment angle the traveller has nothing to do but to compare the base copies of the earlier work with their originals, or to observe the total want of invention in the Renaissance sculptor, wherever he has depended on his own resources. This, however, always with the exception of the twenty-seventh and of the last capital, which are both fine.

I shall merely enumerate the subjects and point out the plagiarisms of these capitals, as they are not worth description.

§ CXXV. TWENTY-SIXTH CAPITAL. Copied from the fifteenth, merely changing the succession of the figures.

TWENTY-SEVENTH CAPITAL. I think it possible that this may be part of the old work displaced in joining the new palace with the old; at all events, it is well designed, though a little coarse. It represents eight different kinds of fruit, each in a basket; the characters well given, and groups well arranged, but without much care or finish. The names are inscribed above, though somewhat unnecessarily, and with certainly as much disrespect to the beholder's intelligence as the sculptor's art, namely, ZEREXIS, PIRI, CHUCUMERIS, PERSICI, ZUCHE, MOLONI, FICI, HUVA. Zerexis (cherries) and Zuche (gourds) both begin with the same letter, whether meant for z, s, or c I am not sure. The Zuche are the common gourds, divided into two protuberances, one larger than the other, like a bottle compressed near the neck; and the Moloni are the long water-melons, which, roasted, form a staple food of the Venetians to this day.

§ CXXVI. TWENTY-EIGHTH CAPITAL. Copied from the seventh.

TWENTY-NINTH CAPITAL. Copied from the ninth.

THIRTIETH CAPITAL. Copied from the tenth. The "Accidia" is noticeable as having the inscription complete, "ACCIDIA ME STRINGIT;" and the "Luxuria" for its utter want of expression, having a severe and calm face, a robe up to the neck, and her hand upon her breast. The inscription is also different: "LUXURIA SUM STERC^s (?) INFERI" (?).

THIRTY-FIRST CAPITAL. Copied from the eighth.

THIRTY-SECOND CAPITAL. Has no inscription, only fully

robed figures laying their hands, without any meaning, on their own shoulders, heads, or chins, or on the leaves around them.

THIRTY-THIRD CAPITAL. Copied from the twelfth.

THIRTY-FOURTH CAPITAL. Copied from the eleventh.

THIRTY-FIFTH CAPITAL. Has children, with birds or fruit, pretty in features, and utterly inexpressive, like the cherubs of the eighteenth century.

§ CXXVII. THIRTY-SIXTH CAPITAL. This is the last of the Piazzetta façade, the elaborate one under the Judgment angle. Its foliage is copied from the eighteenth at the opposite side, with an endeavor on the part of the Renaissance sculptor to refine upon it, by which he has merely lost some of its truth and force. This capital will, however, be always thought, at first, the most beautiful of the whole series : and indeed it is very noble ; its groups of figures most carefully studied, very graceful, and much more pleasing than those of the earlier work, though with less real power in them ; and its foliage is only inferior to that of the magnificent Fig-tree angle. It represents, on its front or first side, Justice enthroned, seated on two lions ; and on the seven other sides examples of acts of justice or good government, or figures of lawgivers, in the following order :

Second side. Aristotle, with two pupils, giving laws. Inscribed :

" ARISTOT * * CHE DIE LEGE."
Aristotle who declares laws.

Third side. I have mislaid my note of this side : Selvatico and Lazari call it "Isidore" (?)†

Fourth side. Solon with his pupils. Inscribed :

" SAL° UNO DEI SETE SAVI DI GRECIA CHE DIE LEGE."
Solon, one of the seven sages of Greece, who declares laws.

† Can they have mistaken the ISIPIONE of the fifth side for the word Isidore ?

Note, by the by, the pure Venetian dialect used in this capital, instead of the Latin in the more ancient ones. One of the seated pupils in this sculpture is remarkably beautiful in the sweep of his flowing drapery.

Fifth side. The chastity of Scipio. Inscribed:

"ISIPIONE A CHASTITA CH * * * E LA FIA (e la figlia?) * * ARE."

A soldier in a plumed bonnet presents a kneeling maiden to the seated Scipio, who turns thoughtfully away.

Sixth side. Numa Pompilius building churches.

"NUMA POMPILIO IMPERADOR EDIFICHADOR DI TEMPI E CHIESE."

Numa, in a kind of hat with a crown above it, directing a soldier in Roman armor (note this, as contrasted with the mail of the earlier capitals). They point to a tower of three stories filled with tracery.

Seventh side. Moses receiving the law. Inscribed:

"QUANDO MOSE RECEVE LA LEGE I SUL MONTE."

Moses kneels on a rock, whence springs a beautifully fancied tree, with clusters of three berries in the centre of three leaves, sharp and quaint, like fine Northern Gothic. The half figure of the Deity comes out of the abacus, the arm meeting that of Moses, both at full stretch, with the stone tablets between.

Eighth side. Trajan doing justice to the Widow.

"TRAJANO IMPERADOR CHE FA JUSTITIA A LA VEDOVA."

He is riding spiritedly, his mantle blown out behind; the widow kneeling before his horse.

§ CXXVIII. The reader will observe that this capital is of peculiar interest in its relation to the much disputed question

of the character of the later government of Venice. It is the
assertion by that government of its belief that Justice only
could be the foundation of its stability; as these stones ot
Justice and Judgment are the foundation of its halls of council.
And this profession of their faith may be interpreted in two
ways. Most modern historians would call it, in common
with the continual reference to the principles of justice in the
political and judicial language of the period,* nothing more
than a cloak for consummate violence and guilt; and it may
easily be proved to have been so in myriads of instances. But
in the main, I believe the expression of feeling to be genuine.
I do not believe, of the majority of the leading Venetians of
this period whose portraits have come down to us, that they
were deliberately and everlastingly hypocrites. I see no
hypocrisy in their countenances. Much capacity of it, much
subtlety, much natural and acquired reserve; but no meanness.
On the contrary, infinite grandeur, repose, courage, and the
peculiar unity and tranquillity of expression which come of
sincerity or *wholeness* of heart, and which it would take much
demonstration to make me believe could by any possibility be
seen on the countenance of an insincere man. I trust, therefore, that these Venetian nobles of the fifteenth century did, in
the main, desire to do judgment and justice to all men; but,
as the whole system of morality had been by this time under-
mined by the teaching of the Romish Church, the idea of
justice had become separated from that of truth, so that dis-
simulation in the interest of the state assumed the aspect of
duty. We had, perhaps, better consider, with some carefulness, the mode in which our own government is carried on,
and the occasional difference between parliamentary and
private morality, before we judge mercilessly of the Venetians

* Compare the speech of the Doge Mocenigo, above,—"first justice, and
then the interests of the state:" and see Vol. III. Chap. II. § LIX.

in this respect. The secrecy with which their political and criminal trials were conducted, appears to modern eyes like a confession of sinister intentions; but may it not also be considered, and with more probability, as the result of an endeavor to do justice in an age of violence?—the only means by which Law could establish its footing in the midst of feudalism. Might not Irish juries at this day justifiably desire to conduct their proceedings with some greater approximation to the judicial principles of the Council of Ten? Finally, if we examine, with critical accuracy, the evidence on which our present impressions of Venetian government are founded, we shall discover, in the first place, that two-thirds of the traditions of its cruelties are romantic fables: in the second, that the crimes of which it can be proved to have been guilty, differ only from those committed by the other Italian powers in being done less wantonly, and under profounder conviction of their political expediency: and lastly, that the final degradation of the Venetian power appears owing not so much to the principles of its government, as to their being forgotten in the pursuit of pleasure.

§ CXXIX. We have now examined the portions of the palace which contain the principal evidence of the feeling of its builders. The capitals of the upper arcade are exceedingly various in their character; their design is formed, as in the lower series, of eight leaves, thrown into volutes at the angles, and sustaining figures at the flanks; but these figures have no inscriptions, and though evidently not without meaning, cannot be interpreted without more knowledge than I possess of ancient symbolism. Many of the capitals toward the Sea appear to have been restored, and to be rude copies of the ancient ones; others, though apparently original, have been somewhat carelessly wrought; but those of them, which are both genuine and carefully treated, are even finer in composition than any, except the eighteenth, in the lower arcade.

The traveller in Venice ought to ascend into the corridor, and examine with great care the series of capitals which extend on the Piazzetta side from the Fig-tree angle to the pilaster which carries the party wall of the Sala del Gran Consiglio. As examples of graceful composition in massy capitals meant for hard service and distant effect, these are among the finest things I know in Gothic art; and that above the fig-tree is remarkable for its sculptures of the four winds; each on the side turned towards the wind represented. Levante, the east wind; a figure with rays round its head, to show that it is always clear weather when that wind blows, raising the sun out of the sea: Hotro, the south wind; crowned, holding the sun in its right hand: Ponente, the west wind; plunging the sun into the sea: and Tramontana, the north wind; looking up at the north star. This capital should be carefully examined, if for no other reason than to attach greater distinctness of idea to the magnificent verbiage of Milton:

> " Thwart of these, as fierce,
> Forth rush the Levant and the Ponent winds,
> Eurus, and Zephyr; with their lateral noise,
> Sirocco and Libecchio."

I may also especially point out the bird feeding its three young ones on the seventh pillar on the Piazzetta side; but there is no end to the fantasy of these sculptures; and the traveller ought to observe them all carefully, until he comes to the great Pilaster or complicated pier which sustains the party wall of the Sala del Consiglio ; that is to say, the forty-seventh capital of the whole series, counting from the pilaster of the Vine angle inclusive, as in the series of the lower arcade. The forty-eighth, forty-ninth, and fiftieth are bad work, but they are old ; the fifty-first is the first Renaissance capital of the upper arcade: the first new lion's head with smooth ears, cut in the time of Foscari, is over the fiftieth capital ; and that capital, with its shaft, stands on the apex of the eighth arch from the Sea, on the Piazzetta side, of which one spandril is masonry of the fourteenth and the other of the fifteenth century.

§ cxxx. The reader who is not able to examine the building on the spot may be surprised at the definiteness with which the point of junction is ascertainable ; but a glance at the lowest range of leaves in the opposite Plate (XX.) will enable him to judge of the grounds on which the above statement is made. Fig. 12 is a cluster of leaves from the capital of the Four Winds ; early work of the finest time. Fig. 13 is a leaf from the great Renaissance capital at the Judgment angle, worked in imitation of the older leafage. Fig. 14. is a leaf from one of the Renaissance capitals of the upper arcade, which are all worked in the natural manner of the period. It will be seen that it requires no great ingenuity to distinguish between such design as that of fig. 12. and that of fig. 14.

§ cxxxi. It is very possible that the reader may at first like fig. 14. the best. I shall endeavor, in the next chapter, to show why he should not ; but it must also be noted, that fig. 12. has lost, and fig. 14. gained, both largely, under the hands of the engraver. All the bluntness and coarseness of feeling in the workmanship of fig. 14. have disappeared on this small scale, and all the subtle refinements in the broad masses of fig. 12. have vanished. They could not, indeed, be rendered in line engraving, unless by the hand of Albert Durer ; and I have, therefore, abandoned, for the present, all endeavor to represent any more important mass of the early sculpture of the Ducal Palace : but I trust that, in a few months, casts of many portions will be within the reach of the inhabitants of London, and that they will be able to judge for themselves of their perfect, pure, unlabored naturalism ; the

freshness, elasticity, and softness of their leafage, united with
the most noble symmetry and severe reserve,—no running to
waste, no loose or experimental lines, no extravagance, and no
weakness. Their design is always sternly architectural; there
is none of the wildness or redundance of natural vegetation,
but there is all the strength, freedom, and tossing flow of the
breathing leaves, and all the undulation of their surfaces,
rippled, as they grew, by the summer winds, as the sands are
by the sea.

§ CXXXII. This early sculpture of the Ducal Palace, then,
represents the state of Gothic work in Venice at its central
and proudest period, i. e. circa 1350. After this time, all is
decline,—of what nature and by what steps, we shall inquire
in the ensuing chapter; for as this investigation, though still
referring to Gothic architecture, introduces us to the first
symptoms of the Renaissance influence, I have considered it
as properly belonging to the third division of our subject.

§ CXXXIII. And as, under the shadow of these nodding leaves,
we bid farewell to the great Gothic spirit, here also we may
cease our examination of the details of the Ducal Palace; for
above its upper arcade there are only the four traceried
windows*, and one or two of the third order on the Rio
Façade, which can be depended upon as exhibiting the original
workmanship of the older palace. I examined the capitals of
the four other windows on the façade, and of those on the
Piazzetta, one by one, with great care, and I found them all
to be of far inferior workmanship to those which retain their
traceries: I believe the stone framework of these windows
must have been so cracked and injured by the flames of the
great fire, as to render it necessary to replace it by new

---

* Some further details respecting these portions, as well as some necessary
confirmations of my statements of dates, are, however, given in Appendix 1.
Vol. III. I feared wearying the general reader by introducing them into the
text.

traceries ; and that the present mouldings and capitals are base imitations of the original ones. The traceries were at first, however, restored in their complete form, as the holes for the bolts which fastened the bases of their shafts are still to be seen in the window-sills, as well as the marks of the inner mouldings on the soffits. How much the stone facing of the façade, the parapets, and the shafts and niches of the angles, retain of their original masonry, it is also impossible to determine ; but there is nothing in the workmanship of any of them demanding especial notice ; still less in the large central windows on each façade, which are entirely of Renaissance execution. All that is admirable in these portions of the building is the disposition of their various parts and masses, which is without doubt the same as in the original fabric, and calculated, when seen from a distance, to produce the same impression.

§ cxxxiv. Not so in the interior. All vestige of the earlier modes of decoration was here, of course, destroyed by the fires ; and the severe and religious work of Guariento and Bellini has been replaced by the wildness of Tintoret and the luxury of Veronese. But in this case, though widely different in temper, the art of the renewal was at least intellectually as great as that which had perished : and though the halls of the Ducal Palace are no more representative of the character of the men by whom it was built, each of them is still a colossal casket of priceless treasure ; a treasure whose safety has till now depended on its being despised, and which at this moment, and as I write, is piece by piece being destroyed for ever.

§ cxxxv. The reader will forgive my quitting our mor immediate subject, in order briefly to explain the causes and the nature of this destruction ; for the matter is simply the most important of all that can be brought under our present consideration respecting the state of art in Europe.

The fact is, that the greater number of persons or societies

18

throughout Europe, whom wealth, or chance, or inheritance
has put in possession of valuable pictures, do not know a good
picture from a bad one,* and have no idea in what the value
of a picture really consists. The reputation of certain works
is raised, partly by accident, partly by the just testimony of
artists, partly by the various and generally bad taste of the
public (no picture, that I know of, has ever, in modern times,
attained popularity, in the full sense of the term, without having some exceedingly bad qualities mingled with its good
ones), and when this reputation has once been completely
established, it little matters to what state the picture may be
reduced : few minds are so completely devoid of imagination
as to be unable to invest it with the beauties which they have
heard attr buted to it.

§ CXXXVI. This being so, the pictures that are most valued
are for the most part those by masters of established renown,
which are highly or neatly finished, and of a size small enough
to admit of their being placed in galleries or saloons, so as to
be made subjects of ostentation, and to be easily seen by a
crowd. For the support of the fame and value of such pictures, little more is necessary than that they should be kept
bright, partly by cleaning, which is incipient destruction, and
partly by what is called "restoring," that is, painting over,
which is of course total destruction. Nearly all the gallery
pictures in modern Europe, have been more or less destroyed
by one or other of these operations, generally exactly in proportion to the estimation in which they are held ; and as,
originally, the smaller and more highly finished works of any
great master are usually his worst, the contents of many of

---

* Many persons, capable of quickly sympathizing with any excellence, when
once pointed out to them, easily deceive themselves into the supposition that
they are judges of art. There is only one real test of such power of judgment.
Can they, at a glance, discover a good picture obscured by the filth, and confused among the rubbish, of the pawnbroker's or dealer's garret ?

our most celebrated galleries are by this time, in reality, of very small value indeed.

§ CXXXVII. On the other hand, the most precious works of any noble painter are usually those which have been done quickly, and in the heat of the first thought, on a large scale, for places where there was little likelihood of their being well seen, or for patrons from whom there was little prospect of rich remuneration. In general, the best things are done in this way, or else in the enthusiasm and pride of accomplishing some great purpose, such as painting a cathedral or a campo-santo from one end to the other, especially when the time has been short, and circumstances disadvantageous.

§ CXXXVIII. Works thus executed are of course despised, on account of their quantity, as well as their frequent slightness, in the places where they exist ; and they are too large to be portable, and too vast and comprehensive to be read on the spot, in the hasty temper of the present age. They are, therefore, almost universally neglected, whitewashed by cus todes, shot at by soldiers, suffered to drop from the walls piecemeal in powder and rags by society in general ; but, which is an advantage more than counterbalancing all this evil, they are not often "restored." What is left of them, however fragmentary, however ruinous, however obscured and defiled, is almost always *the real thing ;* there are no fresh readings : and therefore the greatest treasures of art which Europe at this moment possesses are pieces of old plaster on ruinous brick walls, where the lizards burrow and bask, and which few other living creatures ever approach ; and torn sheets of dim canvass, in waste corners of churches ; and mildewed stains, in the shape of human figures, on the walls of dark chambers, which now and then an exploring traveller causes to be unlocked by their tottering custode, looks hastily round, and retreats from in a weary satisfaction at his accom-plished duty.

§ cxxxix. Many of the pictures on the ceilings and walls of the Ducal Palace, by Paul Veronese and Tintoret, have been more or less reduced, by neglect, to this condition. Unfortunately they are not altogether without reputation, and their state has drawn the attention of the Venetian authorities and academicians. It constantly happens, that public bodies who will not pay five pounds to preserve a picture, will pay fifty to repaint it :* and when I was at Venice in 1846, there were two remedial operations carrying on, at one and the same time, in the two buildings which contain the pictures of greatest value in the city (as pieces of color, of greatest value in the world), curiously illustrative of this peculiarity in human nature. Buckets were set on the floor of the Scuola di San Rocco, in every shower, to catch the rain which came through the pictures of Tintoret on the ceiling ; while in the Ducal Palace, those of Paul Veronese were themselves laid on the floor to be repainted ; and I was myself present at the re-illumination of the breast of a white horse, with a brush, at the end of a stick five feet long, luxuriously dipped in a common house-painter's vessel of paint.

This was, of course, a large picture. The process has already been continued in an equally destructive, though somewhat more delicate manner, over the whole of the humbler canvasses on the ceiling of the Sala del Gran Consiglio ; and I heard it threatened when I was last in Venice (1851–2) to the " Paradise " at its extremity, which is yet in tolerable condition,—the largest work of Tintoret, and the most won-

---

* This is easily explained. There are, of course, in every place and at all periods, bad painters who conscientiously believe that they can improve every picture they touch ; and these men are generally, in their presumption, the most influential over the innocence, whether of monarchs or municipalities. The carpenter and slater have little influence in recommending the repairs of the roof; but the bad painter has great influence, as well as interest, in recommending those of the picture.

derful piece of pure, manly, and masterly oil-painting in the world.

§ CXL. I leave these facts to the consideration of the European patrons of art. Twenty years hence they will be acknowledged and regretted; at present, I am well aware, that it is of little use to bring them forward, except only to explain the present impossibility of stating what pictures *are*, and what *were*, in the interior of the Ducal Palace. I can only say, that in the winter of 1851, the "Paradise" of Tintoret was still comparatively uninjured, and that the Camera di Collegio, and its antechamber, and the Sala de' Pregadi were full of pictures by Veronese and Tintoret, that made their walls as precious as so many kingdoms; so precious indeed, and so full of majesty, that sometimes when walking at evening on the Lido, whence the great chain of the Alps, crested with silver clouds, might be seen rising above the front of the Ducal Palace, I used to feel as much awe in gazing on the building as on the hills, and could believe that God had done a greater work in breathing into the narrowness of dust the mighty spirits by whom its haughty walls had been raised, and its burning legends written, than in lifting the rocks of granite higher than the clouds of heaven, and veiling them with their various mantle of purple flower and shadowy pine.

APPENDIX.

1. THE GONDOLIER'S CRY.

MOST persons are now well acquainted with the general aspect of the Venetian gondola, but few have taken the pains to understand the cries of warning uttered by its boatmen, although those cries are peculiarly characteristic, and very impressive to a stranger, and have been even very sweetly introduced in poetry by Mr. Monckton Milnes. It may perhaps be interesting to the traveller in Venice to know the general method of management of the boat to which he owes so many happy hours.

A gondola is in general rowed only by one man, *standing* at the stern; those of the upper classes having two or more boatmen, for greater speed and magnificence. In order to raise the oar sufficiently, it rests, not on the side of the boat, but on a piece of crooked timber like the branch of a tree, rising about a foot from the boat's side, and called a "fórcola." The forcola is of different forms, according to the size and uses of the boat, and it is always somewhat complicated in its parts and curvature, allowing the oar various kinds of rests and catches on both its sides, but perfectly free play in all cases; as the management of the boat depends on the gondolier's being able in an instant to place his oar in any position. The forcola is set on the right-hand side of the boat, some six feet from the stern: the gondolier stands on a little flat platform or deck behind it, and throws nearly the entire weight of his body upon the forward stroke. The effect of this stroke would be naturally to turn the boat's head round to the left, as well as to send it forward; but this tendency is corrected by keeping the blade of the oar under the water on the return stroke, and raising it gradually, as a full spoon is raised out of any liquid, so that the blade emerges from the water only an instant before it again plunges. A *downward* and lateral pressure upon the forcola is thus obtained, which entirely counteracts the tendency given by the forward stroke; and the effort, after a little practice, becomes hardly conscious, though, as it adds some labor to the back stroke, rowing a gondola at speed is hard and breathless work, though it appears easy and graceful to the looker-on.

If then the gondola is to be turned to the left, the forward impulse is given without the return stroke; if it is to be turned to the right, the plunged oar is brought forcibly up to the surface; in either case a single strong stroke being enough to turn the light and flat-bottomed boat. But as it has no keel, when the turn is made sharply, as out of one canal into another very narrow one, the impetus of the boat in its former direction gives it an enormous lee-way, and it drifts laterally up against the wall of the canal, and that so forcibly, that if it has turned at speed, no gondolier can arrest the motion merely by strength or rapidity of stroke of oar; but it is checked by a strong thrust of the foot against the wall itself, the head of the boat being of course turned for the moment almost completely round to the opposite wall, and greater exertion made to give it, as quickly as possible, impulse in the new direction.

The boat being thus guided, the cry "Premi" is the order from one gondolier to another that he should "press" or thrust forward his oar, without the back stroke, so as to send the boat's head round *to the left;* and the cry "Stali" is the order that he should give the return or upward stroke which sends the boat's head round to the *right.* Hence, if two gondoliers meet under any circumstances which render it a matter of question on which side they should pass each other, the gondolier who has at the moment the least power over his boat, cries to the other, "Premi," if he wishes the boats to pass with their right-hand sides to each other, and "Stali," if with their left. Now, in turning a corner, there is of course risk of collision between boats coming from opposite sides, and warning is always clearly and loudly given on approaching an angle of the canals. It is of course presumed that the boat which gives the warning will be nearer the turn than the one which receives and answers it; and therefore will not have so much time to check itself or alter its course. Hence the advantage of the turn, that is, the outside, which allows the fullest swing and greatest room for lee-way, is always yielded to the boat which gives warning. Therefore, if the warning boat is going to turn to the right, as it is to have the outside position, it will keep its own right-hand side to the boat which it meets, and the cry of warning is therefore "Premi," twice given; first as soon as it can be heard round the angle, prolonged and loud, with the accent on the e, and another strongly accented e added, a kind of question, "Prémi-é," followed at the instant of turning, with "Ah Premí," with the accent sharp on the final i. If, on the other hand, the warning boat is going to turn to the left, it will pass, with its left-hand side to the one it meets; and the warning cry is, "Stáli-é, Ah Stalí." Hence the confused idea in the mind of the traveller that Stali means "to the left," and "Premi" to the right; while they mean, in reality, the direct reverse; the Stali, for instance, being the order to the unseen gondolier who may be behind the corner, coming from the left-hand side, that he should hold as much as possible *to his own right;* this being the only safe order for him, whether he is going to turn the corner himself, or to go straight on; for as the warning gondola will always swing right across the canal in turning, a collision with it is only to be avoided by keeping well within it, and close up to the corner which it turns.

There are several other cries necessary in the management of the gondola, but less frequently, so that the reader will hardly care for their interpretation; except only the "sciar," which is the order to the opposite gondolier to stop the boat as suddenly as possible by slipping his oar in front of the forcola. The *cry* is never heard except when the boatmen have got into some unexpected position, involving a risk of collision; but the action is seen constantly, when the gondola is rowed by two or more men (for if performed by the single gondolier it only swings the boat's head sharp round to the right), in bringing up at a landing-place, especially when there is any intent of display, the boat being first urged to its full speed and then stopped with as much foam about the oar-blades as possible, the effect being much like that of stopping a horse at speed by pulling him on his haunches.

2. OUR LADY OF SALVATION.

"Santa Maria della Salute," Our Lady of Health, or of Safety, would be a more literal translation, yet not perhaps fully expressing the force of the Italian word in this case. The church was built between 1630 and 1680, in acknowledgment of the cessation of the plague;—of course to the Virgin, to whom the modern Italian has recourse in all his principal distresses, and who receives his gratitude for all principal deliverances.

The hasty traveller is usually enthusiastic in his admiration of this building; but there is a notable lesson to be derived from it, which is not often read. On the opposite side of the broad canal of the Giudecca is a small church, celebrated among Renaissance architects as of Palladian design, but which would hardly attract the notice of the general observer, unless on account of the pictures by John Bellini which it contains, in order to see which the traveller may perhaps remember having been taken across the Giudecca to the Church of the "Redentore." But he ought carefully to compare these two buildings with each other, the one built "to the Virgin," the other "to the Redeemer" (also a votive offering after the cessation of the plague of 1576); the one, the most conspicuous church in Venice, its dome, the principal one by which she is first discerned, rising out of the distant sea: the other, small and contemptible, on a suburban island, and only becoming an object of interest because it contains three small pictures! For in the relative magnitude and conspicuousness of these two buildings, we have an accurate index of the relative importance of the ideas of the Madonna and of Christ, in the modern Italian mind.

Some further account of this church is given in the final Index to the Venetian buildings at the close of the third Volume.

3. TIDES OF VENICE, AND MEASURES AT TORCELLO.

The lowest and highest tides take place in Venice at different periods, the lowest during the winter, the highest in the summer and autumn. During the period of the highest tides, the city is exceedingly beautiful especially if, as is not unfrequently the case, the water rises high enough partially to flood St. Mark's Place. Nothing can be more lovely or fantastic than the scene, when the Campanile and the Golden Church are reflected in the calm water, and the lighter gondolas floating under the very porches of the façade. On the other hand, a winter residence in Venice is rendered peculiarly disagreeable by the low tides, which sometimes leave the smaller canals entirely dry, and large banks of mud beneath the houses, along the borders of even the Grand Canal. The difference between the levels of the highest and lowest tides I saw in Venice was 6 ft. 3 in. The average fall rise is from two to three feet.

~~~~~~

The measures of Torcello were intended for Appendix 4.; but having by a misprint referred the reader to Appendix 3., I give them here. The entire breadth of the church within the walls is 70 feet; of which the square bases of the pillars, 3 feet on each side, occupy 6 feet; and the nave, from base to base, measures 31 ft. 1 in.; the aisles from base to wall, 16 feet odd inches, not accurately ascertainable on account of the modern wainscot fittings. The intervals between the bases of the pillars are 8 feet each, increasing towards the altar to 8 ft. 3 in., in order to allow for a corresponding diminution in the diameter of the bases from 3 ft. to 2 ft. 11 in. or 2 ft. 10 in. This subtle diminution of the bases is in order to prevent the eye from feeling the greater narrowness of the shafts in that part of the nave, their average circumference being 6 ft. 10 in.; and one, the second on the north side, reaching 7 feet, while those at the upper end of the nave vary from 6 ft. 8 in. to 6 ft. 4 in. It is probable that this diminution in the more distant pillars adds slightly to the perspective effect of length in the body of the church, as it is seen from the great entrance : but whether this was the intention or not, the delicate adaptation of this diminished base to the diminished shaft is a piece of fastidiousness in proportion which I rejoice in having detected; and this the more, because the rude contours of the bases themselves would little induce the spectator to anticipate any such refinement.

4. DATE OF THE DUOMO OF TORCELLO.

The first flight to the lagoons for shelter was caused by the invasion of Attila in the fifth century, so that in endeavoring to throw back the thought of the reader to the former solitude of the islands, I spoke of them as they must have appeared "1300 years ago." Altinum, however, was not finally destroyed till the Lombard invasion in 641, when the episcopal seat was removed to Torcello, and the inhabitants of the mainland city, giving up all hope of returning to their former homes, built their Duomo there. It is a disputed point among Venetian antiquarians, whether the present church be that which was built in the seventh century, partially restored in 1008, or whether the words of Sagornino, "ecclesiam jam vetustate consumptam recreare," justify them in assuming an entire rebuilding of the fabric. I quite agree with the Marchese Selvatico, in believing the present church to be the earlier building, variously strengthened, refitted, and modified by subsequent care; but, in all its main features, preserving its original aspect, except, perhaps, in the case of the pulpit and chancel screen, which, if the Chevalier Bunsen's conclusions respecting early pulpits in the Roman basilicas be correct (see the next article of this Appendix), may possibly have been placed in their present position in the tenth century, and the fragmentary character of the workmanship of the latter, noticed in §§ x. and xi., would in that case have been the result of innovation, rather than of haste. The question, however, whether they are of the seventh or eleventh century, does not in the least affect our conclusions, drawn from the design of these portions of the church, respecting pulpits in general.

5. MODERN PULPITS.

There is no character of an ordinary modern English church which appears to me more to be regretted than the peculiar pompousness of the furniture of the pulpits, contrasted, as it generally is, with great meagreness and absence of color in the other portions of the church; a pompousness, besides, altogether without grace or meaning, and dependent merely on certain applications of upholstery; which, curiously enough, are always in worse taste than even those of our drawing-rooms. Nor do I understand how our congregations can endure the aspect of the wooden sounding-board attached only by one point of its circumference to an upright pillar behind the preacher; and looking as if the weight of its enormous leverage must infallibly, before the sermon is concluded, tear it from its support, and bring it down upon the preacher's head. These errors in taste and feeling will however, I believe, be gradually amended as more Gothic churches are built; but the question of the position of the pulpit presents a more disputable ground of discussion. I can perfectly sympathise with the feeling of those who wish the eastern extremity of the church to form a kind of holy place for the communion table; nor have I often received a more painful impression than on seeing the preacher at the Scotch church in George Street, Portman Square, taking possession of a perfect apse; and occupying therein, during the course of the service, very nearly the same position which the figure of Christ does in that of the Cathedral of Pisa. But I nevertheless believe that the Scotch congregation are perfectly right, and have restored the real arrangement of the primitive churches. The Chevalier Bunsen informed me very lately, that, in all the early basilicas he has examined, the lateral pulpits are of more recent date than the rest of the building; that he knows of none placed in the position which they now occupy, both in the basilicas and Gothic cathedrals, before the ninth century; and that there can be no doubt that the bishop always preached or exhorted, in the primitive times, from his throne in the centre of the apse, the altar being always set at the centre of the church, in the crossing of the transepts. His Excellency found by experiment in Santa Maria Maggiore, the largest of the Roman basilicas, that the voice could be heard more plainly from the centre of the apse than from any other spot in the whole church; and, if this be so, it will be another very important reason for the adoption of the Romanesque (or Norman) architecture in our churches, rather than of the Gothic. The reader will find some farther notice of this question in the concluding chapter of the third volume.

Before leaving this subject, however, I must be permitted to say one word to those members of the Scotch Church who are severe in their requirement of the nominal or apparent extemporization of all addresses delivered from the pulpit. Whether they do right in giving those among their ministers who *cannot* preach extempore, the additional and useless labor of committing their sermons to memory, may be a disputed question; but it can hardly be so, that the now not unfrequent habit of making a desk of the Bible, and reading the sermon stealthily, by slipping the sheets of it between the sacred leaves, so that the preacher consults his own notes *on pretence* of consulting the Scriptures, is a very unseemly consequence of their over-strictness.

6. APSE OF MURANO.

The following passage succeeded in the original text to § xv. of Chap. III. Finding it not likely to interest the general reader, I have placed it here, as it contains matter of some interest to architects.

"On this plinth, thus carefully studied in relations of magnitude, the shafts are set at the angles, as close to each other as possible, as seen in the ground-plan. These shafts are founded on pure Roman tradition; their bases have no spurs, and the shaft itself is tapered in a bold curve, according to the classical model. But, in the adjustment of the bases to each other, we have a most curious instance of the first beginning of the Gothic principle of aggregation of shafts. They have a singularly archaic and simple profile, composed of a single cavetto and roll, which are circular, on a square plinth. Now when these bases are brought close to each other at the angles of the apse, their natural position would be as in fig. 3. Plate I., leaving an awkward fissure between the two square plinths. This offended the architect's eye; so he cut part of each of the bases away, and fitted them close to each other, as in fig. 5. Plate I., which is their actual position. As before this piece of rough harmonization the circular mouldings reached the sides of the squares, they were necessarily cut partly away in the course of the adjustment, and run into each other as in the figure, so as to give us one of the first Venetian instances of the continuous Gothic base.

"The shafts measure on the average 2 ft. 8½ in. in circumference, at the base, tapering so much that under the lowest fillet of their necks they measure only 2 feet round, though their height is only 5 ft. 6 in., losing thus eight inches of girth in five feet and a half of height. They are delicately curved all the way up; and are $2\frac{1}{2}$ in. apart from each other where they are nearest, and about 5 in. at the necks of their capitals."

7. EARLY VENETIAN DRESS.

Sansovino's account of the changes in the dress of the Venetians is brief, masterly, and full of interest; one or two passages are deserving of careful notice, especially the introductory sentence. "For the Venetians from their first origin, having made it their aim to be peaceful and religious, and to keep on an equality with one another, that equality might induce stability and concord (as disparity produces confusion and ruin), made their dress a matter of conscience, . . . ; and our ancestors, observant lovers of religion, upon which all their acts were founded, and desiring that their young men should direct themselves to virtue, the true soul of all human action, *and above all to peace*, invented a dress conformable to their gravity, such, that in clothing themselves with it, they might clothe themselves also with modesty and honor. And because their mind was bent upon giving no offence to any one, and living quietly as far as might be permitted them, it seemed good to them to show to every one, even by external signs, this their endeavor, by wearing a long dress, which was in no wise convenient for persons of a quick temperament, or of eager and fierce spirits."

Respecting the color of the women's dress, it is noticeable that blue is called " Venetian color " by Cassiodorus, translated " turchino " by Filiasi, vol. v. chap. iv. It was a very pale blue, as the place in which the word occurs is the description by Cassiodorus of the darkness which came over the sun's disk at the time of the Belisarian wars and desolation of the Gothic kingdom.

8. INSCRIPTIONS AT MURANO.

There are two other inscriptions on the border of the concha; but these, being written on the soffit of the face arch, which, as before noticed, is supported by the last two shafts of the chancel, could not be read by the congregation, and only with difficulty by those immediately underneath them. One of them is in black, the other in red letters The first :

> " Mutat quod sumsit, quod sollat crimina tandit
> Et quod sumpsit, vultus vestisq. refulsit."

The second :

> " Discipuli testes, prophete certa videntes
> Et cernunt purum, sibi credunt ese futurum."

I have found no notice of any of these inscriptions in any Italian account of the church of Murano, and have seldom seen even Monkish Latin less intelligible. There is no mistake in the letters, which are all large and clear; but wrong letters may have been introduced by ignorant restorers, as has often happened in St. Mark's.

9. SHAFTS OF ST. MARK.

The principal pillars which carry the nave and transepts, fourteen in number, are of white alabaster veined with grey and amber; each of a single block, 15 ft. high, and 6 ft. 2 in. round at the base. I in vain endeavored to ascertain their probable value. Every sculptor whom I questioned on this subject told me there were no such pieces of alabaster in the market, and that they were to be considered as without price.

On the façade of the church alone are two great ranges of shafts, seventy-two in the lower range, and seventy-nine in the upper; all of porphyry, alabaster, and verd-antique or fine marble; the lower about 9 ft., the upper about 7 ft. high, and of various circumferences, from 4 ft. 6 in. to 2 ft. round.

There are now so many published engravings, and, far better than engravings, calotypes, of this façade, that I may point out one or two circumstances for the reader's consideration without giving any plate of it here. And first, we ought to note the relations of the shafts and wall, the latter being first sheeted with alabaster, and then the pillars

set within two or three inches of it, forming such a grove of golden
marble that the porches open before us as we enter the church like
glades in a deep forest. The reader may perhaps at first question the
propriety of placing the wall so close behind the shafts that the latter
have nearly as little work to do as the statues in a Gothic porch ; but
the philosophy of this arrangement is briefly deducible from the principles stated in the text. The builder had at his disposal shafts of a
certain size only, not fit to sustain the whole weight of the fabric above.
He therefore turns just as much of the wall veil into shaft as he has
strength of marble at his disposal, and leaves the rest in its massive
form. And that there may be no dishonesty in this, nor any appearance in the shafts of doing more work than is really allotted to them,
many are left visibly with half their capitals projecting beyond the
archivolts they sustain, showing that the wall is very slightly dependent
on their co-operation, and that many of them are little more than mere
bonds or connecting rods between the foundation and cornices. If
any architect ventures to blame such an arrangement, let him look at
our much vaunted early English piers in Salisbury Cathedral or Westminster Abbey, where the small satellitic shafts are introduced in the
same gratuitous manner, but with far less excuse or reason : for those
small shafts have nothing but their delicacy and purely theoretical
connection with the archivolt mouldings to recommend them ; but the
St. Mark's shafts have an intrinsic beauty and value of the highest
order, and the object of the whole system of architecture, as above
stated, is in great part to set forth the beauty and value of the shaft
itself. Now, not only is this accomplished by withdrawing it occasionally from servile work, but the position here given to it, within
three or four inches of a wall from which it nevertheless stands perfectly clear all the way up, is exactly that which must best display its
color and quality. When there is much vacant space left behind a
pillar, the shade against which it is relieved is comparatively indefinite,
he eye passes by the shaft, and penetrates into the vacancy. But
when a broad surface of wall is brought near the shaft, its own shadow
is, in almost every effect of sunshine, so sharp and dark as to throw out
its colors with the highest possible brilliancy ; if there be no sunshine,
the wall veil is subdued and varied by the most subtle gradations of
delicate half shadow, hardly less advantageous to the shaft which it

relieves. And, as far as regards pure effect in open air (all artifice of excessive darkness or mystery being excluded), I do not know anything whatsoever in the whole compass of the European architecture I have seen, which can for a moment be compared with the quaint shade and delicate color, like that of Rembrandt and Paul Veronese united, which the sun brings out, as his rays move from porch to porch along the St. Mark's façade.

And, as if to prove that this was indeed the builder's intention, and that he did not leave his shafts idle merely because he did not know how to set them to work safely, there are two pieces of masonry at the extremities of the façade, which are just as remarkable for their frank trust in the bearing power of the shafts as the rest are for their want of confidence in them. But, before we come to these, we must say a word or two respecting the second point named above, the superior position of the shafts.

It was assuredly not in the builder's power, even had he been so inclined, to obtain shafts high enough to sustain the whole external gallery, as it is sustained in the nave, on one arcade. He had, as above noticed, a supply of shafts of every sort and size, from which he chose the largest for his nave shafts; the smallest were set aside for windows, jambs, balustrades, supports of pulpits, niches, and such other services, every conceivable size occurring in different portions of the building; and the middle-sized shafts were sorted into two classes, of which on the average one was about two-thirds the length of the other, and out of these the two stories of the façade and sides of the church are composed, the smaller shafts of course uppermost, and more numerous than the lower, according to the ordinary laws of superimposition adopted by all the Romanesque builders, and observed also in a kind of architecture quite as beautiful as any we are likely to invent, that of forest trees.

Nothing is more singular than the way in which this kind of superimposition (the only right one in the case of shafts) will shock a professed architect. He has been accustomed to see, in the Renaissance designs, shaft put on the top of shaft, three or four times over, and he thinks this quite right; but the moment he is shown a properly subdivided superimposition, in which the upper shafts diminish in size and multiply in number, so that the lower pillars would balance them safely even without cement, he exclaims that it is "against law," as if he had never seen a tree in his life.

Not that the idea of the Byzantine superimposition was taken from trees, any more than that of Gothic arches. Both are simple compliances with laws of nature, and, therefore, approximations to the forms of nature.

There is, however, one very essential difference between tree structure and the shaft structure in question; namely, that the marble branches, having no vital connexion with the stem, must be provided with a firm tablet or second foundation whereon to stand. This intermediate plinth or tablet runs along the whole façade at one level, is about eighteen inches thick, and left with little decoration as being meant for hard service. The small porticos, already spoken of as the most graceful pieces of composition with which I am acquainted, are sustained on detached clusters of four or five columns, forming the continuation of those of the upper series, and each of these clusters is balanced on one grand detached shaft; as much trust being thus placed in the pillars here, as is withdrawn from them elsewhere. The northern portico has only one detached pillar at its outer angle, which sustains three shafts and a square pilaster; of these shafts the one at the outer angle of the group is the thickest (so as to balance the pilaster on the inner angle), measuring 3 ft. 2 in. round, while the others measure only 2 ft. 10 in. and 2 ft. 11 in.; and in order to make this increase of diameter, and the importance of the shaft, more manifest to the eye, the old builders made the shaft *shorter* as well as thicker, increasing the depth both of its capital and the base, with what is to the thoughtless spectator ridiculous incongruity, and to the observant one a most beautiful expression of constructive genius. Nor is this all. Observe: the whole strength of this angle depends on accuracy of *poise*, not on breadth or strength of foundation. It is a *balanced*, not a propped structure: if the balance fails, it must fall instantly; if the balance is maintained, no matter how the lower shaft is fastened into the ground, all will be safe. And to mark this more definitely, the great lower shaft *has a different base from all the others of the façade*, remarkably high in proportion to the shaft, on a circular instead of a square plinth, and *without spurs*, while all the other bases have spurs without exception. Glance back at what is said of the spurs at pp. 84, 85, of the first volume, and reflect that all expression of *grasp* in the foot of the pillar is here useless, and to be replaced by one of balance merely, and you will feel what the old builder wanted to say to us, and how much he desired us to follow him with our understanding as he laid stone above stone.

And this purpose of his is hinted to us once more, even by the position of this base in the ground plan of the foundation of the portico; for, though itself circular, it sustains a hexagonal plinth *set obliquely to the walls of the church*, as if expressly to mark to us that it did not matter how the base was set, so only that the weights were justly disposed above it.

10. PROPER SENSE OF THE WORD IDOLATRY.

I do not intend, in thus applying the word "Idolatry" to certain ceremonies of Romanist worship, to admit the propriety of the ordinary Protestant manner of regarding those ceremonies as distinctively idolatrous, and as separating the Romanist from the Protestant Church by a gulf across which we must not look to our fellow-Christians but with utter reprobation and disdain. The Church of Rome does indeed distinctively violate the *second* commandment; but the true force and weight of the sin of idolatry are in the violation of the first, of which we are all of us guilty, in probably a very equal degree, considered only as members of this or that communion, and not as Christians or unbelievers. Idolatry is, both literally and verily, not the mere bowing down before sculptures, but the serving or becoming the slave of any images or imaginations which stand between us and God, and it is otherwise expressed in Scripture as "walking after the *Imagination*" of our own hearts. And observe also that while, at least on one occasion, we find in the Bible an indulgence granted to the mere external and literal violation of the second commandment, "When I bow myself in the house of Rimmon, the Lord pardon thy servant in this thing," we find no indulgence in any instance, or in the slightest degree, granted to "covetousness, which is idolatry" (Col. iii. 5; no casual association of terms, observe, but again energetically repeated in Ephesians, v. 5, "No covetous man, who is an idolater, hath any inheritance in the kingdom of Christ"); nor any to that denial of God, idolatry in one of its most subtle forms, following so often on the possession of that wealth against which Agur prayed so earnestly, " Give me neither poverty nor riches, lest I be full and deny thee, and say, ' Who is the Lord ?' "

And in this sense, which of us is not an idolater? Which of us has the right, in the fulness of that better knowledge, in spite of which he nevertheless is not yet separated from the service of this world, to speak scornfully of any of his brethren, because, in a guiltless ignorance, they have been accustomed to bow their knees before a statue? Which of us shall say that there may not be a spiritual worship in their apparent idolatry, or that there is not a spiritual idolatry in our own apparent worship?

For indeed it is utterly impossible for one man to judge of the feeling with which another bows down before an image. From that pure reverence in which Sir Thomas Brown wrote, " I can dispense with my hat at the sight of a cross, but not with a thought of my Redeemer," to the worst superstition of the most ignorant Romanist, there is an infinite series of subtle transitions; and the point where simple reverence and the use of the image merely to render conception more vivid, and feeling more intense, change into definite idolatry by the attribution of Power to the image itself, is so difficultly determinable that we cannot be too cautious in asserting that such a change has actually taken place in the case of any individual. Even when it is definite and certain, we shall oftener find it the consequence of dulness of intellect than of real alienation of heart from God; and I have no manner of doubt that half of the poor and untaught Christians who are this day lying prostrate before crucifixes, Bambinos, and Volto Santos, are finding more acceptance with God, than many Protestants who idolize nothing but their own opinions or their own interests. I believe that those who have worshipped the thorns of Christ's crown will be found at last to have been holier and wiser than those who worship the thorns of the world's service, and that to adore the nails of the cross is a less sin than to adore the hammer of the workman.

But, on the other hand, though the idolatry of the lower orders in the Romish Church may thus be frequently excusable, the ordinary subterfuges by which it is defended are not so. It may be extenuated but cannot be denied; and the attribution of power to the image,* in which it consists, is not merely a form of popular feeling, but a tenet of priestly instruction, and may be proved, over and over again, from any book of the Romish Church services. Take for instance the following prayer, which occurs continually at the close of the service of the Holy Cross:

> "Saincte vraye Croye aourée,
> Qui du corps Dieu fu aournée
> Et de sa sueur arrousée,
> Et de son sanc enluminée,
> Par ta vertu, par ta puissance,
> Defent mon corps de meschance,
> Et montroie moy par ton playsir
> Que vray confes puisse mourir."

"Oh holy, true, and golden Cross, which wast adorned with God's body, and watered with His sweat, and illuminated with His blood, by thy healing virtue and thy power, defend my body from mischance; and by thy good pleasure, let me make a good confession when I die."

There can be no possible defence imagined for the mere terms in which this prayer and other such are couched: yet it is always to be remembered, that in many cases they are rather poetical effusions than serious prayers; the utterances of imaginative enthusiasm, rather than of reasonable conviction; and as such, they are rather to be condemned as illusory and fictitious, than as idolatrous, nor even as such, condemned altogether, for strong love and faith are often the roots of them and the errors of affection are better than the accuracies of apathy. But the unhappy results, among all religious sects, of the habit of allowing imaginative and poetical belief to take the place of deliberate, resolute, and prosaic belief, have been fully and admirably traced by the author of the "Natural History of Enthusiasm."

* I do not like to hear Protestants speaking with gross and uncharitable contempt even of the worship of relics. Elisha once trusted his own staff too far; nor can I see any reasonable ground for the scorn, or the unkind rebuke, of those who have been taught from their youth upwards that to hope even in the hem of the garment may sometimes be better than to spend the living on physicians.

11. SITUATIONS OF BYZANTINE PALACES.

(1.) THE TERRACED HOUSE.

The most conspicuous pile in the midmost reach of the Grand Canal is the Casa Grimani, now the Post-Office. Letting his boat lie by the steps of this great palace, the traveller will see, on the other side of the canal, a building with a small terrace in front of it, and a little court with a door to the water, beside the terrace. Half of the house is visibly modern, and there is a great seam, like the edge of a scar, between it and the ancient remnant, in which the circular bands of the Byzantine arches will be instantly recognized. This building not having, as far as I know, any name except that of its present proprietor, I shall in future distinguish it simply as the Terraced House.

(2.) CASA BUSINELLO.

To the left of this edifice (looking from the Post-Office) there is a modern palace, on the other side of which the Byzantine mouldings appear again in the first and second stories of a house lately restored. It might be thought that the shafts and arches had been raised yesterday, the modern walls having been deftly adjusted to them, and all appearance of antiquity, together with the ornamentation and proportions of the fabric, having been entirely destroyed. I cannot, however, speak with unmixed sorrow of these changes, since, without his being implicated in the shame of them, they fitted this palace to become the residence of the kindest friend I had in Venice. It is generally known as the Casa Businello.

(3.) THE BRAIDED HOUSE.

Leaving the steps of the Casa Grimani, and turning the gondola away from the Rialto, we will pass the Casa Businello, and the three houses which succeed it on the right. The fourth is another restored palace, white and conspicuous, but retaining of its ancient structure only the five windows in its second story, and an ornamental moulding above them which appears to be ancient, though it is inaccessible without scaffolding, and I cannot therefore answer for it. But the five central windows are very valuable ; and as their capitals differ from most that we find (except in St. Mark's), in their plaited or braided border and basket-worked sides, I shall call this house, in future, the Braided House.*

(4.) THE MADONNETTA HOUSE.

On the other side of this palace is the Traghetto called "Della Madonnetta ;" and beyond this Traghetto, still facing the Grand Canal, a small palace, of which the front shows mere vestiges of arcades, the old shafts only being visible, with obscure circular seams in the modern plaster which covers the arches. The side of it is a curious agglomeration of pointed and round windows in every possible position, and of nearly every date from the twelfth to the eighteenth century. It is the smallest of the buildings we have to examine, but by no means the least interesting : I shall call it, from the name of its Traghetto, the Madonnetta House.

(5.) THE RIO FOSCARI HOUSE.

We must now descend the Grand Canal as far as the Palazzo Foscari, and enter the narrower canal, called the Rio di Ca' Foscari, at the side of that palace. Almost immediately after passing the great gateway of the Foscari courtyard, we shall see on our left, in the ruinous and time-stricken walls which totter over the water, the white curve of a circular arch covered with sculpture, and fragments of the bases of small pillars, entangled among festoons of the Erba della Madonna. I have already, in the folio plates which accompanied the first volume, partly illustrated this building. In what references I have to make to it here, I shall speak of it as the Rio Foscari House.

* Casa Tiepolo (?) in Lazari's Guide.

(6.) CASA FARSETTI.

We have now to reascend the Grand Canal, and approach the Rialto. As soon as we have passed the Casa Grimani, the traveller will recognize, on his right, two rich and extensive masses of building, which form important objects in almost every picturesque view of the noble bridge. Of these, the first, that farthest from the Rialto, retains great part of its ancient materials in a dislocated form. It has been entirely modernized in its upper stories, but the ground floor and first floor have nearly all their original shafts and capitals, only they have been shifted hither and thither to give room for the introduction of various small apartments, and present, in consequence, marvellous anomalies in proportion. This building is known in Venice as the Casa Farsetti.

(7.) CASA LOREDAN.

The one next to it, though not conspicuous, and often passed with neglect, will, I believe, be felt at last, by all who examine it carefully, to be the most beautiful palace in the whole extent of the Grand Canal. It has been restored often, once in the Gothic, once in the Renaissance times,—some writers say, even rebuilt; but, if so, rebuilt in its old form. The Gothic additions harmonize exquisitely with its Byzantine work, and it is easy, as we examine its lovely central arcade, to forget the Renaissance additions which encumber it above. It is known as the Casa Loredan.

The eighth palace is the Fondaco de' Turchi, described in the text. A ninth existed, more interesting apparently than any of these, near the Church of San Moisè, but it was thrown down in the course of "improvements" a few years ago. A woodcut of it is given in M Lazari's Guide.

12. MODERN PAINTING ON GLASS.

Of all the various principles of art which, in modern days, we have defied or forgotten, none are more indisputable, and few of more practical importance than this, which I shall have occasion again and again to allege in support of many future deductions:

" All art, working with given materials, must propose to itself the objects which, with those materials, are most perfectly attainable; and becomes illegitimate and debased if it propose to itself any other objects, better attainable with other materials."

Thus, great slenderness, lightness, or intricacy of structure,—as in ramifications of trees, detached folds of drapery, or wreaths of hair,—is easily and perfectly expressible in metal-work or in painting, but only with great difficulty and imperfectly expressible in sculpture. All sculpture, therefore, which professes as its chief end the expression of such characters, is debased; and if the suggestion of them be accidentally required of it, that suggestion is only to be given to an extent compatible with perfect ease of execution in the given material,—not to the utmost possible extent. For instance: some of the most delightful drawings of our own water-color painter, Hunt, have been of birds' nests; of which, in painting, it is perfectly possible to represent the intricate fibrous or mossy structure; therefore, the effort is a legitimate one, and the art is well employed. But to carve a bird's nest out of marble would be physically impossible, and to reach any approximate expression of its structure would require prolonged and intolerable labor. Therefore, all sculpture which set itself to carving bird's nests as an end, or which, if a bird's nest were required of it, carved it to the utmost possible point of realization, would be debased. Nothing but the general form, and as much of the fibrous structure as could be with perfect ease represented, ought to be attempted at all.

But more than this. The workman has not done his duty, and is not working on safe principles, unless he even so far honors the materials with which he is working as to set himself to bring out their beauty, and to recommend and exalt, as far as he can, their peculiar qualities. If he is working in marble, he should insist upon and exhibit its transparency and solidity; if in iron, its strength and tenacity; if in gold, its ductility; and he will invariably find the material grateful, and that his work is all the nobler for being eulogistic of the substance of which it is made. But of all the arts, the working of glass is that in which we ought to keep these principles most vigorously in mind. For we owe it so much, and the possession of it is so great a blessing, that all our work in it should be completely and forcibly expressive of the peculiar characters which give it so vast a value.

These are two, namely, its DUCTILITY when heated, and TRANSPARENCY when cold, both nearly perfect. In its employment for vessels, we ought always to exhibit its ductility, and in its employment for windows, its transparency. All work in glass is bad which does not, with loud voice, proclaim one or other of these great qualities.

Consequently, *all cut glass* is barbarous: for the cutting conceals its ductility, and confuses it with crystal. Also, all very neat, finished, and perfect form in glass is barbarous: for this fails in proclaiming another of its great virtues; namely, the ease with which its light substance can be moulded or blown into any form, so long as perfect accuracy be not required. In metal, which, even when heated enough to be thoroughly malleable, retains yet such weight and consistency as render it susceptible of the finest handling and retention of the most delicate form, great precision of workmanship is admissible; but in glass, which when once softened must be blown or moulded, not hammered, and which is liable to lose, by contraction or subsidence, the fineness of the forms given to it, no delicate outlines are to be attempted, but only such fantastic and fickle grace as the mind of the workman can conceive and execute on the instant. The more wild, extravagant, and grotesque in their gracefulness the forms are, the better. No material is so adapted for giving full play to the imagination, but it must not be wrought with refinement or painfulness, still less with costliness. For as in gratitude we are to proclaim its virtues, so in all honesty we are to confess its imperfections; and while we triumphantly set forth its transparency, we are also frankly to admit its fragility, and therefore not to waste much time upon it, nor put any real art into it when intended for daily use. No workman ought ever to spend more than an hour in the making of any glass vessel.

Next in the case of windows, the points which we have to insist upon are, the transparency of the glass and its susceptibility of the most brilliant colors; and therefore the attempt to turn painted windows into pretty pictures is one of the most gross and ridiculous barbarisms of this preeminently barbarous century. It originated, I suppose, with the Germans, who seem for the present distinguished among European nations by the loss of the sense of color; but it appears of late to have considerable chance of establishing itself in England: and it is a two-edged error, striking in two directions; first at the healthy appreciation of painting, and then at the healthy appreciation of glass. Color, ground with oil, and laid on a solid opaque ground, furnishes to the human hand the most exquisite means of expression which the human sight and invention can find or require. By its two opposite qualities, each naturally and easily attainable, of transparency in shadow and opacity in light, it complies with the conditions of nature; and by its perfect governableness it permits the utmost possible fulness and subtlety in the harmonies of color, as well as the utmost perfection in the drawing. Glass, considered as a material for a picture, is exactly as bad as oil paint is good. It sets out by reversing the conditions of nature, by making the lights transparent and the shadows opaque; and the ungovernableness of its color (changing in the furnace), and its violence (being always on a high key, because produced by actual light), render it so disadvantageous in every way, that the result of working in it for pictorial effect would infallibly be the destruction of all the appreciation of the noble qualities of pictorial color.

In the second place, this modern barbarism destroys the true appreciation of the qualities of glass. It denies, and endeavors as far as possible to conceal, the transparency, which is not only its great virtue in a merely utilitarian point of view, but its great spiritual character; the character by which in church architecture it becomes most touchingly impressive, as typical of the entrance of the Holy Spirit into the heart of man; a typical expression rendered specific and intense by the purity and brilliancy of its sevenfold hues*; and therefore in

---

* I do not think that there is anything more necessary to the progress of European art in the present day than the complete understanding of this sanctity of Color. I had much pleasure in finding it, the other day, fully

endeavoring to turn the window into a picture, we at once lose the sanctity and power of the noble material, and employ it to an end which is utterly impossible it should ever worthily attain. The true perfection of a painted window is to be serene, intense, brilliant, like flaming jewellery; full of easily legible and quaint subjects, and exquisitely subtle, yet simple, in its harmonies. In a word, this perfection has been consummated in the designs, never to be surpassed, if ever again to be approached by human art, of the French windows of the twelfth and thirteenth centuries.

understood and thus sweetly expressed in a little volume of poems by a Miss Maynard:

> "For still in every land, though to Thy name
> Arose no temple,—still in every age,
> Though heedless man had quite forgot Thy praise,
> *We* praised Thee; and at rise and set of sun
> Did we assemble duly, and intone
> A choral hymn that all the lands might hear.
> In heaven, on earth, and in the deep we praised Thee,
> Singly, or mingled in sweet sisterhood.
> But now, acknowledged ministrants, we come,
> Co-worshippers with man in this Thy house,
> We, the Seven Daughters of the Light, to praise
> Thee, Light of Light! Thee, God of very God!"
>
> *A Dream of Fair Colors.*

These poems seem to be otherwise remarkable for a very unobtrusive and pure religious feeling in subjects connected with art.

END OF THE SECOND VOLUME.